Changing Realities in Southern Africa

Implications for American Policy

MICHAEL CLOUGH, Editor

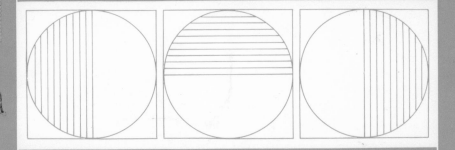

iiS

**INSTITUTE
OF INTERNATIONAL
STUDIES**
University of California, Berkeley

CHANGING REALITIES IN SOUTHERN AFRICA

RESEARCH SERIES
No. 47

Changing Realities in Southern Africa

Implications for American Policy

MICHAEL CLOUGH, Editor

iiS

INSTITUTE
OF INTERNATIONAL
STUDIES
University of California, Berkeley

Library of Congress Cataloging in Publication Data

Main entry under title:

Changing realities in southern Africa.

(Research series, ISSN 0068-6093; no. 47)
Includes bibliographical references and index.
1. Africa, Southern—Relations—United States—Addresses, essays, lectures.
2. United States—Relations—Africa, Southern—Addresses, essays, lectures.
3. Africa, Southern—Politics and government—1975- —Addresses, essays,
lectures. 4. Africa, Southern—Economic conditions—1975- —Addresses, essays,
lectures. I. Clough, Michael. II. Series: Research series (University of California,
Berkeley. Institute of International Studies); no. 47.

DT747.U6C47 1982   327.68073   82-12124
ISBN 0-87725-147-9

CONTENTS

PREFACE

Over the past eight years southern Africa has undergone a rapid and remarkable transformation. Beginning with an April 1974 coup in Portugal and the subsequent decision of the new Portuguese regime to grant independence to its African colonies, a series of regional and international developments has served to undermine the preexisting political balance in the region—one which had been decisively weighted in favor of white rule. By 1980 three former territories—Angola, Mozambique, and Rhodesia—had gained independence; a fourth territory—Namibia—stood on the verge of independence; and the white regime in South Africa was being forced to come to terms with growing pressures for change. During this period a new group of political leaders has emerged whose claims to authority are based on their roles in the long and bitter struggles against white governments claiming to be aligned with Western capitalism. In order to cope with the problems engendered by ongoing liberation struggles in the region and to take advantage of the emergence of new states, southern African leaders have established new regional institutions such as the Southern African Development Coordination Conference (SADCC). At the same time, the South African government has responded to regional change by launching a controversial program of significant (albeit limited) domestic reforms, accepting the inevitability of Namibian independence, and attempting to promote its own regional grand design. These developments constitute a new set of southern African "realities," the nature and implications of which must be clearly understood by American policymakers if they are to formulate a coherent, consistent, and effective policy toward this troubled region.

The idea for this book initially grew out of my belief that the independence of Zimbabwe constituted a particularly salient focal point for an examination of the developments noted above. The need for such a study was increased by the election of Ronald Reagan and his administration's decision to reorient American policy toward southern Africa. In recent years a number of very useful studies have been written on the myriad problems of this region.[1] However, many excellent earlier studies are out of date, while many others are of only limited use to readers trying to understand the practical choices that presently confront American policymakers.

In putting together this book, I have sought to present essays that will help provide answers to four questions:

(1) What has been the nature of recent political changes in southern Africa?
(2) What is the relation between such changes and American interests in the region?
(3) Which processes, actors, and objectives in southern Africa should American policymakers seek to support?
(4) What means can and should be used to promote the desired ends?

These questions are at the heart of the current debate over the future direction of American policy toward southern Africa. Which course of action the Reagan administration ultimately adopts will depend almost entirely on which answers it accepts to these questions.

Given the quantity and quality of studies dealing with South Africa's regime and the potential for political change in that country, I have chosen not to include essays dealing directly with domestic problems in South Africa.[2] That does not mean I believe those problems can be separated from broader regional issues. To the contrary— as most of the essays in this volume make clear—regional problems are in many cases directly related to the continued existence of the apartheid regime in South Africa. However, this book implicitly assumes that change in South Africa—regardless of the form it takes— is likely to be sporadic, uneven, and conflictual; and that therefore the United States must develop a southern Africa policy that can be sustained over a longer term, despite prolonged regional antagonisms stemming from the continuation of white rule in South Africa.

This book ranges from single-country analyses to examinations of regional cooperation projects to questions of foreign—explicitly Soviet and American—involvement in the region. In Chapter 1, "From Rhodesia to Zimbabwe," I use insights borrowed from bargaining theory to explain the long and drawn out conflict in Rhodesia which ended with the successful Lancaster House conference in London at the end of 1979. In Chapter 2, "From South West Africa to Namibia," I attempt to explain shifts in South Africa's Namibia policy, assess the prospects for a near-term settlement of the conflict in the territory, and predict the probable consequences of various American policies. In Chapter 3, "One Namibia, One Nation: The Political Economy of Transition," Reginald Herbold Green examines the likely policies that would result were the South West Africa People's Organization (SWAPO)—the most likely victor of internationally supervised elections in Namibia—to come to power. Green provides a detailed analysis of the structure of the Namibian economy, the political and economic objectives of SWAPO, and the types of opportunities and constraints that would be faced by an independent government in Namibia. Chapters 4 and 5 examine the alternative strategies that have been proposed by different regional actors as potential bases for political and economic cooperation in southern Africa. In "South Africa's Regional Policy," Deon Geldenhuys analyzes the relation between South Africa's domestic objectives and its regional strategies by tracing the evolution of South Africa's policies toward its neighbors. In "Regional Cooperation in Southern Africa," John Ravenhill and I examine the historical antecedents, current program, and future prospects of the SADCC. In Chapter 6, "The Natural Ally," Seth Singleton outlines the Soviet Union's southern Africa strategy and analyzes the strengths and weaknesses of that strategy by examining Soviet relations with nationalist movements and leaders in Angola, Mozambique, Namibia, South Africa, and Zimbabwe. In Chapter 7, "Issues for U.S. Development Assistance Policy," Raymond W. Copson explicitly addresses the question of American interests and options in southern Africa, outlining current American aid programs in southern Africa and discussing the manner in which these programs can serve to promote different policy objectives in the region.

In recent years, one of the major issues in the debate concerning American policy toward southern Africa has been the dependence of the United States and its Western allies on strategic minerals exports from this region. For that reason I have included as an appendix excerpts from a Senate Foreign Relations Committee study of this problem.

All the chapters in this book have benefitted from the careful editing of Bojana Ristich. The preliminary index was ably prepared by Stevens Tucker.

M.C.

NOTES ON CONTRIBUTORS

MICHAEL CLOUGH is Assistant Professor of National Security Affairs and African Area Coordinator, Naval Postgraduate School, Monterey, California.

RAYMOND W. COPSON is Analyst in International Relations at the Congressional Research Service, Library of Congress.

DEON GELDENHUYS is Assistant Director of the South African Institute of International Affairs.

REGINALD HERBOLD GREEN is Professorial Fellow of the Institute of Development Studies, University of Sussex, England.

JOHN RAVENHILL is Lecturer in Political Science, University of Sydney, Australia.

SETH SINGLETON is Professor of Political Science, Ripon College, Ripon, Wisconsin.

Chapter 1

FROM RHODESIA TO ZIMBABWE

Michael Clough

INTRODUCTION

Conflict in Rhodesia became an international crisis on 11 November 1965, when the white settler administration in the then self-governing British colony issued a Unilateral Declaration of Independence (UDI). Through this action, Prime Minister Ian Smith hoped to counter Great Britain's refusal to grant Rhodesia independence without guarantees that there would be progress after independence toward eventual majority rule. After UDI was announced, British Prime Minister Harold Wilson predicted that the rebellious government would collapse in "a matter of weeks, not months." Fourteen years and three British Prime Ministers later, after a civil war costing 20,000 lives, a settlement was finally reached for Rhodesia in London at Lancaster House on 17 December 1979.

Why did it take so long to reach a settlement? Why did the Lancaster House conference succeed while eight earlier diplomatic initiatives had failed? The most useful explanation is in terms of a bargaining approach: the Rhodesian conflict was a bargaining process in which all parties were interested *not* in a negotiated settlement for its own sake, but in maximizing their own long-term positions in Rhodesia. As long as any of the parties believed they could gain from prolonging

The author is grateful to Michael Brown and Helen Kitchen for comments on earlier versions of this chapter and to Albertine Potter and Denise Squires for typing assistance. Completion of this chapter was made possible by a grant from the Research Foundation of the Naval Postgraduate School. The views expressed are strictly those of the author.

1

the conflict, they were not interested in a settlement. Only when all of the main parties came to believe that a negotiated settlement offered them an outcome preferable to continued conflict did a settlement become possible. By focusing attention on the variables that affected the parties' assessments of the relative advantages of a settlement, a bargaining approach makes it possible to explain the causes of the conflict, the failure of earlier initiatives, and the success of the Lancaster House conference.

A BARGAINING FRAMEWORK

Bargaining takes place whenever two or more parties with conflicting claims to the same goods attempt to determine how these goods are to be distributed.[1] It can be either explicit (such as negotiations), in which case the parties communicate their interests and intentions to each other directly, or tacit, in which case they attempt to influence each others' behavior through actions and indirect messages.[2] In these terms, almost all political conflicts involve bargaining. In Rhodesia the goods in question were control over territory and the terms under which that control would be relinquished by the white settler regime.

The ability to affect the distribution of disputed goods in a conflict depends upon each player's relative bargaining power. "Bargaining power," like "power" itself, is a difficult concept to define because its only measure is the ability to achieve results—which can be determined only after the fact. In order to get around this problem, one can distinguish among *inherent* bargaining power, *actual* bargaining power, and bargaining *skill*.[3] Inherent bargaining power is a function of a player's perception of (1) the cost of conceding to an opponent's demand; (2) the possible gains from standing firm; and (3) the possible losses from standing firm. Actual bargaining power is based on "perceived comparative resolve"[4]—i.e., each player's perception of the credibility of his adversaries' threats weighed against the maximum risk he is willing to take from a bargaining breakdown. Thus the more credible an adversary's threats and the higher the potential cost of a bargaining breakdown, the lower will be a player's actual bargaining power. Bargaining skill refers to a player's ability to convert bargaining power into results. A major factor affecting bargaining skill is the internal cohesiveness of the different players—that is, their ability to communicate and act as a unified group. At one extreme would be a player that represents a small homogeneous group with clearly defined, consistent interests and strategic views; at the opposite extreme would be a player that represents a loose coalition of different factions with diverse, even conflicting interests and divergent views of how best to promote those interests. Players representing cohesive interests are less vulnerable to "divide-and-conquer" tactics and better able to maintain the credibility of their threats than are players representing factionalized interests.

The potential influence of external actors on the outcome of a conflict depends upon their ability to alter the resolve of the main protagonists. The extent of external influence is a direct function of the degree of dependence—actual or perceived—of the main protagonists on external supporters. Dependence is measured in terms of the costs of breaking a relationship. To the extent that a group has a large number of potential external supports or can do without external support at a very low cost, it is not very dependent, even though it may receive a large amount of support from a single external actor.[5]

DECOLONIZATION AS A BARGAINING PROCESS

By 1965 Great Britain had either granted or begun to grant independence to all of its African colonies with one exception: Southern Rhodesia. In order to explain why Rhodesia did not follow the same path as the rest of Great Britain's colonies, it will be useful to briefly examine the forces that caused the European powers to hastily withdraw from Africa.[6]

THE GENERAL PATTERN OF DECOLONIZATION

At the end of World War II, all of the European colonial powers except Italy were firmly entrenched in Africa. Even Great Britain's Labour Party, committed in principle to eventually handing over power to Africans, believed complete decolonization would come only after a long period of preparation.[7] Less than twenty years later, only Portugal sought to maintain possession of its African territories.

3

Based on the bargaining framework outlined above, it can be argued that the rapid decolonization of Africa was caused by a radical change in the resolve of the colonial powers. With a few exceptions (discussed in the following section), decolonization involved anticipatory concessions by the colonial powers. Bargaining never even began in many cases. Great Britain, France, and Belgium handed over power to local elites before those elites had mustered enough power to be able to coerce their overlords into concessions.*

Three factors were responsible for the dramatic shift in the resolve of the colonial powers. First, the colonial powers recognized that the future costs of maintaining control over their possessions would be high. There were no major armed liberation movements operating in Africa in the late 1950s (except in Algeria), but protests, strikes, and civil unrest in Africa and developments in other parts of the world—for example, Malaya and Indochina—made the colonial powers realize that violent rebellions were inevitable. At the same time, the relative military and economic strength of the colonial powers was declining, making them less willing to bear the potential costs of standing firm in Africa.[8]

Second, the colonial powers realized that in most cases the costs of concession—i.e., decolonization—were quite low. The benefits of colonial rule were never as large as some have argued,[9] and in the late 1950s the colonial powers began to recognize that the benefits that existed could be maintained without formal control. By coopting nationalist elites and controlling the terms of decolonization, they could establish "neocolonial" relationships with their former colonies while leaving preexisting economic relations intact.[10]

Third, the colonial powers saw that there were advantages to be gained from early concessions. If they delayed until the costs of continued control began to rise, the eventual costs of concession could be expected to rise as well. Delay would inevitably radicalize African elites and politicize the African masses, making it more difficult for the colonial powers to control the terms under which decolonization would occur and less likely that a neocolonial relationship would develop after independence. Thus anticipatory concessions made sense.

*This was particularly the case in the Belgian Congo, where Belgium decided to grant independence at the first sign of possible trouble (see Crawford Young, *Politics in the Congo* [Princeton: Princeton University Press, 1965]).

4

THE EXCEPTIONS TO RAPID DECOLONIZATION

There were three main exceptions to the general pattern of African decolonization—French policy toward Algeria, Portuguese policy toward its colonies (Angola, Cape Verde, Guinea-Bissau, Mozambique, and São Tomé and Principe), and British policy toward Southern Rhodesia. Each of these exceptions can be explained in terms of the bargaining framework. They cannot be attributed to differences in the cost of standing firm since France and Portugal eventually paid a high cost for their failure to make anticipatory concessions, and there are no credible grounds to argue that the expected costs of continued control in these cases were lower than in those where anticipatory concessions were made. The failure to decolonize had to be due to other factors.

In the cases of Algeria and the Portuguese colonies, the most important factor in standing firm was the higher perceived costs of concession. The costs were perceived as higher for two reasons. First, continued control was believed to be important to the prestige and self-image of the two colonial powers. (Their claims to the colonies were bound up with their ideas of national purpose and their role in the world.) Both French and Portuguese policymakers felt that giving up these colonies would mean sacrificing national honor. They emphasized that the colonies were part of the motherland, not mere colonial appendages. In contrast to the British, the French had always put an emphasis on close bonds between the metropole and the colonies: Algeria's symbolic importance went beyond that of France's other colonies, as was stressed by General de Gaulle in a speech in Algiers in October 1947:

> Any policy which . . . would have the effect of reducing the rights and duties of France here, or of discouraging the inhabitants of metropolitan origin who were and who remain the ferment of Algeria, or, finally, of letting the French Muslims believe it could be allowable for them to separate their fate from that of France would in truth only open the doors to decadence . . . Loyal Frenchmen . . . know that in letting our cause be threatened upon this shore of the Mediterranean it is the entire national edifice which risks dislocation.[11]

5

Similarly Portugal's leaders argued that the nation's "very existence and identity" were at stake in the colonial situation.[12]

Second, for various reasons a strategy of anticipatory concessions in Algeria and the Portuguese territories was not likely to yield the kind of results that could be expected in the other colonies. For example, the Portuguese lacked sufficient political and economic strength to ensure a neocolonial relationship with their colonies after independence. For them neocolonialism was a potential danger rather than an opportunity. In 1963 Prime Minister Antonio de Oliveira Salazar warned that the African continent was becoming an arena for economic and technical competition between "the strong State economies" of the East and "the big capitalist syndicates" of the West, each aiming to capture and control markets.[13] Like the Portuguese, the French were concerned about the danger of competition from stronger economic powers like the United States,[14] but they had an additional reason to worry that they would not be able to maintain their ties with an independent Algeria. Before independence the Front de Libération National (FLN) had developed into a mass-based liberation movement. By the mid-1950s it was hopelessly radical in French eyes. Unlike its colonies in West Africa, with whom the French could be relatively confident of continuing close relations after independence, an Algeria governed by the FLN seemed likely to reduce its ties to France.[15]

The consequences of holding on were long, violent struggles. In Algeria the costs of standing firm finally reached the point where France was willing to make the necessary concessions. (It is instructive to note that a settlement was brought about by the French leader—de Gaulle—who could best minimize the damage to French prestige of withdrawal.) In the Portuguese cases, the conflicts ended only after the costs of standing firm had become so high that they precipitated a military coup in Portugal that drove from power all of the leaders committed to hanging on to the colonies.[16]

Some writers have argued that the main factor determining the course of decolonization in Africa was the presence or absence of large white settler populations. While this factor was important, it must be recognized that settlers played different roles in different colonies at different times. In Algeria they were very important. Their existence had a crucial effect on the internal cohesion of France and thus on the ability of the French government to develop and

6

carry out any policy on Algeria. In addition, they were a major catalyst in the radicalization of the Algerian masses and thus indirectly altered the cost of concession for France. However, it must be kept in mind that the settlers were not the only cause of French intransigence. To a certain extent, they were merely part of a larger phenomenon that had its origins in the French mind-set. In the Portuguese case, it would be misleading to argue that Lisbon was forced by the settlers in its African colonies to adopt policies that it would have otherwise rejected. Throughout the conflicts that developed in those colonies, settlers were never the dominant actors. In Kenya, Great Britain was able to carry out a policy of anticipatory concessions despite the opposition of a large white settler population—principally because it had maintained substantial direct control over the local civil service and security institutions, thus making it difficult for Kenyan whites to unilaterally declare independence.[17] In short, the mere presence of European settlers is not significant; rather it is the specific effect of that presence on the bargaining position of the colonial power. This point is particularly important in analyzing the conflicts of Rhodesia, Namibia, and South Africa.

BARGAINING IN RHODESIA

As indicated, Southern Rhodesia differed from other European colonies in several respects, the most important of which was the unique political status of its white settler population. Throughout the colonial period, the territory was never subject to direct British rule.[18] From 1890 until 1923 the colony was administered by the British South Africa Company (BSAC). In 1922 the British Privy Council ruled that Southern Rhodesia belonged to the British crown, not the BSAC, and the settler population was given a choice between union with South Africa and becoming a colony under responsible government—i.e., internal self-government by the settlers, subject to British supervision. They chose the latter, and on 1 October 1923 Great Britain formally annexed the territory. In theory Great Britain reserved control over all legislation governing Africans; in practice, it almost never exercised this control. The entire Rhodesian governmental apparatus—the legislative assembly, civil service, military, and police— was staffed and controlled by the white settlers. As a result, when the British began to consider granting independence to Southern Rhodesia, they had to consider bargaining with an entrenched white settler administration rather than (as in their other colonies) an indigenous African nationalist elite.

British interests in Southern Rhodesia would have been just as well served by the policy of anticipatory concessions adopted for other British colonies. However, implementing that policy in Southern Rhodesia would have required the acquiescence of the white settlers, who perceived the relative costs of concession entirely differently from British policymakers. The primary concerns of most white Rhodesians involved preserving their comfortable lifestyle, holding on to their farms, and keeping their government jobs. Events elsewhere in Africa, such as a civil war in the Congo, reinforced their fears that their interests would be threatened by black rule—and even neocolonialism would involve black rule. In their eyes the potential costs of concession were too high to risk a transfer of government. Unlike their counterparts in Kenya, the white Rhodesians were in a position to veto British concessions that ran counter to their view of their interests. Recognizing this, British policymakers sought to negotiate a transfer of authority with the white settlers that would prevent Great Britain from becoming embroiled in a costly military struggle, satisfy at least minimum black demands, and limit any spillover damage to British interests elsewhere in Africa and the Commonwealth. Achieving even these relatively limited objectives became increasingly difficult for the British as political power in the colony shifted into the hands of the whites most opposed to significant concessions.[19] By 1965 it was clear that white leaders would not be willing to negotiate a settlement that would prove even minimally acceptable to either Rhodesian blacks or African and Commonwealth states. At the time of UDI, intransigent whites, represented by Smith's government and the Rhodesian Front party, were in a strong bargaining position. The period between UDI and the Lancaster House agreement can be divided into seven distinct phases. Let us analyze them in detail.

PHASE ONE: BILATERAL NEGOTIATIONS (NOVEMBER 1965-MAY 1972)

The Rhodesian rebellion began after Smith and his followers realized that the British government would not accept the maximum concessions they were willing to make.[20] The Rhodesians wanted independence on the basis of the 1961 constitution; the British wanted changes that would reduce legal discrimination and expand black political participation, including an increase in potential black seats in the Parliament sufficient to provide blacks with a blocking power over constitutional changes. UDI presented the British with a *fait accompli*. Smith gambled that the immediate British reaction would not be decisive and that eventually London would be forced to offer better terms.

The British response to UDI was constrained by two sets of conflicting concerns. On the one hand, British policymakers were afraid that inaction would threaten Great Britain's extensive economic and political relations with black Africa and possibly even cause the breakup of the Commonwealth. Predictably several Commonwealth states—notably Tanzania and Ghana—called for the use of force against the Rhodesian rebels as soon as UDI was announced. On the other hand, the Wilson government was afraid that military intervention would threaten British economic interests in South Africa, endanger the Labour Party's slender one-vote margin in Parliament, and possibly precipitate a mutiny by members of the military sympathetic with the white Rhodesians. In order to cope with these conflicting pressures, the British "internationalized" the conflict by requesting the UN Security Council to impose economic sanctions on the rebellious regime in Salisbury. At first these sanctions were selective and voluntary for UN member countries; later they were made comprehensive and mandatory.[21] These steps allowed the British to partially deflect pressure from Africa and the Commonwealth and avoid military intervention, but they did little to weaken the resolve of the white Rhodesians.

At the time of UDI, the white settler regime was under no external pressure to settle. Portugal and South Africa were the only countries upon whom Rhodesia was directly dependent because they controlled its only outlets to the sea. There is some evidence that the South Africans disapproved of the UDI strategy, but neither they nor the Portuguese were willing to support coercive measures designed to hasten the collapse of white rule in Rhodesia.[22] Groups that were willing to pressure the Smith regime lacked effective leverage. In 1965 black Rhodesian nationalists were not in a position to credibly threaten the white government; at most they could exercise a very limited veto over prospective British concessions.[23] The impact of sanctions was weakened by South African and Portuguese noncompliance, a lack of effective enforcement mechanisms, and the ability of resourceful

Rhodesian entrepreneurs to develop alternative markets.[24] Only one other player had potential influence: the United States. The U.S. State Department's Africa Bureau urged President Lyndon Johnson to pressure the British for more decisive action, but he decided not to because (as Secretary of State Dean Rusk reportedly remarked) America already had "a full plate." Given the country's other problems—a war in Vietnam in particular—Rhodesia seemed too small a matter to risk alienating the British or overcommitting American resources.[25]

The relative cohesiveness of the different players worked to the Rhodesians' advantage. In Salisbury Smith's Rhodesian Front Party was in firm control. What little liberal opposition existed within the white community was politically powerless. In contrast, political opinion in Great Britain was clearly divided over how hard a bargain London should drive and how much coercion should be applied. With the Labour Party in power, the Salisbury regime could look to the day when a more sympathetic Conservative government would regain parliamentary control. In addition, relative cohesiveness markedly affected the credibility of the two main protagonists. Smith could carry out threats without worrying about his internal political position, whereas Wilson had to keep a close eye on the domestic repercussions of his actions.

The Labour government continued to negotiate with the rebel regime after UDI. Talks were held in December 1966 and October 1968, but on neither occasion was Wilson able to induce Smith to accept British terms.[26] These terms called for a constitutional agreement that would (1) ensure unimpeded progress toward majority rule; (2) guarantee against retrogressive constitutional amendments; (3) immediately improve the political status of the black population; (4) move toward ending racial discrimination; and (5) prove acceptable to the people of Southern Rhodesia as a whole.

The Wilson government was voted out of office in June 1970. The new Prime Minister, Edward Heath, and his Foreign Minister, Sir Alec Douglas-Home, were committed to resolving the conflict even if it meant largely accepting Rhodesian demands. Their willingness to compromise was reinforced by knowledge that the Nixon administration had secretly decided to "tilt" toward the white regimes in southern Africa.[27] When an agreement was reached between Sir Alec and Smith on 24 November 1971, the British had given way on all of the original conditions except the requirement that the settlement be acceptable to the people of Southern Rhodesia as a whole.[28]

Rhodesian opinion on the settlement—which both the British and the Rhodesians believed would be affirmative—was to be determined by a British commission headed by Lord Pearce. The Pearce Commission arrived in Salisbury in January 1972. By March it was forced to conclude that the overwhelming majority of blacks in Rhodesia were opposed to the settlement terms.[29] The commission's final report left the British government with no choice but to cancel the settlement. The Heath government was not willing to apply greater pressure on the whites in order to force more concessions and decided the least costly strategy was to accept the status quo—an illegal regime and a continuation of sanctions—and withdraw from negotiations. Sir Alec reportedly informed Smith that Great Britain would resume negotiations only after Smith could demonstrate that there was black support for a prospective agreement.[30]

PHASE TWO: INTERNAL NEGOTIATIONS AND GUERRILLA WAR
(MAY 1972-APRIL 1974)

The Pearce Commission visit to Rhodesia was a major watershed in the Rhodesian conflict. Until that visit, black Rhodesians had been consulted but not allowed to participate in the negotiations. The Pearce Commission gave them their first genuine opportunity to have a say in the determination of their future. In order to take advantage of this opportunity, a new organization—the African National Council (ANC)—was created inside of Rhodesia.[31] To make it difficult for the Smith regime to ban the new organization, nationalist leaders selected Bishop Abel Muzorewa, leader of the United Methodist Church, to head it.* During the two months that the Pearce Commission was in Rhodesia, the ANC succeeded in tapping the deep undercurrents of black anger that had been suppressed by the white regime. By

*In 1957 the African National Congress of Southern Rhodesia had been formed—the first ANC. This party was banned by Rhodesian authorities in 1959 and replaced by the National Democratic Party (NDP). In December 1961 the NDP was banned and replaced by the Zimbabwe African People's Union (ZAPU), which was banned in September 1962. At this point, the nationalist movement split into two main factions. One faction, led by Joshua Nkomo—the former president of the ANC, NDP, and ZAPU—formed the People's Caretaker Council (PCC); the other faction, led by the Reverend Ndabaningi Sithole, set up the

11

effectively presenting their case to the British commissioners, blacks managed to destroy the Smith-Home agreement and—more important—place themselves at the center of all future bargaining.

After their successful campaign, the ANC leaders decided to transform the organization into a permanent body committed to "universal adult suffrage." Even the myopic Smith began to realize that he would have to negotiate directly with black leaders, and he reluctantly opened negotiations with Muzorewa in 1973. However, Smith was still not willing to make any substantial concessions. Instead he hoped to persuade Muzorewa to accept the terms of the Smith-Home agreement with minor changes.[32]

Although blacks had gained a position at the bargaining table, in 1973 they lacked the inherent power to take advantage of that position. The two main exiled nationalist parties—ZAPU and ZANU—spent more time condemning each other than attacking the Smith regime.[33] Almost all of Rhodesia's major nationalist leaders were in prison. All significant guerrilla activity had ended after the guerrillas had suffered embarrassing defeats in 1967-68.[34] While Muzorewa had grown in stature as a consequence of his part in the defeat of the Smith-Home agreement, he could not claim to represent either ZANU or ZAPU. Were he to have agreed to Smith's terms, he would not have been able to impose an agreement on the black movements, the conflict would have continued, and he would have ceased to be an acceptable nationalist leader. Unfortunately, the black leaders could improve their actual bargaining power only by reviving the war effort.

Just after the Pearce Commission issued its report, representatives of ZAPU and ZANU declared their intention to step up the guerrilla campaign.[35] Unbeknown to most observers, ZANU had been carefully laying plans for a major offensive against the Rhodesian government. From 1970 to 1972, the Zimbabwe African National Liberation Army (ZANLA)—ZANU's military wing—had infiltrated several hundred men into the northeastern region of the country to organize the peasants and workers on white farms. Simultaneously it

Zimbabwe African National Union (ZANU). The PCC and ZANU were subsequently banned in August 1964. In exile the PCC readopted the Zimbabwe African People's Union as its official title. Muzorewa's ANC was not linked to either exiled party, although supporters of both ZANU and ZAPU became involved in ANC activities.

had begun to infiltrate arms and supplies into the region. The ANC campaign against the Smith-Home agreement aided the guerrilla effort indirectly by politicizing blacks throughout the country and creating an environment receptive to guerrilla activity.

The first public sign that the Smith government might be facing a serious military challenge came at Altena Farm near the Mozambique border on 21 December 1972, when ZANLA insurgents began a series of hit-and-run attacks directed against unpopular white farmers.[36] In addition to these attacks, both ZANLA and the Zimbabwe People's Revolutionary Army (ZIPRA)—began to resort to the widespread use of landmines. These new tactics were intended to destroy the white regime's sense of invulnerability and disrupt normal economic activities. For the first time, the conflict began to have a visible effect on Rhodesia. Between December 1972 and December 1973 the Rhodesian Security Forces claimed to have killed 203 guerrillas while losing 57 military and civilian lives. In September 1973 the number of emigrants exceeded the number of immigrants for the first time in seven years, and tourism, a major source of foreign exchange, began to decline. By February 1974 the Rhodesian government had been forced to increase the size of its regular army and double the number of national servicemen being called up.[37]

Despite growing pressures, the Smith regime showed no signs that its internal resolve was diminishing. While the costs of standing firm were rising, Rhodesian officials saw them as manageable, and they still perceived the cost of concession as exorbitant. Thus Smith continued to refuse to consider even moderate black demands.[38] By early 1974 the Rhodesian problem had changed, but no progress toward a settlement had been made. Blacks were now firmly entrenched in the inner circle of negotiations, and they had begun to create new pressures on the Rhodesian government through internal political mobilization and guerrilla warfare. However, they were still too weak to force concessions. A stalemate might have continued indefinitely had it not been for a military coup in Portugal.

PHASE THREE: THE EFFECTS OF MOZAMBICAN INDEPENDENCE AND REGIONAL NEGOTIATIONS (APRIL 1974-SEPTEMBER 1975)

On 25 April 1974, a group of Portuguese officers from the Armed Forces Movement staged a successful coup against the government in

Lisbon,[39] in large part out of increasing dissatisfaction with the government's continuing campaign to hold on to Portugal's African colonies. Once in power, they began negotiations with the leaders of the nationalist movements in the colonies to work out arrangements for a transfer of power. In Mozambique this involved handing over control to the Frente de Libertação de Moçambique (FRELIMO), the only political movement in the colony with a genuine national base.[40]

The emergence of an independent Mozambique governed by FRELIMO had immediate and far-reaching effects on the conflict in Rhodesia. For one thing, combined with several other new considerations—such as the increasing activism of the so-called Frontline States (an informal group consisting of Tanzania, Zambia, Botswana, Mozambique after its independence, and subsequently Angola) and the growing involvement of the Soviet Union in the southern African region—it significantly increased external pressures on Rhodesia. For another, close ties already existed between FRELIMO and ZANLA. When ZANLA stepped up its guerrilla activities against Rhodesia in late 1972, it was assisted by FRELIMO forces. With FRELIMO in power in Mozambique, the entire eastern border of Rhodesia was opened to guerrilla infiltration. In addition, the Rhodesian government had to face the prospect that Rhodesia's rail outlets to the ports of Beira and Maputo (formerly Lourenço Marques) would be closed, leaving it only two rail outlets to the sea—both much longer routes through South Africa. Finally, Mozambique's independence gave the black states in the region significant leverage in the Rhodesian conflict.

The Portuguese coup affected South Africa as well, causing its leaders to reevaluate their policies toward Rhodesia. Before the coup South Africa provided considerable assistance to the Rhodesian government. At a secret meeting in September 1965, South Africa, Portugal, and Rhodesia allegedly had agreed on plans for a common defense of the entire region against "communism" and "nationalism."[41] In 1967 South Africa dispatched members of the South African police to Rhodesia, ostensibly in response to joint military operations by ZAPU and the African National Congress of South Africa. South Africa was not anxious to become directly involved in the conflict, but the prevailing strategic view in Pretoria was that it was better to fight the Communist "onslaught" in Rhodesia than wait for it to reach South Africa—especially if the cost of doing so appeared small.

The Portuguese coup forced South African officials to reconsider this view.

Mozambique, like Rhodesia, had always been regarded as important to South African security. The last thing South Africa's leaders wanted was a radical Marxist state on their northeastern border. However, when such a possibility became a certainty, they found they had few viable options. Unlike in Angola, there was no struggle for power among rival nationalist groups in Mozambique. If South Africa had wanted to support an alternative to FRELIMO, it would have had to create one. Recognizing FRELIMO's strength, Prime Minister Vorster and his cabinet decided not to contest its victory. Instead they decided to attempt to develop a modus vivendi with the new government.[42] Such a strategy would not only ensure South Africa continued access to Mozambican ports and migrant labor, but it would also offer Vorster a chance to prove South Africa's usefulness to other black African states. In this respect the strategy was not entirely new, but rather a resumption of the "outward looking" policy South Africa had adopted in the late 1960s.[43] The goal of that policy had been to improve South Africa's political standing on the continent and reduce pressure for immediate change inside the Republic. The results had been disappointing. With the exception of several very conservative African states—for example, Malawi and the Ivory Coast—South Africa's efforts had been totally rebuffed by black countries in Africa. In 1974 the situation seemed ripe for a second attempt.

Given this strategy, the greatest danger for South Africa was a protracted guerrilla struggle in Rhodesia that would inevitably polarize the entire region. South African officials realized that a white government in Rhodesia would not be able to win such a struggle. As a result, they decided to encourage a negotiated transfer of power. By pressuring Smith to settle, the South Africans hoped to avert a potentially disastrous conflict, provide further evidence of South Africa's usefulness to other African states, and possibly promote the installation of a more "moderate" government in Rhodesia than would otherwise be the case.

As South Africa reassessed its strategy, black states in the region met to consider their options. By late 1974 their discussions had led to the formation of the Frontline States, who assumed responsibility for negotiating with the white regimes. After two visits to Cape Town by Zambian envoy Mark Chona, Vorster informed the Frontline presidents that he would be willing to urge Smith to begin serious negotiations. After talks with Vorster, Smith reluctantly released six detained nationalist leaders—including Nkomo of ZAPU and Robert Mugabe and Sithole of ZANU*—to attend discussions with the Frontline presidents in Lusaka in mid-November. In December the Rhodesian parties agreed to hold a constitutional conference at a later date. [44]

The initiative for a constitutional conference did not have much chance of success. South African leverage was sufficient to get Smith to the bargaining table but not sufficient to convince him to negotiate seriously. Smith agreed to constitutional talks because there were advantages to be gained from appearing to negotiate—especially if he could be fairly certain that the negotiations would break down as a result of disagreements among those sitting on the other side of the bargaining table. By portraying his government as forthcoming and the opposition as unreasonable or double-dealing, Smith sought to increase support for his government from the Western powers and prove to the South Africans that nothing was to be gained by talking to "radicals." Through much of the conflict, Smith as well as the other main protagonists would engage in negotiations while having no intention of making the concessions necessary for a genuine settlement.

For two reasons there was little danger that Smith would be put on the defensive or forced into a settlement in negotiations. First, the success of FRELIMO in Mozambique and later of the liberation efforts in Angola bolstered the resolve of the Rhodesian movements by increasing the nationalists' confidence in the inevitability of their victory. With success on the battlefield seemingly assured, there was little reason for them to make significant concessions. Yet only by making concessions would they have been able to put Smith on the defensive. Second, schisms within the nationalist movement were a serious impediment to a negotiated settlement. Despite extensive efforts on the part of the Frontline States to force the various nationalist groups to come together under a single banner, the nationalist leaders remained bitterly divided. [45]

The December 1974 agreement to hold constitutional talks soon ran into trouble over Smith's contentions that the nationalists were not enforcing a ceasefire which he had demanded as a precondition

*During his time in prison, Sithole had been deposed as the president of ZANU and replaced by Mugabe. After being released, he attempted to reclaim his authority in the organization.

for further talks and his refusal to either attend talks outside of Rhodesia or grant immunity from arrest to exiled black leaders in order to allow them to attend talks in Rhodesia. After considerable maneuvering by South Africa and the Frontline States, a conference was scheduled for 26 August 1975, in a railway car on the bridge over Victoria Falls—midway between Zambia and Rhodesia. Despite the weighty presence of both Vorster and Zambian President Kenneth Kaunda, the talks ended in a deadlock, marking the end of the third phase of the conflict.[46]

As the third phase ended, the resolve of the Salisbury regime was weakening. Smith was beginning to realize that he would have to make some concessions to black demands. South Africa's posture of rapprochement with black governments meant that Rhodesia's costs of standing firm would increase. However, Smith was not yet willing to engage in sincere negotiations. Instead he began to search for a way to reduce the potential cost of a settlement. By playing on the divisions within the nationalist movement, he hoped to induce one of the more "moderate" black leaders to agree to "reasonable" terms. His objective was an "internal settlement" that would allow his regime to rally Western support and defeat the more "radical" elements within the nationalist movement.

PHASE FOUR: INTERNAL NEGOTIATIONS AND GUERRILLA WAR (SEPTEMBER 1975-MARCH 1976)

After the Victoria Falls talks broke down, all illusions of unity in the Rhodesian nationalist movement were shattered. On 11 September 1975 Muzorewa expelled Nkomo from the ANC; Nkomo responded by challenging Muzorewa's authority.* In late September Nkomo held his own ANC congress at Highfields, a black suburb of Salisbury. Six thousand delegates, including forty-three out of sixty-nine members of Muzorewa's ANC executive, attended. On 28 September, they elected Nkomo president of a newly constituted ANC.†

---

*In an attempt to prevent disunity in the nationalist movement, in early 1975 the Frontline States pressured ZAPU and ZANU to merge with the ANC under Muzorewa's leadership.

†This ANC was never anything other than an internal front for ZAPU, which, as always, followed Nkomo. In September 1976 the ANC faction led by Muzorewa renamed itself the United African National Council (UANC).

Shortly thereafter Nkomo began a series of meetings with Smith to discuss the possibility of formal negotiations. [47]

At the same time that Nkomo was involved in internal negotiations, the balance of power within the nationalist groups outside of Rhodesia was shifting. The younger, more militant ZANLA guerrillas were aligning themselves with Mugabe and against Muzorewa and Sithole. In November 1975 an agreement was reached between the liberation movements calling for a common military strategy, the integration of ZANU and ZAPU forces, and an eighteen-member joint military command comprised of nine ZIPRA leaders and nine ZANLA leaders. It was reached without the involvement of any of the external ANC leaders. [48]

The effort to integrate ZANLA and ZIPRA ultimately had to be abandoned because of several violent conflicts in the guerrilla camps. However, the guerrillas were able to intensify the military campaign inside Rhodesia. By 9 March 1976, Rhodesian Deputy Prime Minister Edward Stutton-Pryce estimated that the war zone inside the country had doubled since the beginning of the conflict. [49] In the first four months of 1976 official Rhodesian spokesmen estimated that nine hundred guerrillas had entered the country—a considerable increase over previous estimates. At the same time the guerrillas adopted new tactics. They began to disrupt road and rail traffic and to directly disrupt agricultural activity on the estates and plantations in the eastern highlands. [50] On 18 April, for the first time in the history of the war, ZANU forces managed to cut a rail link with South Africa at the Beit Bridge. During the attack three South African tourists were killed and a woman was wounded. This attack sent shock waves throughout the white community in Rhodesia, shattering the myth of invulnerability that had up until then provided white Rhodesians with a psychological defense against the worsening security situation. Many white Rhodesians point to the Beit Bridge attack as the beginning of the end for white rule in Rhodesia. [51]

On the political front, Smith and Nkomo announced a formal declaration of intent to negotiate a constitutional settlement on 1 December 1975. The declaration was immediately denounced by Sithole and Muzorewa. Despite the fact that Sithole had little or no control over any of the guerrilla forces, he declared that his forces intended to "shoot their way back into Zimbabwe." [52] Behind the scenes the British government attempted to encourage the Smith-Nkomo negotiations. The British had been peripherally involved in the regional initiative of the Frontline States and South Africa, but now they began to play a more direct role. When the talks stalemated in late January 1976, the British—with American cooperation—warned Smith of the consequences of a failure to come to terms with Nkomo. Specifically they sought to convince him that he could not count on any assistance if the war were to intensify.[53] Despite this renewed British pressure, the Smith regime showed few signs of moderating its position. On 20 February, Rhodesia's Minister of Defense and Foreign Affairs, P.K. Van der Byl, said that Rhodesia had never counted on British support. "But," he added, "that does not mean one should not expect the West—in their own interests—to do something about assisting southern Africa to halt Soviet expansionism."[54]

Smith and Nkomo continued to negotiate throughout the first half of March, but on 19 March talks broke down after Smith refused to accept Nkomo's final offer. Nkomo's proposals provided for a 144-seat legislature, with between 36 and 58 seats held by whites. The most Smith was willing to consider was a three-tier assembly in which one third of the seats would be reserved for whites, one third for blacks, and one third selected by voters on a common role. According to Rhodesian estimates, it would have taken at least 10 to 15 years for blacks to gain a majority of the seats under such an arrangement.[55]

Even if Smith and Nkomo had reached agreement, it would not have brought an end to the conflict. Nkomo was not in a position to sign an agreement on behalf of the majority of black Rhodesians. His main political base was the Ndebele tribal grouping, which comprises less than 20 percent of the black population. The other 80 percent is Shona-speaking. Although Nkomo's party (ZAPU) included several Shona speakers among its top leaders, it was ZANU and the ANC faction led by Muzorewa that could claim the support of the Shona masses. Thus unless Nkomo had been able to get an agreement that would give all of the major political leaders an opportunity to play a role in Rhodesia's political future, the war would have continued, but such an agreement was exactly what Smith had hoped to avoid by negotiating solely with Nkomo. The Rhodesian leader still believed that in the event of a final showdown with "Marxist" guerrillas, the West would side with Rhodesia. As long as he and his advisors were able to sustain that belief, they were unwilling to risk the potentially high costs of a comprehensive settlement.

PHASE FIVE: AMERICAN DIPLOMACY AND COMPREHENSIVE NEGOTIA-
TIONS (MARCH 1976-JANUARY 1977)

In 1975, as a result of civil war in Angola, Secretary of State
Henry Kissinger focused American attention on southern Africa. His
belated efforts to prevent the "radical" Movimento Popular de
Libertação de Angola (MPLA) from coming to power failed, and
Kissinger became concerned about the future of the subcontinent.
He feared that events in Angola—including Soviet and Cuban intervention on behalf of the black nationalist groups—might be repeated
in Rhodesia. The United States had been kept informed of the status of
the Smith-Nkomo negotiations by the British; when those talks broke
down, Kissinger decided to take action.

In late January 1976 it had been announced that Kissinger was
planning a trip to Africa at the end of April. At that time no one in
the American government—including Kissinger—knew exactly what
he would attempt to do during this trip. After the MPLA victory in
Angola, Kissinger's speeches had been full of warnings to the Soviets
and Cubans that America would not tolerate another Soviet venture
in Africa. However, U.S. options were severely limited. If the war in
Rhodesia had escalated and the Soviets and Cubans had become involved, the only direct counter for the United States would have been
to provide assistance to the white regime in Salisbury. Such an action
was out of the question. First, Kissinger could not have gotten such
an assistance program through Congress. Resistance would probably
have been greater than in the case of Angola, where Congress had prohibited American intervention. Second, if this program had been
adopted, it would have precipitated a calamitous break between America and most of Africa. Finally, it is doubtful that such a program
would have been able to achieve much more than a delay in the eventual defeat of the Smith government at a tremendously higher cost in
terms of human suffering. Realizing these things, Kissinger, at the urging of the Policy Planning Staff and Africa Bureau of the State Department, began to look for another alternative.*

On 22 March (three days after the Smith-Nkomo talks broke
down), British Foreign Secretary James Callaghan delivered a speech in
Parliament declaring Great Britain's preparedness to become involved

*The information that follows is based on or has been confirmed by interviews
with American and British officials.

in negotiations "with representatives of all shades of Rhodesian opinion, inside and out [of the country]" if Smith would accept four preconditions: (1) majority rule; (2) no independence before majority rule; (3) negotiations must not be long and drawn out; and (4) elections had to be held within eighteen months to two years.[56] In part these proposals were offered as a defensive gesture by the British. Given its precarious political position at the time, the Labour government was fearful of the consequences if it were to appear to be sitting idle while Rhodesia collapsed. At the same time, British leaders were skeptical about the prospects for a settlement. Callaghan's proposals were designed to demonstrate that it was Smith's intransigence, not British policy, that was at fault. Thus when Smith immediately rejected the proposals as "no less extreme than those of the ANC," it was probably what the British had expected.

In preparation for Kissinger's trip to Africa, the Policy Planning Staff had drafted a speech outlining a rather general statement of American support for majority rule without a proposal for substantive action to back up the rhetoric. Kissinger asked for a speech with more teeth in it. The final product of the drafting process was a speech Kissinger delivered in Lusaka on 27 April. In it he announced ten specific steps that the United States would take with regard to Rhodesia:

(1) American support for the March 22 Callaghan proposals;
(2) A declaration of America's "unrelenting opposition" to the Salisbury regime until a negotiated settlement was reached;
(3) A commitment to repeal the Byrd Amendment (1971), which allowed American firms to import chrome and thirteen other strategic materials from Rhodesia in violation of UN sanctions;*
(4) Support for a rapidly negotiated settlement leading to majority rule;
(5) A promise to discourage American citizens from traveling to Rhodesia;
(6) and (7) A promise to give $12.5 million in assistance to Mozambique and other states on Rhodesia's borders who suffered as a result of UN sanctions;
(8) U.S. assistance for Rhodesian refugees;
(9) A promise of economic, technical, and educational assistance to Rhodesia once an agreement had been reached; and

*For more on the Byrd Amendment, see p. 32 below.

(10) Support for the protection of minority rights after independence.[57]

Kissinger's speech marked the beginning of five months of intensive negotiations among all the actors in the conflict.[58] Over this period Kissinger met twice with Vorster, and other American officials made several trips to Africa to talk with other African leaders. In September Kissinger returned to Africa to pin down an agreement. The result was a public statement by Smith on 24 September, in which he accepted what he called the "Kissinger proposals" for a settlement to the Rhodesian conflict. The "package" (as Smith labeled it) included six points:

(1) Majority rule in two years;
(2) An immediate conference with African leaders to organize an interim government;
(3) The interim government was to consist of a Council of State, half of whose members would be black and half white, with a white chairman without a special vote. This council would be responsible for drafting a new constitution. There would also be a Council of Ministers with executive authority during the interim period. The Ministries of Defense and Law and Order on this council were to be held by whites;*
(4) Great Britain would enact enabling legislation once an agreement had been reached;
(5) Once the interim government was established, a ceasefire would begin; and
(6) The international community would provide "substantial economic support" to assure Rhodesia's economic future.

With the exception of number 6, these proposals had been dictated word for word to Smith by Kissinger. However, they had not been approved by either the Frontline States or the nationalist leaders. Within several days of Smith's speech it was clear to most observers that the prospective conference had almost no chance of succeeding. Smith and the African leaders looked at the conference in totally different terms. For Smith the sole purpose of the conference was to implement the "package" presented by Kissinger. For the Africans the purpose was to work out the details of an agreement. The conference opened in Geneva on 28 October—and it quickly stalemated.[59]

*This provision is discussed in detail on p. 25 below.

The Geneva conference adjourned on 14 December 1976. Chairman Ivor Richard (Britain's Ambassador to the United Nations) set 17 January 1977 as the date for resumption and announced that in the meantime he would undertake a comprehensive tour of Africa to attempt to find a basis for agreement. At the same time, Foreign Minister Anthony Crosland announced that Great Britain was considering new proposals that would involve a larger British role during a transition period. Richard met with Smith in Salisbury on 21 January, after having already gotten the firm support of the Frontline States for the new proposals. On 24 January Smith flatly rejected the proposals. "The fact of the matter," Richard said after receiving word of Smith's response, "is that the nationalist delegations accepted our proposals as a basis for discussion. They were prepared to negotiate about it. Mr. Smith apparently is not."[60]

Before Kissinger's efforts can be evaluated, it is important to note several points about his position in the proceedings. Throughout the negotiations Kissinger acted as an interlocutor, not a mediator. He had no choice. All of his leverage—with one exception, to be discussed below—was based on the resources and influence of other actors— South Africa, the Frontline States, and Great Britain—and none of it was sufficient to allow him to impose concessions on the main protagonists. As long as the Smith regime and the black nationalists thought it would be possible to improve the terms of an eventual agreement, they were not interested in making concessions. Negotiations could be used to probe for the weaknesses of the other side, exacerbate known weaknesses, or generate external support. Kissinger was successful in convincing Smith and his advisors of the gravity of their situation. That was a significant breakthrough. However, he underestimated the resolve of the nationalist leaders and overestimated the willingness of the white Rhodesians to make concessions.

Kissinger's initial success was based on three factors. First, he allowed the South Africans to exercise the full extent of their leverage on Smith. Contrary to the contentions of several writers, Kissinger did not have to "bribe" the South Africans into cooperating with him on Rhodesia. As noted above, their desire for a negotiated settlement existed before Kissinger entered the picture. However, there were two major limits on Vorster's ability to pressure Smith: (1) Vorster had to worry about a possible backlash within his own electorate if he were perceived as betraying the "white man's cause." On at least one occasion, Smith had attempted to counter Vorster's pressures by taking his case directly to the South African white community;[61] (2) Vorster could not openly support the international boycott of Rhodesia for fear that it would strengthen the case for applying similar pressure against South Africa itself. Kissinger offered Vorster a "cover." There is no question that Vorster's decisions to limit Rhodesian rail traffic through South Africa to one train a day and to withdraw South African helicopter pilots from Rhodesia were most responsible for Smith's concessions.[62] But it was Kissinger who applied the public *coup de grâce*.

Second, Kissinger took advantage of America's one source of direct leverage. Throughout the conflict Smith and his fellow white Rhodesians had firmly believed they were fighting on behalf of "Western civilization"; sooner or later the West would provide them with support against the "Communist menace" responsible for the guerrilla war. These beliefs had been reinforced by the Nixon administrations's "tilt" toward their position and by the passage of the Byrd Amendment.[63] In early 1976, when Kissinger launched his tirade against Soviet and Cuban intervention in Africa, white Rhodesians grew even more confident that they could count on Western—i.e., American—support. However, by declaring America's support for majority rule and making it clear that the United States would under no circumstances aid the Smith regime, Kissinger dramatically altered white Rhodesian perceptions of the cost of standing firm. (It is important to recognize, though, that once Kissinger had used this leverage and the white regime had adjusted its expectations, further American threats could have no effect on Rhodesian resolve.)

Third, Kissinger was able to deal successfully with the Frontline States. Although the main problem before negotiations got under way was getting Smith to accept majority rule, Kissinger could not have made headway without at least the appearance that he was involving the parties that would ultimately sit across the bargaining table from Smith. Kissinger had been surprised at the receptiveness of Zambia and Tanzania to his initiative. When he made his first trip in April, he got a tentative go-ahead to open discussions with South Africa. At every stage of the discussions he carefully sought African approval. For their part, the Frontline States agreed to "deliver" the various nationalist leaders to a conference once Smith had made the necessary concessions.

Kissinger's efforts had been devoted entirely to getting all of the parties to the conference table—not to producing an agreement. He mistakenly assumed that once the conference began, it would be possible to hammer out a settlement. The ultimate collapse of the Geneva talks can be attributed to three specific Kissinger mistakes. First, in order to get Smith to the conference table, Kissinger "finessed" both Smith and the Frontline States.[64] In Pretoria Smith accepted Kissinger's "package" with one critical provision: white control of the Ministries of Defense and Law and Order during a transition period. This provision had been in some of the earlier drafts of the proposals, but it was not included in the final draft Kissinger presented to Smith. Kissinger did not agree on the spot; instead he said he would have to check with the Frontline States. From Pretoria he flew to Lusaka and Dar es Salaam, where he informed a jubilant Kaunda and Julius Nyerere respectively that Smith had accepted majority rule. While in Dar es Salaam, Kissinger sent a cable to Smith indicating that the provision regarding the ministries "could be included." Kissinger did not tell Smith that the African leaders had in fact accepted this provision earlier. Undersecretary William Rogers later testified before the Senate Foreign Relations Committee that the African presidents had not ever finally agreed to this provision—or any of the other provisions for that matter. Either Kissinger misled Smith into believing that the proposals were a package and not subject to further negotiations, or Smith deliberately misinterpreted the status of the proposals in order to lay the ground for an internal settlement. Regardless of which interpretation is correct, it is clear that Smith was not willing to make the concessions that would have been required to satisfy nationalist demands.

The second specific mistake Kissinger made was to place too much reliance on the British. It had been Kissinger's intention to get the parties to agree to talk and then leave the negotiations to the British. However, the British were not anxious to be dragged in too far. They regarded the proposals that Kissinger took to Smith as a study paper, not official British policy. The proposals had not been given cabinet approval. In their eyes, Kissinger had shown up in the middle of the night with a skeleton plan and said, "Now you deliver." Crosland deliberately distanced himself from the negotiations. Despite African protests, he delegated the task of chairing the Geneva conference to Richard. Furthermore, the British made it clear that they had no intention of becoming directly involved in any transitional arrangements.

Without Britain's willingness to assume some authority during a transitional period, it was highly unlikely that the most critical issues—e.g., who would be in charge of the security forces and who would run the election—could be solved.

The third mistake in Kissinger's strategy was that it provided no solution to the problem of conflict within the nationalist movement. With the exception of Nkomo, Kissinger had no direct contacts with the nationalist leaders, relying on the Frontline States for communication with them. During his first trip, Muzorewa and Sithole had refused to see him on the grounds that there was no prospect for successful negotiations. (Ironically these leaders were then seen by many Western observers as "radicals," while Nkomo was widely viewed as "moderate.") At that point, Kissinger had no knowledge of Mugabe—already the most important ZANU leader.[65] Although the Frontline leaders had considerable leverage over the nationalists, they could not impose unity on them. Just prior to the Geneva conference, they were able to get Mugabe and Nkomo to establish a joint ZANU-ZAPU political alliance—the Patriotic Front (PF). However, in Geneva the competition among Mugabe, Nkomo, Muzorewa, and Sithole was so intense and bitter that they were not able to confront Smith with a united stand and force him to either negotiate seriously or withdraw from the negotiations. Instead they allowed him to use the conference for his own purposes—i.e., to begin movement toward an "internal settlement" that would satisfy South Africa and the West.

Kissinger has offered the following explanation for the failure of the Geneva conference: "After the defeat of [incumbent Gerald] Ford, it was clear that a different policy would be followed by the new administration. As a result, the conference stalemated until the inauguration. Shortly afterward the conference blew up, partly because the radical members escalated their demands and partly because the new administration had lost interest in the existing framework."[66] This explanation misrepresents the situation that existed in late 1976.

As indicated above, the main reason the Geneva conference collapsed was that conditions for a successful settlement did not exist. While the election of Jimmy Carter had an effect on the conference, it is unfair to say that the Carter administration had "lost interest in the existing framework." To the contrary, Carter sent signals to Geneva that he supported the talks. Moreover, Kissinger's contention that the "radical members" were the guilty parties ignores the fact that it was Smith who closed the door on further negotiations when Richard went to Rhodesia in January 1977. Kissinger's argument fails to take into account the fact that Smith, Mugabe, and Nkomo all believed they could gain from standing firm. Smith thought he could get better terms through an internal settlement, while Mugabe and Nkomo believed they could eventually win on the battlefield. At the end of 1976, only Muzorewa and Sithole were committed to an international settlement, and neither was in a position to end the conflict. Even if Ford had won reelection in 1976 and Kissinger had remained Secretary of State, a settlement would not have been possible.

PHASE SIX: INTERNAL NEGOTIATIONS AND GUERRILLA WAR (JANUARY 1977-APRIL 1979)

The collapse of the Kissinger initiative coincided with leadership changes in London as well as Washington. David Owen, a young, bright Labour Party MP became British Foreign Minister after the sudden death of Crosland. Owen was far more willing than the cautious Crosland to directly involve Great Britain in a Rhodesian settlement. His views fit perfectly with those of the men Carter put in charge of America's Africa policy. The appointment of Andrew Young as Ambassador to the United Nations and individuals with Africa experience—for example, Donald McHenry and Anthony Lake—in key middle-level foreign-policy positions signaled a new American interest in southern Africa and a new era of Anglo-American cooperation. Unfortunately the new leaders brought with them no new sources of influence over the main protagonists in Rhodesia.

Even before the Geneva conference had adjourned, Smith had begun to suggest that he might attempt a separate settlement. In Salisbury he announced on 5 November 1976 that he would implement the Kissinger proposals himself if the negotiations in Geneva broke down. Smith hinted at his plan of action when he called Muzorewa's delegation "most responsible" and said that Sithole had been "surprisingly responsible."[67] He provided a frank indication of his strategy in an interview:

It is a fact that in the talks I had with Dr. Kissinger in Pretoria . . . he did give me assurances that if we entered this agreement and it collapsed because of what the black Rhodesians had done, as

27

opposed to myself and my government, that he was absolutely convinced that we would get a great deal of sympathy from the Free World and also tangible assistance. And he believed it would lead to greater material support. [68]

Clearly the cost of the war was increasing rapidly and the Rhodesian economy was deteriorating. [69] In order to survive, the white regime needed Western assistance and the lifting of sanctions. In the past when Smith had negotiated with blacks, he had not felt the need to make major concessions. By 1977 he realized he had no choice. His new goal was to limit the concessions he would have to make and control to whom they would be made. He hoped to make a deal with the blacks in the weakest bargaining position and then go on the offensive against the others. For this plan to succeed Smith had to gain the support of three groups: (1) the South African government, (2) "moderate" black leaders, and (3) the Western powers. All of Smith's actions over the next two and a half years were directed toward this end.

It was not very difficult for Smith to gain South African support. While South African officials wanted an end to the Rhodesian conflict, they did not want to see a "radical" government come to power in Salisbury. An internal settlement appealed to them: it closely paralleled their own objective for a settlement in Namibia. [70] Furthermore, the Carter victory in the United States had served to decrease their interest in squeezing Smith. When the Republicans were in power, the South Africans could hope that an end to the Rhodesian conflict would decrease Western pressure on them. Carter administration officials indicated very early that they would not be willing to provide such a quid pro quo. [71]

South Africa's policy became clear at the beginning of 1977. Just four days after Smith had rejected the latest British proposals, Vorster declared in the South African Parliament that boycotts were contrary to South African policy. [72] On 9 February Smith and Vorster met in Cape Town; the next day Smith announced that he was actively seeking an internal settlement. While he said he would continue to talk with the British and Americans, he said he felt there was "no future" in continuing to talk with the PF. [73] Vorster implicitly supported this decision in a BBC interview: "As far as outside countries are concerned, whether they like the solution is totally immaterial because it is not their country."[74] However, it was too early for Smith to entirely abandon international negotiations at this point.

As noted above, both Great Britain and the United States were busy in early 1977 canvassing Africa to discover grounds for further negotiations. On 11 May, after discussions with American Secretary of State Cyrus Vance, Owen announced that an Anglo-American team headed by British Foreign Office official John Graham and American Ambassador to Zambia Stephen Low would begin one-on-one meetings with interested parties.[75] This new initiative represented a tactical departure from previous Anglo-American efforts. Instead of trying to get general agreement on proposals for a transition period and then trying to hammer out constitutional details at an all-parties conference, the new approach sought to work out a settlement, including a new constitution, through bilateral negotiations; after an agreement had been reached, a conference would be held to ratify the terms. The so-called Anglo-American proposals were made public on 1 September 1977.[76] All sides reacted with caution. None of the key leaders was willing to reject the proposals out of hand, but all had serious reservations about parts of them. The main area of disagreement centered on the issue of control over the police and security forces during a transition period. The PF leaders demanded that it be granted to the guerrilla forces, while the Salisbury government insisted upon retaining it. At the root of the disagreement was one consideration: no group was willing to accept any proposals that might mean it would not be in power after independence. Since there was no formula that could ensure all parties that they would be in power after independence and since all parties still believed they could improve their bargaining power without making any major concessions, the Anglo-American proposals were doomed.

Smith temporarily shelved his plans for an internal settlement to consider the Anglo-American proposals, but by 23 October he was moving ahead again on his plans. Over the previous nine months, he had cleared away a number of obstacles. In late February he had announced plans to eliminate racial discrimination in the country. At the end of April he had purged twelve extreme right-wing rebels from the Rhodesian Front. On 18 July he had dissolved Parliament and called for new elections in which he said he would seek white support for an internal settlement. "As part of this plan," he had told Rhodesians, "I envisage the creation of a broad based Government incorporating those black Rhodesians who are prepared to work peacefully and constitutionally with the present government in order to establish a base from which we would be able to draw up our future constitution."[77] Late in July, South African Foreign Minister R.F. (Pik) Botha had suggested that an election be held to decide the "indisputable leader" of black Rhodesians. After the election, he had argued, the West should give its support to the winner (whom he did not expect to come from the PF). The result would be continued conflict because it was inevitable that the losers would not put down their guns. Botha had declared that the British would then have to decide whether to support "free and open" elections or to placate "the men with the guns."[78]

Smith's plans could succeed only if he were able to induce widely acceptable black leaders to go along. Muzorewa and Sithole were attractive candidates for several reasons. First, their long-standing involvement in the nationalist movement gave them necessary international credibility. Second, Rhodesian intelligence had concluded in late 1976 that Muzorewa would win an open election. Just as important, neither Muzorewa nor Sithole had any guerrilla support, and both were in danger of being cut out of the black struggle by Mugabe and Nkomo. To continue to carry weight they needed either armies or a relatively quick settlement. Since there was little prospect that they could develop their own armies, their best hope was a settlement on the lines of the Anglo-American proposals. Ironically Smith's greatest leverage over these two leaders was his ability to prevent such a settlement: the more dismal the prospects for a settlement, the greater the pressure on Muzorewa and Sithole to develop alternatives, and the greater Smith's bargaining power.

On 9 January 1977 the Frontline States had decided to give their full support to the PF. This decision, later endorsed by the Organization of African States (OAU), was intended to solidify the alliance between ZANU and ZAPU and bolster military pressure on the whites. The Frontline leaders were caught in a dilemma. On the one hand, they were convinced that the only way to get the Salisbury regime to make meaningful concessions was to increase the war effort; on the other, they were interested in ending the war as soon as possible. By siding with Nkomo and Mugabe, they were able to make it more costly for the whites to stand firm, but at the same time they increased the potential intransigence of the PF. In addition, abandoning Muzorewa and Sithole had a dual effect. It reduced conflict within the nationalist involvement, but it gave Smith new alternatives.

At first both Muzorewa and Sithole had refused to enter into negotiations with Smith. By March there had been rumors they were wavering. In July Sithole had returned to Rhodesia from exile. On 24 November, with the Anglo-American proposals seemingly going nowhere, Smith announced that he accepted the principle of majority rule and would begin talks on 9 December with Muzorewa, Sithole, and two traditional leaders—Chiefs Jeremiah Chirau and Kayisa Ndiweni.

The PF leaders' main response to the internal talks was a stepping up of the war effort. Nkomo declared on 24 November: "The British have nothing to talk about. As far as we are concerned, we are going to fight. There will be no negotiations, just a formal signing of surrender instruments."[79] In early December the PF refused to meet with Owen in London. In the face of this deteriorating situation, the leaders of the Frontline States met in Beira on 18 December, reaffirmed their support for the Anglo-American proposals, and began to consider ways to get negotiations back on track. Mozambican President Samora Machel began to apply pressure on the PF to resume negotiations. On 13 January 1978 he called for new talks on the Anglo-American proposals; an unidentified Mozambican official said his government recognized that PF demands for control over the military during a transition period were "unrealistic."[80] Six days later it was announced that PF leaders would meet with Anglo-American representatives on Malta at the end of January. Although American and British officials viewed the Malta talks as a positive development, they had no effect on the more important talks that were being held in Salisbury.

Despite a brief walkout by Muzorewa, the Salisbury talks culminated in an internal settlement on 3 March 1978, establishing a transitional government and setting 31 December 1978 as the date for elections. A new constitution provided for universal suffrage but reserved twenty-eight seats in the one hundred-seat Parliament for whites (enough to provide whites with a veto over constitutional changes) and left whites firmly in control of the civil service.[81] Nine days after they signed the agreement, the participants in the "Salisbury coalition" announced they were not interested in an all-parties conference. With the South Africans and the "moderate" blacks behind it, the coalition focused its attention on the West.

31

Western support for the Rhodesian government had reached an ebb in early 1977. In response to Smith's plans for a separate settlement that would exclude the guerrilla leaders, Vance had told reporters at his first press conference on 31 January 1977 that "the position announced by Mr. Smith has resulted in a new and more dangerous situation regarding the prospects for peace in Rhodesia. The Rhodesian authorities should understand clearly that under no circumstances can they count on any form of American assistance in their effort to prevent majority rule in Rhodesia or to enter into negotiations which exclude leaders of nationalist movements."[82] Furthermore, he had announced that the administration planned to make a major effort to persuade Congress to repeal the Byrd Amendment.

The Byrd Amendment had survived repeated repeal attempts. A coalition of conservatives and steel producers had managed to persuade a majority in Congress that its repeal would cost American steelworkers jobs, raise the price of imported chromium, and make the United States dependent on the Soviet Union. However, armed with an impressive array of well-researched counterarguments and the firm support of the new administration, Senator Dick Clark of Iowa, Chairman of the Africa Subcommittee of the Senate Foreign Relations Committee, succeeded in getting the amendment repealed on 15 March 1977.* The key to the repeal was a voting shift by a number of moderate Congressmen who were no longer convinced that the amendment served American interests. For example, Senator Howard Baker, who had consistently voted against repeal, said the following during the floor debate:

> For the immediate future, neither the strategic nor the economic interests of the United States are served by continuing the abrogation of our legal responsibility to abide by the sanctions imposed on Rhodesia under the charter of the United Nations. Finally, the long term interest of the United States will be adversely affected by a continuance of the Byrd Amendment. Whether by peaceful or violent means, Rhodesia is a territory in transition: sooner or later it will be a nation at least nominally representative of its black majority. . . . If chrome or other natural resources are truly the

---

*The repeal measure passed both houses of Congress by surprisingly comfortable margins—66-26 in the Senate and 250-146 in the House of Representatives (see *Congressional Quarterly Almanac*, 1977, pp. 328-31).

issue at stake, then the interests of the United States are better served by repeal of the Byrd Amendment. This is particularly true, if by repeal we are in a better position to encourage the development of a moderate successor government favorably disposed to the United States.[83]

The internal settlement in Salisbury was designed to reconvert Baker and others like him—i.e., it was designed to appeal to American legislators who could reverse the Carter administration's policy in the United States and to British Conservatives, who were poised to replace the Labour government in Great Britain. Once Muzorewa and Sithole were in the government, supporters could argue that the Salisbury regime was a "moderate," multiracial government committed to Western democratic principles and besieged by "radical Marxist terrorists." An integral part of such a strategy was an effort to portray American and British policymakers as "pro-terrorist." When Owen and Young had sought to head off the internal negotiations in January 1978, Smith had issued a statement calling on the British government to "get off our backs and stop hindering the progress of our country to peace and prosperity."[84] He had accused the British of being unwilling to support a settlement "unless it is acceptable to the terrorists and to the leaders of neighboring states who harbour and nurture the terrorists and to the Russians who arm and equip the terrorists."[85]

The internal settlement put the British and Americans in a severe bind. They were correct in arguing that it would not end the war, but they found it difficult to explain *why* without sounding like they were giving in to the guerrillas. Newspaper editorials in many cities across the United States praised the developments in Rhodesia and asked why the Carter administration was opposing them.[86] Less than a week after the internal settlement was announced, four influential American Senators jointly introduced a resolution calling on the government to give the Salisbury accord serious consideration.

Faced with domestic pressures for acceptance of the internal settlement, the State Department first refused to commit itself. On 8 March, amidst rumors of a rift between the United States and Great Britain, Vance acknowledged that the agreement was "a significant step" toward majority rule in Rhodesia, but added that "a great deal remains unclear about what is involved in that proposal."[87] Counterbalancing these domestic pressures, African leaders pushed for a strong condemnation of the internal settlement. It was vociferously attacked by the leaders of the Frontline States, prompting the State Department to reaffirm its commitment to the Anglo-American proposals and emphasize the "serious inadequacies" of the internal settlement.[88]

The clearest statement of American policy toward the internal settlement was made by Carter during a visit to Nigeria. In a joint communique with Nigerian leader Lt.-Gen. Olusegun Obasanjo on 1 April, the President noted that the settlement "does not change the illegal character of the present regime and is unacceptable as it does not guarantee a genuine transfer of power to the majority."[89] As a result of discussions with the Nigerians and representatives of the Frontline States in Lagos, Carter agreed to dispatch Vance to southern Africa in a renewed effort to get the Anglo-American proposals back on track.

Vance traveled first to Dar es Salaam, where he and Owen met with PF leaders. Based on the discussions in Lagos, Vance and Owen thought that the PF leaders were ready to agree to the details of the Anglo-American proposals, but they quickly discovered that this was not the case. The main point of contention was still over the provisions for control of the police and military during a transition period. A heated meeting with ZANU leaders left both Vance and Owen doubtful that a settlement was possible,[90] although the PF leaders did not close the door on future talks. The two diplomats proceeded to Salisbury, where they were greeted coolly. Now that Muzorewa and Sithole were on the inside, neither saw the need for talks. The Executive Council of the Salisbury regime announced on 25 April that it did not believe new talks would serve any purpose. Instead it proposed that ZANU and ZAPU put down their guns and accept the framework outlined by the internal settlement. In what was to become a constant refrain, the regime insisted that "the leaders of the Patriotic Front were not excluded from our negotiations, they excluded themselves."[91]

The main problem at this point was that all parties believed their bargaining position was improving. PF leaders initially saw the internal settlement as a sign of the white regime's weakness. Time seemed to be on their side. More and more white Rhodesians were leaving the country, and economic conditions inside the country were deteriorating. Bolstering the PF's resolve was a joint announcement on 24 April by the Soviet Union and Cuba that they intended to increase aid to the guerrilla forces.[92] At the same time, signals from London and

Washington indicated that the internal settlement was not likely to get much Western support. As far as Smith, Muzorewa, Sithole, and their associates were concerned, a new game was beginning. While the war was becoming more intense, they evidently believed that large numbers of the "boys in the bush" would be willing to give up once they realized that (as Muzorewa frequently claimed) "the things they are fighting for have been accomplished." Thus on 2 May 1978 the government announced a general amnesty.[93] Moreover, it started a campaign for Western support. Ironically, the one person in the Salisbury regime who appears to have quickly begun to have doubts about the future prospects of the internal settlement was Smith himself.

Smith was informed on 14 June by his military advisors that the military situation was not improving.[94] Few guerrillas had taken advantage of the amnesty. Smith responded in two ways. First, he gave an interview to Canadian and British television in which he admitted the war was getting worse and claimed that Great Britain and the United States could resolve the conflict by accepting the internal settlement and lifting sanctions. "With one act," Smith said, "the British Government would solve our problem. It would bring terrorism to an end."[95] Second, at roughly the same time, Smith approached the PF leader with whom he still thought he might be able to make a deal: Nkomo.

Through the efforts of the British, the Nigerians, and Kaunda a secret meeting was arranged between Smith and Nkomo on 14 August. Smith's interest in such a meeting is obvious: Nkomo was viewed by many as the father of Zimbabwean nationalism; his presence in an internal government would have virtually guaranteed international recognition. He was acceptable to the British, many Africans, and South Africa. Despite the fact that ZAPU received more aid from the Soviet Union than did ZANU, Smith regarded Nkomo as a pragmatist and moderate. Nkomo's interest in a meeting with Smith is less clear. He later claimed he never intended to make a separate deal with Smith, that he wanted only to explore the possibility of a settlement that would include Mugabe. Given the long history of animosity between ZANU and ZAPU and the possibility that ZANU (with many more guerrillas inside the country) might end up in control as a result of a military denouement, Nkomo's explanation drew a skeptical response from many observers. The details of the Smith-Nkomo meeting and its aftermath are still in dispute.[96] The meeting became public only after Muzorewa and Sithole, who had not been consulted by Smith, leaked information to the press. If there had been any prospects for a Smith-Nkomo deal, they were destroyed on 4 September, when guerrillas shot down an Air Rhodesia passenger plane; forty-eight people were killed. Nkomo announced that his forces were responsible, and the public outcry in Rhodesia was so strong that it prevented Smith from even considering reopening the talks with him.[97]

The Smith-Nkomo meeting and the attack on the Air Rhodesia plane gave the internal settlement regime a tremendous boost. The former created tensions within the Frontline States and further heightened antagonisms between ZAPU and ZANU. Recognizing that an impasse had developed, British and American officials met in London on 9 September and decided to temporarily reduce their efforts to promote a settlement in conjunction with the Anglo-American proposals.[98] More important, the plane incident increased the momentum behind efforts to win Western support for the internal settlement by reinforcing the "terrorist" image of the PF. After the repeal of the Byrd Amendment, the Carter administration had been confident that its policies were supported by Congress. This confidence was seriously shaken when Senator Jesse Helms came within six votes of gaining Senate approval of a measure that would have forced the Carter administration to lift sanctions against Rhodesia by 31 December 1978.[99] Helms quickly launched a concerted effort to garner the additional votes needed. Largely at Helms's invitation, Muzorewa came to Washington in July to lobby on behalf of the internal settlement.[100] Rather than risk a defeat that might destroy its policy entirely, the Carter administration decided to accept compromise legislation proposed by Senators Clifford Case and Jacob Javits.

The Case-Javits Amendment to the International Security Assistance Act of 1978 was adopted by the Senate on 26 July. It called for the removal of sanctions against Rhodesia after 31 December 1978

provided that the President determines that (1) the Government of Rhodesia has demonstrated its willingness to negotiate in good faith at an all-parties conference, held under international auspices, on all issues; and (2) a government has been installed, chosen by free elections in which all political and population groups have been allowed to participate freely, with observation by impartial, internationally-recognized observers.[101]

At a joint House-Senate Conference Committee session on 15 August, the House agreed to accept the Senate amendment.

The Rhodesian regime was also given a boost by developments in London. The Conservative Party's foreign policy spokesman, John Davis, told Conservative back-benchers on 25 June that a Tory government would be ready to send a full-scale diplomatic mission to Rhodesia to help frame a constitution, guide the rulers in the internal settlement, and generally help establish confidence in the settlement.[102] On 2 August the Labour government barely defeated a Conservative amendment criticizing its Rhodesia policy and calling for an end to sanctions.[103] Elliot Gabellah, Co-Minister of Foreign Affairs in the Rhodesian regime, commented in Salisbury: "I am absolutely delighted and most encouraged by the rising tide of support in both Britain and the United States for the Transitional government."[104]

The Case-Javits Amendment redefined the terms of the U.S. debate over Rhodesia and put the Carter administration on the defensive. The two conditions it set were entirely different from the considerations that underpinned American policy. Even if they had been met, the war would have continued. Recognition of the internal settlement regime and the lifting of sanctions would have bolstered the resolve of the internal parties, but they still would not have been able to win the war. To the contrary, the war would have continued to escalate, polarizing the entire region and leaving the United States hopelessly caught in the middle.[105] By accepting the Case-Javits Amendment, the Carter administration weakened its ability to defend its policy in the best possible terms. It was forced to debate on the grounds the Salisbury regime preferred.

After the amendment was adopted, the Salisbury regime became less concerned with genuine progress toward a negotiated settlement and more concerned with projecting the right appearances. As long as it could appear to meet the two conditions, it had no incentive to negotiate seriously. In order to give the Salisbury leaders an opportunity to present their case to the American public, on 14 September twenty-seven American Senators invited them to visit the United States.[106]

The four leaders of the Salisbury regime — Smith, Muzorewa, Sithole, and Chirau — arrived in the United States on 7 October and immediately went on the offensive against the Carter administration. In a nationally televised interview Smith argued that the real reason for the failure of the 2 May ceasefire established by his government was the fact that the American and British governments are supporting the Patriotic Front of Marxist terrorists instead of supporting the internal settlement by peaceful people, to try to bring Rhodesia into the Western camp. There is no doubt, I want to promise you, that if we got the support which we should get because of previous commitments, terrorism would have collapsed by now.[107]

For the next eleven days the Rhodesians took advantage of every opportunity to present their case to the American public. The culmination of their trip was a meeting in Washington with British and American officials to discuss a revised version of the Anglo-American proposals. After the meeting, Smith announced that his regime was willing to attend an all-parties conference—a reversal of prior statements by Muzorewa and Sithole forecasting (for example) that such a conference would be another "Geneva fiasco."[108] The supporters of the Salisbury regime could now claim that it would be in compliance with the terms of the Case-Javits Amendment as soon as internal elections were held.

By their visit to the United States, the Rhodesian leaders forced the British and American governments to increase their efforts to get the rival parties to resume negotiations. In a move designed primarily to counter the Rhodesian government's campaign (now Prime Minister) Callaghan asked Cledwyn Hughes, former Labour Minister for Commonwealth Affairs, to visit southern Africa to assess the prospects for renewed negotiations. Hughes reported back on 20 December that a sufficient basis for convening an all-party meeting did not exist:

All the parties would come to a conference now with profound reservations. Each side in the war is convinced that it can reach its goal—or at least not lose—by continuing to follow its own present policies. Thus the Patriotic Front would attend believing that it can achieve its aims by war, but that there is nothing to lose by attempting to achieve them by negotiation before military victory comes. The Salisbury parties would attend believing that they would lose nothing by again offering a place to the Patriotic Front within the internal settlement. They doubt at present whether there is any future for them in a country ruled by the Patriotic Front, and they think that, if the latter will not abandon its claims, they can hope to survive by following the path they have mapped

38

out for themselves in the 3 March agreement. The chief motive at the moment of each side in the negotiation will, I am afraid, not be to seek an understanding but rather to demonstrate that the other is unreasonable and intransigent, and thus to strengthen its own claim to external support and sympathy.[109]

Hughes concluded that the conditions he described were not likely to change until after the internal election.

Inside Rhodesia the situation continued to deteriorate. The internal parties were unable to use their successes abroad to make progress at home. In late September Rhodesian officials had publicly acknowledged that the level of hostilities in the rural areas made it virtually impossible to register voters in time for a December election.[110] On 29 October, evidently without consulting Muzorewa and Sithole, Smith announced that elections would be delayed until April 1979 for "purely mechanical reasons."[111] Despite mounting Rhodesian strikes against guerrilla base camps in Mozambique and Zambia, the influx of guerrillas into Rhodesia continued.[112] Large areas of western and southern Rhodesia were placed under martial law on 31 October. Guerrillas began to hit previously untouched targets in urban areas; in one particularly important incident on 11 December, they destroyed twenty-eight oil tanks at a bulk storage depot in Salisbury.[113] Reacting to these events, whites left Rhodesia in record numbers in each of the final three months of 1978.[114] When confronted on the seriousness of the situation, Smith admitted Rhodesia was not winning the war but argued that his forces would be able to contain it "for a long time."[115]

The Salisbury regime was able to maintain its resolve for two reasons. First, it continued to believe it would eventually win Western support. On 18 January 1979 Van der Byl explained: "The Rhodesian view is that once the new constitution has been accepted by the white voters, and once one-man, one-vote elections have been held next April 20, international opposition to the country will be indefensible."[116] This view was reinforced by conservatives in both the United States and Great Britain. For example, in late January Helms sent the following note to Sithole: "There are many members of the United States Congress who are wholeheartedly behind you. . . . We shall continue to do our utmost to remove the impediment of sanctions, preferably quickly, but certainly not later than immediately after your elections."[117] Second, Rhodesian hopes were buoyed by support from South Africa. The success of the internal settlement had become linked to Prime Minister P.W. Botha's design for "a constellation of states."[118] In order to bolster the Salisbury regime, South Africa committed substantial amounts of money, military supplies, and manpower to the war effort, making it easier for the internal parties to afford the rising costs of resisting a settlement.[119] With Rhodesia counting on external support to reverse its declining fortunes, there was—as the Hughes report had suggested—nothing positive for policymakers in Washington and London to do except wait for the April elections.

The results of the election for the seventy-two seats in the new Parliament were announced on 24 April. Muzorewa's UANC was the landslide winner, capturing fifty-one seats and 67 percent of the votes; Muzorewa became Prime Minister. Earlier in the month, in a separate election, the Rhodesian Front had won all twenty-eight of the white seats.[120] The results of the election were almost of secondary importance. The internal parties had agreed the previous December that regardless of the outcome of the election, the new government would be "a coalition of national unity" with cabinet portfolios distributed on the basis of the number of parliamentary seats each party won in the election.[121] Thus the whites would retain at least one quarter of the cabinet posts. This agreement, in conjunction with built-in restrictions in the independence constitution, limited the power of a new black prime minister regardless of the size of his parliamentary majority.[122]

More important than the election results was how the election appeared to the outside world. In order to satisfy the terms of the Case-Javits Amendment and win Western support, the Salisbury parties needed a large voter turnout and a "free and fair" process. The voter turnout—roughly 63 percent—was considerably higher than had been anticipated; the majority of the international observers present sent home favorable reports on the election process;[123] only a few pointed out subtle biases and coercive features that were built into the political system.[124] Despite charges of fraud by Sithole, whose party did far worse than he had expected, there were no signs of it. Given that the country was at war, there were surprisingly few major incidents of any sort during the voting. Thus from the standpoint of the internal parties the election was a success.

40

After the election, Rhodesian officials began to predict that sanctions would be lifted soon—Smith said within two months.[125] One official commented, "Our opponents are running around like headless chickens. They're on the defensive, and our friends are on the offensive."[126] When Margaret Thatcher and the Conservative Party defeated the Labour Government in British parliamentary elections on 3 May, Rhodesians grew even more confident that the tide of events was flowing in their favor.

The significance of the elections was not lost on the leaders of the PF. They immediately began to make plans to recapture lost ground by stepping up the war effort. Mugabe and Nkomo met in Addis Ababa under the watchful eye of the Soviet Union's firmest supporter in Africa, Ethiopian leader Lt. Col. Mengistu Haile Mariam. After three days of talks, the two leaders announced that a joint military operations command would be formed to coordinate the actions of ZANLA and ZIPRA.[127] In an amazingly frank interview Mugabe said:

> Our unity is now a reality. I accept that past efforts have failed to unify the two wings of the Patriotic Front but both sides felt that unity was imperative now. The forces against us in Salisbury are gathering momentum. The Smith-Muzorewa-South African alliance is seeking recognition and the indications are that they might get it, in which case the internal regime will receive further military and financial support from abroad. We have to reverse that trend.[128]

The April elections marked the end of the sixth phase of the conflict. Vance acknowledged in London on 23 May that "a new reality" now existed in Rhodesia.[129] In January 1977 Smith and his white government had been in their weakest bargaining position since the beginning of conflict. Twenty-seven months later, they appeared to have regained the initiative, albeit at the expense of a major strategic concession in the form of the internal settlement—their version of a "neocolonial" solution. A negotiated settlement seemed to be out of the question since the main protagonists were convinced they could improve their position by standing firm.

PHASE SEVEN: TOWARD A SETTLEMENT (MAY 1979-APRIL 1980)

A major irony of the Rhodesian conflict is that the April 1979 elections, which the internal parties thought would be their salvation, ultimately caused their downfall. The reasons are quite simple. The internal parties were able to generate a surprisingly large turnout in the elections by promising war-weary Rhodesians an end to the war, yet the leaders continued to believe that the main problem was a lack of international support, not the war. In effect, they were looking for an external solution to an internal problem. As it became clear to both their potential external supporters and the Rhodesian population—blacks and whites—that the new government could not end the war, the internal parties began to lose support.

The Thatcher government in Great Britain had become the internal parties' main source of hope. After the British elections, Muzorewa said, "Our victory would not have been complete without Mrs. Thatcher's victory."[130] Before Thatcher's election, one senior Conservative MP had noted the following: "There is a substantial chance—no, a probability—that she will say to Smith, 'OK, you've fulfilled what we asked, so now we will recognize you.'"[131] However, almost immediately after the British election, officials in the new Conservative government—in particular moderate Foreign Secretary Lord Carrington—set about developing plans that were certain to disappoint Rhodesian leaders.

Vance flew to London for meetings with the new government on 21 May. He was prepared for a major dispute over Rhodesia because the Carter administration had evidently already decided to resist Congressional efforts to lift sanctions.[132] To Vance's surprise, he soon discovered that the British had no intention of taking precipitate action on Rhodesia.[133] Carrington and Vance, with Thatcher's support, developed a new Anglo-American posture toward the conflict.

Britain assumed the dominant role in negotiations for several reasons: (1) Rhodesia still was primarily a British legal responsibility; (2) the political situation in the United States severely limited action by the Carter administration; and (3) the British had the necessary access and credibility in Salisbury. In mid-May the British dispatched Sir Anthony Duff, a well-respected Foreign Office official with considerable Rhodesian experience, to southern Africa to survey the situation. This mission was the first not to include an American negotiator since 1975.[134] Now in a supporting role, the Carter administration's most important task was to prevent Congress from lifting sanctions and thus further increasing Rhodesian intransigence.

In a carefully worded, probably intentionally vague policy statement, Lord Carrington outlined British intentions to the House of Lords on 22 May: "It is our responsibility to try to bring Rhodesia to legal independence in conditions which will afford that country the prospect of a more peaceful future. To that end it will be our objective to achieve a return to legality in conditions of the widest possible internal recognition."[135] On 27 May, Lord Harlech, a distinguished British diplomat who had served as deputy chairman of the Pearce Commission, was appointed as "a high level emissary" to Africa.[136] Shortly thereafter, Harlech traveled to Africa to consult with the leaders of the countries most directly involved in the conflict. The British let it be known that contrary to Rhodesian hopes, they would not make a decision in Rhodesia before the Commonwealth summit met in Lusaka in August.

In Washington after the Rhodesian elections, no less than five Congressional resolutions and bills were introduced calling for the lifting of sanctions.[137] The greatest setback for the Carter administration came on 15 May, when the Senate voted overwhelmingly (75-19) to instruct the President to lift sanctions. Meanwhile, the White House and State Department were preparing Carter's official findings as mandated by the Case-Javits Amendment.

Carter announced on 7 June that lifting sanctions would not be in the best interests of either the United States or the people of Rhodesia. Although there had been "very encouraging progress made," he said, "the action taken has not been sufficient to satisfy the provision of the United States law described in the so-called Case-Javits Amendment."[138] Citing inadequacies in the Rhodesian constitution and the failure of the new government to win the diplomatic recognition of any other government, Carter announced that he would do "everything . . . within his power" to prevent the lifting of sanctions.[139] Carter's statement drew a hostile response from Congress. The *Washington Post*, generally supportive of the administration's policy in Rhodesia, called it a blunder:

Many Americans are appalled by the *impression* of its policy the administration has conveyed. They think the administration is ignoring fairness and impartiality in order to court those black African states, mostly petty dictatorships or paper democracies, that insist that no Rhodesian government with even one white fingerprint on it deserves the time of day.[140]

The main problem facing the administration was that the debate over Rhodesia had become an ideological issue. The Byrd Amendment was repealed because the administration had been able to persuade a critical bloc of moderate legislators that repeal was in America's best economic and strategic interests. By mid-1978 the internal settlement's supporters had been able to transform the debate from one of interests to one of "radical terrorism" versus "moderate democracy." Ironically the Carter administration, genuinely committed to the promotion of human rights, was losing the debate to individuals who were on record in support of many of the world's most repressive right-wing dictatorships and who had consistently backed Smith when he had no intention of allowing blacks any political power. The administration's best and only hope was to redefine the terms of the debate once again. By emphasizing that his decision was based on "what is right, what is decent, and what is fair," Carter did the opposite. Disastrous consequences were averted only through a deft restatement of the administration's position by Vance and legislative maneuvering by administration supporters in Congress—particularly Congressman Steven Solarz, Chairman of the House Foreign Affairs Committee's Africa Subcommittee.[141]

In his statement, the major turning point in the legislative debate over the removal of sanctions, Vance first bowed to those who felt the administration was biased against the internal parties by emphasizing that "there has been encouraging progress in Zimbabwe-Rhodesia." Although the President had included the same phrasing in his own statement, it had been overshadowed by the general tone of his remarks. In addition, Vance provided more subtle and convincing reasons than Carter to explain why the Salisbury government had not met the conditions specified in the Case-Javits Amendment. More important, he restated American objectives: "Our challenge is to build on the progress to help create the conditions which can bring an enduring peace."[142] To do this, the administration would (1) consult closely with the British, (2) communicate with "all parties to the conflict," (3) "support any peace agreement which the parties themselves might reach—whether it is based on open, impartially supervised elections or on some other form of political accommodation," and (4) "keep the sanctions questions under constant review in light of progress toward a wider political process and more legitimate and genuine majority rule." Vance succeeded in redefining the debate by pointing out the following:

> Our primary national interest . . . is in a peaceful settlement. Growing conflict would bear a heavy toll. It would radicalize the situation further. It would deepen divisions within the country and throughout the region. And it would create greater opportunities for outside intervention. Progress has been made in Salisbury. But without further progress and accommodation, there will not be peace.

Finally Vance argued that "premature lifting of sanctions" would (1) undermine the new British initiative, (2) "diminish the chances for a peaceful settlement" by encouraging Salisbury to expect American support in the military struggle and hardening the external parties' view that "their only option was a military one," (3) undermine America's relations with the rest of Africa, (4) create new opportunities for "others" to expand their influence in Africa, and (5) mark "a retreat from the principles of racial justice which we have strived to achieve in our own country."

Vance's statement came too late to avert defeat in the Senate, but on 28 June the House voted in favor (350-37) of legislation that essentially abandoned the Case-Javits conditions. It authorized the President to make a decision to lift or maintain sanctions on the basis of the "national interest";[143] this criterion was eventually accepted by the Senate. Thus after a year of gains, the supporters of the internal settlement finally lost the debate. In consequence, the British government's ability to maneuver in Rhodesia was increased.

In London Carrington was reportedly told that there was strong opposition to the Zimbabwe-Rhodesia constitution throughout Africa, even in relatively moderate African states.[144] Nigeria began sending clear signals to both Great Britain and the United States that it would feel compelled to respond negatively to any move to lift sanctions.[145] In order to make sure there was no doubt about the seriousness of their concerns, the Nigerian government nationalized British Petroleum holdings on the eve of the Commonwealth Conference meeting in Lusaka. Nigeria's position was important since (as the Foreign Office had certainly informed Thatcher) British economic and political interests in sub-Saharan Africa are substantial—particularly in Nigeria. In a ninety-page report to the Commonwealth Heads of Government released in mid-July, Commonwealth Secretary-General Shridath Ramphal emphasized that "nothing that has been agreed between former Premier Ian Smith and his black colleagues can be considered other than of marginal or cosmetic consequence."[146] Throughout June and July the British consulted with a wide range of African and Commonwealth leaders.

When the Commonwealth conference convened in Lusaka on 1 August, officials in Salisbury almost without exception were convinced that the British were planning to lift sanctions and grant recognition in exchange for constitutional concessions.[147] They—along with their South African allies—were shocked when Thatcher announced on 3 August that her government intended to work for a comprehensive settlement involving "all parties." In private talks among Thatcher, Australian Prime Minister Malcolm Fraser, Nigerian External Affairs Commissioner Maj. Gen. Henry Adefope, Jamaican Prime Minister Michael Manley, Nyerere, and Kaunda, the basic outline for a settlement was developed. On 6 August a document was unanimously approved by the thirty-nine heads of delegation at the conference. In essence it called upon Great Britain to convene "a constitutional conference to which all parties would be invited" in order to adopt "a democratic constitution including appropriate safeguards for minorities" and "to bring about a cessation of hostilities and an end to sanctions."[148]

The immediate response of the main protagonists to this new initiative was not encouraging.[149] In Salisbury Smith denounced the conference as an "overabundance of hot air," and Muzorewa protested that the proposals were "totally unfair and in fact an insult."[150] Nkomo rejected British-supervised elections, reminding reporters that the British were "the reason we are in this mess."[151] ZANU issued a statement on 7 August outlining three fundamental principles from which it would not deviate: (1) "the Smith-Muzorewa illegal regime and its iniquitous constitution must be liquidated"; (2) "the constitution must contain no racist or other abridgement on the power of the people acting either directly or through their representatives in parliament to freely alter it or abolish it"; and (3) "before reaching any agreement the racist Rhodesian army and police forces must be disarmed, barracked and demobilized to give way to our forces."[152] Thus neither side seemed ready to make the compromises that would be required for a successful settlement. Nonetheless, by 20 August both sides had accepted an official British invitation to attend an all-parties conference in London.

How was it possible to get all of the parties to return to the negotiating table at a time when each side seemed committed to carrying on the struggle? Some observers have given most of the credit to brilliant British diplomacy. However, even the best diplomat can produce a negotiated settlement only if the underlying conditions for a settlement exist; in the final analysis, such conditions are a function of the bargaining power of the main protagonists in the conflict. In sum, both sides in the Rhodesian struggle finally believed that a continuation of the conflict might be more costly than the concessions required for a negotiated settlement—especially for the side that appeared to be the more intransigent.

The internal parties were in the weakest position to resist external pressure to negotiate. Since 1977 the Salisbury regime's sources of resolve had changed radically. Before 1977 Smith had been able to resist external pressures for a settlement because the internal costs of standing firm were relatively low. As these costs rose, he was forced to opt for the internal settlement. Once it became clear that the settlement could not reduce the internal pressures behind the rising costs, the new regime began to count on external support. To a certain extent, it had no choice; however, the focus on external support exacerbated the regime's problems. Instead of seeking to deemphasize its dependence on external support—as Smith had done in the past—the new regime made that dependence an integral part of its policy and rhetoric. Thus it was inevitable that it would have no alternative but to negotiate when it realized that Western support would not be forthcoming.

Continuing to stand firm in the face of Western pressure to negotiate would have been extremely costly for the internal regime. By mid-1979 the only alternative to negotiations would have been an escalation of the military campaign against the guerrillas and the Frontline States. Support for such an effort would have had to come from South Africa and would have created three problems. First, increased dependence on South Africa would have reinforced arguments that Muzorewa had become a South African puppet, making it more difficult for the internal regime to win support from the West. Second, greater South African involvement would have provided a degree of legitimacy for greater Soviet and Cuban assistance to the guerrillas (as it had done in Angola). Third, the Rhodesians could not have counted on South African assistance indefinitely. Faced with a widening conflict in Namibia and internal racial problems, South Africa might decide to cut off support to Rhodesia (as it had done before) if the situation continued to deteriorate.

Even before the Commonwealth conference, many Rhodesians—black and white—had begun to question whether the lifting of sanctions and diplomatic recognition of the new regime would bring an end to the war. At best, these actions would have made it easier for Rhodesia to bear the rising material costs of the war. However, they could not have reduced the war's tremendous human costs—and these were the only costs that mattered to most Rhodesians. Not only had the April 1979 elections not ended the war, but also Muzorewa had not delivered on any of his other major campaign promises.[153] The jobs that were supposed to materialize after blacks gained power did not. Blacks continued to earn lower wages than whites. Whites continued to control the civil service, the police, and the military. Confronted with the need to give black Rhodesians a reason to rally behind his regime, Muzorewa asked them to "pray to God that we will discover oil in this country" and continued to promise that Africans would have "the fat of the land and sufficient money"once sanctions were lifted.[154] Making matters worse, Muzorewa was having problems keeping his government intact. After protesting the election, Sithole and his party refused to take the twelve seats they had gained in the new Parliament; members of Ndiweni's Matabele-based United National Federal Party (UNFP), which held nine seats in the Parliament, openly expressed pro-Nkomo sentiments; in June seven members of the UANC broke away to set up a new party.[155] For all these reasons, Muzorewa and his government could not refuse Thatcher's call for renewed negotiations; they could only hope that the British move was a clever ruse to isolate the guerrillas and make it easier to counter opposition to eventual recognition of the Salisbury regime.

Although the choices facing the PF leaders were not as limited as those facing the internal leaders, they too had clear reasons to favor negotiations. In mid-1979 the guerrilla leaders evidently believed the war had reached a military stalemate.[156] Despite substantial gains throughout the rural areas, they were not in a position to threaten the internal regime's control of the urban areas. At the same time, the PF's political standing among black Rhodesians was probably at an all-time high. With Muzorewa discredited for the reasons mentioned above, the PF had good reason to feel confident that it would win a genuinely open election. However, there was a danger that its political support would wane if it was blamed for the continuation of the war. Furthermore, Mugabe and Nkomo were realistic—at least privately—about the tenuous nature of their alliance. They could not deny the possibility that an escalation of the war might provide either ZAPU or ZANU with an incentive to break the alliance, possibly setting the stage for a civil war many observers continually predicted. Any incentives the PF might have had to resist negotiations were outweighed by external pressures from the Frontline States.

As discussed above, contrary to the contentions of Smith's supporters, the Frontline States had consistently favored a negotiated settlement—as originally outlined in the Lusaka Manifesto.[157] By mid-1979 they were particularly anxious for an end to the conflict and realized that the British invitation might be the last chance for a negotiated settlement. Three of them—Botswana, Mozambique, and Zambia—had been hit especially hard by the war in Rhodesia, and further escalation could have threatened the survival of their governments.[158] Furthermore, for the region as a whole, peace in Rhodesia was a necessary precondition for economic progress.[159] Thus the Frontline leaders were willing to work with the British once they were assured that the British were sincerely interested in a comprehensive settlement.

The Frontline leaders assumed responsibility for "delivering" the PF to the all-parties conference. In the early stages Nyerere took the lead. At the Commonwealth conference he hinted that an intransigent PF might lose Frontline support.[160] When Mugabe and Nkomo initially responded somewhat negatively to the new proposals, Nyerere quickly announced that the PF was not rejecting the idea of elections or a new constitution. In Dar es Salaam Nyerere and representatives of the other Frontline States reportedly told the guerrilla leaders in no uncertain terms that they should attend the proposed conference and negotiate in good faith; shortly thereafter the PF announced that it would attend. Once the conference began in Lancaster House, Mozambique assumed the dominant role behind the scenes, evidently intervening on several occasions to ensure that the negotiations did not break down.

The leverage of the Frontline leaders over the PF was based on (1) their ability to affect the flow of assistance to the guerrillas, and (2) their de facto authority to legitimize the PF's position. This leverage was very important, but it can be easily overestimated. By mid-1979 ZIPRA forces in Zambia had grown so large that it would have been difficult for Zambia to halt ZIPRA activities as it had done on several previous occasions. The same was true to a lesser extent in the case of ZANLA forces in Mozambique. Moreover, by August 1979 the guerrillas inside Rhodesia were sufficiently well entrenched that they would have been able to carry on operations without base camps in Mozambique and Zambia. The Frontline leaders were able to use their leverage to maximum advantage because (as outlined above) the PF had its own reasons for favoring negotiations. By threatening to increase the potential costs to the PF of standing firm, the Frontline leaders were able to ensure that it did not decide to hold out in hopes of further internal gains.

In short, the British government and the Frontline States were able to take advantage of the weakened resolve of both sides to get them to the bargaining table in London on 10 September 1979. However, as the Geneva talks in 1976 had demonstrated, agreeing to talk is not the same as agreeing to settle. By mid-1979 the relative bargaining power of the two sides was balanced at a point that made a settlement possible. The task facing the British was to prevent either side from reconsidering its critical risk and adopting an intransigent negotiating posture.

The basic outline of British strategy became apparent before the conference opened. The British induced the two sides to gradually commit themselves to the negotiating process through a subtle combination of threats, concessions, and implicit promises. An unnamed "British official" cautioned Muzorewa and his supporters in the widely read *Time* magazine that "Any attempt to implement the Conservative party's desire to lift sanctions and recognize the government in Salisbury would result in an unmitigated diplomatic disaster."[161] At the same time, hints were dropped that a forthcoming attitude on the part of the internal parties would be rewarded. In Salisbury Rhodesian officials began to predict that the PF would "hang themselves" by making unreasonable demands, thus providing the Thatcher government with a justification for recognition of the internal government.[162] On the eve of the opening session in London, the Voice of Zimbabwe (broadcast from Maputo) warned, "According to the plans of the Thatcher government, they would welcome a boycott of the London conference by the Patriotic Front so that Britain would be free to hold another round of bogus elections in Zimbabwe with what would appear to be Commonwealth backing. . . . Part of the plan has been foiled by the Patriotic Front's acceptance to attend the London conference."[163] The ambiguity of British statements and actions encouraged both sides to be forthcoming. By using each side's interest in *not* being held responsible for the breakdown of the negotiations and by focusing on the most tractable issues first, the British hoped to build up a momentum toward a settlement that would be impossible to reverse.

Throughout the negotiations Lord Carrington assumed direct responsibility for producing an agreement. He continually shifted his attention from one side to the other, first praising the cooperativeness of the PF in order to extract concessions from the internal parties, then turning on the PF once the internal parties had made concessions and pressuring it to go a step further. This pattern was clear in negotiations over the conference agenda and the independence constitution.

Muzorewa had insisted that the talks were to be a "constitutional conference," not a "peace conference." He had backtracked slightly on 1 September, when he seemed to accept the possibility that the talks might cover "ceasefires and all sorts of things"; he even reluctantly acknowledged that new elections might be required. However, on the day the conference opened, a source close to the Salisbury delegation leaked word that Muzorewa was prepared to walk out of the talks rather than accept any change in the basic proposals. At a press conference three days later, Muzorewa continued to maintain that he had come to London to discuss a new constitution and nothing else. "As soon as what we are talking about is over," he said, "I believe it is quite logical to leave."[164]

Muzorewa's position was obviously unacceptable to the PF. On the second day of the conference, PF leaders requested that it be expanded into a full "peace conference" covering all the most controversial issues separating the contending factions in London. While emphasizing his willingness to work with Great Britain, Nkomo argued that "the critical period leading to independence is as vital as the

51

independence constitution."[165] Edson Zvogbo, a spokesman for the PF, outlined his group's fears: "We feel . . . that if we reach agreement on a constitution and only a constitution, it might be possible for Britain to then adjourn the conference and start waving the document in front of the rest of the world, saying 'an agreement on a constitution has been reached,' and then place less importance on other matters that are vital to us." The PF wanted an agenda that would show "the ground that has been covered and the distance to go."[166]

The PF proposed a four-point agenda. The British accepted the concept of a comprehensive agenda but imposed a different order of precedence from that outlined by the PF. The final agenda called for the following: (1) discussion of the independence constitution, and (2) "Pre-independence agreements, divided into three sectors (a) elections under the new constitution (b) the ceasefire and military arrangements and (c) administrative arrangements and maintenance of law and order during the transition."[167] Neither side was entirely happy with the agenda, but it made it possible to begin to discuss substantive matters. Once the agenda was fixed, the British circulated an outline of proposals for a new constitution based on the existing constitution in Zimbabwe-Rhodesia as well as on independence constitutions of other former British colonies. The content of the proposed constitution closely followed the outline suggested in the British invitation to the conference. Using the now familiar tactic of praise-plus-pressure, the British leaked their game plan to the press, who obliged with reports such as the following: "British sources close to the conference said the [Patriotic] Front had shown 'reasonableness,' especially in the 'manner and presentation' of its proposals. The sources said that so far Muzorewa's delegates had not shown similar reasonableness and 'seem to be speaking with divided voices.' It was noted, however, that the 'crunch' for the Front would come later in the conference."[168]

A potential stumbling block in British efforts to get the internal parties to go along with the proposed constitution was the presence of Ian Smith in the Rhodesian delegation. For 15 years the Rhodesian Front had been firmly united behind him. As the pressures for a settlement mounted, the internal cohesion of the whites began to break down. After Smith rejected British proposals to water down white guarantees in the constitution, another white member of the Rhodesian delegation privately referred to Smith as a frustrated, embittered man; "I'm not going back without [a settlement]," he added.[169] Inside

Rhodesia there were growing indications that continuing military call-ups, a skidding economy, and a deteriorating security situation had convinced whites of the need for concessions. Some white farmers felt that lifting sanctions and deescalation of the war were absolutely imperative as a matter of survival.

On 19 September the British decided to begin bilateral discussions with each group. Just in case the Rhodesian delegation was counting on a boost from the Conservative Party's back bench, it was informed that "technicalities in British sanctions law ... makes 90% of the present sanctions measures removable only by administrative action." On 21 September the Salisbury delegates voted 11-1 in favor of accepting the constitution proposed by the British. In exchange, Muzorewa demanded the lifting of sanctions, but he received only praise for his "constructive attitude" and an announcement that the conference would continue.

The PF expressed serious reservations about the proposed constitution and tabled its own proposals, whose most important differences were as follows: (1) no special representation for whites; (2) provision for an executive president with wide-ranging powers—including the power to appoint members of public service, defense, and police commissions; (3) no protection of private property rights; (4) no guarantees for the pension rights of civil servants, and (5) stringent citizenship requirements.

After the internal parties accepted the British proposals, pressure on the PF began to build. "We will never be able to negotiate a constitution with the Front," a British official said. "It will be a question of getting Muzorewa's agreement, then putting it squarely on the table for the Front, take it or leave it."[170] An African "close to the situation" nudged the PF. "There is always the danger," he warned, "that the guerrillas, by being too intransigent, would simply deal themselves out of the talks altogether."[171] The PF reluctantly accepted the principle of reserved seats for whites, but serious difficulties remained.

On 1 October Zvogbo announced that the PF was unwilling to accept the proposed constitution without changes. Two days later, Carrington presented a more detailed version of the British proposals which did not incorporate any of the PF's suggestions; he gave the PF five days to make a final decision. Mugabe countered that the PF would not be "threatened into a 'yes' or 'no' deal." The British, he said, "invited us here to create peace. If they don't want to create peace, fine, we go back and fight."[172] Slowly, however, the PF came around. On 10 October Mugabe and Nkomo presented a joint statement: "We are now satisfied that the conference has reached a sufficiently wide measure of agreement on the independence constitution to enable it to proceed to the next item on the agenda. If we are satisfied beyond doubt as to the vital issues relating to transitional arrangements, there may not be a need to revert to discussion on the issues we have raised under the constitution." The PF objective was to maintain as much bargaining leverage as possible, but Carrington refused to go along. He adjourned the conference and made it clear that when it reopened it would be to discuss implementation of the constitution, with or without the PF.[173]

Once again timely leaks appeared in the press. The *New York Times* reported that Carrington was resigned to an eventual walkout by the PF and was preparing a second-level solution that would involve recognizing the Muzorewa government.[174] However, the PF leaders had no intention of allowing themselves to be isolated. Nkomo retorted, "Carrington has no right to throw us out of our own conference. We have a right as members of that conference to continue, and we want to continue."[175] The PF finally accepted the British constitutional proposals on 18 October. Three considerations influenced its decision: (1) a fear that the British would recognize the internal government; (2) a joint American-British promise to provide financial assistance after independence to defray the costs of the constitutional provisions that guaranteed white pension rights and compensation to white farmers for land that might be expropriated; and (3) pressure from the Frontline States.

The rest of the conference followed a similar pattern of temporary stalemates quickly overcome by concerted pressure from the British, Americans, and Frontline States.[176] It appeared to be nearing a successful conclusion when the PF leaders agreed to a transition plan on 5 December, but talks stalemated over the exact terms of a ceasefire agreement. In a bit of last minute brinksmanship, on 14 December the British dispatched the interim governor-in-residence, Lord Arthur Soames, to Rhodesia to begin preparation for a transition period even though a final agreement had not been signed. The British intended to make it clear to the PF that they were going ahead with the plans no matter what. The gamble paid off. After the British made several relatively minor symbolic concessions, the PF leaders signed the final peace terms on 17 December.

For the two-month transition period Soames adopted the same resolute stance that Carrington had displayed during the Lancaster House negotiations.[177] His task was complicated by a decision of Mugabe and ZANU to run separately in the elections rather than in coalition with Nkomo and ZAPU. On several occasions the agreement seemed to be on the verge of collapse; however, as in the negotiations, the British and the Frontline States (especially Mozambique) were able through a virtuoso display of bargaining skill to prevent either side from beginning to believe it could gain by pulling out. The task was made easier by the fact that until the very eve of the elections, each of the three major rivals for power—Mugabe, Nkomo, and Muzorewa—genuinely believed he would emerge as the new Prime Minister of Zimbabwe.

The bargaining process culminated on 4 March 1980 with the announcement that Mugabe's party, officially listed as ZANU-PF, had won an overwhelming victory—62.9 percent of the 2.7 million votes cast by an estimated 93.6 percent of the black electorate.[178] It thus had a clear majority of the black seats (fifty-seven out of eighty) in the new one hundred-seat Parliament (twenty seats were reserved for whites), eliminating a need for a coalition government. Twenty of the remaining seats went to ZAPU, which had run as the Patriotic Front, and only three went to the UANC.

Prior to the election, there was considerable speculation that a Mugabe victory would lead to a coup by the Rhodesian military, a black-against-black civil war, or a combination of the two. It did not. Because Mugabe and his party had won by such a large margin, any attempt to oppose their victory would have been widely regarded as illegitimate. It is certain that the war would have resumed and Mugabe's opponents would have been in a far worse predicament than the Muzorewa regime had been in before the settlement. No outside state except South Africa would have been likely to consider aiding the opposition, but many would have been willing to assist ZANU-PF. Mugabe further shifted the balance in his favor by extending an olive branch to whites and his erstwhile ally Nkomo, decreasing the costs to them of accepting a ZANU-PF victory.

Based on the criteria used by both the Ford and Carter administrations, the outcome in Zimbabwe had to be judged a success. The conflict was ended; a direct East-West confrontation had been avoided; and the final settlement had come at the negotiating table, not the ballot box. Elections produced a government clearly backed by a majority of the people of Zimbabwe, and that government immediately reassured whites that there was a place for them in the country. It made it clear that it did not intend to radically reorient the existing capitalist economic system; it launched a major drive to attract Western investment; it shunned the Soviet Union. While Western countries soon opened embassies in Salisbury, neither the Soviet Union nor East Germany were encouraged to do so. Prime Minister Mugabe personally pledged not to allow his country to be used as a base for guerrilla operations against South Africa. One of his first major international trips was a well-received visit to the United States.

Despite a satisfactory outcome to the conflict, the situation in Zimbabwe is not ideal. As in almost all other African countries, the government is certain to move to consolidate its political position at the expense of its opponents. A *coup d'état* or widespread civil unrest cannot be discounted. However, such problems would have existed regardless of who had won the independence elections; they could have been far worse if the government had had to be based on a fragile multiparty coalition that did not command majority support. Thus it would be a mistake to reserve judgment on the Lancaster House settlement. Regardless of the fate of the Mugabe government, the settlement has been a success.

CONCLUSIONS

The Rhodesian conflict was not a struggle between advocates of violent change and advocates of peaceful change or between "radicals" and "moderates." The leaders involved had one main objective: the best possible outcome for themselves and the groups they represented. In pursuit of that objective they were willing to use every available means—including peaceful negotiations and military force.

In the late 1950s and early 1960s the black opposition to Smith used almost entirely peaceful means. Only after Smith refused to make any concessions and systematically repressed all black political opposition, locking up the most important nationalist leaders and banning the major nationalist parties, did blacks turn to armed struggle. Smith continued to refuse to make concessions until 1976 (Phase

Five), when an escalating civil war left him little alternative. After the internal settlement was signed (Phase Six), Smith sought Western support for a military campaign to defeat the guerrillas and force them to accept the internal settlement terms. Had the internal parties received that support, there is a strong likelihood that Smith would not have gone along with the Lancaster House initiative.

Until 1975 the major black leaders supported the "boys in the bush." In late 1975-76 (Phase Four), while Nkomo negotiated with Smith, Sithole and Muzorewa attempted to gain control over the guerrilla forces. When Smith refused to make sufficient concessions, Nkomo began to build up guerrilla backing. Once Muzorewa and Sithole realized they could not gain the support of the guerrillas, they became firm proponents of negotiation. By 1977 (Phase Six) ZANU had the greatest guerrilla strength inside Rhodesia, and Mugabe was willing to engage in international negotiations only if Smith would make substantial concessions. Nkomo, with a significantly smaller guerrilla presence in the country, was evidently at times willing to consider a separate deal with Smith. In contrast, after signing the internal settlement with Smith and thus gaining the backing of the Rhodesian military, Muzorewa and Sithole disdained further negotiations and supported military efforts to force the Frontline States to abandon the PF and compel it to surrender. The various parties considered abandoning the military option only after it no longer seemed to offer them a chance to improve their bargaining position. Under the circumstances outside observers had to be either naive or disingenuous to argue that one party was less willing to resort to violence than another. Furthermore, all were guilty of sanctioning the military option for the party they supported while condemning it for the parties they opposed.

A policy genuinely intended to encourage a negotiated settlement could succeed only by convincing all parties that they could not, or did not have to, use the military option to improve their position. There were two prerequisites for such a policy to be effective. First, foreign powers had to clearly communicate their commitment to a negotiating process rather than to a particular leader or party. As long as some of the parties believed they could count on external support, they had an incentive to stand firm, while their opponents were likely to attempt to retaliate by seeking external support for themselves. Second, these powers had to convince all parties that they were able and willing to use the leverage they had to punish intransigence and reward cooperation on a neutral basis. Until they established the credibility of such a commitment, none of the main protagonists had an incentive to engage in genuine negotiations. Either they would refuse to negotiate without substantial preliminary concessions out of fear that the process would be stacked against them, or they would negotiate without any intention of making significant concessions, confident they would be able to veto any agreement that did not satisfy their demands. Until mid-1979 (Phase Seven), foreign powers were not able to satisfy these two conditions.

As we have noted, prior to 1976 no foreign power was in a position to coerce the Smith regime into substantial concessions—the necessary condition for a comprehensive settlement. UN sanctions were costly, but they were not undermining the regime's control over the country. Only two external actions could have shaken the inherent resolve of the Smith regime: British military intervention or South African and Portuguese compliance with UN sanctions. Since the British had foresworn intervention even before UDI and South Africa and Portugal had clearly signaled their support for Rhodesia, whites had little reason to be concerned about external pressure.

After the independence of Mozambique and escalation of the guerrilla war inside Rhodesia, the Smith regime became more sensitive to external pressure. In late 1974 (Phase Three) South African pressure forced Smith to engage in the first round of comprehensive negotiations since UDI. However, there were limits to South Africa's leverage. Smith was aware that the Vorster government was constrained by fears of a white backlash inside South Africa and a reluctance to accept UN sanctions. Nonetheless, the combination of Rhodesia's weakening internal position and South African pressure was sufficient to convince Smith to seek a settlement with then "moderate" Nkomo (Phase Four). By late 1976 (Phase Five) the Salisbury regime's internal position had deteriorated significantly, and for the first time it was extremely vulnerable to external pressure. By the time Smith met Kissinger in Pretoria in September 1976, he and his advisors had realized they could no longer afford the costs of standing firm. The issue now became what kind of settlement could be reached.

The conflict did not end in 1976 because Smith believed he could exploit divisions within the nationalist movement to isolate guerrilla leaders and work out an internal settlement on terms more favorable to whites than those required for a comprehensive settlement. He was convinced that an internal settlement would allow him to counter rising internal pressure and win external support. Kissinger and the South African leaders encouraged this belief; they were not committed to a genuine negotiating process *regardless* of the outcome. For example, Kissinger began with the assumption that certain groups—e.g., ZANU—were inherently "radical" and deserved to be excluded. He later explained:

> My plan was to co-opt the program of moderate evolutionary reform, that is to say majority rule and minority rights. At the same time we sought to create a kind of firebreak between those whose radicalism was ideological and those whose radicalism was geared to specific issues. We could meet the demands for majority rule; we never thought we could co-opt the ideological radicals; our goal was to isolate them. [179]

It is clear from this statement that Kissinger's objective was to create an alliance of "cooptable" black leaders willing to accept the definition of "majority rule and minority rights" that he and Smith agreed upon. Smith's internal settlement was a logical outgrowth of Kissinger's thinking. The demands of black leaders whom Kissinger classified as "ideological radicals" were in his view illegitimate by definition. Therefore those leaders had only two choices: accept the terms outlined by Kissinger and Smith, or attempt to bolster their bargaining position. Predictably they chose to do the latter, leaving the United States and other external players with three options: (1) leave the conflict and let each side test its bargaining power; (2) choose sides; or (3) attempt to pressure both sides to negotiate a comprehensive settlement.

The Carter administration and the Callaghan government had decided in favor of the third option, but they were in effect forced to adopt the first. Contrary to the allegations of supporters of the internal settlement, the Anglo-American proposals did not give the PF a veto over an agreement; negotiations never reached the stage where veto rights became an issue—in spite of the "shuttle diplomacy" that took place between January 1977 and April 1979. The major problem was that neither the British nor the American government was in a position to credibly coerce either side into negotiations. For one thing, conservatives in both countries had undermined their countries' leverage over the internal parties, while the South Africans encouraged the internal parties not to make concessions by underwriting the costs of the escalating war. For another, the British and Americans had to depend on the Frontline States to convince the PF to negotiate, and the Frontline leaders could not be expected to do so without some indication that the internal parties were willing to compromise. In such a situation, the Anglo-American proposals were basically a delaying tactic that made it more costly for the main protagonists to *appear* to be intransigent. Without the illusion of negotiations, each side would have probably made a total commitment to the military option. In these terms the Anglo-American proposals were the best response to a bad situation. Had the advice of conservative opponents of this policy been followed, the result would almost certainly have been an international crisis comparable to the Angolan civil war.

A settlement became possible in 1979 (Phase Seven) because the new Conservative government in Great Britain was able to convince the internal parties that they would not be recognized unless they demonstrated a sincere willingness to make the concessions necessary for successful comprehensive negotiations and to convince the PF that it would receive a fair hearing. The Thatcher government's position was credible because (1) no group could seriously threaten to overturn a policy supported by the Conservative Party leadership; (2) the Carter administration had defeated Congressional efforts to lift sanctions; and (3) the Frontline States were committed to coercing the PF to negotiate. Had Thatcher listened to those who argued that the war in Rhodesia was a struggle between "radicals" and "moderates," the war would have continued to escalate with potentially disastrous consequences. Luckily the views that prevailed were of those advisors who understood that the underlying problem was a complicated conflict of interests—some legitimate, some not—involving a number of groups, none of which could claim a monopoly on truth and justice. British—and American—policy was ultimately successful because it focused on ending the conflict, not supporting the "right" side.

Chapter 2

FROM SOUTH WEST AFRICA TO NAMIBIA

Michael Clough

Since 1976 the prospects for a negotiated settlement of conflict over the future of the South African-controlled territory of Namibia (South West Africa) have appeared to fluctuate radically. On several occasions seemingly imminent agreements have failed to materialize. In order to understand why the search for peace in Namibia has proven so long and tortuous, it is necessary to focus on the motivations, perceptions, and relative bargaining position of the South African government.

In Namibia, now as always, the South African government stands in a commanding position. Neither the South West African People's Organization (SWAPO), the United Nations, the Frontline States, nor the Western powers possess sufficient leverage to compel South Africa to agree to an international settlement. During 1976-81 the differences over the terms of an agreement could have been resolved if South Africa had been convinced that the costs of a settlement would be lower than a continuation of the diplomatic stalemate.

South Africa has consistently sought to protect its interests in Namibia by maintaining a high degree of control over developments in the territory; it has loosened its hold only when the cost of standing firm has appeared to increase substantially. Throughout the conflict South African officials have based their estimates of this cost on three interacting factors: (1) the international political climate; (2) the

The author is grateful to Helen Kitchen for comments on earlier versions of this chapter and to Denise Squires for typing assistance. The views expressed in this chapter are strictly those of the author.

level of black unrest in Namibia; and (3) the effect of Namibian developments on the political situation in South Africa. These factors have acted as constraints on South African policy, and as they have changed, South Africa's policy toward Namibia has changed. Over the past sixty years that policy has gone through several phases, each successive phase marking an attempt by South African policymakers to develop a new strategy that would allow them to minimize the costs of accommodating changing political realities.

PHASE ONE: THE DRIVE FOR INCORPORATION (1920-62)

South Africa gained control over South West Africa (SWA) at the end of World War I under the provisions for "Class C" mandate territories in Article 22 of the League of Nations Covenant.[1] The terms of the mandate represented a compromise between South Africa's desire to annex the territory outright and President Woodrow Wilson's efforts to establish the principle of international accountability with regard to dependent territories. As a mandatory power, South Africa was entrusted to "promote to the utmost the material and moral well-being and social progress of the inhabitants" of the territory.[2] Although it was allowed to administer the territory as an integral part of the Union of South Africa, the South African government was required to submit annual reports on performance of its duties to the League Council. As far as South Africa was concerned, its obligations were pro forma. Shortly after the terms of the mandate were announced, South Africa's representative at the Versailles peace talks (and future Prime Minister), Jan Smuts, remarked that "the relations between the South West Protectorate and the Union amount to annexation in all but name."[3]

A conflict developed in 1946, when the League of Nations was dissolved and its successor, the United Nations, set up a trusteeship system designed to strengthen the principles of self-determination and international accountability. The United Nations asserted its right to assume authority over former mandates and requested that all mandatory powers sign trusteeship agreements. Only South Africa refused. Its leaders proposed instead that they be allowed to annex SWA, arguing that the territory would never be ready for "ultimate self-government and separate statehood" because of its lack of economic resources and the backwardness of its inhabitants.[4] In

December the United Nations refused South Africa's request. South Africa rejected the UN claim to authority over SWA, but it agreed not to proceed with incorporation and to continue to submit reports on its administration of the territory. This accommodation was short-lived.

On 26 May 1948 the Afrikaner-dominated National Party, led by D.F. Malan, came to power in South Africa—an event which had an immediate impact on the SWA issue.[5] The new government was much less concerned with international sensibilities than had been the United Party administration headed by Smuts, who had played an important role in the creation of the League of Nations. Shortly after the United Nations criticized South Africa's administration of SWA, the new government announced that it would not submit any further reports on the territory. At the same time, the South African Parliament passed the South West Africa Affairs Amendment Act of 1949, transferring control over native affairs in the territory from the Administrator for South West Africa to the South African Parliament and giving SWA six seats in the South African Assembly and four seats in the South African Senate. All the seats were quickly won by the National Party, thus enabling the new government to consolidate its slim parliamentary majority. The fate of SWA was now irreversibly entangled with South African politics.

In response to South Africa's actions, the UN General Assembly requested a ruling on SWA's status from the International Court of Justice (ICJ), setting in motion one of the longest and most complex court battles in international legal history.[6] Between 1950 and 1960, a series of nondefinitive ICJ rulings and fruitless UN diplomatic initiatives produced no major change in the situation. In an attempt to increase pressure on South Africa, in 1960 Liberia and Ethiopia—the two oldest African states—filed suit with the ICJ to force the Pretoria regime to place the territory under trusteeship. Six years later the court ruled that the plaintiffs lacked legal standing in the case and refused to rule on the merits of the suit. Disappointed with this result, the United Nations changed its strategy. On 27 October 1966 the General Assembly by overwhelming majority passed Resolution 2145, which terminated the original mandate and made SWA a direct UN responsibility.[7] (The only negative votes were cast by South Africa and Portugal, while France, Great Britain, and Malawi abstained.) Despite the overwhelming majority, the United Nations was not in a position to take decisive action. However, rising international opposition had made South Africa aware of a need to reassess its strategy in SWA.

PHASE TWO: THE ODENDAAL STRATEGY (1962-74)

In 1962 Prime Minister Hendrik Verwoerd appointed a five-member commission of inquiry to develop a final solution to the SWA problem that could protect South Africa's interests and counter growing international pressure. The result was the Odendaal Report, released in December 1963. It recommended that the policy of "separate development," the proposed solution to South Africa's internal racial problems, be extended to SWA.[8] Separate homelands were to be created for each of the territory's ethnic groups, with the largest share of the territory's most fertile farming areas reserved for whites. As in South Africa, each homeland was to be given gradually greater powers of self-government and each would have the right to self-determination, culminating eventually in full independence. (Ironically South African leaders now maintained that the homelands would be economically viable, although seventeen years earlier they had argued that the territory as a whole could never achieve economic independence.) During the transition to independence the territory was to be governed as an integral part of South Africa. The recommendations of the Odendaal Report were made into law in the Development of Self-Government for Native Nations of South West Africa Act, No. 54 of 1968, and the South West Africa Affairs Act, No. 25 of 1969. Implicit in the Odendaal strategy was the assumption that a white homeland controlling most of the territory's economic resources would eventually opt for incorporation into South Africa, leaving the black homelands free to choose independence. By 1973 two homelands—Ovambo and Kavango—had become self-governing territories.

While South Africa was attempting to carry out the Odendaal strategy, the United Nations was taking steps to implement Resolution 2145. On 19 May 1967 the General Assembly established a UN Council for Namibia to administer the territory, and it set June 1968 as a target time for the territory's independence. Although only two countries voted against the latter decision, thirty (including all of the major Western countries) abstained because of their belief that setting a time for independence was impractical. In 1968 the General Assembly formally changed the name of the territory to Namibia. The UN actions were legitimized by ICJ rulings, including a determination on 21 June 1971 stating the following: "The continued presence of South Africa in Namibia being illegal, South Africa is under obligation to withdraw its administration from Namibia immediately and thus put an end to its occupation of the territory."[9]

A special meeting of the UN Security Council held in Addis Ababa in February 1972 approved two new resolutions dealing with Namibia. One (Resolution 309) instructed Secretary-General Kurt Waldheim "to initiate as soon as possible contacts with all parties concerned with a view to establishing the necessary conditions so as to enable the people of Namibia, freely and with strict regard to the principles of human equality, to exercise their right to self-determination and independence."[10] The other (Resolution 310) reaffirmed the illegality of South Africa's presence in the territory, called on all member states to observe a voluntary arms embargo against South Africa, and called for a future meeting to discuss possible action under Chapter VII of the UN Charter (which provides for sanctions in cases where there is a threat to international peace) if South Africa failed to withdraw. These resolutions established the pattern for all subsequent UN actions concerning Namibia—i.e., veiled threats accompanied by proposals for further negotiations.

Prime Minister John Vorster responded to the Security Council resolutions by inviting Waldheim to visit South Africa. Waldheim's visit was the first of three rounds of talks between the United Nations and South Africa from March 1972 to April 1973.[11] The main objective of the United Nations was to convince South Africa to abandon the policy of separate development in Namibia and to accept the principle of self-determination for a unitary Namibia. Although South Africa claimed that it no longer envisaged separate independence for the individual population groups in the territory, it continued to grant them greater powers of self-government on an ethnic basis. In February 1973, in a White Paper introducing the Development of Self-Government for Native Nations of South West Africa Amendment Bill, the South African government reaffirmed its "oft-repeated assurance that it is the firm and irrevocable intention of the Government . . . to lead individual nations in South West Africa and the Eastern Caprivi to self-government and independence."[12] Confirming that he had no intention of meeting UN demands, Vorster told the National Party Congress in Windhoek (capital of Namibia) in October 1973 that "If and when the peoples of South West Africa have had ample experience in self-government, then it will be for them to decide . . . about a unitary state or whatever. Those who do not want to be in a unitary state will not go in. About your future, neither Pretoria nor Capetown nor the glass palace of the UN will make a decision. The Legislative Assembly on the hill in Windhoek will decide."[13] Waldheim reported that South Africa's position was at odds with UN objectives, and the Security Council formally terminated the negotiations on 12 December 1973. The negotiations failed because South Africa's leaders felt no serious compulsion to make significant concessions. The threat of UN sanctions was not yet credible and—more important—South Africa's position in the territory seemed secure.

In Namibia opposition to South African rule had begun in the mid-1950s with the formation of the South West Africa Progressive Association.[14] In 1959 black leaders in Namibia formed two new parties: the South West Africa National Union (SWANU) and the Ovamboland People's Organization, which changed its name to SWAPO in 1960. Neither organization was able to mount an effective internal political campaign against South Africa in the early 1960s. In 1965 SWAPO decided its only hope was to launch a guerrilla effort. The first contact between the South African Defense Forces (SADF) and SWAPO occurred on 26 August 1966; however, it was not until May 1973 that the first SADF soldier was killed. Serious black unrest began in December 1971, when 13,000 Ovambo contract laborers working in the Namibian mines went on strike over living conditions, but the political groundwork necessary to transform a labor strike into a national revolt did not then exist.

South Africa's sense of security began to weaken in 1974, when international pressures increased dramatically. In two moves signaling the beginning of a more concerted international campaign against South Africa, the General Assembly in December 1973 recognized SWAPO as the "authentic representative of the Namibian people" and appointed Irish activist Sean MacBride as UN Commissioner for Namibia.[15] During 1974 the Council for Namibia under MacBride's direction began to play a more active role. Several international organizations, such as the World Health Organization (WHO) and the United Nations Education, Science and Cultural Organization (UNESCO), granted the territory associate membership through the council. On 27 September 1974 the council enacted a decree that prohibited the exploitation of the territory's resources without council approval; called the Decree on the Natural Resources of Namibia, its main objective was to allow the council to use domestic courts in countries other than Namibia and South Africa to recover natural resources exported from Namibia and thus discourage international firms from operating in the territory. At the same time, the major Western powers began to increase pressure on South Africa to reconsider its policy toward Namibia. On 4 December 1974 the British government announced that it had decided to accept the 1971 ICJ ruling that South Africa's presence in Namibia was illegal, although it disagreed with the ICJ's reasoning. Subsequently Great Britain, France, and the United States joined with the other members of the Security Council to unanimously pass a resolution on 17 December calling for South Africa to begin a withdrawal from the territory.[16] Pending a final transfer of power, the resolution demanded that South Africa abolish all racially discriminatory and politically repressive laws— particularly those on Bantustans and homelands—and release all Namibian political prisoners. The Security Council announced that it would meet on or before 30 May 1975 to review South Africa's compliance with the resolution.

South Africa's position in Namibia was most seriously affected by a military coup in Portugal in April 1974 and a subsequent announcement by the new Portuguese government that it would grant independence to Angola, Namibia's northern neighbor. Psychologically, the announcement of Angola's independence shattered the aura of invincibility that had bolstered the self-confidence of whites in southern Africa. More practically, it forced South Africa's leaders to think seriously about the possibility of an escalating guerrilla war, a danger that became apparent at an Organization of African Unity (OAU) Council of Ministers meeting in April 1975, when Tanzania proposed increased support for SWAPO's liberation struggle.[17] Also in April British, French, and American representatives in Pretoria met with South Africa's Foreign Minister Hilgard Muller to convince him of the seriousness of the situation. South Africa's Ambassador to the United States, R.F. (Pik) Botha, reported their message to a private meeting with whites in Windhoek in early May; he added: "I personally doubt whether these three countries will much longer resist attempts in the Security Council or elsewhere to intensify the onslaught on us. In fact, I have reason to believe that very soon they might become indifferent toward possible drastic proposals with regard to the South West issue."[18]

PHASE THREE: THE TURNHALLE STRATEGY (1974-77)

By mid-1974 South Africa had begun to develop a new strategy to deal with the growing pressures. On 14 September 1974, A.H. du Plessis, leader of the National Party in SWA and Minister of Community Development in the South African government, proposed that whites in the territory hold talks with other population groups in order to reach agreement on the future of the territory.[19] Enlarging upon this proposal, Dirk Mudge, the National Party leader in the territory's all-white Legislative Assembly, called for a constitutional conference, to be attended by representatives of all ethnic groups (but no political parties), in which "all options" would be considered.[20] The relation between the developments in SWA and South Africa's new strategy became clearer in 1975 as South Africa prepared to respond to the UN review of its policies. In a key statement on 20 May, Vorster claimed that South Africa was in agreement with the UN and OAU positions on self-determination, independence, and the maintenance of SWA's territorial unity. "Where we do differ," he said, "is in regard to the role claimed for the UN and SWAPO."[21] In a letter to Waldheim on 25 May, Muller noted that South Africa was now committed to a transfer of power to the inhabitants of the territory as a single body. However, he added that his government would not accept UN authority over the territory or allow the United Nations to supervise a transfer process. Instead South Africa would directly transfer power to the participants in the proposed constitutional conference.[22] In this way, South Africa hoped to maintain as much control as possible over the outcome of the transfer of power, exclude all radical elements, and still improve its international position.

The Turnhalle Conference—named for the building in which the meetings were held—opened on 1 September 1975.[23] All ethnic groups in the territory were represented at the opening meeting; however, the composition of the assembly failed to reflect the population as a whole, even on the basis of the most narrow criteria. Fully one third of the delegates were from the Herero tribe, which comprises less than 7 percent of the total population, while less than 15 percent came from the Ovambo tribe, which represents 45 percent of the total population. Moreover, very few of the delegates could claim to have been chosen by the people they allegedly represented. Neither the recognized leaders of the Damara tribe—the second largest ethnic group in Namibia—nor the leaders of any of the nonethnic-based political parties in the territory, such as the Namibian National Front (NNF; one of the two major black opposition parties in Namibia) and "internal" SWAPO,* participated in the Turnhalle meetings.

On 12 September, the Turnhalle Conference unanimously endorsed a declaration of intent to draft a constitution for SWA—if possible within three years. The objective of the constitution would be to create a state "which will guarantee to each population group the greatest maximum say over its own and national matters."[24] After several abortive sessions, on 18 August 1976 a general outline for a three-tiered government was unveiled:

(1) A central government with a ceremonial president, an eleven-member Council of Ministers as the executive, and a sixty-member National Assembly. Each of the eleven officially recognized ethnic groups would elect representatives to the National Assembly. Twelve seats were apportioned to the Ovambos, six to the whites, five each to the Caprivians, coloreds, Damaras, Hereros, Kavangos, and Namas; and four each to the Basters, Bushmen, and Tswanas. In addition, each ethnic group was given one seat on the Council of Ministers.
(2) Separate "ethnic legislatures" with "regional" responsibilities for matters such as primary education and other local and group concerns.
(3) Metropolitan Councils with authority over local issues in urban areas and responsibility for the coordination of separate municipal councils for Africans, whites, and coloreds.[25]

A final agreement on the constitution was announced on 18 March 1977.[26] The Turnhalle participants set 31 December 1978 as the

*Throughout the conflict an "internal" wing of SWAPO has operated openly inside the territory. Although clearly identified with the external SWAPO headed by Sam Nujoma, it avoided any connection with guerrilla activities and was widely regarded as a moderating force in the conflict. However, by 1979 most of internal SWAPO's leadership had been either imprisoned or forced into exile.

date for independence for Namibia and formed themselves into an interim government to administer the territory until that date. South Africa was to continue to control defense, internal security, communications, foreign affairs, currency, and external trade until independence, but all other internal functions would be transferred to the interim "internal" government.

After the Turnhalle agreement was announced, the five Western members of the Security Council—Canada, France, Great Britain, the United States, and West Germany—assumed the role of a "contact group" in order to persuade South Africa to resume negotiations with the United Nations and thus avoid a further polarization of the conflict.[27] Secretary of State Henry Kissinger had briefly raised hopes of a settlement in 1976, when he addressed the Namibian issue during discussions with Vorster.[28] In fact, most observers—and many participants—initially believed that Kissinger was much more likely to achieve a breakthrough on the Namibian problem than on the Rhodesian problem. However, they failed to take into account that the level of hostilities in Namibia was far lower than in Rhodesia, and that South African officials still rightly believed they had plenty of room within which to maneuver. Little had changed by the time the Western contact group decided to launch its initiative in April 1977. The contact group's only leverage over South Africa derived from the Vorster government's desire to avoid a total diplomatic break with the rest of the world. This leverage was sufficient to convince South Africa to delay formation of an interim government in SWA; but it was not sufficient to convince it to accept the UN's claims to authority over the territory. Instead in June South Africa appointed an Administrator-General, Justice Marthinus Steyn, to govern the territory until elections could be held.[29] This concession marked the beginning of a new phase in South African policy.

PHASE FOUR: THE "DUAL TRACK" (1977-81)

Over the years 1977-81 South African policy toward Namibia moved along a "dual track": the Pretoria government continued to grant the internal parties greater authority and autonomy while at the same time engaging in negotiations with the United Nations and/or Western governments over the terms for an international settlement. As a result, a pattern emerged: (1) South Africa threatened to abandon the international track or quietly nudged the internal parties a little further toward independence; (2) the United Nations and the Western contact group condemned South Africa's action, intensified diplomatic pressure on it, and compromised on settlement terms; (3) South Africa either retreated slightly or announced that its action was not intended to affect movement toward an international settlement. By stringing the negotiations along, South Africa was able to forestall a clear break with the United Nations and buy time to strengthen the position of the internal parties. However, a dual track approach is not a viable long-term strategy; rather it is a short-term expedient. Eventually a point must be reached where South Africa will be forced to either accept a negotiated settlement or grant independence to the internal parties. By bending over backwards to meet South African settlement demands, the United Nations, Frontline States, and Western contact group appeared on the verge of bringing the negotiations to such a decisive point in late 1980.

The basic terms for an international settlement in Namibia were laid out in Security Council Resolution 385. It called for (1) free elections in Namibia under the supervision and control of the United Nations; (2) withdrawal of South Africa from the territory; and (3) a complete transfer of power to the Namibian people.[30] Discussions to carry out Resolution 385 did not begin in earnest until February 1978, when the Western contact group presented South Africa with draft proposals for a settlement. A first round of talks opened on 9 February in New York. Representatives from the Western contact group met in separate sessions with officials from SWAPO and the South African government. South African Foreign Minister Botha joined these so-called "proximity talks" two days later, only to pull South Africa out of them the following day. He called aspects of the Western proposals "totally unacceptable," but left the door open for further negotiation.[31] However, on 15 February Vorster announced that he was committed to granting SWA independence by the end of 1978, even if this ran counter to the Western proposals.[32] On 30 March the Western contact group presented the two sides with a revised set of proposals. These were accepted in principle by South Africa on 25 April and by SWAPO on 8 July.[33] On the basis of the acceptance, the Security Council adopted Resolution 431, which requested the Secretary-General to appoint a Special Representative for Namibia and to submit a report with detailed recommendations for implemen-

71

tation of Resolution 385.[34] In order to allay SWAPO concerns about the status of Walvis Bay, Namibia's main port, the Security Council adopted Resolution 432, which declared its support for Walvis Bay's eventual reintegration into an independent Namibia.* This resolution sparked an immediate protest from South Africa, even though it implicitly acknowledged that Walvis Bay would not be included in an independence agreement.[35]

On 6 August the newly appointed UN Special Representative for Namibia, Maarti Ahtisaari, arrived in Windhoek with a fifty-member mission to work out the details of a final agreement. Based on Ahtisaari's findings, Waldheim presented a set of proposals to the Security Council. Waldheim's proposals envisaged a UN peacekeeping force in a transition period in Namibia of 7,500 troops and up to 2,000 civilians, and elections seven months after a UN Transitional Assistance Group (UNTAG) was dispatched to the territory.[36] South Africa protested that the proposals deviated from the original terms of agreement; specifically it objected to (1) the large size of the UNTAG force, (2) the proposed inclusion of 360 civil police officers, and (3) the seven-month transition period.[37] Shortly thereafter, Vorster simultaneously announced his resignation and his cabinet's decision to go ahead with plans for internal elections in the territory in December without UN participation.[38] In spite of this decision, on 29 September the Security Council adopted Resolution 435 approving the Waldheim proposals.[39]

Seeking to avoid a total collapse of the negotiations, all five of the foreign ministers of the Western contact group travelled to Pretoria in October to confer with South Africa's new Prime Minister, P.W. Botha. After three days of talks, on 19 October the South African government and the five ministers issued a joint statement announcing that the elections would go ahead, but that they would be only "an internal process to elect leaders" and that "the South African government will thereafter use its best efforts to persuade them to consider

---

*Walvis Bay was not part of the original German colony; Great Britain had exercised authority over it as part of the Cape Colony. Therefore South Africa claims that Walvis Bay is part of South Africa and need not be handed over to an independent Namibian government. Although it had previously administered Walvis Bay as an integral part of the territory, on 31 August 1977 South Africa formally transferred administrative authority to the Cape Province in South Africa.

ways and means of achieving international recognition through the good offices of the Special Representative and the Administrator-General [of the territory]."[40] In addition, the statement indicated that some of the sticking points in the negotiations had been resolved and that it was therefore "appropriate for ... Mr. Ahtisaari to resume his discussions with the South African Administrator-General of Namibia within the framework of Security Council Resolution 435."[41] At the time, this rather confusing and complicated compromise appeared to be little more than a postponement of the inevitable collapse of the contact group initiative. Until the elections, the contact group pressed South Africa for assurance that they were to be an "internal process" and nothing more. As a result, the group was able to get a public commitment from South Africa that it would "retain authority in Namibia" after the elections, pending implementation of the UN proposals.[42]

The elections were held on 4-8 December. They were boycotted by all three of the nonethnic parties in Namibia—internal SWAPO, the NNF, and SWAPO-Democrats.* According to the South African government, 81 percent of all registered voters turned out, although both the opposition political parties and leaders of the major black Namibian churches claimed that reluctant voters had been intimidated by the army and police.[43] The clear victor in the elections was the Democratic Turnhalle Alliance (DTA), which won forty-one out of the fifty seats in the ethnically apportioned Constituent Assembly. (The DTA had been formed on 5 November 1977, after Mudge, who had chaired the Turnhalle Conference, and seventy-five other National Party members broke away to form a new, all-white Republican Party, which then joined with the ten black ethnic parties that had participated in the Turnhalle proceedings to form the DTA.)[44]

After discussions with the newly elected "internal" leaders, South Africa informed the United Nations on 22 December that these leaders had "expressed their support for an internationally acceptable settlement" and that it therefore had "decided to cooperate in the expeditious implementation of Security Council resolution 435."[45]

---

*SWAPO-Democrats was formed in 1978 by former SWAPO leader Andreas Shipanga, who had been detained (as a result of a leadership struggle with Nujoma) in Zambia and Tanzania from 1976 until his release by Tanzanian President Nyerere in May 1978.

In addition, South Africa reiterated its position on five disputed elements of the Waldheim proposals:

(1) There shall be no reduction of the South African troop strength in the Territory until there has been a comprehensive cessation of violence and hostilities.

(2) A date for an election will be determined in consultation between the Special Representative of the Secretary-General and the Administrator-General on the understanding that the election will take place not later than 30 September 1979.

(3) Questions on which there should be further consultation, such as the size and composition of the military component of UNTAG, and other matters which have already been brought to the attention of the Western powers, should be resolved satisfactorily with the Administrator-General. Special reference is made to paragraph 12 of the settlement plan accepted by the South African Government on 25 April 1978 with a view to monitoring of SWAPO bases in neighbouring states.

(4) The maintenance of law and order in South West Africa/Namibia remains the primary responsibility of the existing police forces.

(5) The Administrator-General shall exercise the legislative and administrative authority in South West Africa/Namibia during the transitional period until independence.[46]

In an accompanying letter, South Africa outlined the major concerns of "the leaders of South West Africa":

(1) The recognition by the United Nations of SWAPO as the sole and authentic representative of the inhabitants of South West Africa/Namibia.

(2) The financial and other assistance which SWAPO receives from the United Nations.

(3) The encouragement which SWAPO receives directly and indirectly from the United Nations to persist with its violent activities against the people of South West Africa/Namibia.

(4) The making available by some countries of their territory to SWAPO for bases for the perpetration of violence against the people of South West Africa/Namibia.[47]

Over the next fifteen months, South Africa and the United Nations continued to spar over what can only be regarded as relatively technical matters which could have been easily resolved if a genuine commitment to a negotiated settlement had existed. The real stumbling block was South Africa's desire to wait and see how Prime Minister Abel Muzorewa's "internal" government would fare in Zimbabwe/Rhodesia. If the Salisbury regime had been able to win international support, South Africa would in all likelihood have abandoned negotiations with the United Nations and proceeded to grant the Namibian internal regime independence on the basis of the March 1977 Turnhalle formula. However, it was forced to reassess the situation in Namibia by the overwhelming victory of Robert Mugabe and the Zimbabwe African National Union (ZANU) in the February 1980 Zimbabwe elections. The failure of Muzorewa's internal coalition to gain international recognition made South African leaders realize that support for a similar solution in Namibia was equally unlikely; at the same time, the amazingly poor showing of Muzorewa in the Zimbabwe elections made them realize that the DTA would probably lose to SWAPO if open elections were held as part of an international settlement. Thus the potential costs to South Africa of adopting either an internal or an international option were significantly increased.

Throughout the summer and fall of 1980 the prospects for an international settlement seemed to be better than ever before. By 20 June the United Nations, the Frontline States, and SWAPO had acceded to virtually all of South Africa's substantive demands regarding the proposals for implementation of Resolution 435[48] — as was implicitly acknowledged by R.F. Botha in a letter to Waldheim on 30 August.[49] Botha made no new substantive demands; instead he reiterated South African complaints of UN partiality and demanded equal treatment for all parties. Despite the inflammatory language of the letter, the United Nations and the Frontline States regarded the South African response as a potential breakthrough. Secret discussions were held between Angola and South Africa,* and a UN mission headed by Under-Secretary-General for Special Political Affairs Brian

*Angola has never publicly acknowledged that it participated in such discussions; however, that it did so has been confirmed in several confidential conversations of the author with informed parties.

Urquhart met with the South African government in Pretoria on 20-25 October.[50] Based on the Urquhart discussions, Waldheim reported to the Security Council on 24 November that he believed "a decisive phase" had been reached and announced that a "preimplementation multiparty meeting [including] the parties concerned in the envisaged election" would be held 7-14 January 1981.[51] The ostensible objective of such a conference was to create a "climate of confidence and understanding" in order to overcome the "acute mutual distrust and lack of confidence" which was blocking progress in the negotiations.[52]

Hopes of an imminent settlement were soon dashed. Before the multiparty conference opened, the main protagonists began arguing over its nature, purpose, and venue. SWAPO leaders insisted they would attend only to negotiate the final terms of agreement on implementation of Resolution 435 with South Africa,[53] while South African officials maintained they would play only an indirect, advisory role in the negotiations, leaving center stage to an "internal" delegation led by Danie Hough, then Administrator-General for Namibia.[54] Most observers discounted these squabbles as preconference posturing. However, when the conference got under way in Geneva—ironically the scene of abortive Rhodesian talks in 1976—it quickly became apparent that South Africa and the internal parties—i.e., the DTA—had no intention of genuinely negotiating a settlement. According to most observers, both SWAPO (under pressure from the Frontline States) and the United Nations were prepared to make substantial concessions to satisfy South African and DTA demands regarding UN "impartiality" and postindependence guarantees.[55] However, no demands were placed on the table.

To explain the unwillingness of South Africa and the DTA to negotiate a settlement in Geneva and to assess the prospects for a future settlement, it is necessary to consider four factors which determine South African policymakers' perceptions of the relative costs of opting for either an internal or an international settlement: (1) the South African view of its stakes in Namibia; (2) the internal political balance in Namibia; (3) the military situation in Namibia; and (4) the international political climate.

FROM SOUTH WEST AFRICA TO NAMIBIA

SOUTH AFRICA'S STAKES IN NAMIBIA

There are two views—the optimistic and the pessimistic—of how the South African government defines its interests in Namibia. The optimistic view—i.e., the one that holds out the most hope for a near-term settlement—is that South Africa has few intrinsic interests in Namibia that would cause it to stand firm once the costs of a stalemate began to increase. According to this view, South African policymakers believe that a SWAPO government in Namibia would be too weak, vulnerable, and economically dependent on South Africa to constitute a military or economic threat to it. Like Mozambique and Zimbabwe, an independent Namibia, regardless of who was in power, would be forced to reach an accommodation with its neighbor. (Support for this contention comes from the widely recognized fact that the border between South Africa and Namibia is particularly unsuitable for guerrilla incursions.)* In the optimistic view, the most important costs to South Africa of a SWAPO victory in Namibia would result from the effects of such a victory on the political situation in South Africa—specifically the possibility that a SWAPO victory might (1) unleash a right-wing backlash against the Botha government which might endanger its domestic reform program, and (2) provide a psychological boost to black opposition forces in South Africa.

According to the optimistic view, South Africa would be willing to accept an international settlement as long as it could shift responsibility for a SWAPO victory to others (i.e., the internal parties and the West) and gain something in exchange for its efforts—e.g., the removal of Cuban troops from Angola and Western support for its internal reform program. The key to a settlement would thus be to provide South Africa with a "cover" that would allow it to deflect attacks from both its right and left that such a settlement would be a "defeat" for the South African government and for the white cause in the southern African region. This optimistic view is at the heart of the Reagan administration's strategy for resolving the Namibian conflict.

*It is interesting that Moses Garoeb, Administrative Secretary of SWAPO, recently referred to this fact when asked about potential SWAPO support for the African National Congress of South Africa (*Windhoek Advertiser*, 11 December 1980).

The pessimistic view holds that South Africa considers the emergence of a SWAPO government in Namibia as a direct threat to its interests and that it therefore perceives the costs of a settlement that would produce such a government as extremely high. If this is the case, it would not be possible to satisfy South African demands by merely changing the terms of an agreement—unless the terms in effect precluded a SWAPO victory—and the only means of convincing South Africa to accept a settlement that would include SWAPO and other interested parties would be to raise the costs to it of continued intransigence—i.e., by an escalation of the guerrilla war in Namibia and an increase of international pressure on the Botha government.

Significantly two of South Africa's most important policymakers—Minister of Defense General Magnus Malan and R.F. Botha—gave a joint interview to the influential Afrikaans newspaper *Die Transvaler* in which they stressed that South Africa had a very large stake in developments in Namibia.[56] Boldly titled "Why Must South Africa's Sons Die for South West Africa?," the interview presents the most detailed official explanation of South African thinking on Namibia published to date. According to Malan and Botha, "The security interests of South Africa and South West Africa are irrevocably and inseparably tied to each other." Declaring that "SWAPO strategy in South West Africa is prescribed by the Soviet Union, and successful resistance to it in that territory is part of South Africa's struggle for survival," they argued that a South African withdrawal from the territory would involve the following:

(1) "Entail a loss of credibility for the South Africa government" in Africa and the world, as well as in Namibia;
(2) "Encourage the Soviet Union into a stronger attempt at a wider territorial expansion in Southern Africa in order to reach its central goal—South Africa";
(3) "Substantially reduce the time scale for large scale hostile actions against South Africa";
(4) Provide "a moral victory for the enemies of South Africa";
(5) "Give SWAPO a substantially freer hand to wage its terror campaign against the inhabitants of that area";
(6) Place "the enemy closer to the heart-land of the Republic" and possibly give Russia a naval base at Walvis Bay;

(7) "Contribute to a high degree to the intensification of the revolutionary climate and ... fill the conservative elements among all the population groups with a spirit of defeatism"; and

(8) "Contribute substantially to the disintegration of South Africa's ability to withstand a full scale attack."

As if in direct response to the optimistic view that South Africa's interests would be best served by a conciliatory policy toward SWAPO and the United Nations, Botha and Malan noted that "A withdrawal from [South West Africa] would entail certain short term advantages for South Africa—which are of a tactical nature—, which would not compensate at all, however, for the long term strategic disadvantages of such an action and for the consequences which such an action would have in the future." Although they repeated the claim that South Africa was interested in "actively [pursuing] a peaceful settlement which would enjoy international recognition," they emphasized that it would not "participate in a plan, which would allow Moscow to rule over Windhoek, for the sake of shortlived international popularity."

The Malan-Botha interview was especially important because it was directed not at the international community, to whom South Africa has said similar things on many occasions, but at the main political base of the National Party. Even if it was campaign rhetoric designed to gain the support of potential voters in the elections held at the end of April 1981—as some might argue—it cannot be disregarded. By publicly making the case for a continued South African military presence in Namibia in strident tones, Malan and Botha have raised the domestic ante: they have increased the potential domestic costs of a SWAPO victory and made it more difficult for their government to accept it, no matter how well the acceptance is camouflaged. This problem has become even more serious as a result of the split in the National Party and the emergence of a potential right-wing alternative to the Botha regime. The newly formed Conservative Party, headed by former National Party minister, Dr. Andries Treurnicht, would be almost certain to use a SWAPO victory in Namibia as a campaign issue. Thus the Botha regime's perception of its stakes in Namibia makes an accommodation with SWAPO unlikely in the near term unless the counterbalancing costs of a failure to reach a settlement increase markedly.

THE INTERNAL POLITICAL BALANCE IN NAMIBIA

One of the reasons for the success of the Lancaster House conference on Zimbabwe is that all three of the principal black leaders—Mugabe, Muzorewa, and Joshua Nkomo (head of the Zimbabwe African People's Union—ZAPU)—believed they had a good chance of becoming the Prime Minister of an independent Zimbabwe under the election formula provided in the final agreement. Had Muzorewa and Nkomo been able to anticipate the result of the February 1980 elections, it is far less likely that they would have signed the agreement. In Namibia everyone appears to agree—at least in private—that SWAPO would defeat the DTA and all other interested parties in open elections, regardless of the election formula used.

It is extremely difficult to make confident estimates of the extent of popular support in Namibia for SWAPO, the DTA, or any of the many other parties in the territory. However, it is possible to piece together a fairly good picture of the general political situation. Moderate newspapers in both South Africa and Namibia have consistently argued that SWAPO would be the most likely victor of internationally supervised elections. For example, Alistair Sparks wrote that "There is hardly a serious political observer in South West Africa today who doesn't believe SWAPO would win any free election there, if not as overwhelmingly as Mugabe did then at least comfortably."[57] Prior to the Geneva conference it was reported that "The DTA is in no shape at present to fight and win a major election and there is every reason to believe that this may cause it to drag its feet."[58] During the conference, the London *Times* reported that Mudge had told a black African observer that "he would need at least eighteen months to build up the alliance into a viable alternative to SWAPO."[59] After the conference collapsed, the widely read newsletter *Africa Confidential* concluded that SWAPO was likely to win an election for the following reasons:

(1) The DTA is in a state of disarray;
(2) The centrist revival based on middle-of-the-road parties who are anti both SWAPO and the DTA never materialised, and the centrist groupings themselves have all but collapsed;
(3) SWAPO has maintained the best discipline and organisational skill throughout the nationalist struggle;
(4) In ethnic terms SWAPO has an overwhelming advantage;
(5) SWAPO has greater support outside Ovamboland than is often assumed.[60]

The strongest direct evidence of the DTA's weakness is in the results of internal elections held in November 1980 to select representatives to the ethnic legislatures created as part of the original Turnhalle agreement.[61] Because of the war, no elections could be held in Ovamboland, the country's most populous area and SWAPO's most important base of support. Embarrassingly, Mudge's Republican Party was able to win only seven of eighteen seats in the white Legislative Assembly, the majority going to the ultraconservative National Party. In addition, DTA member parties lost elections for the Damara Legislative Assembly and the Rehoboth Basters. Overall DTA parties won majorities among the Herero, Kavango, Caprivian, Nama, Tswana, and colored peoples, which together account for only 30 percent of the total population. Moreover, black turnout in all areas was relatively low—ranging from 33 percent among the colored to 53 percent among the Herero.

In early 1981 it seemed fairly clear that South African and DTA officials shared the media assessments noted above, and as a result were unwilling to agree to a settlement that would provide for elections within fifteen to eighteen months. Instead they appeared intent on stalling, in hopes that the political prospects of the internal parties would improve and eventually allow them to win open elections, thus leading to an internationally acceptable DTA government in Namibia.[62] In order to foster such a development, South Africa launched a concerted effort to bolster both the internal and international credibility of the internal parties.

The first and most important aspect of this effort involved the transfer of increasingly more authority in Namibia to the DTA-dominated National Assembly (which was created by the Turnhalle agreement). On 1 July 1980 a DTA Ministerial Council was sworn in by then Administrator-General Gerritt Viljoen and put in charge of twenty government departments.[63] Control over the military and police was formally transferred from South Africa to the territorial administration in the early months of 1981.[64] Finally, on 14 September, in a surprisingly underpublicized move, South Africa transferred almost all the Administrator-General's day-to-day authority over the territory to the Ministerial Council. Commenting on the changes, Mudge said, "Now [the Ministerial Council] has effective control over all of the government's powers."[65] It is questionable that such efforts will serve to boost internal support for the DTA. It should be noted that Muzorewa's popularity in Zimbabwe declined precipitously once he assumed control of the government and found himself unable to satisfy the expectations of his constituents.

A second crucial part of South Africa's effort to boost the DTA's credibility has been an attempt to force the United Nations to grant the DTA equal status with SWAPO. Evidently this was one of the main reasons South Africa and the DTA agreed to attend the Geneva conference. Despite the failure of the conference to make headway toward a settlement, South African officials proclaimed the conference a success. For example, Malan and Botha noted the following in their interview:

> The South African government agreed to the [Geneva] conference because it would provide the democratic parties of SWA the opportunity to discuss the feasibility of Security Council Resolution 435 and other practical proposals on an equal footing and on the same basis as SWAPO. . . . The activities in Geneva were given substantial international coverage and rather favorable reports and comments appeared especially in certain British and American newspapers. In that manner the [internal] parties widely proclaimed their existence. . . . They effectively struck a deeply felt blow to the myth of SWAPO as the sole and true representative of the people of SWA.[66]

Ultimately the DTA's political prospects will be determined by its ability to (1) disassociate itself from South Africa, (2) decisively defeat SWAPO's guerrilla effort, and (3) unite the internal parties under an anti-SWAPO banner. For reasons discussed below, the first two endeavors may be irreconcilable, while the third seems unlikely because the most important other internal parties have shown little willingness to throw in their lot with the DTA despite concerted attempts by the South Africans to induce them to do so.*

THE MILITARY SITUATION IN NAMIBIA

A major factor in South African calculations regarding alternative policy options in Namibia is the level of conflict inside the territory. Although the war is largely confined to the Ovambo area in northern Namibia, over the years 1976-80 it steadily intensified. In 1979 the

*The DTA's hopes of expanding its support inside Namibia were dealt a serious blow in March 1982, when its President and chief black spokesman, Peter Kalangula, resigned and formed yet another internal party.

number of incidents involving insurgents doubled over the previous year, land-mine detonations in the first quarter of 1980 were higher than in any previous three-month period, and total SADF casualties for 1980 were apparently more than double the total for 1979.[67]

Beginning in 1979, the SADF stepped up its military campaign against SWAPO forces—the People's Liberation Army of Namibia (PLAN)—by carrying out increasingly deeper raids into southern Angola, where PLAN bases are located. As a result of a series of three operations between July 1981 and March 1982—Proteus, Daisy, and Super—in which SWAPO losses were said to exceed 1,000 lives, South African officials had begun to speak of wiping PLAN out entirely as a military force. However, in April PLAN surprised most observers by infiltrating 100 guerrillas into the Tsumeb area in northern Namibia, making it the most extensive incursion in the sixteen-year history of the war. This development is consistent with past trends, whereby PLAN has periodically cut back its operations substantially, only to resume them later at a higher level of intensity.[68] (In this respect, it is instructive to compare the Rhodesian experience: until the very last stages of the conflict Ian Smith and his military aides continued to insist that the war was under control.) One indicator that the SADF campaign is not making lasting inroads into SWAPO support is a failure of its amnesty program to induce defections from the guerrilla forces. In over a year less than seventy individuals responded—and the majority of them were part of a Caprivi faction that split with Nujoma and the main SWAPO leaders as a result of internecine disputes.[69]

In the past SADF leaders themselves have stressed that the conflict cannot be settled on the battlefield. At most the military can buy time for political leaders to work out an "acceptable" solution. Over the longer term, an escalation of the conflict—or even a stabilization of hostilities at current levels—will cause the costs to steadily increase for South Africa, primarily in two ways.

First, as the number of South African casualties increases, the government is likely to face rising protest at home and deteriorating morale in the field. The Malan-Botha interview is a clear indication that South African officials are concerned about the problem of increased internal pressures. In an attempt to minimize this problem, the SADF has sought to transfer more of the war burden to the Namibian internal government. For example, on 1 January 1981 a military draft of blacks in Namibia was instituted. So far, however, it appears to have been counterproductive. The major black churches in the territory as well as several of the major non-DTA political parties have protested against it.[70] More important, the move appears to have provided an unintended boost for SWAPO. Shortly after the draft was to take effect, an estimated 5,000 draft-eligible blacks fled the country, many of them to join the guerrillas.[71] As a consequence, South Africa was forced to exempt Ovamboland, Kavango, Caprivi, and Kaokoveld from the draft.

Second, an escalation of the war is likely to increase political support for SWAPO. As guerrillas move into more areas of the country, SWAPO will have an opportunity to expand and solidify its political base outside of Ovamboland. As in Zimbabwe, the war-weariness of peasants who are caught between the guerrillas and the South African security forces will almost certainly work to SWAPO's advantage. By further polarizing the situation in Namibia, an escalation of the war will force those in the middle to choose sides, which can only hurt South Africa. A senior leader of the NNF was reported to have said the following:

> Our position in the middle is now beginning to be an impossible one. If we go by the way Namibian politics are now developing there will simply not be a role for us to play. As a politician and a leader of my people I will have to decide for myself where I am going. . . . Despite my objections to SWAPO, I can tell you that I will never go along with the DTA.[72]

In similar terms, the Johannesburg *Sunday Times* predicted that "every additional day that South Africa remains in the territory means another 20 votes for Sam Nujoma."[73] In addition, it is important to note that one Namibian newspaper concluded that blacks in the territory viewed South Africa's July 1980 raid into Angola negatively.[74]

THE INTERNATIONAL POLITICAL CLIMATE

Contrary to the arguments of many conservative analysts, South Africa has been quite responsive to international pressure, particularly with regard to Namibia. In fact, almost every major change in South Africa's policy toward the territory has been as a result of changes in the international political climate. For example, although it is difficult to recognize the Odendaal Report as a response to international pressure, its adoption was based on South Africa's realization that incorporation of Namibia along the lines it originally intended was internationally unacceptable. The formulation of the report began precisely when serious opposition to South Africa was developing in the United Nations and (more important) the United States. Following its adoption, there was a long period of stalemate during which South Africa showed few signs of making further changes in its policies. Not coincidentally, in this period the United States and its Western allies showed little willingness to lend their support to UN efforts to pressure South Africa. The situation did not change until 1974-75, when the Angolan civil war made independence struggles in southern Africa a major international issue and gave substantial credibility to SWAPO's military campaign. After warnings from its Western "allies," South Africa initiated the Turnhalle strategy, which from its perspective represented a major concession to international opinion.

From 1977 to 1980, South African policymakers engaged in ongoing, substantive negotiations with the United Nations and for the first time accepted in principle a UN-supervised transition process in Namibia (Resolution 435). Despite frequent attacks on the United Nations and the Carter administration, the South African government was not willing to risk the consequences of breaking off negotiations. Conservative analysts who point to the fact that no final settlement was reached as proof of their contention that the Carter administration's policies were a failure overlook the important question: Would South Africa have been more likely to agree to an international settlement had other policies been followed? Based on experiences during the Nixon administration, when a policy of "constructive engagement" or "quiet diplomacy" was tried, the answer is no. In the absence of international pressure, it is doubtful that South Africa would have accepted Resolution 435 even in principle.

Events in 1980 clearly demonstrate South Africa's sensitivity to international pressure. After the Zimbabwe settlement, negotiations over Namibia were reaching a decisive point. The Western contact group warned South Africa that it was uncertain how much longer it would be able—or willing—to resist UN pressure for sanctions if South Africa failed to agree to a settlement. Had Carter been reelected, South Africa would quite probably have been forced to choose between an internal and an international settlement. However, the election of

Ronald Reagan cut the costs of intransigence for South Africa and obviated the need for a clear choice. By assuring South Africa that it would veto any attempt by the Security Council to take decisive action against it, the new administration virtually guaranteed that the Geneva conference would fail.

OPTIONS FOR THE UNITED STATES

Any U.S. program intending to promote a negotiated settlement in Namibia must begin from the assumption that the key to such a settlement is South Africa. As should be clear from the evidence we have presented, South Africa is presently in a position to effectively veto any agreement that is not to its liking. At the same time, the other main protagonists in the conflict—SWAPO, the Frontline States, and the United Nations—would be likely to accept any agreement as long as it provided for internationally supervised elections on a one-man, one-vote nationwide basis. Thus the likelihood of a settlement is largely a function of the South African government's estimation of the relative costs of (1) a continued stalemate, (2) an internal settlement, or (3) an international settlement.

If American policymakers are interested in promoting an international settlement, they have a choice between two basic strategies. On the one hand, they can attempt to induce the South African government into an agreement by reducing its costs of an international settlement; on the other hand, they can attempt to pressure that government into an agreement by increasing its costs of both a continued stalemate and an internal settlement. In theory there is no reason why both strategies cannot be used simultaneously—i.e., why both "carrots" and "sticks" cannot be offered; in practice a dual strategy is very difficult to orchestrate. Generally speaking, the Carter administration sought to offer South Africa some carrots but basically relied on the threat of the stick.

As indicated above, the Carter administration's Namibia policy was not the failure its critics make it out to be. This can be understood more clearly with reference to Zimbabwe. Prior to August 1979 many observers—especially those who now charge that the Carter administration's policy in Namibia was a failure—believed the administration's Rhodesian policy had not brought any progress toward a settlement. However, Carter's refusal to ease U.S. pressure on the

Muzorewa government was a critical element in the ultimate success of the British initiative which led to the Lancaster House conference and final agreement. A seeming stalemate in Rhodesia from 1977 through mid-1979 was a time of internal sorting out during which Smith and his black allies searched for an alternative to a negotiated settlement.[75] If international pressure had been decreased—thus reducing the internal parties' costs of holding out—it is doubtful that a settlement would have been possible in 1979. Moreover, the British were able to bring about a final agreement only by threatening to increase the costs of holding out for all parties. Some carrots were offered to both sides—for example, reserved seats in the legislature for whites and postindependence economic assistance to the new government—but in the final analysis it was the threatened sticks that were by far the more important forces behind the settlement. Because the situation in Namibia holds many parallels to that in Zimbabwe, it would be a mistake to conclude that the Carter policy in Namibia was a failure or that a reversal of that policy is likely to succeed.

Contrary to the expectations of many observers, the Reagan administration has not abandoned the basic approach followed by the Carter administration. After several months of uncertainty, in May 1981 Secretary of State Alexander Haig and President Reagan informed South Africa that the United States remained committed to a Namibian settlement under the terms of UN Resolution 435. After receiving assurances from the Botha regime that it was seriously interested in a settlement, the United States began a series of intense discussions with all of the important actors in the conflict. As this book goes to print, those discussions continue.

The Reagan administration's strategy for achieving an internationally acceptable settlement differs from the Carter administration's approach in three respects: (1) Drawing on what they perceived to be the lessons of the Rhodesian negotiations, Reagan's advisors—Assistant Secretary for African Affairs Chester Crocker in particular—have placed greater emphasis on satisfying South African concerns about postindependence constitutional arrangements and developing an electoral formula that could provide the internal parties in Namibia some hope that they would not be totally routed by SWAPO at the polls. Negotiations over these matters proved more difficult than the Reagan administration had anticipated, and SWAPO, supported by the Frontline States, grew suspicious of a complex voting formula proposed by the United States for the election of members of a constituent assembly whereby half would be elected by a system of proportional representation and half by majority vote in single-member districts.

It would be a serious mistake to overestimate the importance of measures such as these which seek to speed an agreement by cutting the costs of an international settlement for South Africa. In the case of Namibia a policy that focuses on cutting the costs to South Africa (and all other participants) rather than maintaining and increasing the costs of delaying such a settlement is almost certain to fail. It would be very difficult, if not impossible, to cut the costs of agreement for South Africa and still produce an international agreement because, as noted above, an international agreement would have to provide for open elections which would probably result in a SWAPO victory.

If a SWAPO victory were the only cost that mattered to South Africa, no international agreement could be crafted so as to reduce that cost. If (in line with the optimistic view of South Africa's interests in Namibia) the South African government were willing to countenance the possibility of a SWAPO government as long as the domestic repercussions of such an outcome could be minimized, it might be possible to cut the costs of a settlement. However, one way of doing so would be to maintain pressure on the South African government so that it could argue that its "friends"—i.e., the Western powers— "forced" it to accept a settlement, absolving it of responsibility for the emergence of a "terrorist, Marxist" government in Namibia.* Moreover, the South African government would prefer any alternative to a SWAPO government that it thought could be sustained at an acceptable cost. Thus decreasing its costs of a failure to agree to an international settlement would undoubtedly encourage its leaders to stall.

(2) The Reagan administration has chosen to emphasize positive inducements (carrots) rather than negative pressures (sticks) in its discussions with South Africa. In order to gain the confidence of the Botha regime, the administration has taken a number of actions, including the following: vetoed a Security Council resolution condemn-

---

*This is exactly what R. F. Botha did in 1975 to convince whites to go along with the Turnhalle plan. Similarly in 1976 the Vorster regime used Kissinger's public pressure as a "cover" for the far more important pressure that was being applied on Smith. (For details, see Chapter 1 above.)

ing South African raids into Angola; allowed a South African rugby team to visit the United States; lessened restrictions on exports of nonlethal equipment for use by South African security forces; and discussed the possibility of exports of nuclear materials for use by South Africa's nuclear power industry. In having taken these actions, the administration has gambled that the long-term payoffs from a Namibian settlement will exceed the short-term political costs of being perceived as having "tilted" American policy in favor of the white regime in Pretoria. If a settlement is achieved, this gamble will probably succeed. However, if a settlement is not achieved relatively soon—i.e., by the end of 1982—this strategy may prove very costly since to a very great extent the overall credibility of the Reagan administration's Africa policy now hinges on its ability to win South African acceptance of a settlement.

(3) The Reagan administration has directly linked a Namibian settlement to the withdrawal of Cuban troops from Angola. In a major policy address on 29 August 1981, Crocker outlined the administration's position as follows:

> Our diplomacy recognizes openly the intimate relationship between the conflicts in Namibia and Angola. We have repeatedly made clear our position that progress toward a Namibia settlement could set the stage for withdrawal of Cuban forces from Angola. There is little debate about the logic of this proposition, which the Angolan Government itself accepts in part. But we do not share the view that there is anything automatic or predictable about that relationship, as some would argue. The assumption that Cubans will depart— or that UNITA will evaporate like the morning dew—as South Africa withdraws from Namibia is problematical. . . . We are convinced that a satisfactory outcome can only be based on parallel movement in both arenas.[76]

Although administration officials have been intentionally ambiguous on the exact nature of this linkage, they have not wavered in their insistence that progress on the Cuban troop issue must accompany a Namibian settlement. On several occasions, Angolan officials have said publicly that once South African troops were withdrawn from Namibia, there would no longer be a need for Cuban troops to remain in Angola.[77] However, there is considerable reason to doubt that the Angolans will be able to agree to a withdrawal of Cuban troops so long as the MPLA regime in Angola continues to be threatened by an insurgency led by Jonas Savimbi and his UNITA party.*

Despite over forty hours of direct discussions between American and Angolan officials as of June 1982, the issue of Cuban troops in Angola appeared to be still unresolved. If a solution is not found, there is a danger that South Africa will use the issue to shift blame for failure to reach a settlement to SWAPO and the Angolan government. It could then push forward on the implementation of an internal settlement that excluded SWAPO. Were this to occur, it would constitute a major blow to the Reagan administration's standing in Africa.

The only sure means of promoting an international settlement in Namibia is to maintain and (if necessary) steadily increase international pressure on the South African government to agree to such a settlement. It is important to note here that one very important form of pressure would be to make clear to South Africa that it would have to bear the costs of an escalation of the guerrilla war in Namibia without U.S. aid, even if the escalation were fueled by significantly increased Soviet and Eastern bloc arms transfers to SWAPO. If this is not made clear, the United States will be in danger of finding itself in another no-win situation such as it did in the spring of 1976, when the Angolan civil war radically escalated. By making it clear that aid will not be forthcoming, the United States should be able to alter South African policymakers' perceptions of the relative costs of alternatives enough to cause them to accept an international agreement sooner rather than later. In this respect, the Reagan administration is in a particularly favorable position to pressure South Africa because, unlike the Carter administration, it can credibly argue that no future administration would be more likely to come to South Africa's aid.

As the Reagan administration clearly recognizes, the Namibian problem is a matter of great urgency. If an international agreement is not reached in the near future, it may soon become much more difficult—primarily for two reasons—to reach such a settlement, with the result that many more lives—most of them innocent Namibian peasants—will be lost and a significantly more dangerous international

---

*The conflict between the MPLA and UNITA is an extension of the struggle that occurred in 1975 when the MPLA, with Cuban and Soviet assistance, defeated UNITA and another Angolan nationalist party—the FNLA—who were backed by South Africa and the United States (discussed in John Marcum, *The Angolan Revolution* [Cambridge, Mass.: MIT Press, 1977], vol. 2).

situation will be created. First, South Africa's ability to impose a settlement on its internal allies—i.e., the DTA—will inevitably decline. As the DTA assumes more administrative control in Namibia—especially over the police and the army—it will be in an increasingly stronger position to veto any prospective international settlement. Furthermore, for the DTA the cost of an agreement involving a SWAPO victory would be a matter of its political survival (which, despite Malan and Botha's statements, it would in the final analysis probably not be for South Africa); were a SWAPO victory likely, the DTA would strongly resist an international settlement. At best, it would prolong the conflict; at worst, it would create a situation in which the battlefield was the only arena in which a resolution could be reached.

Second, a prolongation and intensification of the conflict will shift the balance of power within SWAPO in favor of the factions most hostile to the United States and least willing to compromise. As Secretary of State Alexander Haig and Assistant Secretary for African Affairs Chester Crocker have acknowledged, SWAPO is not a monolithic, pro-Soviet organization irrevocably committed to a military victory in Namibia. To the contrary, the majority of SWAPO's leadership is at least as pragmatic and nondoctrinaire as Mugabe in Zimbabwe. However, if the prospects for a negotiated settlement wane, the more militant factions within SWAPO will be certain to gain influence. To expect anything else would be incredibly naive.

In conclusion, it would be a serious and potentially very costly mistake to reduce U.S. pressure on South Africa for an immediate negotiated settlement in Namibia. Do those who argue for doing so believe such a policy would increase the chances of a negotiated settlement? Or do they believe that *American* interests would be threatened by a SWAPO victory and that the United States should therefore help South Africa bear the costs of preventing such an outcome?

Chapter 3

ONE NAMIBIA, ONE NATION: THE POLITICAL ECONOMY OF TRANSITION

Reginald Herbold Green

The future of South West Africa is inextricably tied to that of South Africa. Nothing except war can alter this association between South West Africa and South Africa.

– Prime Minister Jan Smuts, 1947[1]

We made South West. Why should we give it to you?

– Settler employer to Namibian employee, 1960s[2]

We do not believe in a system that sells people.

– Striking contract workers, 1971

A nation which is dependent on another country for the food consumption of its population cannot be but a dependent hostage of the particular country which feeds its population.

– SWAPO, *Political Programme*, 1976[3]

It must be borne in mind that the Namibian people are shedding blood to liberate each and every inch of the Namibian soil, thus each and every inch of the Namibian land must and will belong to the Namibian people.

– Sam Nujoma, President of SWAPO, 1979[4]

TRANSITION TO WHAT?

Namibia is in transition from South African colonial rule. Neither occupation forces now approaching 100,000 nor a flirtation with a South African-guaranteed "unilateral declaration of independence"

The analysis and views expressed in this chapter are the personal responsibility of the author. They are not necessarily those of the South West African People's Organization (SWAPO), the United Nations Institute for Namibia (UNIN), or the Southern African Development Coordination Conference (SADCC), to whom the author has served as advisor or consultant.

(UDI) can avert that. Speculations about timing or the balance of violence, negotiation, and election are not very fruitful. However, it is reasonable to assume that Namibia will be independent by 1985 with a radical African government dominated by the liberation movement SWAPO.

SWAPO is committed to socialism and self-reliance.[5] Its practice in refugee camps, base camps, and semi-liberated areas is consistent with that commitment and relatively similar to that of the Frente de Libertação de Moçambique (FRELIMO).[6] The protraction and nature of the liberation struggle since SWAPO's founding in 1960 (as an association of contract workers led by young former students) have radicalized it. Algeria and Mozambique, Guinea-Bissau and Angola are now the comparable experiences for Namibia—not Zambia or Kenya, Botswana or Tanzania.

The history of Namibia and especially the duration and bitterness of its liberation struggle have ensured that "moderation" and "gradualism" are no longer marketable products in that country. This is not to say that SWAPO is committed to overnight transition— presumably to chaos—nor that it wishes to substitute unilateral dependence on any other state for its present dependence on South Africa. A distinct awareness of the need to set priorities, to keep key sectors running, and to retain access to foreign skills, markets, and personnel exists. In large part, how rapid and far-reaching initial transition measures are will depend on how and how soon Namibia attains independence, whether there is a mass exodus of skilled personnel, what attitudes are adopted by foreign firms and their governments (especially in respect to the status of post-1966 mines—discussed below), and which governments are perceived by an independent Namibian government as willing to cooperate or act in solidarity with it. In these respects Zimbabwe and the Zimbabwe African National Union-Patriotic Front (ZANU-PF) are the most relevant precedents for interpreting the options Namibia and SWAPO will see as open under an "optimistic" scenario, while Angola and the Movimento Popular de Libertação de Angola (MPLA) figure in a "pessimistic" one.

Even a brief survey of Namibia's natural resources, ecology, present economic structure, patterns of technology and employment, size, and external environment raises questions as to the constraints on and possible meaning of socialism and self-reliance.[7] With a population of about 1.4 million, 90 percent of physical output (70 percent of Gross Domestic Product—GDP) exported, over two thirds of middle- and high-level manpower expatriate or settler European, and a very skewed (albeit not ungenerous) natural resource endowment, it can be argued that transition either to socialism or to self-reliance is impossible or so expensive economically as to be undesirable.

THE WEB OF VIOLENCE

The history of Namibia since European entry in the latter half of the nineteenth century has been one of exceptional violence. This violence has not been only military and physical, but equally social and political. It has not been episodic but virtually continuous. For most Namibians it has not been optional or avoidable but always actually or potentially present and inescapable.

The first wave of violence was the manipulation and destruction of the emerging state systems of Namibia by traders, missionaries, settlers, the German South West Africa Company, and imperial Germany.[8] This was quickly followed in the first years of the twentieth century by the violence of reconquest after Herero, Nama, and Damara revolts—with Ovambo support—almost threw the Germans into the sea. These revolts gave the world the term genocide, and in them perished over half of the Herero, Nama, and Damara.[9] South Africa expelled Germany from Namibia, and a new wave of violence followed. Partly this was to subdue the Namibians, who misguidedly expected liberation from the new invaders. Partly it was to complete territorial conquest in the north and northeast, which Germany effectively had not ruled.

Parallel to the military violence were social and economic violence. Social violence encompassed the destruction of social systems; ethnic groups were relegated to reserves and penetrated by appointed chiefs, who served as means of coercive control. More important, social violence was built on the old Transvaal tradition of apartheid— No equality [between black and white] in Church or State, before God or man, in life or death, now or forever—a tradition which was carried out more fully and longer in Namibia than in the Republic itself.

94

The political economy of colonial Namibia has been the political economy of theft—theft of land for settlers; theft of mineral, water, and fishing rights for the colonial state and foreign firms; theft of cattle and more land to ensure that the only options open to Africans were "work or starve"; theft of the right to choose employers or negotiate terms of employment to ensure that work would be on settler and company terms. The violence of naked exploitation was built on that of theft. Apartheid and reserves were one side of the coin; the other was the unity of exploitation. The Namibian territorial economy was built on African labor. As a result of land theft and the coercive contract system, it was forced labor paid below family subsistence levels.

By the mid-1970s about 100,000 African workers were employed on term contracts of from six to eigthteen months.[10] They had come—and were separated—from 150,000-odd reserve households. Neither they nor their families could survive in the reserves. By allowing some production of food and shelter, the reserves lowered "necessary" wages. By being unable to provide full subsistence, they ensured a labor force. Contract workers' employers are designated for them; effective organization is forbidden; residence is in prison-like compounds. Cosmetic amendments in 1972-81 have not altered the basic characteristics of the contract system. Its purpose is to acquire cheap labor—vital to ranching, fish processing, and (at least until the 1970s) mining.

The contract system has built the colonial political economy of cattle, karakul, fish, copper, lead, zinc, diamonds, and uranium. It has also doomed it. Large compounds—now "no go" areas for the occupation authorities except in large, armed units—have proven foci for resistance organization. The involvement of most peasant households in the system and the circulation from reserve to job has created a national consciousness and communications network. The mechanism of exploitation has been so brutally clear and so evidently systemic that worker consciousness has gone from seeking better conditions to challenging the contract system to organizing against the whole colonial system.*

*In 1971 a general strike against the term contract, single channel recruitment and compound residence system swept Namibia. While broken, it left a distinctly higher level of political bitterness and consciousness.

In its own terms the colonial political economy has been success-ful. After a slow start GDP, exports, remittances, and settler and corporate incomes have risen precipitately since 1945. For South Africa the remittances and the captive market (all paid in foreign exchange from globally oriented exports) have been significant. One basic reason that South Africa has fought so hard to hang on to Namibia is quite simple: it pays—or did so until the explosive rise in the cost of repression from the late 1970s. The cost reached perhaps R1,000 million for 1981.

ECONOMIC STRUCTURE: PRODUCTION

In territorial terms, Namibia after independence will not be a poor economy. GDP exceeds $1,750 million.[11] Even on a population estimate of 1.4 million, this gives $1,250 per capita.[12] Gross National Product (GNP) is about one third lower—$1,200 million and $825 per capita.

In recent years constant price GDP has been virtually stagnant, and in 1981 it probably declined. However, this is the result of factors that would not necessarily pertain after independence:

(a) Reduced South African quotas for Namibian cattle and lack of adequate territorial slaughtering capacity to raise exports to other markets, followed by severe drought, problems of desert encroachment, and falling karakul prices;[13]

(b) Near destruction of the fishing industry by overcatching (South African inshore and dominantly Russian and Spanish offshore); a "rest" of perhaps three years is required to rebuild stocks;

(c) A 1974-78 slump in base metal prices and slumps since 1980 in uranium oxide and gem diamond prices;

(d) Above all, political and legal uncertainties and a growing physical insecurity have deterred new investment, whether in residential buildings or the rail link to Botswana, and have prevented the development of irrigation or the opening of new mines on the basis of recently proven ore bodies.

Production is dominated (47 percent) by mining. Mineral exports in 1979 were of the order of $1,050 million. Diamonds contributed over half of this and uranium oxide about a third, although with Rossing, Namibia's single uranium mine, now producing at its full 5,500 short ton (5,000 metric ton) yellowcake capacity and selling at $40 per pound term contract prices, the difference should narrow. Copper, lead, and zinc contributed $125 million to 1979 exports, but at full capacity their production could exceed $200 million.

As far as value of output is concerned, agriculture is centered on large karakul and cattle ranches. Crop output on European commercial units and on African subsistence (more accurately semi-subsistence) holdings is very low. In the former case this results partly from state-managed price structures and partly from ecological factors. In the latter, a combination of discouraging African cash production, a lack of agricultural services, infrastructure, or inputs, and the barren nature of much reserve land (especially in central and southern Namibia) have resulted in astoundingly low yields per unit and total production.

As noted, the fishing industry is now a disaster. While up to 1,500,000 tons is a sustainable catch (half inshore and half offshore), the inshore catch has declined to perhaps 250,000-300,000 tons. The Metal Box Company has closed its tin plant, all but two or three of ten canneries are shut or operating fitfully, and trawler use is limited both by quota limits and lack of fish to be caught even within them.[14]

Secondary sector output turns largely on fish tinning and meat packing, with brewing, printing, and machinery and vehicle repair among the larger of the other production units. Together with construction (hampered by political uncertainty) and electricity/water, manufacturing contributes about one ninth of GDP.

The tertiary or service sector is about three tenths of GDP (most of domestically used GDP). It is characterized by a high proportion related to servicing imports and exports and a low proportion of general government. The latter (which excludes RSA military spending) is caused by the very limited provision of services to the over 90 percent of Namibians who are not Europeans.[15]

POLITICAL ECONOMIC STRUCTURE: DISTRIBUTION AND USE

The aggregate level of GDP and its average per capita level give a very partial picture of Namibian economic reality. The distribution is perhaps the most unequal and the use the most skewed of any substantial territorial unit. The production mix is a textbook illustration of an economy which produces what it does not use and uses what it does not produce. About 90 percent of all physical production is exported—100 percent of minerals and karakul, 90 percent of cattle and fish, about 50 percent of manufacturing. Excluding meat and milk, Namibia is self-sufficient in nothing. Even staple grain is imported—40-50 percent in good years and up to 70-80 percent in drought years.

Personal income distribution is dominantly on racial lines. In 1979 the average European household income was about $15,000, while that of the average African household was about $700 (including subsistence production). African personal income stood at one eighth of GDP and one third of total personal incomes, even though over 85 percent of the population is African. The $700 average contrasts starkly with urban poverty-line data: $1,800 has been suggested as the minimum necessary household income.[16]

The profile of the economically active population is equally daunting. Of over 500,000 economically active in 1977, about 475,000 were African (including coloreds). Of that number, 240,000 were in pseudo-subsistence agriculture (2 percent of GDP) and another 75,000-odd in domestic service (1 percent of GDP). In the categories of administrators, proprietors, and professional-technical-paraprofessional workers, 20,000 of 27,000 were European, and 5,000 of the 7,000 Africans were primary school teachers and nurses.[17]

The financial and corporate economic relations structures are as heavily externally oriented as the production structure.[18] The currency is the South African Rand. The banks (with one minor exception) are branches of South African units. The key operating companies are transnational corporations (TNCs). One group—(Anglo-American)—engrosses diamonds, chunks of base metals, fish processing and export, much of karakul export, and a melange of subsidiary activities. A "gang of five" dominates productive activity: Anglo, RTZ, Amax-Newmont, Falconbridge (mining), and the South African state (cattle marketing; railways, harbors, telecommunications; much rail transport, power, and water; a dominant interest in several mines, and codomination with RTZ of the Rossing mine); the gang extends to nine if Standard, Barclays, Shell, and BP are included.

Very few enterprises are complete. Namibia has not been treated as a territorial economy at all but as a corner of South Africa where it was convenient to carry on some aspects of South African business. The major diamond sorting and valuing company, the main workshops of the railways, the largest copper refinery, and the processing and auction of karakul pelts—all are located in the Republic.

Except for uranium oxide and base metals, exports go through the Republic and are handled by South African-based firms. In the case of cattle up to 80 percent are sold to the Republic as live beasts— an economically unsound approach which may help the railway and South African packing plants but is hardly cost-efficient (nor a base from which to shift markets). Ninety percent of imports go through the Republic, and 70 percent are from there. Importing is a preserve of South African-based firms.

The patterns of services and infrastructure are as distorted as those of personal income. Presently there is no usable national language. The Afrikaaner tribe's conduct has ruled out Afrikaans; English, "the language of freedom" (or "of terrorism," as the Afrikaans press put it recently), is not widely spoken; no Namibian language is broadly national. African education is deplorable in quantity (especially beyond the primary level) and quality, as are the African health services. Productive services—e.g., agricultural planning and extension—are very close to being for whites only. Of over 7,000 boreholes (deep, drilled wells), only 500 are in African areas. There is an all-weather road net in African areas—to allow the army to combat liberation forces. There is a rather good vaccination service for African cattle—to ensure they are not reservoirs of contagion for settler ranch herds.

SWAPO'S POLITICAL ECONOMY OF LIBERATION

The proposals for a radical transformation of the Namibian economy are uniquely those of SWAPO.[19] While present church thinking is certainly supportive of radical change, it is not articulated into a program of political economy. With the exception of the National Union of Namibian Workers—which is affiliated to SWAPO— worker critiques of the system have been far-reaching but proposed changes have been either very general or within an immediate demand, workplace-centered, human dignity/economic gains framework.[20]

SWAPO's firmness in respect to principles and goals can be sensed in part from a selection of quotations dealing with its goals:

Transition to a socialist mode of production—immediate nationalisation of land, mineral and fishing rights, of South African state property and of illegally acquired assets. Joint ventures and TNC operations to operate within a Namibian framework.

Land to the tillers. The abolition of all forms of exploitation of man by man . . . and aggrandisement of wealth and power by individuals, groups or classes. Greater equality—including universal access to basic health and education and to pure water. Opportunities for full productive employment.

Abolition of "contract" labour, child labour, "humiliating servant systems." Right of workers to organise and to have an effective voice in all decisions directly affecting them.

Sever all relations with the South African racist regime until there is a democratic government in that country based on the principles of majority rule.[21]

SWAPO's *Political Programme* spells out not only a set of goals, but also rough guidelines for achieving them. It has been carried further in dialogues, seminars, work in refugee and base camps, and training and technical assistance contacts, but this evolution is both ongoing and unpublished. Six main themes can be identified: (1) Mode of production; (2) Rural development; (3) Distribution (exploitation and equality); (4) National economic integration/self-reliance; (5) Basic services; (6) Participation.

The basic *mode of production* set as a goal is socialism—specifically "bringing all the major means of production and exchange into ownership of the people" and "planning and development . . . governed by the principles of scientific socialism." A transitional period with state, cooperative, joint-venture, and private ownership is equally clearly stated, however. The initial minimum public directly productive sector is envisaged as including land, mineral and fishing rights, banking and finance, public utilities, and mass media. Private ownership of productive assets will be allowed within a national planning framework subject to consistency with the interests of the people and economic development.

Joint venture arrangements with existing private enterprises are specifically foreseen. Full nationalization for all assets acquired is neither specified nor clearly implied. Compensation related to value is envisaged for acquired assets except in respect to land, mineral and fishing rights, and South African state and state corporation assets. Continued private ownership of "justly acquired" nonproductive assets (dwelling houses, savings accounts) is guaranteed. For settler ranchers compensation would appear to imply payment for herds, equipment, and the 50 percent of the value of improvements not subsidized by the colonial state—subject to running the ranch properly up to an orderly handover. For small businesses compensation is not a likely early major issue. Currently SWAPO does not seek to nationalize small stores, repair shops, lodging houses, etc. Indeed clear statements to the contrary have been made, notably to the Federal German delegation and to Namibian residents of German ancestry at the time of the 1981 Geneva Pre-Implementation Conference. For major ventures (mines, factories) predating the 1966 revocation of the mandate over South West Africa entrusted to South Africa by the League of Nations, partial acquisition with compensation to create joint ventures is likely to be the preferred transition. This applies to Consolidated Diamond Mines and Tsumeb in particular. For post-1966 mines—illegal *ab initio*, and the possession of which constitutes fraud or theft under the 1971 International Court of Justice (ICJ) decision—there is much less likelihood of long-term joint ventures with existing operators or substantial compensation. Falconbridge Nickel (Oamites) and its owner Superior Oil (Etosha Petroleum), Johannesburg Consolidated (Otjihase), and RTZ and partners (Rossing) are perceived differently from the pre-1966 entrants. SWAPO has no illusions that it could run the mines itself, but would probably seek new managing agents—e.g., in Scandinavia or Yugoslavia. In interviews during the 1981 Geneva talks—including a substantial television discussion of the economy—President Nujoma stressed that SWAPO sees a large role for joint ventures. Secretary-General Moses Garoeb made the same point at least as forcefully in a November 1981 interview in Zimbabwe.[22]

SWAPO is most unlikely to accept South African state or state corporation claims for assets (e.g., power, railway, harbor, as well as shares in Rossing and other mines), still less the (largely spurious) South African claim for asserted subsidies to South West African budgetary spending. Recent South West Africa/Namibia data show a surplus of revenue over capital and recurrent expenditure through 1979/80. Very large 1980/81 and 1981/82 overall deficits appear to relate to massive transfer payments to ranchers to keep them in place for security reasons and to expanded "bantustan" employment to buy support, as well as to drought and diamond price related revenue falls. With the possible exception of some of the mining shareholdings, such claims have few if any precedents in previous colonial transitions.

"Comprehensive agrarian reforms aimed at giving the land to the tillers" are seen as a precondition for *rural development*. All colonial land "rights" are to be terminated. Continued use of part of the land by present holders will be subject to negotiation. Peasant and farmer cooperatives and collectives are presented as one form of organization to be developed, and state ranching and crop farms as another. Self-sufficiency in food is an explicit goal. Better knowledge, more inputs, and agricultural industries (both to produce inputs and to process outputs) are cited as means to improve the productivity and the incomes of the rural sector.

"The abolition of all forms of exploitation of man by man . . . and aggrandisement of wealth and power by individuals, groups or classes" is linked to the equality aspects of *distribution*, including differences between towns and rural areas and regional imbalances in the distribution of wealth. Measures specifically cited are price control and general surveillance (to prevent "parasitic means" of making profits) and opportunities for full, productive employment. Linked to the latter are provisions for nondiscriminatory wage and salary scales and protection of workers' economic and organizational rights. This protection is to be undertaken by unions, which are to be free to defend workers' interests and to participate in economic management. The contract labor system, child labor, and "humiliating servant systems" are to be abolished. The degree of equality in earnings envisaged is not very clear. "Payment according to one's contribution," linked to a clear opposition to substantial unearned or property income and to broad rural/urban income differentials, implies narrower limits than those in a majority of African countries. How much narrower is a debated issue.

National economic integration and *self-reliance* are treated as integral parts of national development (social, political, cultural, defense). Equality of access to work, the removal of rural/urban inequalities, and the provision of education and training are seen as having an economic content as well as being necessary to making the SWAPO motto of "One Namibia, One Nation" a reality. Some present economic setups (e.g., the "residual sector" and "domestic service") are seen as both politically excluding and humanly degrading. The attainment of basic self-sufficiency in food and the buildup of natural resource-based and/or input-producing industries are set in the context of increasing national economic balance and self-reliance. Public sector control of fiscal, monetary, and financial policy and institutions is set out as a major means toward integration (and general operation of planning). Neither autarchy nor (it would appear) general reduction of the absolute levels of production for export is envisaged.

The priority use of meat and fish to meet Namibia's nutritional needs and the processing of present raw material exports to build up value added and employment are stated or implied guidelines. In mining, fishing, and ranching, meeting Namibian requirements first could imply lower exports than those associated with maximum enterprise surpluses, but drastic retreat from the world economy is neither posited nor practical if the state is to have the resources to finance other facets of social and economic transformation.

The most radical guideline—and in the short run perhaps the most difficult—relates to selective delinking to "sever all relations with the South African racist regime until there is a democratic government in that country based on the principles of Majority Rule." The context and detailed wording leave open the possibility of selective interim use of personnel who are South African and renegotiated relations with private South African firms on a case-by-case basis. Certainly both options are discussed by SWAPO cadres. Garoeb in his November 1981 interview goes somewhat further in contemplating an "extremely pragmatic" set of renegotiations and phasing of changes.[23]

Basic services provisions are presented in terms of health and education. Urban services, including housing, do not receive specific attention (somewhat surprisingly, given the shift from contract to resident household nonagricultural labor force patterns). Health is presented in preventive as well as curative terms, paramedical as well as highly specialized, decentralized rural as well as urban. The presentation is evidently heavily influenced by SWAPO's own rural medical program in refugee and base camps and in northern and northeastern

Namibia, and the perspective this work has provided on needs and possibilities. Education is related to self-reliance (managerial and technical), universal productive employment (functional and literacy), and nation-building (primary and adult, creation of a national cadre of educators).

UNIN has carried out a substantial body of work on national language development and educational system preindependence planning. SWAPO both has a substantial educational system of its own and places students abroad—indeed with 3,000 at senior secondary schools and 800 at tertiary levels, its system at these levels is larger than the South African one in Namibia.

Participation is a recurrent theme. "The economic reconstruction aims at the creation of a classless society." Trade unions are seen as worker organizations to serve worker interests and participate in economic management—"to unite all Namibian people particularly the working class, the peasantry and progressive intellectuals into a vanguard Party capable of safeguarding . . . and building." Cooperative and community action are stressed. Decentralization is implicit rather than explicitly articulated. This is the result of South Africa's "divide and rule" policy and its attempts to create pseudo-territorial, pseudo-decentralized ethnic mini-states which has required central stress on attaining the unity of people, nation, and state—not because a highly centralized bureaucratic model lies behind the guidelines. SWAPO itself is highly collegiate in key decision-making but relatively decentralized in implementation.

Women's participation is not treated in the *Programme* but has received explicit attention from SWAPO.[24] Its nominations for programs demonstrate greater participation by women at all levels than that achieved by any independent African state. Its first draft legal code is on family law, in response to and largely prepared by its women cadres. There are women political commissars in combat units as well as senior women technical personnel.

LOOSENING THE TIES THAT BIND

Namibia's position in respect to South Africa is aptly summed up in "Southern Africa: Toward Economic Liberation," the intergovernmental declaration founding the SADCC:

Southern Africa is dependent on the Republic of South Africa as a focus of transport and communications, an exporter of goods and services and as an importer of goods and cheap labour. This dependence is not a natural phenomenon nor is it simply the result of a free market economy. The nine States and one occupied territory of Southern Africa . . . were, in varying degrees, deliberately incorporated—by metropolitan powers, colonial rulers and large corporations—into the colonial and sub-colonial structures centering on the Republic of South Africa.[25]

Namibia is the most extreme case of territorial dis-integration. It has been treated as a subprovincial unit without even full-fledged territorial or divisional headquarters of many departments, parastatals, and firms. The one exception is migrant labor: the contract system is virtually totally internal (there is some inflow from Angola). Very few Namibians work in the Republic. In addition, Namibia is the most extreme case of artificial links—the economic logic of integration into the Republic's economy is far from self-evident. However, that does not necessarily make reduction of concentrated unilateral dependence in personnel, institutions, knowledge, transport and communications, markets, sources, and finance all that much easier—at least in the short run.

The 36,500 economically active Europeans in Namibia include a majority of South African expatriates. Almost half are on South African public- or private-sector contracts. SWAPO is willing to negotiate their selective secondment from the South African to the Namibian public service and gradual phasing out, but this may not be practicable in the public sector. A majority of the settlers probably see themselves as South African and may depart thither. Indeed the problem is not seen so much in terms of reducing the South African personnel presence as of training Namibians and recruiting alternative expatriates to keep the economy and public services operating.

Namibia will inherit few complete institutions—albeit South Africa's slow-motion UDI threat and private firms' hedging against change have modestly improved the situation. Planning, accounting, financial control, research, and maintenance are largely in RSA. How much can be "repatriated" is unclear. How quickly new institutions which are more self-contained can be created is a key question.

105

Knowledge about general technical subjects can evidently be fairly easily secured from non-RSA sources. But specialized knowledge linked to Namibia—e.g., the very detailed farm planning mechanism and its data banks, the construction and civil engineering research and survey results—are another matter.[26] They can be reproduced only by trial and error if access is lost (as it probably will be in the absence of substantial personnel secondment). SWAPO hopes to retain a high proportion of German-ancestry civil servants, who are believed to be more receptive to change and to hold territorial attachment to Namibia rather than South Africa.

Transport and communication links with South Africa are omnipresent but hardly economically rational and—once Walvis Bay is secured—clearly can be reduced to secondary significance. The railroad is not self-contained. If it were, the long haul to the Cape would make no kind of sense to Namibia. In road transport the dependence is on RSA transport firms and lorry fleets. Even in respect to trade with South Africa the logical routes are dominantly sea (Maputo or Durban or Cape Town to Walvis Bay), not land. While Namib Air is South African-owned, it would be relatively easy to create a territorial and regional airline and to secure some intercontinental service (e.g., appended flights from Europe to Luanda, Lusaka, or Salisbury). Present communication links are almost all via the Republic. However, construction of VHF (short-wave telecommunication) links to Angola, Zambia, and Botswana, erection of a Class B Earth Satellite Station near Windhoek, and rerouting mail via new regional and intercontinental connections could reverse that fairly rapidly and easily.

South Africa is Namibia's dominant market for live cattle. To reduce ranching dependence requires adequate abbatoir facilities, an EEC beef quota (SWAPO's current intent is to seek both Commonwealth and ACP membership), and new outlets in non-EEC Europe and the Middle East. Fish and products sales to RSA are substantial but usually at below world prices (for required deliveries). For other products (e.g., karakul, diamonds) shipments to RSA are neither necessary nor economically logical, except to Republic marketing firms, as the ultimate markets are in Europe and North America. The real problem—which UNIN and SWAPO have begun to explore—is to devise a new set of marketing institutions and/or induce European, North American, and Far Eastern firms to buy directly from Namibia rather than via Republic intermediaries and branch offices.

While (as noted) about 70 percent of Namibia's imports come from the Republic, this is more the result of a customs union and South African dominance of the wholesale and import trades than because of availability or cost considerations. Switching sources of grain and coal (areas in which self-reliance would seem likely to take a decade to achieve) might pose cost problems but hardly insuperable ones. For other goods knowledge of alternative sources, presence of sellers, and an independent tariff would result in significant short- and medium-term shifts in sources.

The net financial flow—excluding the war bill—is from Namibia to South Africa. An economically functioning Namibia could—like Botswana—float and manage a national currency independent of the Rand. For reasons of both the control of capital outflow and general economic management, there is a need for separate Namibian financial institutions (including territorial branches of private, non-RSA firms), a target which will prove harder to achieve because of personnel and knowledge constraints.

On balance a substantial reduction in dependence on the Republic can be achieved within five years of independence. In large part this would be the result of a more diversified set of international relationships, but some of the changes would represent direct substitution of Namibian personnel, resources, and institutions for South African. There is a danger of South African (public and/or private) withdrawal before workable alternatives are in place; in a sense, such a withdrawal would speed dependence reduction, but at the cost of severe interim dislocations. Experiences in Zimbabwe suggest there is both a possibility of orderly disengagement and a danger of deliberate destabilizing actions in relation to transport, fuel supply, and trade by South Africa.

SOUTHERN AFRICAN DEVELOPMENT COORDINATION

South Africa's attempts to float an economic "constellation" of dependent African states to provide room for its economic expansion and a *cordon sanitaire* against external pressure have failed. No independent African state has responded positively, and the disappearance from office of former Prime Minister Abel Muzorewa has knocked out the key star.[27] New efforts to refloat the same scheme with an overtly private-sector content have begun but seem unlikely to be more than very partially successful from a South African point of view.[28]

The SADCC—which grew out of the Frontline States' experience that economic dependence on the Republic hampered the pursuit of regional political liberation and national economic development—affords a number of opportunities for collective self-reliance to Namibia. The nine members have specifically listed support for liberation movements in training and preplanning in the Lusaka Declaration[29] and provided for their associate status in the Southern African Transport and Communications Commission. Namibia's accession on independence is seen both by SADCC and SWAPO as virtually certain—a position reaffirmed at SADCC's 1981 annual conference in Blantyre.[30]

The SADCC is a very new grouping. Its first prefounding ministerial conference was in May 1979, its founding declaration in April 1980,[31] and its first conference with potential cooperating states and institutions (at which $650 million was pledged) in November 1980.[32] It has a clear strategy based on practical sector by sector cooperation to achieve the following: reduce dependence (especially on the Republic of South Africa); create operational and equitable regional integration; mobilize resources (domestic and external) to achieve regional coordination and to secure international understanding of and cooperation with the strategy (i.e., treating southern Africa as an entity in its own right and not as an appendage of South Africa).[33]

The areas which have advanced furthest are transport and communications[34] and agrarian (foot and mouth and the livestock diseases, soil conservation and land use planning, semi-arid agricultural research, food security).[35] In both areas concrete projects are already being implemented. Industrial development, human resources (manpower) development, regional financial mechanisms, energy, and bank note, check, and stamp printing are other areas in which explorations toward joint action are proceeding.[36] For a country as small—and as near a strong former colonial power—as Namibia, the concrete technical/economic and solidarity approaches of the SADCC are strong attractions.

The most important regional links for Namibia are likely to be with Botswana and Angola. In the case of Botswana they turn on the Trans-Kalahari Railroad and an Okavango Waters Agreement (also involving Angola). The latter is critical to fuller Okavango Valley development in Namibia and to allowing Botswana to develop its main arable potential and water source—the interior delta of the Okavango. The Trans-Kalahari Railroad is critical to integrating Botswana's north and west (agriculture, cattle, several secondary mineral desposits) into the present north-south axis. It could be viable on the basis of Botswana coal exports and a reorientation of existing external trade routes, and it could provide Zimbabwe with access to an Atlantic port.[37] For Namibia it would provide a better route to its own coast, a source of coal, a direct tie to a neighbor, some transit revenues, and opportunities for broader coordination (e.g., in railroad maintenance and personnel training). The railroad is not in practice an alternative to a new heavy-duty line from Botswana via Zimbabwe to Maputo since that line could not integrate Botswana but would be optimal for Far Eastern-oriented coal (and soda ash) shipments, as distinct from those destined for Europe.*

Certain joint ventures—e.g., in petroleum refining and cement—may prove attractive to Botswana and Namibia. If Namibia's coal proves to be low grade or expensive to mine, Botswana will be a logical supplier. Namibian exports to Botswana of fish and dairy products are secondary but need not be insignificant. In addition, agrarian concerns and contexts are similar enough to suggest the value of technical research and training coordination and exchange.†

In the short term Angolan links may be more critical for Namibia. This will be especially true if South Africa seeks to hold on to Walvis Bay, in which case access to Puerto Alexandre and Mocamedes may become critical. Angola has plans for a central north-south rail link connecting with the Namibian system at Tsumeb. Namibia might find Angola at least an interim source for petroleum products and a market for meat.

---

*As Zimbabwe needs a heavy duty line from Bulawayo to Maputo, by strengthening the existing line to Bulawayo, a link from the Botswana coalfields to Maputo may be a desirable interim measure (the Trans-Kalahari's earliest completion date is circa 1988) and a subsequent complement allowing Botswana and Zimbabwe direct access to both the Atlantic and Indian Oceans.

†Via the growers' co-op, South Africa has thwarted Botswana from entering the karakul industry by an artificial longitude restriction on pelts. Namibia (the world's dominant karakul producer) might reverse that decision after independence.

Zimbabwe's economy is of interest to Namibia as an alternative import source to South Africa and as a potentially significant market for fish and fish meal. While Zambia is a neighbor, immediate links may be limited as its logical Atlantic port is Lobito and the scope for trade may not be great.

Certainly SADCC links will never be comparable to those now existing with South Africa. However, over a decade they could be of value in reducing dependence on the Republic and come to be significant in themselves and last as long as (or longer than) residual RSA ties.

THE UNFORGIVING LAND

Namibia is a territory and will be a state subject to a series of rigid constraints which can be ignored only at a high cost. Ecology, technology, geopolitics, and history are for Namibia neither malleable nor forgiving.

Desert encroachment is a present reality and—under conditions of breakdown in the large-scale ranching sector—could have results as dramatic as those caused by reckless overfishing, but with one difference: desertification would be largely irreversible. Only in the extreme north and east and in a few small pockets elsewhere is there a significant margin for error (or bad luck) in the rural sector. Namibia's ecology is such that misuse leads to short-run loss of output and longer-term destruction of the potential to produce.

Technology is not much more malleable. Retreat to subsistence, which has limited the worst effects of modern sector dislocation elsewhere, is not open to Namibia. Modern production or starvation are the alternatives in most of the country. This is particularly true of mining. Almost half of Namibia's production, exports, and surplus are derived from seven mines, a smelter, and a uranium oxide plant. Failure to understand, maintain, and operate this technology properly will be disastrous. The price will not merely be financial: mining accidents kill. This technological constraint is compounded by the fact that grave doubts exist as to adequacy in terms of worker health and environmental impact of the underground mining and processing procedures at Rossing.[38]

110

The ranching economy, while technically less complex than mining, is neither simple nor self-contained. It depends on vehicles and boreholes, sophisticated land-use planning, and complex service and marketing systems.[39] Furthermore, production neither is, nor in many parts of rural Namibia can be, directed to rural consumption, as opposed to urban consumption or export; thus transportation is necessary to realize the value of production and to secure food to eat.

The Windhoek urban water system is an example of the constraints imposed by existing urban technology. One quarter of the water deliveries are purified and recycled sewage. To take that source out of use would worsen a severe water shortage (which is already likely to result from a post-independence urban population increase as families move to join former contract employees). To operate it without technical competence and proper servicing would practically guarantee a cholera epidemic.

Namibia's location and most valuable resources hold potential problems as well as opportunities. With Namibia's independence the Orange River will become a front line of the South African liberation struggle. On the Namibian side of the estuary, the Oranjemund diamond complex is literally in range of South African guns at Port Alexander. Granted that neither Rhodesia nor South Africa has found cross-border raids to be of much use in bolstering internal security for any length of time—a fact illustrated (not contradicted) by the 1980-81 pattern of increasing SWAPO military activity in Namibia despite massive RSA invasions of Angola—Namibia's proximity to South Africa, combined with its commitment to liberation, will entail costs. They may not be as high as is sometimes supposed because the strategy of the South African liberation movements (and the Frontline States) does not turn on transborder-based guerrilla action starting at the peripheries of South Africa. Rather the vision is of urban and peri-urban strikes, demonstrations, and risings eroding confidence, sapping output, and stretching military and police forces ever thinner.* Under such a scenario, raids across the Orange (or Limpopo or Pongola) would become an expensive and irrelevant

*If the 1980 riots in South Africa had all taken place at one time, the military and police forces available to control them would have been numerically inadequate without withdrawing forces from Namibia or using different and more sanguinary tactics. The point has not been missed by Generals Geldenhuys and Malan.

luxury for RSA, albeit it is not clear that South Africa would see them in that light.

Uranium is not a normal product. While internationally traded oxide is not in a form directly usable for any purpose and 99 percent of it is destined for power production, major oxide producers attract the eye of official as well as amateur strategists and security services. How real a constraint this proves to be depends on how well SWAPO's position is understood: that uranium oxide is a key national resource to be exploited and marketed like any other mineral—i.e., commercially and at the best attainable price. It implies a commercial technical management and term contracts with power companies or their procurement agents—hardly a prospect logically troubling any state's security planners.*

Namibia's history of the past century is unforgiving as well. As noted, it is a virtually unrelieved record of theft and violence, blood and iron—African blood shed by European iron. That history does not necessarily require a total exodus of Europeans nor guarantee a xenophobic new society. SWAPO and many Namibians are nonracist in word and spirit. But what will happen at independence is problematic. A mass European exodus based on fear (however unfounded) and accompanied by sabotage could both cripple the economy and create xenophobia. Similarly the difference between reversal of land theft and action on the 1971 ICJ ruling on post-1966 mines, rather than generalized confiscation of European assets, may be much clearer to Namibians than to external observers, let alone Europeans and foreign firms in Namibia. Given the complexities of state infrastructures and corporations, land titles (as opposed to improvements), and post-1966 natural resource exploitation investment, a "constitutional property clause" cannot resolve and could exacerbate this problem.†

*For capacity to produce power-grade—or a fortiori weapon-grade—enriched uranium, different considerations apply. However, it is neither technically nor economically feasible for Namibia to go beyond the present yellowcake stage in the foreseeable future.

† SWAPO is certainly willing to agree to fair compensation for property legitimately acquired by present owners. The precedents on transfer of colonial state assets to successor states do not suggest compensation in such cases (except perhaps for shareholdings in directly productive sectors), nor, in the light of the ICJ opinion, can a case be made that post-1966 mines represent legally acquired

How severely past history does in fact constrain the first years of independent Namibia will depend very much on the duration and nature of the present final chapter of transition to independence.

"WAITING FOR SWAPO"

Namibia is a country in waiting—waiting for SWAPO. . . . One of the most consistent trends [among] a wide range of Namibians representing all shades of the motley political and economic spectrum was an acceptance—sometimes eagerly expectant sometimes resigned and fearful—that a SWAPO government is on the way.[40]

That quotation is not from an independent African newspaper or even a European social democratic newspaper but from the Johannesburg press. Nor is it atypical of the direction and present resting point of informed South African opinion. Two other recent headlines have been "Pretoria's Choice: SWAPO or Sanctions" and "SWA's Choices Narrow Down."[41] Nor is it only the English-speaking press and the business community that can see the handwriting on the wall. It has been two years since Foreign Minister Pik Botha admitted that "The people of the Territory will have to get independence sooner or later. The political momentum has been set in motion."[42]

In Namibia itself the perception of an inevitable transition to a SWAPO government within five years is even stronger.[43] Indeed at least the English language press now treats the return of Nujoma as President of the country as a fait accompli.[44] At the Geneva talks in 1981 Dirk Mudge admitted that early elections would reproduce the Zimbabwe result and stated that the Democratic Turnhalle Alliance (DTA) government needed two years of peace with no SWAPO presence to have a chance to win.[45]

A shift in outlook has been emerging for several years. It has accelerated sharply since 1979 for two reasons:

property. Furthermore, a property rights clause so rigid as to block change would either lead to perfectly legal steps to wipe out the "market price" of the property (as done by Botswana in respect to certain mineral and urban "concession" rights) or set up pressures for avoiding or abrogating the clause (as appears to be happening in Zimbabwe).

(1) The war in Namibia is going badly for South Africa. The parallels with Zimbabwe of (say) 1977 are increasingly evident and the willingness to play out a lost cause increasingly dwindling— at least among those most directly affected;

(2) The ZANU-PF electoral victory in Zimbabwe has dashed hopes of installing a safe "white government with black faces." If Muzorewa, who originally had genuine nationalist credentials, proved a broken reed, who can believe that the much more tawdry puppets in the Mudge entourage would make any showing in a free and fair election? If an internationally observed election contested by the liberation movements so totally reversed the "verdict" of an "internal settlement" poll, who can suppose any South African-run election in Namibia would carry the least international credibility?

At first glance this pattern of perception suggests a relatively speedy and orderly transition via a UN-supervised election. However, that is an oversimplification of a more complex reality, and one in no basic way altered by the 1981 U.S. initiatives and South African responses.

South Africa has for years been playing for time in Namibia— partly because continued occupation was profitable, partly to try to devise a loss-limiting formula for withdrawal. While the gains have shrunk and the options narrowed, the tactics and goals remain unchanged. South Africa's sudden enthusiasm for "direct talks" with SWAPO late in 1980 fitted squarely in this model, as does its "in principle" acceptance of U.S./Western contact group proposals to "strengthen" (i.e., water down) Security Council Resolution 435 and to "build confidence" (i.e., placate South Africa).

South Africa can hold the following hopes:

(1) That SWAPO or the Frontline States will act in a way perceived externally as "unreasonable" (a weakening hope in that they have already agreed to the broad outlines of the proposals precisely because after the Zimbabwe precedent they are sure SWAPO can win a two thirds majority in any nonfraudulent election);

(2) That a breakdown can be engineered by continuing its war of aggression against Angola and insisting on involving its "Major Hadad"—Jonas Savimbi—in the demilitarization process (a

course of action which has dangers as it is South Africa which tends to be seen as "unreasonable"—except, perhaps, in Washington);

(3) That by some miracle the DTA can create a popular (or bought) electoral base (of which to date there is no sign);

(4) That time can be bought to continue the war—which, while unwinnable, will not quickly be lost—and to cast about for a better time or set of terms (a route which has worked to date; 1981's respite of effective Western pressure is a year gained without any clear action by RSA demonstrating a good faith intent to negotiate or settle); and

(5) At worst, that if SWAPO-RSA negotiations can be shifted from modalities for electing a constitutional assembly to parameters of a constitution, certain key South African interests might be safeguarded (on the Lancaster House model).

Except for the last point, and perhaps the third, these are RSA concerns—not those of European residents or firms in Namibia. Many of them are as cynical and bitter about South Africa's tactics as SWAPO. But they too have an unrealistic wish for a painless transition to independence which would ensure retention of their own privileges. Anglo-America's "man in Namibia," Douglas Hoffe of Consolidated Diamond Mines, is not atypical in noting that "Both sides would have to make major compromises in their political philosophies and reach a compromise constitution which would be administered by a coalition formed by the colonial power and SWAPO. I know it's wishful thinking but by God I wish it."[46] Under the circumstances the headline "Cynics Hold Sway Over Hope of Success for Multi-Party Talks" is still only too accurate, both as a description of South African and Namibian views and as an evaluation of the short-term outlook for negotiations.[47]

FOCI OR FLASH POINTS?

There are four elements in the transition to independence in Namibia and its immediate aftermath which could alter SWAPO's present strategy and tactics in the directions of greater speed, lesser flexibility, and increased harshness in respect to internal and external

115

doubters, neutrals, and apparent opponents. These concern the process and timing of independence, the status of Walvis Bay, the settler response to independence, and the external reaction to steps taken in respect to the three post-1966 mines (four counting Superior Oil's Etosha Pan operation).

In respect to process and timing the general principle is that the longer the delay, the greater the escalation in military action, and the more the attempts to limit the freedom of the electorate (e.g., by a "pre-baked" constitution to be presented to the Assembly), the poorer will be the basis for an orderly, relatively tolerant and gradual transition. Apparently rigid limits set by constitutional clauses—e.g., to protect property rights—are likely in practice to build up pressures in a way leading to an explosion, not to resolve underlying problems.

Similarly South African trick-or-trap proposals engender deep suspicion and ill will which bode ill for subsequent negotiations. To propose to include in talks representatives of the União Nacional para a Independência Total de Angola (UNITA) in Namibia (paid, uniformed, equipped, and officered by RSA, and to a significant degree Rhodesian and Portuguese African mercenaries, not Angolans) is either a joke in very poor taste or a deliberate attempt to prevent talks. To create a "separate" South West Territorial Force supposedly not subject to regulation of external forces during elections when its personnel remain on the RSA roster and its command structure is an integral part of the overall RSA forces is to plant a booby trap to be exploded at will.[48]

Walvis Bay is Namibia's main port and has been an integral part of the territory for over sixty years, although South Africa inherited it from the United Kingdom rather than conquering it from Germany. For SWAPO to govern Namibia with its external trade passing through a South African enclave is not practicable for more than a very brief period. If South Africa seeks to hang on to Walvis Bay, SWAPO contemplates four lines of response:

(1) Appeal to the international community via the United Nations and ICJ;

(2) Reactivation of Swakopmund (the main German port which was once able to handle 8,000 ton vessels) by use of artificial breakwaters, lighters, dredging, and jetty repairs;

116

(3) Establishment of road—and later rail—links to the southern Angolan port of Mocamedes and perhaps (depending on the problems of equipping it) Puerto Alexandre;

(4) Requests for external assistance to construct one of the artificial ports to the north of Walvis Bay (e.g., Hentiesbaai, Cape Cross) for which South African studies already exist.

The last response illustrates the self-defeating nature of South African perceptions. South Africa fears a foreign naval presence at Walvis Bay and hopes a lock on external trade would "moderate SWAPO." The reality is rather different. SWAPO has no present intent to allow bases of any foreign state. However, if the price of securing construction of an artificial harbor to replace a South African-occupied Walvis Bay included providing naval base (or fishing) facilities, it would be difficult for any nationalist Namibian to refuse.

Settler responses are complex and unpredictable—especially in the short run. When in 1978 a UN election briefly seemed imminent, 3,000-odd ranchers (mostly of German ancestry) applied for SWAPO membership. In fact, the "optimal" rancher response would probably be one in which one third to one half wished to transfer their operations in return for compensation for herds, equipment, and buildings, plus one year "advisory" contracts, with the remainder taking the same decision over a five-year period. The worst scenarios would be 100 percent cut-and-run (complete with asset stripping and sabotage—as in Angola and Mozambique), or if 90 percent decided to "die on their land" and had to be forced off. Neither an instant takeover (for production reasons) nor a failure at a substantial, early start to land recovery (for political credibility reasons, as well as the need to get land into African hands to set rural reconstruction in train) is desirable.

Civil servants' decisions pose comparable problems. A substantial number are personally unacceptable; a new set of senior officials (whether citizens or SWAPO-chosen expatriates) is needed. But the basic technical personnel—most of whom are personally acceptable if they accept a change in employer and in relations to black Namibians—are needed until Namibians can be trained and/or new expatriates recruited. Company personnel and small businessmen are more likely to stay—at least for a time. That is necessary to keep production going and to provide basic amenities for the remaining Europeans and for new expatriates more generally.

SWAPO makes a distinction between pre- and post-1966 mines.[49] The Rossing, Oamites, Otjihase, and Etosha mines fall into the latter category. While in pre-1966 cases SWAPO appears to consider joint ventures and regulation as practicable options, its stand on post-1966 cases has hardened since the late 1970s, when attempts to negotiate with RTZ failed.* Even in these cases SWAPO does not envisage overnight acquisition and self-operation.[50] The technical problems of securing new managements and marketing channels are not insuperable. The problems turn on overseas reaction.

Certain Rossing customers—notably in Germany—have seemed to view actions against RTZ as threats to themselves.[51] That appears somewhat unwise and may be receding. Access to uranium oxide for power supplies and security of contractual arrangements arrived at equitably and legally are of concern to them, but it is less clear why RTZ operation, or an asserted "mining right" which the ICJ has found invalid on standard bourgeois legal principles, should be.†
But if the reaction to SWAPO action in respect to post-1966 mines is attempted isolation or destabilization, SWAPO will be forced to reassess its economic strategy and pattern of internal economic relations. It would be unlikely to do so from the viewpoint of seeking accommodation.

CONCLUSION

A checklist of probabilities in respect to Namibia and to SWAPO has become clearer since 1980:

(1) Namibia will be independent before 1985, and the independence government will be formed wholly or dominantly by SWAPO;

---

*SWAPO sought a public statement by RTZ accepting the illegality of the existing contracts and immediate negotiations on new ones; RTZ sought a private commitment by SWAPO to allow Rossing (at least so far as RTZ's involvement went) to continue basically unchanged after independence.

†SWAPO statements at the UN uranium hearings and elsewhere suggest it would decline to honor "sweetheart contracts" entered into by RTZ. They do not indicate any intent to halt production or to decline to enter into term contracts subject to acceptable price formulas.

(2) SWAPO is committed to substantial and rapid social and political economic transformation of a type which can reasonably be described as "transition to socialism";

(3) In respect to timing, tactics, and sequences, SWAPO's political economic program includes substantial elements of flexibility and of adjustment to perceived constraints;

(4) In principle SWAPO's political economic program is implementable;

(5) Reduction of dependence on South Africa would be both practicable and economically desirable for an independent Namibia and could include significant southern African regional aspects;

(6) The constraints on change and, equally, on failure to change in Namibia are numerous and severe. In the context of a delayed transition, of destabilization by South Africa and/or other external states, or of economic breakdown, they could become unmanageable and result in a much harsher, simpler, and (at least in the short run) dramatically less successful political economic program than that now envisaged by SWAPO. While not in the interests of the Western contact group or the OECD states more generally, such a result might be seen as desirable by South Africa. A bankrupt, hostile, xenophobic Namibia might be seen to pose less of a challenge (especially in terms of international and internal South African response) than a prosperous, nonracial one rapidly reducing dependence on RSA while increasing domestic and regional self-reliance. In March 1982 Prime Minister Botha threatened a "scorched earth" withdrawal.[52]

PRIORITIES FOR YEAR ONE: A CHECKLIST

The immediate requirements of Namibia on independence will far exceed available resources: human, knowledge, institutional, physical, and financial. This will be especially true if South Africa pulls out its personnel, settlers, and portable assets to achieve an initial destabilization and/or if major private-sector interests do likewise. There will be an overriding need to establish priorities and sequences. What is desirable but not essential, or essential but not immediately critical, will have to be postponed if energy, attention, and resources are to be adequate to accomplish what is both critical and urgent.

The following checklist is the author's—not SWAPO's. However, from discussions with SWAPO cadres and from their participation in international meetings and seminars, it would appear that most—perhaps all—of the items figure on their shortlists and are in many cases perceived in relatively similar terms.

- Keeping *mineral production* going—notably in diamonds, uranium, and the main copper, lead, and zinc mines. This is the backbone of government revenue, export earnings, and investible surplus. Its output is readily salable—and for diamonds and uranium oxide, readily exportable by air. The mineral TNCs are used to being forced to renegotiate historic unequal contracts. There are alternative operators to be had if existing companies will not accept reasonable new arrangements.

- *Ranching* is the heart of rural production. Together with mining, it is critical to employment. It is likely to be hit by cattle exodus or killing—which might be mitigated if SWAPO publicly agrees to pay market value for cattle and created assets which are turned over in good order, and also indicates an intent to prosecute for sabotage. If the industry is in reasonable working order, it will face marketing problems; more packing facilities (or possibly cattle boats to the Middle East) and new markets will be needed.

- It is highly probable that the *fishing* fleet will be in Table Bay, not Walvis Bay, on the day the latter becomes Namibian. To save jobs in the processing industry, contract fishing, training for skippers, and boat building (abroad and at the Walvis Bay base) are urgent necessities. So are conservation measures, both inshore and to the two hundred mile economic zone limit to allow restoration of fish stocks.

- Additions to *basic services* will be required. An acceptable national language (presumably English) must be taught. Adult education—especially rough-and-ready gap-filling and upgrading courses—must have top priority so that the number of expatriates can be reduced rapidly from 36,500 to 15,000. The ground must be laid for radical expansion of the educational system. Health services—especially vaccination, health education, preventive medicine, and first aid—must be made available nationally; these will build on the experiences of Zambia and Angola and "semi-liberated" area clinics and first aid teams.

- With the end of contract labor, 100,000 families will seek to be reunited at places of work. Many will wish to move rapidly. *Urban layout* and *services,* as well as the *construction* (even on an artisanal and communal basis) of (say) the first quarter of the homes needed during the first year, are minimum requirements to retain credibility and to avoid the instant creation of permanent urban slums to replace the prison compound and shack pattern.

- *Personnel* must be mobilized more vigorously and allocated more carefully than any other resource. Every Namibian with a special skill is a scarce asset. Namibians must hold and be seen to hold power. In the rural sector failure to act on this principle would render land reform unacceptable no matter how technically desirable it might be as a first step. Use of expert technical support teams, each servicing a score of ranches with Namibian production level management, might be feasible. But expatriates in a wide range of positions will be needed and will have to be identified, recruited, and supervised—and promptly fired if unsuitable.

- *Income distribution* will pose problems. African wages and salaries must be raised, but not to present European levels (which Namibia could not afford). Because separate scales by race must be ended—a different thing from separate scales for expatriates— a dilemma will exist in respect to would-be citizens of European ancestry.* It will be necessary to raise agricultural incomes (by redistribution in ranching and by initial measures to raise

*Zimbabwe has tried to avoid cutting any public-sector salaries in nominal terms, to reduce all top salaries by incomes policy, and to avoid any expatriate allowances. Given the very high top salaries (up to $40,000), this approach poses severe problems if services are to be expanded and a de facto dual-salary system based on race eliminated by equalizing at the "white" rates.

121

productivity and prices for field crops) to avert a wholesale rural exodus and to avoid a hugh urban/rural income gap.

- The *public sector* will need to be large, quick on its feet, and business-like. It must be dominant in finance (beginning with a central bank) and external trade (beginning with marketing ranching and fishing products, and organizing critical imports). In addition, it will need to encompass former South African statal/parastatal production units and any other key enterprises whose former owners have been expelled or who have abandoned them (including probably at least one of the major post-1966 mines). All this will require the creation of Namibian-controlled institutions, even if these have to be staffed initially by expatriate technical agents.

Chapter 4

SOUTH AFRICA'S REGIONAL POLICY

Deon Geldenhuys

INTRODUCTION

The South African government's proposed "constellation" of southern African states has renewed attention on South Africa's relations with its neighbors, both in the Republic and abroad. Analysts are bound to interpret the idea of a constellation in different ways. There are those who would brand it as apartheid on a new "offensive," as the latest version of a long-standing expansionist desire which aims at reducing black southern African countries to client states of South Africa.* Others would tend to dismiss a constellation as little more than a change in semantics: a new name for an old and only marginally successful regional policy aimed at promoting closer relations between South Africa and surrounding black states. The optimistic counterpart of the latter interpretation would be that a constellation is an imaginative yet realistic and viable formula for extending and further institutionalizing cooperation between South Africa and black countries. Still others would be inclined to see a constellation primarily in domestic terms—i.e., a device to restructure economic and political relations between South Africa and its independent former homelands of Transkei, Bophuthatswana, and Venda.[1]

---

*In 1967 President Kenneth Kaunda of Zambia responded to Prime Minister B.J. Vorster's announcement of a new "outward movement" by saying that "Apartheid is on the offensive" (quoted in G.M. Cockram, *Vorster's Foreign Policy* [Pretoria; Academica, 1970], p. 126). In November 1979 Kaunda referred to South Africa's proposed constellation as follows: "South Africa is to become the king-pin of all of us, and all of us—Zambia, Mozambique and Angola—are going to be satellite or puppet states of South Africa" (*Rand Daily Mail*, 26 November 1979).

Finally, some analysts are likely to associate a constellation with what may be termed South Africa's garrison option; a constellation then becomes synonymous with a fortress designed to safeguard South Africa (and its allies) against external attack. Although most of these interpretations no doubt contain some measure of truth, no one by itself provides an adequate basis for assessing South Africa's regional policy. In short, single-factor explanations or narrowly based premises represent a harsh oversimplification of the complex process of interaction which produces the Republic's foreign and regional policies.

In common with other states, South Africa's foreign policy cannot be analyzed without reference to its domestic base. However, the impact of domestic policy on foreign policy is far more profound in South Africa's case because of the very nature of the country's internal political order. Put differently, a domestic racial policy universally condemned places severe constraints on South Africa's foreign policy. As will be shown below, the detrimental, obstructive effects of domestic policy are evident in the country's regional policy as well. Creating a favorable external environment is therefore far more difficult in South Africa's case. Nonetheless, South Africa's ruling elite has consistently been guided by a desire to create an environment in southern Africa which would be favorable to the Republic's political, economic, and military/strategic interests. Inevitably this has meant (*inter alia*) the safeguarding of South Africa's domestic political order. The concern with creating an acceptable regional environment can be regarded as the paradigm within which South Africa's regional policy— and indeed its Africa policy generally—has been formulated through the years.

The ways in which South Africa has sought to shape an agreeable regional environment have changed as circumstances in the region and the world, as well as within the Republic, have changed. Its regional policy should therefore be seen as the product of the interaction of a wide range of variables. Yet while the policy has not been static, it has retained some enduring and fundamental objectives.

Before examining the development of South Africa's regional policy, let us note that we shall consider only the postwar period in detail because South Africa's present international position and the state of its relations with other countries in southern Africa are primarily outcomes of the postwar international political environment.

Within this time frame, the focus will be strictly on interstate relations at the governmental level; the South African perceptions and actions referred to will therefore be those of the government of the day. This does not mean that official views and actions are the only relevant ones; however, in the context of this study, which presents a broad overview of South Africa's regional relations and cannot therefore lay claims to completeness, the authoritative and operative official perceptions and actions will suffice. Finally, we shall examine the evolution of South Africa's regional policy from the perspective of the country's long-standing objective of establishing a context favorable to its security, prosperity, and domestic political order.

SOUTH AFRICA'S REGIONAL POLICY FROM SMUTS TO VORSTER

GENERAL J. C. SMUTS: FROM PAN-AFRICAN TO REGIONAL COOPERATION (1939-48)

Before 1945 South African ideas on relations with neighboring African territories were rather grandiose in conception. Prime Minister J. C. Smuts was an ardent advocate of pan-African cooperation, and he urged that relations in Africa be conducted "in the spirit of a small League of Nations."[2] Since Africa at the time was largely under colonial rule, Smuts was in fact proposing a relationship between South Africa and the European colonial powers. South Africa's identification with the colonial powers was the result not only of their common interests in Africa; white South Africans' historical and cultural ties with their European countries of origin made close political relations with them natural. Smuts clearly wanted relations to be of more than merely symbolic significance. Accordingly, in 1943 he suggested a scheme of "colonial re-organisation" in the British empire to create new "colonial groups" in which neighboring dominions (of which the Union was one) would actively involve themselves, thus making them "sharers and partners" in the empire.[3] Such an arrangement would obviously have given South Africa a direct hand in plotting the political future of colonial Africa. Some years earlier Oswald Pirow, Minister of Defense in the government of J. B. M. Hertzog, had expressed South Africa's political and military interests in Africa in his vision of two or three federations between the Union and the

Sudan, linked to South Africa "by a common Native policy" and (directly flowing from that) "a common defence policy."[4] The idea of a common racial policy was one to which the postwar National Party governments became particularly attracted. They and Pirow shared the conviction that South Africa was entitled to take the lead in establishing such policies because the country had a large permanent white population and was, moreover, economically the most advanced in Africa.

Given South Africa's peculiar domestic political order and its close identification with the European colonial powers, the Union understandably had considerable difficulty adjusting to the vastly changed postwar international environment—above all in Africa. Smuts suggested that a commission composed of colonial powers and others with economic and military interests in Africa (thus including South Africa) be established to formulate a common policy for the continent[5]—probably an attempt to bridge the emerging differences between colonial and South African views on the course of political development in Africa, and on race relations in particular. In addition, Smuts's proposal was consistent with the paradigm shaping the country's policy toward the rest of Africa. On a more modest level, Smuts stated his commitment to the "knitting together" of southern Africa[6] in a manner which would ultimately lead to an organization for regional cooperation along the lines of the Pan-American Union.[7] Of course such an organization would have been essentially intercolonial. Nonetheless, Smuts's emphasis on closer regional relations was an important new theme, and it is not unlikely that his scaleddown ideas on cooperation in Africa resulted from a realization that his grandiose designs for continental cooperation in a colonial context were simply not feasible—not least because of political considerations on the part of the colonial powers.

DR. D. F. MALAN AND THE AFRICA CHARTER (1948-54)

The growing differences between South African thinking on the status of colonial Africa and of black Africans generally, on the one hand, and international trends in the first postwar decade, on the other, were vividly illustrated in the so-called Africa Charter drawn up by Smuts's successor, D. F. Malan. An anachronistic statement of policy, the charter sought in effect to consolidate the colonial order in Africa by (*inter alia*) declaring that the development of the continent should be guided along the lines of "Western European Christian civilization" and that the militarization of the "native of Africa" should be prevented since it could endanger "our white civilization."[8]

South Africa's commitment to the creation of a beneficial African environment found further expression in its participation in a series of talks in the 1950s on the defense of Africa and the Middle East involving the colonial powers, the Commonwealth, and the United States.[9] South Africa's ideal, which it actively but unsuccessfully canvassed, was the formation of an African Defense Organization for anti-Communist states with interests in Africa.[10] It should be explained that the combating of communism has been a major foreign and domestic policy objective of Nationalist governments since they came to power in 1948. The Nationalists typically perceived international politics in terms of a struggle between Communist and anti-Communist forces; moreover, communism was seen as a genuine threat to South Africa, both externally and internally, as well as to Africa generally. In the 1950s the Union saw its defense responsibilities extending well beyond its borders—indeed beyond the perimeters of southern Africa—and prepared itself (by building up an armored task force) to fight Communist aggressors in Africa.[11]

J. G. STRIJDOM: EXPORTING APARTHEID (1954-58)

In the mid-1950s a familiar theme was revived with the official assertion that South Africa had a "right" to show Western European colonial powers the way in structuring race relations.[12] Prime Minister J. G. Strijdom made no secret of his conviction that apartheid was exportable to Africa (and not merely to territories in southern Africa) and that this policy provided the only acceptable formula for structuring white-black relations.[13] E. H. Louw, Minister of External Affairs, provided yet another illustration of South Africa's preoccupation with its external environment with his suggestion of periodic ad hoc discussions on common interests—of which racial policy was one—among foreign states with African interests (i.e., colonial powers), South Africa, and Rhodesia.[14] Given its concern about race relations, South Africa had not surprisingly long been cultivating links with other white communities elsewhere in Africa.[15] Not only had race thus been made a powerful factor of cohesion between South Africa and some colonial territories, but racial policy had also been elevated to a primary component of what South Africa would consider a favorable external milieu.

When Ghana became Britain's first black African colony to achieve independence in 1957, it demonstrated better than anything else the irrevocability of the process of decolonization which had been set in motion after the war. In South Africa there developed a gradual if grudging realization that its fortunes in Africa no longer lay in a close and exclusive relationship with the colonial powers. Thus in a celebrated policy statement in March 1957, Louw urged that South Africa must "accept its future role in Africa as a vocation and must in all respects play its full part as an African power." At the same time, however, South Africa could become a "permanent link between the Western nations on the one hand and the population of Africa south of the Sahara on the other."[16] In other words, South Africa began trying to bridge the gap between the disappearing and emerging orders in Africa by keeping one foot in each.

South Africa gave effect to its "role in Africa" by participating in the activities of the Commission for Scientific Cooperation in Africa South of the Sahara (CSA), the Commission for Technical Cooperation in Africa South of the Sahara (CCTA), and the Fund for Mutual Assistance in Africa South of the Sahara (FAMA).[17] It considered itself a leader in providing African territories with aid and cooperation and in fact used its economic and military capabilities to impress the Union's importance in Africa upon the colonial powers.[18] In addition, South Africa enjoyed consular representation in a number of African territories.[19] In a formal sense, these organizational and consular links were a relationship between South Africa and the colonial powers. However, there can be little doubt that South Africa was relying on its reputation as a dispenser of aid as an entrée to the emerging black political elites in colonial Africa.

As we have suggested, although South Africa acknowledged the need to adjust to the new realities in Africa, it did not view the process of colonial liquidation with enthusiasm. It had serious misgivings about both the direction and speed of decolonization and was thus unwilling to identify unequivocally with the emerging order in Africa.[20]

Its attitude resulted from fears about the impact of events in colonial Africa on its domestic political status quo.

DR. H. F. VERWOERD: DOMESTIC DECOLONIZATION AND COLONIAL LIQUIDATION (1958-66)

Against a backdrop of unremitting hostility of emergent black African countries toward white-ruled South Africa and the latter's growing international political isolation, Prime Minister H. F. Verwoerd in 1959 announced a radical departure in the policy of apartheid. In expounding his so-called new vision, Verwoerd was at pains to associate the policy of separate development with trends in Africa. By providing for Bantu homelands which could ultimately become independent states, Verwoerd's policy offered "precisely what those countries of Africa which attack us desire to have themselves." He made particular reference to Basutoland, where, he claimed, Britain was introducing a similar policy.[21] Far from denying Africans human rights and dignity, separate development "intended to give them dignity and rights in the highest form, namely through self-government and self-determination."[22] Verwoerd envisaged that a Commonwealth-type relationship would eventually develop between South Africa and the states-to-be: they would be politically independent but economically interdependent.[23]

Verwoerd's desire to equate separate development with developments in colonial Africa indicates that foreign opinion had influenced him in shaping domestic policy. The importance of external considerations is borne out by the following remark:

> We must ensure that the outside world realizes and that the Bantu realizes, that a new period is dawning, a period in which the White man will move away from discrimination against the Bantu as far as his own areas are concerned; that the White man is leading him through the first steps towards full development.[24]

Furthermore, the Prime Minister was frank enough to admit that the price to be paid in an attempt to accommodate external opinion was higher than South Africa would have hoped:

> The Bantu will be able to develop into separate Bantu states. That is not what we would have liked to see. It is a form of fragmentation

which we would not have liked if we were able to avoid it. In the light of the pressure being exerted on South Africa there is however no doubt that eventually this will have to be done, thereby buying for the White man his freedom and the right to retain domination in what is his country, settled for him by his forefathers.[25]

In sum, Verwoerd saw separate development as a counter to the opposition of both black African countries and the rest of the international community to South Africa's racial policy.

The homelands formula also formed the basis of Verwoerd's policy toward southern Africa. What is more, the separate development "grand design" elevated relations with territories in the region to a new prominence. In effect South Africa's focus narrowed from "Africa south of the Sahara" to its immediate neighbors. However, it would be wrong to consider this a shift in foreign policy orientation; it was essentially a realignment in domestic policy which had regional implications. In due course, however, the foreign policy features of the Prime Minister's design gained in prominence.

The regional dimension of Verwoerd's grand design is to be found in his desire to draw the three British High Commission Territories—Basutoland, Bechuanaland, and Swaziland—into the homelands scheme. Under South African guardianship, these territories would be led to independence in the same way as the Bantu homelands. Such a design would prevent the adoption of policies in the High Commission Territories which would be in conflict with separate development.[26] In addition, it could be interpreted as another way of securing for South Africa an external environment conducive to its interests.

Britain refused to transfer its political guardianship of the High Commission Territories to South Africa and chose instead to lead them to independence according to its own design. Nonetheless, Verwoerd saw a role for the newly independent countries in his scheme for regional cooperation. In the political sphere, he reiterated the idea of a commonwealth as a consultative body of independent states, while economic links could be formalized in a coordinating body along the lines of a common market.[27]

Verwoerd's plans for regional cooperation were initially confined to white South Africa, future independent homelands, and the High Commission Territories, but in due course he expanded the scope of a common market as far north as the Congo (later Zaire).[28] Southern Rhodesia, with which South Africa had long had an ambivalent love-hate relationship, began drawing closer to its southern neighbor upon the dissolution of the Central African Federation (CAF) in 1963. Given the politico-racial proclivities of whites in Southern Rhodesia, they had little option but to see their hinterland to the south. The long-standing divisive factors between the two countries—white Rhodesians' traditional Anglophilic sentiments against the Afrikaners' republican sympathies; Southern Rhodesia's entry into the CAF and its pursuit of a racial policy of partnership, which was anathema to the supporters of apartheid or separate development—began to decline in light of what was being perceived by both countries as a new identity of (white) interests. Verwoerd lost no time in suggesting in 1963 that if Southern Rhodesia could become an independent state, it could lead to a closer relationship with South Africa, whether "in some form of organised economic interdependence" (as in the European Economic Community) or "for common political interests" (an arrangement on the lines of the Commonwealth).[29] However, these suggestions came to naught because it was politically inexpedient for South Africa to associate closely and formally with a country which in 1965 declared itself unilaterally independent and thereby attracted universal disapprobation.

The Portuguese territories of Angola and Mozambique were by and large excluded from Verwoerd's regional design. It was only in the latter half of the 1960s, during the premiership of Vorster, that growing economic ties and the perception of a common military threat encouraged closer relations between them and South Africa.

It can be argued that through his grand design Verwoerd had reformulated Smuts's ideas on regional cooperation above all to meet domestic political exigencies and external demands secondarily. An added feature of Verwoerd's Africa policy was an assumption about the primacy of economic over political considerations in South Africa's relations with black African countries.[30] Indeed the notion that divisive political factors would in the end submit to powerful economic forces of cohesion has become a basic tenet of South Africa's regional policy. However, Verwoerd was not relying only on normal trade relations as an instrument in South Africa's policy toward black African states. Like his predecessors, he emphasized the Republic's willingness to provide direct, bilateral aid to black countries. (South

Africa had withdrawn from the CSA, CCTA, and FAMA, so it could no longer channel aid through these organizations.) Realizing the depth of political alienation between South Africa and black Africa, Verwoerd saw aid as a means of contact, although he made it conditional upon black states muting their hostility toward the Republic.[31]

Although Verwoerd accorded Africa—specifically southern Africa—a new priority in South Africa's foreign policy and based his policy toward black African countries on an acknowledgment of the demise of colonialism, he nonetheless adhered to the old notion of South Africa serving as a link between Africa and the West.[32] Relations with Western countries remained South Africa's major foreign policy preoccupation. Verwoerd no doubt hoped that relations would improve by his introduction of a domestic policy which he maintained was in line with Western colonial policy. Despite South Africa's continuous Western fixation, the idea of its acting as a bridge between Africa and the West points to a "schizophrenic" element in its external orientation; faced with increasing hostility from both the old and the new worlds, the country engaged in a search for a new identity and role.

B. J. VORSTER AND THE OUTWARD MOVEMENT (1966-78)

The independence of Botswana and Lesotho in 1966 (formerly Bechuanaland and Basutoland respectively) and Swaziland in 1968 appeared to offer the ideal opportunity for giving effect to the Verwoerdian design for a commonwealth-cum-common market arrangement in southern Africa. However, Prime Minister B.J. Vorster thought in less ambitious terms than his predecessor—at least initially—and merely committed himself "to maintaining the closest economic and technological co-operation among the countries of the [southern African] region, for their mutual benefit and joint development." He insisted that each country should retain its political autonomy and therefore "the right freely to choose its own political, racial, cultural and economic systems."[33] This was a restatement both of the established notion of political independence amid economic interdependence, and of South Africa's professed adherence to the principle of noninterference in other countries' internal affairs. The object in each case was exactly the same—i.e., the safeguarding of South Africa's domestic political status quo. Vorster was in effect saying that regional cooperation had to be based on the existing political order in South as well as southern Africa. For the Republic the political order included future independent black homelands which would be entitled to full participation in cooperative regional arrangements. In this respect, Vorster subscribed to his predecessor's stance of linking regional policy with separate development.

South Africa's cautious regional policy was soon overtaken by and indeed absorbed into the so-called outward movement on which Vorster embarked in 1967. As Barber has argued, the outward movement was a "broad based attempt by the South African government to improve its international status and position,"[34] but its major thrust was unmistakably directed at Africa, the hope being that a *rapprochement* with Africa would improve South Africa's foreign relations over a wide front.

Like the Verwoerdian grand design, the outward movement was in the final analysis aimed at creating a favorable external environment for South Africa. However, there was a significant difference between the two. Within the grand design—albeit as a secondary consideration—there was an attempt to devise a domestic policy commensurate with the demands of foreign policy; by contrast, the outward movement was essentially externally oriented and implicitly denied that foreign policy demanded a domestic corollary.

The timing of the outward movement was not incidental. By the time Vorster had succeeded Verwoerd, the highly unsettled domestic conditions which had prevailed in the aftermath of the Sharpeville shootings of 1960 and the banning of the African National Congress (ANC) and Pan-Africanist Congress (PAC) seemed things of the past. Verwoerd's "politics of security" had paid handsome dividends in terms of suppressing internal violence, restoring white confidence, and steering the economy firmly toward growth.[35] In short, South Africa was ready to face the world with renewed confidence and approach Africa from a position of strength.[36] The emergence of moderate and friendly black governments in neighboring Botswana, Lesotho, and Swaziland, as well as in distant Malawi, seemed to augur well for a South African attempt at establishing a rapprochement with black African states. The government had painstakingly been preparing its followers to accept the "price" for such a rapprochement: the stationing of black diplomats in the Republic.[37]

Although the extension of South Africa's ties with countries in southern Africa was part of the overall outward movement, it appeared that the Republic was more interested in "bigger stakes"—i.e., establishing relations with black states further north which carried greater diplomatic weight than those in the region and which could not in any sense be labelled client states or captive allies of South Africa. However, it was only in southern Africa that South Africa succeeded in strengthening and in some cases formalizing its links with black countries. In some instances success was owing to the outward movement; in others, it was brought about by circumstances not related to it. Among the successes related to the outward movement were South Africa's establishment of diplomatic ties with Malawi in 1967—the first and to date the only link with a black African state (except for links with independent former homelands of South Africa)—and the revision in 1969 of the Customs Union Agreement between South Africa and the three former High Commission Territories.[38] In addition, for the first time South Africa was able to give effect to its long-standing offer of aid to its neighboring black states;[39] it was on such nonpolitical ties, together with trade links, that the Republic relied to prepare the ground for the establishment of new formal cooperative structures, in both the economic and political fields. South Africa's approach was essentially functionalist, relying on the so-called spillover effect of nonpolitical ties.

While South Africa was moving outward to independent black states, circumstances began drawing the Republic and other white-ruled territories in southern Africa closer together in the late 1960s. The reasons for the growing cohesion were partly military/strategic and partly economic. "Communist-inspired terrorism" was seen as a common threat facing Angola, Mozambique, Rhodesia, Namibia, and South Africa. Although no formal defense agreement existed, evidence points to limited South African involvement in counterinsurgency operations in Angola and Mozambique;[40] furthermore, the Republic dispatched police units to Rhodesia in 1967, ostensibly to intercept ANC guerrillas en route to South Africa.[41] In Namibia the destruction of a South West Africa People's Organization (SWAPO) guerrilla training camp by the South African military in August 1966 heralded the beginning of what developed into a protracted low-intensity war between South African troops and SWAPO guerrillas.[42] On the economic front, South Africa's private and public sectors contributed financially to the construction of the Ruacana Falls (Angola) and Cabora Bassa (Mozambique) hydroelectric projects, and the Republic agreed to purchase power from them.[43] Embattled Rhodesia, subjected to mandatory UN sanctions, depended for its very survival on the economic lifeline provided by South Africa.[44]

The increasing importance of military/strategic considerations in South Africa's regional policy was borne out in a statement by Vorster that the Republic would not tolerate terrorism or "communist domination" in southern Africa and was determined to fight it even beyond the country's borders.[45] In addition, South Africa sought to combat the Communist threat by offering nonaggression pacts to black states in 1970.[46] Such pacts—for which there were no takers (except for independent former homelands in the later 1970s)—would have meant that black countries would deny insurgents facilities for operating against South Africa.

As already suggested, the outward movement was not associated solely with southern Africa, but also with black states further north. On this more ambitious diplomatic plane, the "dialogue initiative"—as the outward movement subsequently became known—appeared to produce some initial results in that a good number of black states indicated a willingness to enter into a dialogue with South Africa.[47] The initiative soon petered out, however. For one thing, there was strong opposition in black Africa to any rapprochement with South Africa; the opposition was expressed (*inter alia*) in the Lusaka Manifesto of April 1969[48] and the Mogadishu Declaration of October 1971.[49] For another, it became evident to both supporters and opponents of dialogue that the black states and South Africa had essentially conflicting objectives with the dialogue initiative: the former saw it primarily as a means of persuading South Africa to abolish apartheid; the latter's main objective was a rapprochement with black Africa; insofar as apartheid were to feature in the dialogue—and Vorster declared himself willing to discuss apartheid[50]—it would merely be as an opportunity for South Africa to explain—and hopefully justify—the policy.

Despite the failure of the dialogue initiative and the regional problems demanding South Africa's attention, the Republic did not abandon its attempts at establishing a rapprochement with black states outside the region. It was in fact in the aftermath of the dialogue era that Vorster scored two of his most spectacular diplomatic coups in Africa: in September 1974 he held talks with Ivory Coast President Félix Houphouët-Boigny in Yamoussoukrou, and in February 1975 he met with Liberian President William Tolbert in Monrovia.[51] These breakthroughs failed to produce any substantive and lasting political benefits for South Africa, however.

In the aftermath of the unsuccessful dialogue initiative, South Africa set its sights lower and began concentrating on consolidating its position in the subcontinent. This "inward movement" was not prompted simply by the failure of the outward movement. The course of events in southern Africa had given the Republic cause for concern because for the first time its *cordon sanitaire* appeared to be under serious threat.

South Africa was not slow in realizing that a *coup d'état* in Portugal in April 1974 held potentially far-reaching consequences not only for Angola and Mozambique, but indeed for southern Africa as a whole. In Rhodesia the dispute remained unresolved, and the guerrilla war gradually intensified. South Africa's continued presence in Namibia heaped a growing torrent of international censure upon it, while South African troops remained engaged in a low-intensity armed conflict with SWAPO guerrillas. South Africa sensed that the security situations in both Rhodesia and Namibia could be directly and adversely affected by the course of events in Mozambique and Angola.

The new phase in South Africa's Africa policy was introduced on 5 October 1974, with the first in a series of meetings between the Republic and Zambia in a joint endeavor to resolve the international deadlock over Rhodesia's "illegal" independence.[52] In a now famous Senate speech on 23 October 1974, Vorster said, "Southern Africa has come to the cross-roads" and had to choose between peace and escalating conflict;[53] UN Ambassador R. F. Botha stated to the Security Council the following day that the Republic was committed to the elimination of racial discrimination;[54] and Vorster made an appeal to "give us six months" in November 1974;[55] all were designed to set the scene for a new era of détente.

Like the dialogue initiatives, South Africa's efforts at détente encountered strong opposition in black Africa. For example, in April 1975 the Organization of African Unity (OAU) Council of Ministers adopted the Dar es Salaam Declaration on Southern Africa, which stated (*inter alia*) that "any talk of détente with the *apartheid* regime is such nonsense that it should be treated with the contempt it deserves."[56] Despite the obstacles, the meetings between the Republic and Zambia continued, culminating in a conference at Victoria Falls in August 1975 between the Rhodesian government and the black nationalists. Also present at the historic meeting were Vorster and Kaunda.[57]

The efforts at détente were carried on in Namibia as well, where a South African-initiated constitutional conference got under way in September 1975.[58] The Turnhalle Conference, as it became known, was representative of the various ethnic groups in the territory. However, it was this very ethnic composition (which gave the conference the image of an exercise in South Africa's brand of separate development), together with SWAPO's refusal to participate, that undermined Turnhalle's credibility abroad. The conference nonetheless represented a significant departure in that all races were for the first time drawn into the process of political decision-making on Namibia's future.

The era of détente was short-lived, its demise caused primarily by the collapse of a joint Vorster-Kaunda settlement initiative for Rhodesia (which in turn was mainly the result of the Rhodesian government's intransigence), and South Africa's intervention in the civil war in Angola in 1975-76. The failure of détente was a severe setback for South Africa, which had entertained high hopes for the initiative. For South Africa détente went beyond a mere Rhodesian settlement. Hilgard Muller, Minister of Foreign Affairs, had spoken hopefully of detente drawing the states of southern Africa together in a strong bloc which could present a united front against its common enemies.[59] Vorster envisaged an "economic power bloc,"[60] and he coined a new expression: "a constellation of politically completely independent states" with close economic ties.[61] In addition, South Africa was not oblivious to the wider foreign-policy benefits which might accrue from a breakthrough in southern Africa. Progress in a regional context, it was hoped, would serve to improve the Republic's foreign relations in Africa and beyond. This had in fact become conventional South African foreign-policy wisdom.

South Africa's involvement in the Angolan war had wide-ranging diplomatic and military/strategic implications for the Republic. The Republic's decision to send its forces into an armed conflict in an independent black state—the first such involvement ever—can be explained in terms of three sets of considerations—i.e., safeguarding its interests in the region (particularly military/strategic), promoting détente, and fulfilling its perceived duty toward the "free world."

To understand South Africa's consideration of safeguarding its interests, it is important to understand the situation in Angola in 1975. A transitional government had been set up in Luanda on 28 March in terms of the Alvor Agreement of the previous January, composed of the country's three liberation movements—the Movimento Popular de Libertação de Angola (MPLA), the Frente Nacional de Libertação de Angola (FNLA), and the União Nacional para a Independência Total de Angola (UNITA); it barely survived a month because of large-scale fighting between the MPLA and FNLA. Efforts by the OAU to resolve the conflict and promote cooperation toward independence among the liberation movements resulted in the Nakuru Agreement of 15 June. The agreement was of no avail, and in the same month "the barely viable political situation collapsed entirely."[62] By then large quantities of Communist bloc arms had reached the MPLA, while Zaire contributed to the FNLA's arms buildup. As violence escalated, the FNLA and UNITA formed an uneasy alliance against the MPLA.[63]

In the beginning of October 1975 a new phase began in the Angolan war when MPLA forces were reinforced by Cuban troops. On 23 October South African forces entered Angola in combat strength to join the FNLA-UNITA alliance against the MPLA and its Cuban allies. In the meantime, American aid had been reaching the FNLA. When Portugal granted Angola its independence on 11 November 1975, it did not formally transfer power to an incoming government. The MPLA, controlling Luanda, proclaimed the People's Republic of Angola, whereas the FNLA and UNITA established the Social Democratic Republic of Angola, seated in Huambo. "Clearly, therefore, no legal government existed in Angola at independence—only two rival claimants," Legum and Hodges rightly point out.[64] South Africa, it should be noted, was one of the first states to recognize the independence of Angola.[65]

Prior to its October 1975 intervention in Angola, South Africa had been militarily involved in the far south of Angola for some months on a limited scale—limited, that is, in terms of manpower, arms, and geographic area. The official explanation for this small-scale activity was that South Africa was protecting the Ruacana Falls project, deflecting "the effects of the Angolan civil war from the northern border of SWA [South West Africa]," and inhibiting SWAPO from exploiting the unstable situation in southern Angola.[66]

South Africa's relatively large-scale intervention* and its active participation in the war against the MPLA-Cuban forces were motivated by wider considerations than those behind its initial small-scale involvement. As mentioned, the major consideration concerned the safeguarding of South African interests in the face of what was typically described as an "alarming" situation in Angola which posed a "serious threat to the neighbouring states" because of Communist involvement in the war.[67] In the South African view, there was an "excessive build-up of [Soviet] arms . . . completely out of proportion to the requirements for the war in Angola."[68] The objective behind this buildup was clear: "The Russians and the Cubans have for a long time been openly supporting and advocating the use of force against South Africa," according to Muller.[69] By invading Angola, South Africa hoped to counter Soviet and Cuban advances and at best to drive the Cuban troops out altogether. This could presumably have been achieved by preventing the MPLA from scoring a victory over its rivals and creating a government subservient to Communist interests. Although Muller stated that—as in the case of Mozambique—the type of government elected by the Angolan people— even if it was a Marxist or communist one—"is simply none of our business,"[70] there can be little doubt that South Africa's preference was an FNLA-UNITA government in Luanda because these movements had pro-Western inclinations and contacts with South Africa.[71] Failing this, South Africa would probably have been content to see a government of national unity in Luanda which would lead to an end to the hostilities as well as to the Cuban presence. One of South Africa's basic concerns revolved around the effect of events in Angola on SWAPO's armed struggle against the South African presence in Namibia. Ideally the Republic wanted a government in Luanda which would deny SWAPO bases from which to operate against Namibia.

---

*Estimates of the number of South African troops involved ranged between 2,500 and 12,000. From various accounts the former figure would appear to be more accurate.

With the second set of considerations—the promotion of détente—South Africa hoped to prove itself a reliable ally of black states opposed to Communist intervention in African affairs. Intervention on the side of the pro-Western FNLA-UNITA movement against the MPLA "has furnished proof of our *bona fides*," Muller argued.[72] Moreover, the Republic was encouraged by some black states to send forces into Angola.[73] (It should be noted that member states of the OAU were initially deeply divided about recognizing the MPLA as the sole governing party in Angola—a fact not lost upon South Africa.)[74] South Africa was at pains to prevent its actions in Angola from being represented as a color conflict with black Africa. "It is in fact a struggle between Africans, White and Black on the one hand, and White Russian and Cuban imperialists on the other," Muller explained.[75]

Finally, in accordance with the third set of considerations, South Africa publicly maintained (and no doubt privately believed) that "we have a duty to members of the free world"—meaning the West—to react to Soviet and Cuban involvement in the Angolan war.[76] Angola seemed to offer the ideal opportunity for South Africa to give tangible effect to its oft-repeated commitment against Communist aggression: there was extensive Cuban and Soviet involvement; the war might adversely affect Zambia and Zaire—key states from a Western point of view—and might even draw other African and foreign states into the conflict; and a Soviet satellite in Angola might threaten various other African states. The dangers of the war in Angola extended even further, South Africa claimed. Muller presented the following apocalyptic scenario:

> I cannot emphasize strongly enough that the non-communist world should wake up and should realize that this time it is not merely another minor civil war in Africa, thousands of miles away, in which they have no real interest and which does not affect them. What is in fact happening is that Russian and Cuban actions in Angola are causing a completely new situation to arise in Africa, but also a completely new situation in the epic struggle between communism and the free world. It is the beginning of a new offensive, which is aimed at control over Africa in order to facilitate the conquest of the West.[77]

In addition to the factors noted, South Africa had ample other reasons to intervene. The notion of serving Western interests—and thereby earning some reward—was strengthened by the U.S. blessing of South Africa's intervention and Pretoria's belief (if not understanding) that Washington was committed to providing material support for the combined South Africa-FNLA-UNITA offensive.[78]

In the end, three main developments compelled South Africa to withdraw its forces from Angola without achieving any of its major objectives. First, on 11 February 1976 the OAU Council of Ministers decided (by simple majority) to recognize the MPLA as Angola's legal government, although only weeks before an OAU summit had ended in deadlock, with half the members supporting the immediate recognition of the MPLA as the legal government and the other half calling for a government of national unity.[79] Second, the OAU summit was nearly unanimous in condemning South Africa's intervention in Angola and demanding its withdrawal.[80] Third, the U.S. military assistance on which South Africa relied in Angola did not materialize. Although South Africa's withdrawal was traumatic because intervention had failed to produce the desired results, it was not due to a military defeat. In the face of determined Cuban and Soviet support for the MPLA and the absence of tangible American support for the opposing side, South Africa fully realized that it could not sustain its military offensive without committing a much larger force and heavier weaponry.

South Africa's intervention in Angola not only undermined détente, but also helped to ensure a government in Luanda strongly hostile to South Africa. SWAPO benefited considerably from a sympathetic MPLA government and no doubt from the Cuban presence as well. The U.S. refusal to support South African actions in Angola had repercussions for relations between Washington and Pretoria. There were bitter recriminations from South Africa that it had been left in the lurch by the Americans, proving that the latter were not reliable allies.[81]

Why had South Africa allowed itself to get militarily involved in Angola when it had so carefully abstained from similar intervention in Mozambique? There seem to be a number of plausible reasons. First, since the departure of the Portuguese, Angola had been a springboard for guerrillas operating against South Africa (in Namibia), whereas Mozambique had not. Therefore South Africa had no need to invade Mozambique to prevent insurgents from setting up bases or amassing arms near the South African border.[82] In other words, South Africa perceived no immediate military threat from an independent Mozambique. Vorster had made it plain in August 1974 that it was not his policy to prescribe to Mozambique "what kind of government they should have there or who should serve in that government."[83] In addition, he gave public assurance "that it is by no means South Africa's objective to interfere in the affairs of Mozambique and that South Africa has no intention of invading Mozambique."[84] Furthermore, the South African government was emphatic that it would not permit the local recruitment of mercenaries intent on making a bid for power in Mozambique.[85] When the Portuguese handed over power to a Marxist-leaning Frente de Libertação de Moçambique (FRELIMO) government, South Africa was quick to accord it official recognition,[86] although such a regime was decidedly not what South Africa would have preferred. South Africa, Vorster explained, was not seeking a quarrel with the new state, "just as long as there was a stable government and that country was not used as a base for an attack on South Africa."[87] It is worth noting that South Africa used its diplomatically "correct" position on Mozambique as evidence of its opposition to colonialism: "There ought to be no doubt that we do not identify ourselves with colonialism, 'that we hold no brief whatsoever for colonialism in any shape or form,'" Muller asserted in September 1974. "Traditionally and in principle we are opposed to all forms of it."[88]

Second (and related to the absence of a military threat from Mozambique), there was no Soviet or Cuban military involvement in Mozambique as there was in Angola.[89] Therefore South Africa could not intervene in Mozambique under the guise of protecting the "free world's interests" against Communist aggression and promoting détente with black African states.

Third, in Mozambique the Portuguese were able to effect a smooth transition by handing over power to a single liberation movement (FRELIMO). By contrast, they left it to the three rival liberation movements in Angola to try and resolve matters—which they eventually did by force.[90] Mozambique therefore did not experience the kind of instability that Angola suffered upon independence; furthermore, the emergence of the FRELIMO regime did not cause a division in OAU ranks as had the MPLA's assumption of power in Angola.

Fourth, South Africa assumed that the economic ties it had developed with colonial Mozambique were of such importance to

Mozambique that they would temper the FRELIMO government's relations with South Africa; alternatively economic ties would provide South Africa with a lever which could be used to induce moderation in the new Mozambique government's policy toward its neighboring state.[91] South Africa's economic links with Angola were much weaker.[92]

Finally, if South Africa had entertained the possibility of intervening in Angola primarily to deal with SWAPO, Pretoria would have had to come to the conclusion that a new involvement in Mozambique would become too costly in military and economic terms; in short, the Republic would have been overextended. In addition, South Africa had to consider the situation in Rhodesia and the implications for the Republic of intensified guerrilla war in that country. Vorster acknowledged as much, but in a familiar context: "It is very clear to one that the communist strategy for South Africa is to cause South Africa to fight simultaneously or as much as possible on these three fronts, namely on the Mozambique, Rhodesian and Angolan front."[93] Expressing satisfaction that "owing to level-headed action, nothing came of the planning on the Mozambique front," he listed the grave consequences that would have followed had South Africa been "compelled" to fight on three fronts: "It would have meant total mobilization; it would have meant the large-scale conversion of factories to the manufacture of armaments; it would have meant a tremendous increase in the defence budget and the disruption and halting of the country's economy."[94]

The independence of Mozambique and Angola represented a watershed in the history of southern Africa and accordingly heralded a new era in South Africa's foreign relations. By 1976 the Republic was left with a regional environment more unfavorable to its perceived interests than ever before. The emergence in Luanda and Maputo of regimes politically and ideologically avowedly hostile to Pretoria meant that South Africa had lost two vital links in its cordon sanitaire. Moreover, the new Angolan government was quick to demonstrate its moral and material support for SWAPO. Even worse, the MPLA government allowed Cuba and the Soviet Union to retain a massive military presence in Angola. These results were the very antithesis of what South Africa had set out to achieve by intervening. Furthermore, as noted, one consequence of South Africa's military involvement in Angola was the end to its détente initiative with black

African states. Although some of them had initially given covert support to South Africa's intervention, they soon closed ranks in condemning the Republic's actions; eventually they rallied around the MPLA government, according it official recognition. Another consequence (as noted) was South Africa's severe disillusionment with the West—specifically the United States—for allegedly letting the Republic down. As Vorster put it, "When it comes to the worst, South Africa stands alone."[95]

As South Africa had anticipated, events in Angola and Mozambique had a profound impact on the situations in Rhodesia and Namibia. In the former case, Muller emphasized that "a settlement of the Rhodesian question had become more imperative than ever before in view of the Russian and Cuban presence in a neighbouring state."[96] The Soviet Union, he argued, could not be allowed to exploit another "problem-situation" which might turn Rhodesia into "a second Angola."[97] In the latter case, the MPLA victory undoubtedly caused a setback to South Africa's plans for launching Namibia on the road to self-determination. With a hostile neighbor to Namibia's north and SWAPO intensifying its guerrilla activities, South Africa was much less inclined to leave Namibia to its own devices.

The strain caused by the Angolan war in South Africa's relations with the United States was aggravated by a statement in February 1976 by the presidents of the so-called Frontline States (Angola, Mozambique, Tanzania, Zambia, and Botswana) that efforts at resolving the Rhodesian issue peacefully had run their course and that armed struggle deserved their unqualified support;[98] however, the seriousness of the situation in Rhodesia compelled South Africa to support an American diplomatic offensive in 1976 aimed at resolving the conflict situations in white-ruled southern Africa.[99] America's new activist role in southern Africa was primarily in response to the Soviet-Cuban success in Angola and a consequent fear that the Soviet Union might extend its involvement to other regional conflicts. South Africa no doubt shared these apprehensions, but its involvement in the American-sponsored Rhodesian initiative—publicly known as the Anglo-American settlement proposals—was probably primarily attributable to the crucial influence it could exert over the Rhodesian government.

Indeed Rhodesia, where repeated British settlement attempts had come to grief, was the main focus of the American-led search for peace in southern Africa. Of less immediate concern to the United States (although still matters of great importance) were Namibia and the situation in South Africa itself. In Namibia the Turnhalle Conference had failed to obtain international recognition as a genuine constitutional conference, and SWAPO remained committed to armed struggle. With Angola supporting SWAPO, there was fear that the war in Namibia could escalate dangerously and provide new opportunities for intervention by the Soviet Union and its Cuban allies. In South Africa massive unrest and violence in black townships all over the country began to erupt in mid-1976, only days before high-level American-South African talks were to begin, thus thrusting the Republic's serious domestic political problems to the fore. But however much the United States wanted South Africa to mend its ways both at home and in Namibia, it realized that the primary aim at hand was to achieve a Rhodesian settlement. For this, Vorster's backing was crucial, and it was not likely to be forthcoming if he was at the same time being pressured to make concessions internally and on Namibia.

Meetings between Henry Kissinger, American Secretary of State, and Vorster were held in June and September 1976 in West Germany and Switzerland respectively.[100] The Anglo-American proposals culminated in a tripartite meeting of Kissinger, Vorster, and Ian Smith, the Rhodesian Prime Minister, also in September 1976. At this meeting, Smith accepted the Anglo-American plan for majority rule in Rhodesia within two years—a *volte face* in no small measure due to South African influence.[101] However, the hopes for peace in Rhodesia soon foundered when the British-sponsored Geneva Conference (October-November 1976) of all parties involved in the conflict failed to reach agreement on ways of proceeding toward majority rule.[102] In consequence, there was a continuation and indeed an intensification of the Rhodesian war.

The collapse of the American-directed peace initiative in Rhodesia was a matter of grave concern to South Africa, which above all feared that the Soviet Union might take advantage of the continuing war, but the Republic's interest in a Rhodesian settlement was motivated by other considerations as well. It was well aware of the diplomatic cost of being seen internationally as the principal foreign state sustaining the Rhodesian "rebellion." By cooperating with the American efforts, it probably hoped to receive a reward in the form of some relaxation in pressure over both Namibia and its domestic policies—particularly from Western powers but from black Africa as well. In other words, with the Rhodesian issue out of the way, South Africa expected an improvement in its foreign relations with both Western and African states.[103]

While South Africa publicly declared its willingness "to bring about an atmosphere amenable to peaceful discussions and . . . to bring the parties together,"[104] Vorster at the same time spelled out the limits of South African involvement: "We shall under no circumstances participate in a boycott and a closing of borders, and . . . I am not prepared to pressurize Rhodesia in any respect."[105] The Republic firmly adhered to Vorster's first two commitments, but it is difficult to believe that it could have refrained from pressuring Rhodesia "in any respect." As for the nature of a Rhodesian settlement, South Africa maintained that the parties involved "should settle their own case";[106] the Republic could not prescribe a constitutional arrangement or concern itself with the type of government, party, or ideology which the people in Rhodesia chose to support.[107] Nonetheless, there could have been no doubt that Pretoria preferred a future Zimbabwean government which would adopt a moderate and cooperative policy toward South Africa (thus at least denying South African exile movements guerrilla bases in Zimbabwe), maintain stability in that country, and retain white confidence.

After the failure of the Anglo-American settlement proposals, the Rhodesian government embarked on its own domestic settlement initiative, leading to the so-called internal agreement of March 1978 between the Smith government and three internal black political leaders—Bishop Abel Muzorewa, Ndabaningi Sithole, and Chief Jeremiah Chirau. South Africa was remarkably guarded in its reaction to the internal agreement.[108] "In our opinion the Salisbury Agreement is a step in the direction of a solution, and any development that is a step forward is welcomed," R. F. Botha, now Foreign Minister, declared;[109] however, he added, "We remain in favour of a solution that will attract the widest possible international acceptability," indicating some reservations about the agreement.[110] On the whole, in the South African view the agreement represented some movement in an otherwise depressing situation; moreover, it was an agreement among moderates who could be relied upon to adopt a friendly attitude toward South Africa. Displaying an appreciation of both the possibilities and the shortcomings of the internal agreement, Botha went on to appeal to Joshua Nkomo, exiled leader of the Zimbabwe Africa People's Union (ZAPU), to return and join the parties to the internal agreement.[111]

In 1977 a quick succession of major events had a profound impact on South Africa's international position. In the United States the Carter administration took office in January, bringing new tensions to the already troubled relationship with South Africa. The Republic's foreign relations suffered heavily as a result of black consciousness leader Steve Biko's death in detention in September, followed in October by the Vorster government's sweeping ban on a wide range of political organizations, newspapers, and individuals. The UN Security Council responded in November with a mandatory arms embargo against South Africa, and the country was forced onto the defensive more than ever before. Domestically it resorted to the politics of survival; externally it considered introversion and dissociation, expressed in sporadic official suggestions that it become "neutral" in the East-West conflict and side with the "Fifth World."[112] These alternatives reflected a deep sense of disillusionment, anger, and anxiety, but it would be wrong to dismiss them simply as emotive rhetoric. The so-called Fifth World or pariah option has in fact been taken seriously by South Africa, as shown by Vorster's official visit to Israel in April 1976 and by the cultivation of particularly cordial ties with Taiwan in the late 1970s.[113*] Regional relations attained a new prominence and Foreign Minister Botha reiterated the ideal of "a constellation of states . . . which peacefully co-operate with one another."[114] Given the conflict situations on South Africa's borders and the ever-mounting international censure against the Republic, consolidating its already embattled position in the region became a major priority, perceived as not only attractive but indeed also imperative.

---

*Sun Yan-suan, Prime Minister of Taiwan, paid a state visit to South Africa in March 1980, and Prime Minister P. W. Botha made a reciprocal visit to Taiwan in October 1980. During the Taiwanese Premier's visit, the two countries concluded a series of scientific and technological agreements, in addition to a contract for the sale of R400 million worth of South African uranium to Taiwan (*Rand Daily Mail*, 14 March 1980, and *The Citizen*, 18 March 1980).

P. W. BOTHA'S CONSTELLATION OF STATES (1978-)

Although a preoccupation with regional relations is not new in South African foreign policy, the post-Vorster emphasis on closer regional ties has to be seen in the context of the vastly changed southern African environment. First, by 1978 South Africa's domestic base was under greater threat than ever before. Internally the scars of massive racial unrest which had flared up intermittently in the latter half of 1976 were only too noticeable. In the government's view, the country was facing a "total onslaught" of internal and external forces committed to the violent overthrow of the existing domestic order, and it demanded a "total national strategy" in response. One of the components of this strategy is, significantly, the creation of "a peaceful constellation of southern African states with respect for each other's cultures, traditions and ideals."[115] Second, South Africa's position in southern Africa has become less secure with the loss of Angola and Mozambique, crucial links in its cordon sanitaire. Third, the war escalated in Rhodesia, another link in the cordon sanitaire. Fourth, South Africa's fortunes in Namibia fluctuated greatly. In April 1978 South Africa accepted Western proposals for a settlement of the conflict in the territory. The Security Council endorsed the proposals in July 1978, but repeated UN attempts at reaching an agreement with SWAPO and South Africa on implementing a settlement failed. South Africa blamed the failures on Western duplicity, UN bias toward SWAPO, and SWAPO intransigence.[116] In short, on the one hand, South Africa's confidence in the other parties involved was not high. On the other, the other parties expressed doubts about South Africa's commitment to an international settlement in Namibia. Fifth, as noted, South Africa's relations with the West had deteriorated considerably after 1976-77, and the impasse over Namibia merely added to the alienation. Finally, South Africa itself contributed to changing the political complexion of southern Africa by granting independence to Transkei, Bophuthatswana, and Venda.[117] In the South African government's view, the emergence of these states added impetus to its new regional orientation and paved the way for implementing the Verwoerdian design for regional cooperation through formal interstate structures.

On the whole, it can be argued that the recent changes in South Africa's external environment have been to its detriment and that these changes, together with the unsettled internal situation, have probably left the domestic base less secure than ever. Under the circumstances, it is not surprising that the Republic has resorted to a defensive strategy at home and regionally: it has been forced, as it were, to retreat behind the perimeters of southern Africa.

P. W. Botha, who succeeded Vorster in September 1978, made closer regional ties in southern Africa a major foreign policy initiative. Whereas his predecessor had neither used the concept of a constellation of southern African states consistently nor given it any real substance, Botha has given it a definite content. (It should immediately be noted that the constellation initiative has not been static, but has in several vital respects been amended as policymakers have tried to adjust it to rapidly changing and previously unforeseen circumstances.) One of the earliest authoritative statements on the Botha government's constellation design is in an address by Foreign Minister R. F. Botha.[118] In this and subsequent statements a set of clear assumptions has emerged about the nature and objectives of this form of regional relations. Among them are the following:

(1) A constellation would offer an opportunity for finding regional "solutions" to regional problems. Having made no secret of its disillusionment with repeated Western failures at settlement in Namibia and Rhodesia, South Africa considered a constellation at best a viable alternative to Western peace initiatives, and at worst a fallback position in the event all settlement efforts failed.[119] South Africa maintained that it carried a special responsibility toward the internal political leaders in Namibia (i.e., the Turnhalle participants) and Rhodesia (i.e., the parties to the internal settlement): "If we let [them] down," Foreign Minister Botha said, "the whole of Southern Africa is going to disintegrate."[120]

(2) Closely related to South Africa's misgivings about the West's role in the search for peace in Namibia and Rhodesia was the notion that the "moderate" countries of southern Africa were facing a common "Marxist threat" and could not rely on the West for support.[121] The security and well-being of blacks and whites in the region was perceived as indivisible, and unless they joined forces, common enemies would (in Foreign Minister Botha's words) "shoot us off the branch like birds, one after the other."[122] As an alternative to the grave and evil consequences flowing from a "Marxist order," the Prime Minister advocated "a regional order within which

149

real freedom and material welfare can be maximised and the quality of life for all can be improved."[123]

(3) Given a common threat, members of a constellation would engage in military cooperation. As R. F. Botha saw it, they would "undertake joint responsibility for the security of the region,"[124] which would mean "a joint decision to keep communism out of Southern Africa."[125]

(4) Apart from security considerations, the countries of southern Africa would share interests in trade, agriculture, transportation, health, labor, power and energy, and scientific and technological development.[126] Cooperation in most of these fields in fact existed in practice and was in some cases institutionalized—e.g., the Southern African Customs Union (SACU) and the Southern African Regional Commission for the Conservation and Utilization of the Soil.[127] In future cooperation would become increasingly institutionalized, and it was assumed that it would spill over into the political field.

(5) R. F. Botha visualized that between seven and ten states south of the Kunene and Zambezi Rivers, representing some forty million people, would join a constellation—including (in addition to South Africa) Botswana, Lesotho, Swaziland, Rhodesia, Namibia, Transkei, Bophuthatswana, and Venda.[128] It was hoped that Zambia too would join,[129] while the possibility of including Marxist states (a clear reference to Mozambique) was left open.[130] The Foreign Minister stated that international recognition for Transkei, Bophuthatswana, Venda, Rhodesia (under internal settlement leaders), and Namibia (when independent—presumably under Democratic Turnhalle Alliance [DTA] leadership)* was unlikely and that they and South Africa had to join forces against "radical onslaughts."[131] The statement probably reflects a realization that there was very little chance of a comprehensive constellation being created. In addition, it creates the impression of a constellation as a defensive association of outcast or pariah states.

(6) A constellation based on the existing regional order would reflect the "realities" of South African society—as seen by the government. The most fundamental reality for South Africa is that of

---

*The DTA is a multiethnic political grouping which won a landslide victory in the December 1978 one-man, one-vote election for a constituent assembly in Namibia. SWAPO refused to participate in the election.

"multinationalism," with its concommitant notions of "vertical differentiation" and "self-determination."[132] There is a clear link between a constellation and South Africa's racial policy, which has inevitably led to suggestions that a constellation is being propagated as a device to resolve certain dilemmas in the policy of separate development (see below).

(7) Relations among members of a constellation would be formalized through a "Council of States" and "international secretariats." Although the functions and powers of these institutions have not been spelled out, the Council of States would apparently be an essentially deliberative organ composed of all members of a constellation, and the secretariats would be charged with some executive functions.[133]

The premises upon which a constellation was originally based had a distinctive ring of determinism about them: a constellation was portrayed not merely as desirable but indeed as inevitable. The implicit—and often explicit—assumption was that the centripetal forces at work in southern Africa—particularly economic but political and security as well—were inexorably steering the countries in the region (or most of them at any rate) toward ever closer and more formal relationships; the centrifugal elements would in the end submit to these forces. In typical Verwoerdian fashion, the South African government placed reliance on the primacy of economic forces and, in line with functionalist thinking, anticipated that cooperation in this field would spill over into the political and military areas. Closely related to this brand of economic determinism was a tendency to assume shared perceptions among prospective constellation partners, particularly with regard to the nature of external (that is, extraregional) threats and the need for a common military-cum-political response. Aside from these assumptions, the official expositions of a constellation have been characterized by a considerable measure of vagueness and contradiction, indicating that the proposals have not been officially thought through. The extent of cooperation envisaged by South Africa was summed up in a suggestion by Foreign Minister Botha that the countries in southern Africa should develop "a common approach in the security field, the economic field and even the political field."[134]

It is not surprising that the hoped-for constellation of seven to ten states has failed to materialize. The basic reason for the failure is that the political and ideological divisions between South Africa and black African states are such that the latter are unwilling to formalize relations with the Republic beyond their current level—least of all in the political and military areas. In addition, internationally recognized black states (who are members of the OAU) would not consider joining a formal association in which internationally unrecognized former "bantustans," Rhodesia (prior to 1980), and South African-controlled Namibia would be their equal partners. In other words, the divisions militated against the notion of a spillover factor and against the assumption of shared perceptions regarding the nature of external threats and the need for a common military-cum-political response. Botswana, Lesotho, and Swaziland served notice that they would not consider joining a constellation for as long as South Africa adhered to its present racial policies.[135] A more important setback to South Africa's constellation plan was the emergence in 1980 of an independent Zimbabwe under the premiership of Robert Mugabe. Mugabe not only made it plain that Zimbabwe had no intention of playing the key role South Africa had reserved for it in a constellation,[136] but he was also quick to demonstrate his political distance from the Republic by joining forces with the Frontline States in their attempt to form a new economic grouping—the Southern African Development Coordination Council (SADCC)—aimed at reducing black states' dependence on the South African economy and transportation and communications networks. Lesotho and Swaziland too joined the SADCC, which has been dubbed a counter-constellation— a designation which reflects the black states' opposition to South Africa's proposed constellation.

In consequence South Africa has had no option but to amend its ideas on a constellation and to reduce an initially grandiose design to what is essentially a device to restructure relations between present and former parts of the South African state.[137] What remains can be designated an inner constellation, with the outer constellation rendered unfeasible by the prevailing political climate in southern Africa. However, South Africa has not abandoned its long-held notion of creating an association of friendly, closely cooperating, and interdependent states in the region. A favorable external environment remains a central objective of South Africa's foreign policy, but the chances of success have become extremely poor. Nonetheless, South African spokesmen continue to argue that the desired state of affairs will in time emerge, and they base their claims on some of the assumptions upon which the constellation idea was originally formulated by the Botha government.[138]

The inner constellation has in the meantime been formalized. At a summit meeting among the leaders of South Africa, Transkei, Bophuthatswana, and Venda in Pretoria in July 1980, it was agreed to promote cooperation in the economic, social, and security spheres. Economic cooperation was the top priority, and South Africa appointed a high-powered Special Constellation Committee to give effect to the agreements on economic cooperation. The three primary areas of economic cooperation are the following: (1) the establishment (with public and private capital) of a Southern African Development Bank, which was scheduled to open in 1981; (2) a Small Business Development Corporation, established in November 1980 with R100 million in public and private funds; and (3) the creation of "regional growth points" transcending political (i.e., South African and independent homeland) boundaries. Related agreements concluded at the Pretoria summit concerned the promotion of free enterprise, the advancement of manpower training and tertiary education, and the joint planning of a transportation system.[139]

Although the constellation has a strong economic orientation, South Africa is anxious for closer cooperation in other areas, as well as greater institutionalization of relations among the four partners (and others who may join in the future—e.g., Ciskei).* The government's predeliction is evident in a significant new addition to its political vocabulary—i.e., "confederation."[140] As the word suggests, a confederation would involve more than merely economic cooperation. In 1979 Prime Minister Botha had stated that talk of a confederation was "premature,"[141] but in the course of 1980 it became common official usage to equate a constellation with a confederation.

Prime Minister Botha has proposed that the members embark on a program involving "simultaneous advance on the four broad fronts of interstate political relations, economics, social affairs and security."[142] Such a statement tends to support the contention that the inner constellation has in essence become an instrument to restructure

---

*In a referendum in December 1980, Ciskeian citizens voted overwhelmingly in favor of independence for the homeland; Ciskei became independent in December 1981.

relations between South Africa and its former homelands. On the economic plane, the constellation's emphasis on creating regional growth points is based on an acknowledgment of the integrated nature of the economies of the member states and amounts to a tacit admission of the failure of the Verwoerdian plan to create separate viable homeland economies.* On the political level, there has been speculation that a confederation might merely be an intermediate stage in a process of reintegrating the former homelands into the South African state in a federal arrangement.† If this should be true, it can be argued that the constellation is an instrument to join together what apartheid has put asunder.

The scaling down of the constellation design from the regional plane to what is now essentially an internal political and economic instrument does not represent as profound a departure from the initial proposals as may appear because the constellation proposals have from the very outset had a dual character—i.e., a regional and an internal dimension. The internal dimension is apparent both in the concept of a "total national strategy" and in the policy of separate development.

The total national strategy is today formulated in terms of the so-called "twelve policy principles," the first six of which deal with racial policy. The first and second principles—concerning "the recognition and acceptance of the existence of multinationalism and of minorities in the Republic of South Africa" and "the acceptance of vertical differentiation with a built-in principle of self-determination at as many levels as possible"—respectively—provide the key to government thinking.[143] The eighth principle deals with the creation of "a peaceful constellation of Southern African states."

---

*In a powerful indictment of the economics of separate development, the influential semi-official Bureau for Economic Research: Cooperation and Development (BENSO) in August 1980 reported that separate viable economies cannot be created for the homelands (*Rand Daily Mail*, 19 August 1980).

†Consider the following observation of L. Oppenheim: "History has shown that confederated States represent an organisation which in the long run gives little satisfaction." It is for this reason, Oppenheim argues, that three important "unions of confederated States"—the United States of America and the German and Swiss confederations—"turned into unions of federal States" (*International Law: A Treatise*, 8th ed.; ed. H. Lauterpacht [London: Longmans, 1961], p. 173).

The link between a constellation and South Africa's domestic political order becomes more apparent when official suggestions about the composition of a constellation are considered. Initially the government perceived a constellation of southern African states in a literal sense—i.e., a grouping of independent states only; in other words, independence was to be a condition of membership.[144] (In South Africa's view, Transkei, Bophuthatswana, and Venda of course qualified.) In due course, the base of a constellation was broadened to include self-governing black homelands (e.g., KwaZulu, Gazankulu, and Lebowa), as well as so-called urban (i.e., non-homeland) blacks.[145] It is this extension of membership which has prompted the view that a constellation was being seen as a means of resolving crucial dilemmas in the policy of separate development—notably, the political status of homelands refusing to accept independence, the political status of urban blacks, and the issue of blacks' nationality.[146] In addition, it can be argued that South Africa had hoped to acquire international recognition for independent former homelands—and by implication international legitimacy for the policy of separate development—by creating a formal association of states in which OAU member countries and former South African homelands participated as equal partners. Furthermore, although the regional dimension of a constellation failed to materialize, it does not follow that an inner constellation has all along been a deliberately devised fallback position. The initial enthusiasm and conviction with which the South African government expounded the theme of a regional constellation left little reason to think that it seriously entertained the possibility of its failure. The outcome indicates a remarkable misreading of the political climate of southern Africa and an inability to anticipate events—specifically those in Zimbabwe.

As a foreign policy objective, the inner constellation is of limited relevance to South Africa's foreign relations. It will make little difference to its relations with black states because they have never recognized the independence of Transkei, Bophuthatswana, and Venda. Nonetheless, South Africa hopes that the black states in the SADCC will in due course be attracted by the material benefits offered by the constellation.[147] In the meantime, Namibia has been drawn into the activities of the constellation, albeit in an apparently tentative fashion and not on the same basis as Transkei, Bophuthatswana, and

Venda.* Clearly South Africa would like an independent, hopefully internationally recognized Namibia to formally join the constellation, but participation will depend on the political complexion of the new state's government.

If a comprehensive southern African constellation is unlikely to develop, it can be argued that South Africa will have to concern itself more with the nonmembers than the members of the inner constellation in order to create a regional environment favorable to its interests. Its relations with the recognized black states in southern Africa are characterized by a duality of economic closeness and political distance.[148] Even those countries most heavily dependent on South Africa—Botswana, Lesotho, and Swaziland—have been outspoken in their condemnation of its domestic policies. As noted, economic links have to a considerable extent been formalized in such organizations as the SACU, but they have not spilled over into the more contentious political sphere. Malawi is the only internationally recognized black state which maintains diplomatic links with South Africa. Mozambique's relations with South Africa reflect the duality, but the political alienation is much more pronounced and the economic dependence is not as heavy. Much the same is true of South Africa's relations with Zambia and Zaire. With Angola, South Africa has an actively hostile relationship, owing to the conflict over Namibia. Angola and Tanzania are the only two of the SADCC's nine member states with which South Africa maintains no overt trade links.

In the region South Africa's relations with Zimbabwe are plainly the most problematic. For one thing, the new Zimbabwe is still something of an unknown quantity. For another, South Africa had close ties with the Unilateral Declaration of Independence (UDI) government of Rhodesia. Furthermore, the Republic had entertained high hopes about including an independent Zimbabwe in its constellation. It is understandable therefore that events in Zimbabwe have necessitated a profound readjustment in South Africa's relations with it. The extent of the readjustment is captured in the following

*In October 1980 Namibia was represented at a meeting of the constellation in Pretoria, where guidelines for economic cooperation were formulated (*Beeld*, 21 October 1980). In November 1980 Namibian representatives attended a meeting of the constellation's committee on transport in Bophuthatswana (*ibid.*, 28 November 1980).

comment of Foreign Minister Botha: "It would be a lie, it would be deceit for me to claim that I enjoyed the result of the last election in Zimbabwe. I did not at all. I would have preferred Bishop Muzorewa to have won. Let me be very frank about that."[149]

South Africa's deep disappointment at Muzorewa's defeat and its serious apprehensions about Mugabe are reflected in the Republic's cool response to Mugabe's election victory. There was only a terse statement from P. W. Botha: "It is not for me to say whether the result was attained in a just way or not; . . . [the people of Zimbabwe] will have to work it out for themselves and live with it."[150] Reiterating South Africa's oft-stated commitment to noninterference, he went on to add a stern warning to Mugabe: "Any neighbour . . . which allows its territory to be used for attacks on or the undermining of South Africa and its security will have to face the full force of the Republic's strength."[151]

For his part, Mugabe gave an early assurance that Zimbabwe would not provide sanctuary to insurgents operating against South Africa;[152] in addition, he made a firm commitment to retain Zimbabwe's extensive economic ties with the Republic,[153] although Zimbabwe, like the other SADCC states, is determined to reduce economic dependence on South Africa. However, the new Zimbabwean government left no doubt about its implacable opposition to South Africa's domestic policies and demonstrated it by replacing the diplomatic ties between Salisbury and Pretoria with trade representation only.[154] Zimbabwe gradually became increasingly outspoken in its support for the "liberation struggle" against South Africa and in its condemnation of its neighbor's domestic political order.[155]* In short, Zimbabwe has become one of a chain of black states surrounding South Africa which are committed to the "liberation" of the last white-ruled state in Africa.

Mugabe's assumption of power undoubtedly created new apprehensions in South Africa about Namibia's movement toward independence. South Africa and the leading internal political groups in Namibia—particularly the moderate DTA—feared that SWAPO might emulate Mugabe's Zimbabwe African National Union (ZANU) and

*In October 1980 Mugabe was reported to have said that if African countries could devise some way of protecting Zimbabwe against military attacks by South Africa, he would allow military bases for operations against South Africa on his territory (*Beeld*, 24 October 1980).

emerge victorious if it were to contest an election. Like the United African National Council (UANC) electoral triumph in Rhodesia in April 1979—won in the absence of the Patriotic Front alliance between ZANU and ZAPU—the DTA electoral success won in the absence of SWAPO might prove an equally hollow victory. The prospect of a SWAPO government in Windhoek has all along been unpalatable to South Africa, as well as to the vast majority of Namibia's whites and a considerable number of the territory's black political groups. The South African government clearly fears it would be difficult to explain to its own constituency how the whites of Namibia could be subjected to the rule of an organization branded as "Marxist" and "terrorist." Foreign Minister Botha expressed his country's viewpoint in May 1980: "This Government is not . . . prepared to be a party to the installation, through an unfair process, of a dictatorial, tyrannical Marxist regime in South West Africa."[156] Such a possibility "is worrying the people of South West Africa most after the Rhodesian elections, . . . They are terrified at such a prospect."[157] So is South Africa, he could have added.

It is outside the scope of this chapter to examine the protracted, confusing, and often tortuous international negotiations over Namibia,[158] but it is relevant to consider some implications of the Namibian situation for South Africa's regional policy. First, as noted, South Africa is eager to see an independent Namibia which would formally join the constellation of states; such an event would require an anti-SWAPO government. The least South Africa would like is a Zimbabwe-type relationship between it and an independent Namibia. There are indications from both political and military circles in South Africa that the Republic is preparing for the likelihood of a SWAPO government taking power,[159] despite Pretoria's continuing anti-SWAPO rhetoric. Second, no doubt aware of the international political cost it has to bear over Namibia, South Africa hopes that a resolution will earn it some diplomatic rewards, not only in the region but also internationally—notably in the West. Third, a settlement in Namibia, involving a South African withdrawal, is likely to affect UNITA adversely in its war with the MPLA regime in Angola. A significant deescalation of, if not an actual end to, the conflict in Angola might lead to a reduction in the Soviet-Cuban military presence in that state, which in turn might reduce the danger of a spillover of Communist involvement in southern Africa. Fourth, South Africa is bound

to place increasing emphasis on effective economic integration between it and Namibia as the territory approaches independence to
impress on SWAPO Namibia's dependence on and (by implication)
vulnerability to pressure from South Africa. Existing economic ties
can be presented as evidence of the success of cooperation and thus
as an incentive to maintain them. On the whole, South Africa is only
too aware that the course of events in Namibia can have a far-reaching
impact on both the Republic's regional policy and domestic politics.
A SWAPO-ruled Namibia would complete the chain of politically and
ideologically antagonistic black states on the Republic's frontiers.
South Africa would then be forced more onto the defensive, encouraging a siege mentality. If a non-SWAPO government should be
elected, it would probably provide South Africa with a northern
neighbor at least moderate in its policy toward the Republic; moreover, it would check the tide of noncollaborationist armed conflict
politics which has swept southern Africa since Mugabe's victory in
Zimbabwe.

SOUTH AFRICA'S FUTURE REGIONAL ENVIRONMENT

The unfavorable turn of political events in southern Africa in
the latter half of the 1970s has resulted in South Africa's switching
its foreign policy objectives from an ambitious formal cooperative
association of states to the more modest yet fundamental aim of
enhancing its security. "Our most important priority is the struggle
against Marxism, the struggle for the safety of South Africa," P. W.
Botha stated in February 1980.[160] The objective is now commonly
portrayed as a "struggle for survival."[161] South Africa has in effect
been forced to redefine the requirements of a favorable regional
milieu. The main features of the kind of regional environment which
South Africa can now reasonably expect—and which are close to the
minimum requirements of its perceived security interests—can be
summarized as follows:

(1) Preventing neighboring states from being used as spring-
boards for guerrilla or terrorist attacks against South Africa. Ideally
South Africa would want neighboring governments to give official
assurances to this effect and ensure that they are enforced. It follows
that South Africa would also want to prevent guerrilla training camps

from being set up in adjacent countries.[162] Since 1970 it has alternately offered black states nonaggression pacts[163] or given frequent stern warnings that it would retaliate severely if they were to allow their territories to be used as sanctuaries for guerrillas.[164]

(2) Preventing Soviet bloc countries from establishing a political and especially a military foothold in neighboring states. South Africa's major concern is that the Soviet Union would succeed in creating what Vorster termed "a string of Marxist states across Africa from Angola to Tanzania,"[165] which would place South Africa's security in grave jeopardy.

(3) Ensuring that South Africa's economic ties with black states are maintained, and strengthened if possible. Not only do economic relations provide the only link between South Africa and these states (except for Malawi), but they are also a potentially useful strategic lever to achieve other objectives. South Africa's economic ties with black states have in fact become a political issue within the Republic—an obvious response to the pronounced hostility of some black countries who rely heavily on imports from South Africa.[166] One of the possible levers which has been mentioned in government circles is the supply of food to African states.[167]

Southern African politics will in the near future probably be characterized by the existence of two groups—i.e., the constellation and the SADCC. Although there is an undoubted element of opposition and some measure of competition between the two, considerable intergroup economic ties are bound to be retained because of the heavy economic dependence of many SADCC members on South Africa. Furthermore, the existence of these two groups does not in itself enhance the region's conflict potential, for there are actual and potential sources of conflict independent of the constellation and the SADCC. Rather than promoting conflict, the two associations have a potential for conflict prevention: by contributing to wider regional economic development, they can perhaps promote stability. In addition, the constellation might serve as an instrument for political reform of the present and former parts of the South African union. If it does, the structuring of regional relations on the basis of a constellation would have been converted to an essentially internal device for restructuring the South African state.

Chapter 5

REGIONAL COOPERATION IN SOUTHERN AFRICA: THE SOUTHERN AFRICAN DEVELOPMENT COORDINATION CONFERENCE

Michael Clough and John Ravenhill

Cooperation among African states has traditionally taken place at three levels: the continental, where the focus has been on reinforcing the image of an African identity and regulating the interactions between Africa and external actors as well as among African states themselves; the regional, where cooperation has primarily taken the form of customs unions aimed at exploiting the advantages of an expanded market; and the bilateral, where the principal objective has been to jointly exploit common resources or to share the expenses of constructing and operating costly infrastructural facilities. Some of these objectives are shared by the Southern African Development Coordination Conference (SADCC), but the principal motivation underlying this organization distinguishes it not only from previous attempts at regionalism in Africa, but also from similar endeavors among other groups of less developed countries (LDCs): in the SADCC for the first time regional cooperation has as its primary objective the reduction of the dependence of participating states on a neighboring state within the region.* The manner in which the SADCC

*There have been attempts in some regional integration schemes among LDCs to reduce dependence on metropolitan countries—for example, the Andean Pact's Decision 24 and the Caribbean Common Market's Draft Agreement on Foreign

The authors are grateful to Stevens Tucker for research assistance and to Irene Dixon for typing assistance. Research for this chapter was made possible in part by a grant to Michael Clough by the Research Foundation of the Naval Postgraduate School. The views expressed in this chapter are strictly those of the authors.

161

has chosen to pursue this objective also distinguishes it from previous regional schemes in Africa; its methods may be more propitious for attaining its objective than the "grand design" of previous African regional customs unions.

ORIGINS OF THE SADCC

The origins of the SADCC can be traced to an informal grouping, the Frontline States, founded in 1974 to pursue a specific political objective—the legitimate independence under black majority rule first of Rhodesia and later of Namibia (South West Africa). Efforts to unite the peoples of eastern, central, and southern Africa in order to rid the southern part of the continent of colonial rule and/or white minority governments date from the waning days of the colonial era. The Frontline States were a descendant of the Pan-African Freedom Movement of East, Central, and Southern Africa (PAFMECSA; founded at the time of Tanganyika's independence in December 1961) and its successor, the Conference of East and Central African Heads of State. In a sense, a joint declaration issued at the founding conference of the SADCC in 1980, "Southern Africa: Towards Economic Liberation"—known as the Lusaka Declaration—is a partial realization of hopes originally expressed at the first PAFMECSA summit, at which many of the leaders currently involved in the SADCC were present.

The Conference of Heads of State (whose first meeting was held in Nairobi in 1966) was intended to be an informal forum where the major problems of the day could be discussed.[1] It was not intended to be a decision-making institution; accordingly its annual summits did not have fixed agendas. However, two subjects came to assume a dominant role in discussions—regional economic cooperation and the liberation struggle in southern Africa. As conflicts intensified in Rhodesia, Angola, and Mozambique, the conference's leaders were forced to consider developing a strategy with which they might best pursue their objectives in southern Africa—in particular, how to respond to the concerted effort that an increasingly confident South Africa had

Investment and Development of Technology (see Andrew Axline,"Underdevelopment, Dependence and Integration: The Politics of Regionalism in the Third World," *International Organization* 31 [Winter 1977] : 83-105).

launched to woo its black neighbors with promises of economic assistance and cooperation.[2] By 1967 Malawi had succumbed to South African promises of financial assistance, and Zambia had held discussions with South Africa to explore possibilities for the development of a regional modus vivendi.[3] Many of the conference leaders realized that South Africa, Portugal, and Rhodesia would be the most likely beneficiaries if African states responded to South Africa's initiatives in an uncoordinated, ad hoc manner. Presidents Kenneth Kaunda of Zambia and Julius Nyerere of Tanzania took the lead in developing a strategy. At the fifth Conference of Heads of State (held in Lusaka, 14-16 April 1969), they persuaded the conference to adopt its first comprehensive statement on southern Africa.[4] The final document, now known as the Lusaka Manifesto, was remarkable for its carefully measured tone and incisive analysis of the barriers to peaceful change in the region.

The Lusaka Manifesto begins with a clear statement of African objectives in southern Africa.[5] Using the language of Jefferson and Wilson rather than Marx and Lenin, the signatories declared that "all men are equal, and have equal rights to human dignity and respect, regardless of color, race, religion or sex. We believe that all men have the right and duty to participate, as equal members of the society, in their own government."[6] Fulfillment of these principles would ultimately require the transformation of the white states in southern Africa, but the manifesto recognized "that for the sake of order in human affairs, there may be transitional arrangements while a transformation from group inequalities to individual equality is being effected." However, in 1969 the white regimes were unwilling to accept even the principle of equality as an ultimate objective:

If the commitment to these principles existed among the states holding power in Southern Africa, any disagreements we might have about the rate of implementation, or about isolated acts of policy, would be matters affecting only our individual relationships with the states concerned. If these commitments existed, our states would not be justified in the expressed and active hostility towards the regimes of Southern Africa such as we have proclaimed and continue to propagate. The truth is, however, that in Mozambique, Angola, Rhodesia, South-West Africa, there is an open and continued denial of the principles of human equality and national self-determination. This is not a matter of failure in the implementation of accepted human principles. The effective Administrations of all these territories are not struggling towards these difficult goals. They are fighting the principles; they are deliberately organizing their societies so as to destroy the hold of these principles in the minds of men.

Nonetheless, the manifesto's authors stressed their preference for peaceful change:

We would prefer to negotiate rather than destroy, to talk rather than kill. . . . If peaceful progress to emancipation were possible, or if changed circumstances were to make it possible in the future, we would urge our brothers in the resistance movements to use peaceful methods of struggle even at the cost of some compromise on the timing of change.

The Lusaka Manifesto was intended as a statement of the conditions under which its signatories would be willing to engage in a "dialogue" with South Africa. Of the fourteen nations represented in Lusaka, only Malawi refused to sign the final document. In September 1969 the Organization of African Unity (OAU) approved the manifesto, implicitly recognizing the Conference of Heads of State as Africa's spokesman on southern Africa.

South Africa responded to the Lusaka Manifesto in a disappointing, albeit predictable manner. Instead of indicating that it would be willing to reform apartheid and assist in the resolution of the conflicts in Rhodesia and the Portuguese colonies, South Africa focused its attention on winning support from conservative African states like Malawi and the Ivory Coast, which were less insistent on a commitment to substantial change.[7] A debate over whether to enter into "dialogue" with South Africa continued throughout 1970 and 1971, stirring up considerable dissension within the OAU,[8] until "dialogue" was finally rejected by the Heads of State in October 1971 at a summit conference in Mogadishu, Somalia.[9] In what is now known as the Mogadishu Declaration, the conference leaders detailed their conclusions. In their view, South Africa's response to the Lusaka Manifesto demonstrated that dialogue was "a parody aimed at blinding the African population" and that consequently "there remains no means of liberating Southern Africa other than the armed struggle. . . . We are determined to grant our material, diplomatic and moral support to the national liberation movements in conformity with the resolutions of the UN and the OAU, until the final victory." [10] Again the OAU accepted the conference's position as African policy.

The debate over dialogue marked the beginning of the conference's demise; the call for armed struggle in the Mogadishu Declaration undermined the paper consensus which had been possible as long as no decisive action was called for. Four member states — Malawi, Kenya, the Central African Republic, and Burundi — expressed reservations on the final text of the Mogadishu Declaration. To a certain extent, it was inevitable that the conference would collapse once it was faced with a need to act decisively. As noted above, it was not designed to be a decision-making body. Its membership was too diverse and had too many conflicting interests for it to develop the sense of common purpose necessary to play an active role in the unfolding conflicts in southern Africa.

When the Conference of Heads of State met in Dar es Salaam in September 1972, there were indications that support for it was waning — for example, a decision to hold summits every two years instead of annually. [11] Although it was not foreseen at the time, the ninth summit, held in Brazzaville from 31 August to 2 September 1974, turned out to be the final meeting of the conference. The imminent independence of Angola presented the members with a completely new set of problems. By the fall of 1974, divisions within and among the rival nationalist movements in Angola were threatening to ignite a full-scale civil war. In an attempt to forestall such an eventuality, the conference's leaders made "an urgent and fraternal appeal to all the liberation movements for greater vigilance and for the creation, particularly with respect to Angola, of a joint national front that would lead the nation to independence. [12] However, the conflict in Angola escalated, and the members of the conference ended up choosing sides among the different movements instead of acting in concert to bring them together. [13] This in turn exacerbated the ideological differences that already existed in the organization, and the conference was quietly dissolved.

The conference's role in southern African developments was quickly assumed by the Frontline States (Tanzania, Zambia, Botswana, and ultimately Angola and Mozambique). [14] The immediate impetus for the creation of this group was South Africa's decision to seek a settlement in Rhodesia. According to Nyerere,

> Independence in Mozambique appeared at first to achieve what the
> Lusaka Manifesto had failed to do. The Government of South Africa
> indicated a willingness to talk, on one subject, on the basis we had
> set out—that is, on the basis of how, not whether, majority rule
> would come in Rhodesia. In accordance with the Lusaka Manifesto,
> the governments of Tanzania, Zambia and Botswana therefore
> accepted the responsibility of acting as intermediaries with the
> Rhodesian nationalists, with Vorster assuming a similar function
> with the Smith regime. [15]

The Frontline States met for the first time in Lusaka from 21-25 October 1974—the opening session in a lengthy negotiating process
that led to the Lancaster House settlement on Rhodesia in 1979. [16]
Throughout the negotiations, the group acted as the official representative of the OAU. Without the efforts of the Frontline States, there
would not have been a political settlement in Rhodesia. They were
responsible for keeping the nationalist movements from withdrawing
from negotiations with the West when there appeared to be no hope
for a settlement, and for forcing them to make the concessions necessary for a final settlement. Although there have been frequent conflicts over strategy among the members of the group, the conflicts
have not caused the group's collapse, nor have they prevented decisive
action during critical periods, such as the 1979 Commonwealth Conference.

Between 1975 and 1979 the Frontline States' influence in southern Africa grew steadily. Several factors account for their relative
success. First and foremost, the group has focused on achieving
clearly defined objectives—i.e., negotiated settlements in Rhodesia
and Namibia—which were of concern to all its members; since their
creation their common interest in bringing costly conflicts to an end
has outweighed differences over strategies. Second, all five states
have a somewhat similar political outlook, so that ideological cleavages
have not been a major problem. As a consequence, their preferences
regarding rival nationalist leaders in Rhodesia and Namibia have been
less divisive than was the case with the Conference of Heads of State
during the civil war in Angola. Finally, the group is small enough to
permit flexibility, and the degree of trust and mutual respect among

the members has been sufficient for the group to reach genuine accommodations. In short, in the late 1970s the Frontline States, unlike the Conference of Heads of State, was evolving into a viable political institution.

As the liberation of Rhodesia appeared increasingly imminent, the Frontline States focused on the development of a strategy for attaining black majority rule in the two remaining territories under white domination—Namibia and South Africa. Acknowledging that the struggle for majority rule in the latter would entail a long-term commitment, Frontline leaders sought to institutionalize the informal cooperation within the group. In addition, they explicitly recognized the importance of economic factors, giving priority to removing the constraints that economic dependence on South Africa placed on Frontline policymaking toward the Republic. As the late President of Botswana, Sir Seretse Khama, stated: "Economic dependence has in many ways made our political independence somewhat meaningless."[17] Economic constraints were particularly clear in 1978, when Zambia felt obliged to reopen its border with Rhodesia in order to relieve Zambian transport difficulties. Given the damage to communications links during the struggles for Zimbabwean and Namibian independence, the region had by 1979 become more dependent on South Africa's transport facilities.

Economic independence for the black states in southern Africa might best be attained through the development of the subcontinent as an integrated region "rather than a cluster of impoverished little chauvinistic entities."[18] A regional approach in the late 1970s was attractive because (among other things) it appeared to offer an effective alternative to South Africa's proposals for a "constellation of states"; in addition, it was advocated by many of the bilateral and multilateral agencies on which the southern African states would have to rely for development assistance. (Indeed if the African states did not put forward regional schemes of their own, there was a danger these would be imposed on them by donors such as the U.S. Agency for International Development and the European Economic Community [EEC], both of which had undertaken feasibility studies to consider the possibility of developing a regional approach to aid for southern Africa.)

At a meeting of the Frontline States in Arusha, Tanzania, on 3-4 July 1979, the SADCC was launched. Attending the meeting were the development ministers from Botswana, Mozambique, Tanzania, and Zambia, and representatives from nine aid donor countries, UN agencies, the Commonwealth Secretariat, the Economic Commission for Africa (ECA), the EEC, and the African Development Bank. An Angolan delegation en route to the conference was stranded in Europe—an illustration of the transport difficulties that stand in the way of regional cooperation.

An initial problem faced by the Frontline States was whether to invite nonmember neighboring countries to participate in the SADCC. There is no natural "southern African region." Many of the states that academic commentators group under this rubric have very little in common and could just as easily be considered part of some other African "region."[19] * Regions are not merely objective geographic or economic entities. Although geographic and economic factors obviously are very important, they are probably less significant than the perceptions and aspirations of national leaders. A state's attempts to associate with one region rather than another, or to associate with more than one region, reflect its leaders' sense of national identity and interests. For instance, by all objective criteria Tanzania would be considered part of eastern rather than southern Africa, but its leadership has given priority to the liberation struggle in southern Africa, leading Tanzania not only to identify with that region, but also making it a key actor there.

For the Frontline States a sense of regional identity was not in question. By their commitments in 1974-79, they had demonstrated that they perceived their futures to be inextricably linked to developments in the southern part of the African continent. However, to offer membership in the SADCC to other countries would run the risk of diluting the sense of common purpose that had prevailed and of rendering the SADCC vulnerable to the kinds of problems that had plagued the Conference of Heads of State. Yet to exclude some of the neighboring states made little sense given the nature of the communication links between them and the common resources that some shared, and in any case it would almost certainly offend some potential aid donors.

---

*One difficulty faced by proponents of regionalism in southern Africa has been that external agencies have favored conflicting definitions of the region. For instance, the subregional office of ECA is responsible for seventeen countries, extending from Ethiopia to Lesotho and including the Indian Ocean islands.

Accordingly an invitation to join was extended to Lesotho, Malawi, and Swaziland, and it was announced that Namibia and Zimbabwe would be welcome once they had attained "genuine independence."

POLICIES OF THE SADCC

The rapid unfolding of events in Zimbabwe which led to its independence in April 1980 greatly strengthened the SADCC, especially vis-à-vis the South African alternative of a "constellation of states." After Zimbabwe's independence, SADCC members were faced with the challenge of formulating a workable policy toward South Africa. Essentially there were three options: accommodation, confrontation, or selective disengagement. These will be discussed in some detail.

ACCOMMODATION

An accommodation strategy would entail normalizing economic relations with South Africa, increasing diplomatic and other contacts with it, and limiting support for black South African opposition movements. An accommodation approach has been advocated by leaders in Malawi, Swaziland, the Ivory Coast, and other conservative African states, who have presented accommodation—or "dialogue"—as a means of encouraging political change in South Africa. However, these leaders have probably been motivated by other considerations, the foremost of which have been a belief that political change in South Africa was unlikely in the near term, and knowledge that cooperation with South Africa could be very profitable.[20] Prior to the coup in Portugal in April 1974 (which resulted in the independence of Angola and Mozambique) and riots in the suburb of Soweto in South Africa in June 1976, arguments by the conservative leaders could not be easily dismissed. However, those events, along with the collapse of white rule in Rhodesia, have dimmed South Africa's aura of stability and invulnerability and created a new set of "realities" which have made accommodation a less attractive option since 1980. Even Malawi and Swaziland have felt it necessary to hedge their bets—as evidenced by their efforts to improve relations with their more radical neighbors and their decision to sign the Lusaka Declaration, despite its anti-accommodation tone.

MICHAEL CLOUGH AND JOHN RAVENHILL

CONFRONTATION

A confrontation strategy would involve a determined effort to isolate the white regime in South Africa and force it not only to abandon apartheid, but also to transfer political power to the country's black majority. Advocates of confrontation envisage a repetition of the events that occurred in Zimbabwe—i.e., a guerrilla war carried on with external support and culminating in the collapse of white rule. They view regional cooperation as a means of bolstering the wherewithal of South Africa's neighbors to break economic ties with South Africa and extend direct support to South African liberation movements. However, were such a strategy to be adopted, it would lead to the speedy collapse of the SADCC.

A strategy of confrontation would demand a degree of common purpose and resolve far beyond that which exists among the SADCC members. These countries are neither equally dependent on South Africa nor dependent on it in the same ways (see Table 1); thus the potential cost of confrontation with South Africa would vary from state to state. Some leaders have more reason to worry about the repercussions of confrontation for their countries; if they believe they are being asked to shoulder an unreasonable burden, their support for regional cooperation will weaken. Several member states have openly challenged the desirability of a confrontation strategy. If the costs of confrontation were high (which they are certain to be), these states could be expected to break with the other members.[21] In theory the problem of unequal burdens could be minimized by compensating the states required to bear inordinate losses in the course of fulfilling regional commitments. Realistically, it is extremely doubtful that the other countries in the region would be able to agree to share the compensation costs—in part because only a small number of them would not be able to claim losses as a result of an economic break with South Africa, and in part because none could afford the luxury of making considerable sacrifices in support of its neighbors.

Outside of compensation, the only other hope of successfully sustaining a strategy of confrontation would be to get nonregional actors to foot the bills. Experience in the case of the Rhodesian conflict suggests that this is not a viable alternative. While some assistance was provided to Zambia and Mozambique at that time, it fell far short of the losses incurred (Zambian losses were estimated at over £1 billion

Table 1

DEPENDENCE OF SADCC MEMBER COUNTRIES ON SOUTH AFRICA: REGIONAL TRADE, 1976

[Millions of dollars]

SADCC Member Country	Imports from		Exports to		Workers in South Africa[a]	Degree of Economic Vulnerability[c]	Degree of Military Vulnerability[c]
	SADCC Countries	South Africa	SADCC Countries	South Africa			
Angola	$ 9.7	—	$ 0.4	—	NA	Low	Moderate
Botswana	22.9	$152.7	16.0	$ 26.7	$ 34,000[b]	High	High
Lesotho	—	167.3	0.1	15.2	160,630	Absolute	Absolute
Malawi	17.7	54.6	7.1	8.3	18,000	Moderate	Low
Mozambique	2.1	40.5	13.9	11.5	40,000	High	High
Swaziland	0.9	118.3	1.7	38.7	17,000[b]	High	Absolute
Tanzania	3.0	—	5.0	—	—	None	Low
Zambia	12.5	12.2	8.6	0.6	NA	High	High
Zimbabwe (Rhodesia)	16.7	174.9	32.1	109.6	30,000	High	High

Sources: For regional trade: "Economic Dependence and Regional Cooperation"; Southern Africa Development Coordination Conference Sectoral Paper, Arusha, Tanzania, 2-4 July 1979; for workers in South Africa: Kenneth Grundy, "Economic Patterns in the New Southern African Balance," in Southern Africa: The Continuing Crisis, eds. Gwendolen Carter and Patrick O'Meara (Bloomington: Indiana University Press, 1979).

[a]Figures are for 1977.

[b]Figures are for 1975.

[c]Based on the authors' judgments of a number of key factors such as transportation alternatives, existing trade patterns, ability to absorb economic losses, and strategic location. Given the paucity of reliable data and the difficulty of integrating them into a single matrix, we are forced to rely on rough measures.

for the period 1965-78). The potential losses in the event of a confrontation with South Africa would be greater than those experienced as a result of the imposition of sanctions on Rhodesia; thus the provision of relief assistance would give external donors an implicit say in regional decisions, and there would be a possibility that assistance would dry up if regional strategies were not in accord with the views of the donors—and the idea of confrontation has few supporters among Western governments. Domestic pressures would increase on the different governments if economic conditions were to worsen—or even just fail to improve. The longer the struggle in the region, the more likely it would be that problems would develop. Furthermore, potential difficulties could be exacerbated by South African measures (either punitive or positive) designed to induce some states to break with the others. Accordingly there is little support for a strategy of confrontation among SADCC members.

SELECTIVE DISENGAGEMENT

The most viable option open to South Africa's black neighbors is a strategy of selective disengagement. It would entail gradually reducing dependence on South Africa on the basis of a sector-by-sector analysis of the costs and benefits of disengagement. Ties would be maintained only where the costs of disengagement could not be easily absorbed—but such costs cover a wide range of relations. In contrast to an accommodation strategy, selective disengagement assumes that change is inevitable in South Africa, that such change is likely to involve violent conflict and economic dislocation, and that any short-term benefits that might be derived from economic cooperation with South Africa are likely to be outweighed by the damage resulting from future turmoil. Moreover, this strategy explicitly rejects the accommodation argument that dialogue with South Africa can serve as a positive pressure for political change. In contrast to a confrontation strategy, selective disengagement would be primarily defensive, the object being to "delink" the political and economic future of the region from South Africa. It would involve an implicit (if not explicit) recognition that political change in South Africa must come primarily from internal pressures and that other states in the region lack the resources and power to significantly hasten such change.

The greatest merit of the selective disengagement strategy is its ability to reconcile the conflicting objectives and interests of the black states in the region. Even the more "radical" SADCC leaders such as President Samora Machel of Mozambique have acknowledged that "it is incorrect to make comparisons between the political situation which existed in Rhodesia and that which prevails in the Republic of South Africa."[22] They have accepted the fact that South Africa is an independent state, not a colony, and that unlike colonialism, apartheid is an internal rather than external problem. "The struggle we are waging," Machel has noted, "is not directed against a country—South Africa—but against apartheid. Our struggle is not against the whites who are not foreigners in their country, but against the racial and racist discrimination which is practiced against the overwhelming majority of the South African people."[23] Prime Minister Robert Mugabe of Zimbabwe has stated that "The question of the struggle in South Africa is primarily one for the people of South Africa themselves to consider."[24]

Southern African leaders are realistic about the limits within which they must operate. Responding to a question about his country's cooperation with South Africa, Mozambique's Foreign Minister Joachim Chissano said, "We will never accept apartheid and have told the South Africans that. However, it has to be admitted that some countries have no choice. The ties which their former colonizers had established with South Africa involve their very infrastructures. These ties are such that it is now impossible to reject cooperation without disastrous consequences for our economies."[25] Zimbabwe's Minister of Finance Enos Nkala aptly summed up the dilemma confronting the states that are most dependent on South Africa: "No one can ask us to hang ourselves to help our friends. If we commit suicide how do we aid our allies?"[26] Zimbabwe has refused to allow South African liberation movements to establish guerrilla bases on its territory and has been reluctant to support economic sanctions against South Africa.

SADCC leaders have recognized that their ability to coerce the white regime in Pretoria is very limited. Their militaries are too small and too weak (see Table 2) and their economic relations with South Africa too one-sided for them to represent a threat to Pretoria. Just as important, many do not believe that the guerrilla tactics used against Portugal, Rhodesia, and currently being used in Namibia are well suited for the struggle in South Africa, where effective opposition is

Table 2

MILITARY BALANCE IN SOUTHERN AFRICA

Country	1978 Military Expenditures		Total Armed Forces (July 1981)	Combat Aircraft (July 1981)	Tanks (July 1981)	Arms Imports[e] [Millions of dollars]	
	Total [Millions of dollars]	Percent of GNP				1970-75	1976-78
Angola[a]	$ 98[c]	—	33,000	41	285	—	$619
Botswana	14[d]	3.8%	2,000	—	—	$0	10
Lesotho	0	0	1,000	—	—	0	0
Malawi	18	2.1	5,000	—	—	0	4
Mozambique	45	2.4	26,700	35	350	—	151
Swaziland	4	1.4	2,000	—	—	0	0
Tanzania	148	4.2	44,850	24	131	82	167
Zambia	71	3.1	15,500	49	60	89	106
Zimbabwe[b]	444	—	34,000	39	20	—	—
South Africa	1618	4.2	92,700	239	310	659	366

Sources: The Military Balance 1981-82 (London: ISS, 1981); World Military Expenditures and Arms Transfers, 1969-78 (Washington, D.C.: ACDA, 1980).

[a]Figures for Angola do not include approximately 15,000-20,000 Cuban troops currently in the country.

[b]Given the recentness of Zimbabwe's independence, figures on military expenditures and total armed forces are not truly indicative of the country's potential military strength.

[c]Figures are for 1979.

[d]Figures are for 1977.

[e]Of the countries listed here, only South Africa has a sizable indigenous defense industry.

more likely to develop from urban unrest, industrial labor action, and a selective assault on high-visibility targets.[27]

In sum, the southern African states are in a precarious position. They have little if any potential control over developments in South Africa, although these developments could have a serious effect on their political and economic future. Both accommodation and confrontation strategies would serve to increase rather than decrease their vulnerability. Therefore SADCC leaders realize that selective disengagement is their most viable option.

Having by 1981 agreed that selective disengagement would be the informing principle in the choice of future strategy toward South Africa, the SADCC needed to decide what form of regional cooperation would best serve its purposes. The starting point had to be an acknowledgment of the diversity among its member states—both in terms of their individual factor endowments and their respective dependencies on South Africa. Table 3 presents basic economic data on SADCC member states and (for purposes of comparison) on South Africa and Zaire. As can be seen, there are tremendous disparities among the SADCC members. For instance, Angola has a geographical area seventy two times that of Swaziland. The disparities between SADCC member states and the Republic are even more marked. The combined GNP of the SADCC states is less than half that of the Republic, whose exports, moreover, are twice those of the SADCC states.

While it is true that all SADCC members have some dependence on the Republic—in the words of one observer, "Regarded purely in economic terms, the Southern African region without South Africa is rather like a wheel without a hub"[28]—as we have noted, both the type of dependence and its intensity differ significantly. For Botswana, Lesotho, and Swaziland—South Africa's so-called "economic hostages"—dependence is nearly complete in terms of markets, communication links, and employment opportunities for migrant workers; for example, Lesotho's foreign exchange earnings from migrant workers are three times those from commodity exports. Malawi and Mozambique have in recent years considerably curtailed the number of migrant workers they send to South Africa (currently each country sends about 25,000), but Mozambique depends on South African purchases (and to some degree technical expertise) for the viability of its railroads and the Cabora Bassa dam. Like Malawi and Zambia, Mozambique has relied on South Africa for key imports. During the

Table 3

BASIC ECONOMIC DATA FOR SADCC MEMBER STATES, SOUTH AFRICA, AND ZAIRE

Country	Area (000 km.²)	Population, mid-1978 (Millions)	GNP per capita, 1978 (Dollars)	GNP, 1977 (Millions of dollars)	GDP Growth, 1970-78 (Percent)	Gross Domestic Investment Average Annual Growth, 1970-78 (Percent)	Value Added in Manufacturing (Millions of 1970 dollars) 1970	1976	Structure of Production Distribution of GDP, 1978 (Percent) Agriculture	Industry	Services
Angola	1,247	6.7	$ 300	$ 2,804	-10.0%	-10.9%	$ 80	$ 38	50%	21%	29%
Botswana	600	.7[a]	480	392	15.8[b]	—	—	2	36[a]	15[a]	49[a]
Lesotho	30	1.3	280	318	6.5	29.3	2	2	43	19	38
Malawi	118	5.7	180	826	6.5	-1.1	38	53	45	16	39
Mozambique	783	9.9	140	2,005	-3.2	-9.6	104	82	45	16	39
Swaziland	17	.5	440	271	6.2[a]	—	—	—	51	13	36
Tanzania	945	16.9	230	3,400	5.0	1.9	116	156	51	13	36
Zambia	753	5.3	480	2,337	2.3	-2.9	181	213	20[a]	35[a]	45[a]
Zimbabwe	391	6.9	480	2,995	3.4	-0.8	297	—	8	45	47
South Africa	1,221	27.7	1,480	37,941	3.6	—	3,959	—	9	23	68
Zaire	2,345	26.8	210	4,822	1.3	0.6	155	170	27	20	53

Sources: World Bank: *World Tables,* 2nd ed, 1980, and *World Development,* 1981.

[a]Figures are for 1977.
[b]Figures are for 1970-77.

period of the Unilateral Declaration of Independence (UDI) in Rhodesia, South Africa assumed a dominant role in Rhodesia's trade, and it will take the new government a long time to undo the links established in that period. In the absence of reliable alternatives, Malawi, Zambia, and Zimbabwe are highly dependent on South African railroads and ports for the movement of their imports and exports. Angola and Tanzania have the least direct dependence on South Africa; however, support for the liberation struggle in Zimbabwe and Namibia has cost them dearly; for example, Tanzania's investment in transport facilities primarily to support Zambian delinking from South Africa in the period 1965-75 was in excess of $400 million—over 20 percent of total fixed investment in these years. Over one quarter of the total imports of SADCC member states are derived from South Africa.

While economic and political diversity among SADCC states did not preclude regional cooperation for mutual benefit, it ruled out certain types of regional schemes—in particular, the creation of a free trade area. This strategy, which has been the predominant form of integrative efforts among LDCs, has been an almost universal failure. In a lucid background paper prepared for the initial SADCC meeting, the following was noted:

> The failure of grand aspirations in the field of economic integration among peripheral economies has been all too frequent and has usually led—at least for a time—to cold reaction against cooperation, making new starts ever harder to achieve. Southern and Eastern Africa have been no exception to that pattern of experience.[29]

Indeed customs unions previously established in eastern and southern Africa which included members of SADCC had demonstrated all of the problems associated with this type of arrangement. For example, gains from regional cooperation tended to accrue predominantly to the strongest state within the union—Southern Rhodesia in the Central African Federation (CAF), Kenya in the East African Community (EAC), and the Republic of South Africa in the Southern African Customs Union (SACU). In none of the cases had the stronger states shown willingness to forego significant benefits in order to induce the less privileged parties to maintain the arrangements.

Ironically SACU, the only one of the three southern African customs unions still operating, manifests the most extreme forms of dominance and dependence and ideological heterogeneity. Its continued existence owes little to South African commitment to integrated regional development: while Botswana, Lesotho, and Swaziland have benefited since 1969 from a larger share of customs duties than they would be entitled to on a strict division according to shares of extraregional imports, and while they are allowed to protect infant industries, South Africa has clearly indicated that it is unwilling to see them develop into a base from which the South African market might be supplied. SACU survives because of the institutionalized dependency relations that have been built up over the years, and because of the fears of Botswana, Lesotho, and Swaziland that South Africa might take retaliatory actions should they withdraw from the union—e.g., a curtailment of transport links or a termination of labor migration from these countries to the Republic.[30]

If SADCC had decided to create a free trade area, it would have faced problems similar to those which led to the demise of the EAC— i.e., severe imbalance in the distribution of gains from regional cooperation. Zimbabwe's economy is dominant among SADCC members (it is 50 percent larger than the second largest economy, Zambia's, and has an unusually even balance among mining, agriculture, and manufacturing). Its industries are more developed and diversified than those of other SADCC states—in part a consequence of forced import substitution during the UDI period. The country currently has considerable excess manufacturing capacity, which is ready to be brought on stream if the necessary spare parts become available.[31] (Prior to UDI, over one third of Rhodesian exports consisted of intraregional trade, and over half of these were manufactured goods.) Thus political stability in Zimbabwe could produce the conditions which would lead to its becoming the dominant growth pole in the region. Although other SADCC member states might initially have welcomed a substitution of Zimbabwean for South African products, tensions would inevitably have occurred as the result of an uneven distribution of gains that a free trade area would have created. Furthermore, it would not have been realistic to expect Zimbabwe to take unilateral measures to counteract the uneven distribution because even under optimistic assumptions it is unlikely that its economic growth will keep pace with its growing population.

Such weaknesses of free trade areas were clearly recognized by representatives of the Frontline States who established the SADCC:

No form of *free trade area* (or customs union) is a desirable first step nor even a very promising medium term goal. A standard free trade zone among states as diverse as those of Southern (or Southern and Eastern) Africa would generate cumulative inequalities registered by rising imbalances in trade. Further, given the very different attitudes to TNC's [transnational corporations] in general (and specific TNC's like Lonrho in particular), unplanned free trade area *[sic]* would give rise to acrimonious charges and counter charges. These would almost certainly lead to cumulative restrictions and breakdowns.

The case against a free trade area is partly historic and ideological. The failure of the CAF's Common Market and of the EAC's are seen—partly if not wholly accurately—as demonstrating that a free trade area means "to him who hath shall be given".[32]

Furthermore, it was pointed out, none of the southern African states accords the right of unhindered access to their markets to exports from the industrial economies, so it was unlikely that they would be more willing to accord it to dominant regional economies such as that of Zimbabwe.[33]

All the member states of SADCC face severe economic problems—especially as regards the availability of foreign exchange. None of them could afford a net loss or even an absence of short-term gains as a result of regional cooperation. Accordingly the only way to establish successful regional cooperation was on a project basis, whereby each participating state could weigh the relative benefits that might be derived from each cooperative endeavor. As Khama noted: "The basis of our cooperation, built on concrete projects and on specific programmes rather than on grandiose schemes and massive bureaucratic institutions, must be the assured mutual advantage of all participating states."[34]

PRIORITIES OF THE SADCC

The SADCC's strategy was outlined in detail at its first summit conference in Lusaka on 1 April 1980, which was attended by the heads of state of the Frontline States and Zimbabwe, plus representatives of Lesotho, Malawi, and Swaziland, the OAU Secretary-General, and the ECA Executive-Secretary.[35] The Lusaka Declaration acknowledged that "Our urgent task now is to include economic liberation in our programs and priorities." It continued:

> In the interest of the people of our countries, it is necessary to liberate our economies from their dependence on the Republic of South Africa to overcome the imposed economic fragmentation and to coordinate our efforts toward regional and national economic development. . . . It is not the quest for liberation, but the entrenched racism, exploitation and oppression which is the cause of conflict in Southern Africa. The power behind this is in large measure economic. Economic liberation is, therefore, as vital as political freedom.
>
> We, the majority-ruled States of Southern Africa, do not envisage this regional economic coordination as exclusive. The initiative toward economic liberation has flowed from our experience of joint action for political liberation. We envisage regional coordination as open to all genuinely independent Southern African States. [36]

A set of strategic goals was put forward which included the following:

(1) Reduction of external dependence and in particular dependence on the Republic of South Africa;
(2) Creation of operational and equitable regional integration;
(3) Mobilisation of domestic and regional resources to carry out national, interstate and regional policies to reduce dependence and build up genuine regional coordination;
(4) Joint action to secure international understanding of, and practical support for, the SADCC strategy. [37]

The SADCC established that priority was to be given to the transport and communications sector. The rationale for this was set out in a strategy paper prepared for the second SADCC summit:

(1) Without better communication within and among the member states both national and regional development are severely constrained. This is generally true whether in respect of mineral development for export or of food production and storage for national and regional food security;
(2) Because six of the SADCC states are landlocked, transportation for them necessarily has critical multistate coordination aspects;

(3) Regional fragmentation of transport and communications and their incorporation into the Republic of South Africa's transport and communications network has been and remains the key factor in national and regional dependence on the Republic of South Africa and one which that country seeks to strengthen and expand;

(4) Multistate and regional transport and communications projects—even excluding the Trans Kalahari Railway—are likely to cost about $2,000 million during the current decade, by far the largest single sectoral requirement for SADCC investment.[38]

However, the SADCC did not intend to limit regional cooperation to a single-sector strategy concentrating solely on physical infrastructure. Other proposed cooperation included the creation of a regional control program against hoof and mouth disease, the establishment of a subcenter of the International Crops Research Institute on Agriculture in the Semi-Arid Tropics, coordination of national and regional food plans in order to promote food security in the region, coordination of policies in the energy field, identification of industrial surplus capacity in the region and an exchange of information on national industrial projects, study of the means by which proposed projects could be financed (including the possibility of establishing a southern Africa development bank), and the preparation of an inventory of national training facilities in order to promote regional manpower development. Members of the Frontline States and Swaziland were each given responsibility for drawing up proposals in one or more of the sectors of proposed cooperation.

At a SADCC ministerial meeting in Salisbury in September 1980, a draft convention on the establishment of a Southern African Transport and Communications Commission was approved and submitted to the member states for ratification. The commission established the following priorities for the transport sector: (1) Rehabilitation of all existing transport and communication facilities, including the major interstate rail links; (2) Establishment of telecommunications links and civil aviation infrastructures; (3) New road, rail, air, and lake transport systems for which feasibility studies are completed; and (4) feasibility studies for further major regional road, rail, internal marine, air, and ocean shipping facilities. A list of projects in this sector was drawn up and presented to a meeting of potential donors in Maputo in November 1980.

Giving priority to the transport and communications sector was undoubtedly sensible because most other cooperative projects would fail in the absence of an efficient transportation system. Major gaps exist in the transport network within the region, a result of the countries having historically belonged to two separate colonial trading networks, as well as their being integrated with South Africa. The infrastructure in existence has been damaged—in some cases severely—by the struggles for the liberation of Zimbabwe and Namibia, or has been of limited utility because of various bottlenecks—e.g., at the ports; Dar es Salaam is a particularly notorious example.

In order to reduce the dependence of Zambia and Zimbabwe on South Africa, it was critical that the Benguela and Tanzania-Zambia (TAZARA) railroads be restored to full operating order and the lines between Zimbabwe and Mozambique be reopened. Future rail construction might include a Zimbabwe/Botswana-Namibia (Trans-Kalahari) line, which would be essential if the mineral deposits in western Botswana are to be exploited and would provide Botswana and Zimbabwe with access to an Atlantic Ocean port. In the region's road network the most notable gaps are between Tanzania and Mozambique, Tanzania and Malawi, Namibia and Zambia, Namibia and Angola, and Zimbabwe/Botswana and Namibia. Their elimination is essential if intraregional trade is to move beyond its presently low levels. There are a number of common assets which might profitably be jointly exploited. These include four rivers: the Kunene (Angola and Namibia); the Ruvuma (Mozambique and Tanzania); the Zambezi (Namibia, Botswana, Zambia, Zimbabwe, and Mozambique); and the Shashi (Botswana and Zimbabwe). Consumption within the region of some of the electricity produced by the Cabora Bassa dam would reduce Mozambique's dependence on South Africa.

As we have noted, SADCC members made a conscious choice not to attempt to construct a grandiose free trade area or customs union. For matters of trade they have adopted an approach which appears to be modeled on one developed successfully by Mozambique and Tanzania over the years 1975-80—i.e., an identification of the needs of one state that might be filled by another, and negotiation of an annual trade protocol which specifies quantities and values. This restricted notion of trade expansion offers considerable potential within the region. Angola, Mozambique, Zimbabwe, and Zambia possess surplus industrial capacity whose production could be used to meet the needs of other states for products currently imported from extraregional sources (including South Africa). Similarly, Zimbabwe and Swaziland have the potential to produce considerable quantities of maize, sugar, and dairy products which might be exported to member countries with deficits.

PROBLEMS AND PROSPECTS OF THE SADCC

Regional cooperation for self-reliance continues to attract African governments despite the disappointments of the last two decades. The Lagos Plan of Action, adopted by the OAU in April 1980, makes regional economic groupings the centerpiece of its strategy for improving Africa's disastrous economic performance of recent years. It focuses on the same basic concerns as those expressed at the first summit meeting of the SADCC—i.e., food production, energy, industry, and transport and communications.

As we have noted, the SADCC's strategy marks a novel approach to regional cooperation in Africa. It is a conscious effort to build "from the bottom up"—to establish viable cooperative projects between two or more member states and to use the goodwill and sense of common interest that these generate to move toward wider-ranging and longer-term objectives. The SADCC is more flexible than is the Economic Community of West African States (ECOWAS) in that it has abandoned the traditional fixation with creating free trade areas and has shown willingness to include nonmembers in its discussions. (For example, a meeting among Zimbabwe, Zambia, Mozambique, and Zaire was held in June 1980 and led to a pact on improving transport and communications links.)

Nevertheless, the SADCC faces some formidable problems, some of which derive from its particular organizational form, and others from the goals that it has set. The most fundamental is a need to raise huge sums of money if SADCC's ambitious transportation projects are to be implemented. There are two facets to this problem. First, there is considerable doubt in a period of financial stringency whether donors will come close to providing the aid required. At the donor meeting in Maputo, pledges amounting to $650 million were made— just over one quarter of what the SADCC had sought. Most of these funds did not involve substantial new commitments, and there was some doubt as to the firmness of the pledges since donors reserved the right to review project proposals. Western aid officials questioned whether any of the countries in the region could develop enough trade to warrant new roads or railways for at least a decade, and asserted that existing arteries of trade were underutilized because of poor planning and inefficiency.[39] Second, should substantial aid be forthcoming, the SADCC will be heavily dependent on external agencies, which may attempt to dictate policy to the group. Ironically, a counterdependency effort may, at least in the short term, create new dependencies.

Apparently the pledges of aid made at Maputo were sufficient to maintain the momentum of the SADCC in the short term, but some significant symbolic achievements may be necessary if member states are to remain convinced of its long-term viability. The key to SADCC's success will be whether it can break out of the vicious circle where its actions are inhibited by the costs of its efforts to decrease dependence on South Africa yet where failure to delink tends to reinforce existing dependencies. For countries such as Lesotho, Swaziland, and Namibia (and to a lesser extent Botswana), the risks of breaking with South Africa are too great to shoulder until there are viable alternatives. South Africa's ability to increase the costs of regional cooperation should not be underestimated. Communications facilities are particularly vulnerable to attack by South African forces or guerrilla groups backed by the Republic, as the history of the Benguela railroad illustrates.

For the first fifteen months of its existence, the SADCC was dependent entirely on national civil services for exploratory studies. Following the ministerial meeting in Salisbury, it was announced that Botswana had been asked to prepare details concerning the functions, structure, conditions of service, and budget of a permanent secretariat, and that these details would be reviewed by the Council of Ministers in 1981. While there is a great advantage to a type of regional cooperation that is sufficiently flexible to handle individual projects between a limited number of member states, there is a danger that such projects will not generate momentum toward further cooperation in the region. For example, a road link between Angola and Namibia will do little to promote trade between Lesotho and Mozambique. There is also a danger that some projects will throw into question the viability of existing cooperative arrangements—for example, Zambia's use of ports in Mozambique would cast doubt on the viability of the

TAZARA railroad; if Zimbabwe installs a link to the Cabora Bassa dam, it will almost certainly result in a loss of foreign currency earnings for Zambia, from which Zimbabwe currently purchases significant quantities of electricity; and in November 1979 there were reports that Mozambican officials were uneasy over a five-year development program to upgrade port facilities at Dar es Salaam, fearing that it would adversely affect its own ports. As a Zimbabwean engineer noted with respect to the choice of a future source of electricity supply, "Regional cooperation can be a cut-throat business."[40] Thus there is a clear need for a dynamic secretariat which can not only seize the initiative in identifying possible cooperative projects, but can also ensure that projects are carefully constructed so that they are complementary and optimize the use of existing regional resources. Furthermore, adroit balancing by a secretariat might prevent national sensitivities from being unduly aroused, and if a secretariat can maintain close working relations with national ministries, it will minimize the possibility of an emergence of bureaucratic rivalries.

Much remains to be done in the sphere of commercial cooperation before a significant increase in trade can be expected. At present in SADCC none of the national bureaucracies possesses competence in long-term planning of trade, and it cannot be expected that a Secretariat (once created) will immediately acquire such a capability. Generally tariffs are not a significant barrier to increased intraregional trade, although membership in SACU requires Botswana, Lesotho, and Swaziland to give an institutionalized preference for South African goods. A serious problem (as noted) is the lack of foreign exchange, which severely affects all states in the region. Delays in central bank payments—which often amount to periods from twelve to thirty months and which appear to particularly affect regional creditors since they are least able to exert international pressure—have caused considerable friction within the region in the past. Ideal solutions would be to allow commercial credit or to conduct trade in local currencies—as Mozambique and Tanzania have done since January 1977.

Finally there is the problem of political diversity and the extent to which political feuding will spill over to disrupt regional cooperation. The extension of cooperation from the comparatively homogeneous Frontline States to the larger SADCC has increased the ideological diversity of the group. The members of the SADCC have in common only their dependence on South Africa; as we have noted, it varies a great deal from state to state, and the degree of a state's dependence partly determines its commitment to an active strategy of delinking. There is a danger that the SADCC will be split in the same way as was the Conference of Heads of State, leading to deadlock and inactivity. While the SADCC's concentration on projects between a limited number of states would appear to be an approach most likely to minimize the problem of ideological diversity, it does not guarantee that one regional project will be immune from interstate disputes over others. It would be ideal to insulate the projects from each other so that a dispute over one would not disrupt cooperation in another. Past experiences within the region—particularly the EAC—suggest that however desirable such insulation may be, it is impossible to achieve in practice. While one's best wishes might be extended to the SADCC for its success, the history of cooperative efforts in Africa gives one few reasons to be sanguine.

Chapter 6

THE NATURAL ALLY:
SOVIET POLICY IN SOUTHERN AFRICA

Seth Singleton

The 1975 civil war in Angola provided an opportunity for the Soviet Union to establish its presence and influence in southern Africa, and the Soviets grabbed it. Since then the spectacle of Cuban soldiers, East German propagandists and security police advisors, Soviet weaponry, and occasional effusive African rhetoric about the disinterested nature of Soviet and socialist friendship and support has boggled Western Africanists and Sovietologists. Western anxieties increased. Has Soviet influence reached the point where the United States must choose between helping white racist South Africa or abandoning the region to indirect Soviet control? Will every tanker rounding the Cape of Good Hope soon be shadowed by a Soviet submarine based in Luanda, or in Walvis Bay? What will happen to the Western economic and financial structure if a Soviet-sponsored takeover in South Africa makes the heirs of Lenin the mineral kings and goldbugs of the world?

Such fears of Soviet power in southern Africa are often exaggerated, but this does not mean that Soviet policy is inconsequential. The Soviets have become an important actor in southern Africa. However, the capability of the Soviet Union and its allies to control the flow of events is limited. The Soviets do not possess means to enforce an *un*-natural alliance in southern Africa. Soviet success depends on African needs for weapons and for the military and internal security training provided by the Soviets and primarily their Cuban and East German allies; weapons and training are all the communist nations can offer. If economic development needs replace those of armed struggle, and if the West provides alternatives to armed struggle as a means toward African independence and majority rule,

Soviet influence will wither. In fact the Soviet Union as the natural ally and armorer of liberation has been losing influence since 1977-78. The Soviet problem in the early 1980s is to hold on to the gains of socialism in Angola and Mozambique and to maintain enough presence elsewhere among the Frontline States to take advantage of the next upsurge of violent conflict. As Leninists, the Soviets expect violent conflict to recur, for they believe that the United States and the West are driven by the economic imperatives of "imperialism" to fight any liberation of southern Africa which transfers control of its mineral wealth. The end of war and peaceable establishment of African majority rule in Zimbabwe arranged by the British in 1979 seemed to prove the Soviets wrong. Namibia, the current case, is the next test. The ultimate test will be South Africa.

What the Soviets are trying to do in southern Africa and how they are trying to do it is quite clear to anyone who bothers to take Soviet sources seriously. Their deeds have matched their words. This essay will begin with an analysis of Soviet objectives and policy concepts. It will then describe the arrival of the Soviet Union and its allies in southern Africa and their attempt to pursue a strategy for "liberation" of the region under Soviet guidance. Finally, it will try to explain how and why that strategy has thus far fallen short.

SOUTHERN AFRICA IN SOVIET POLICY

As Leninists, Leonid Brezhnev and his Politburo colleagues refer to "the world revolutionary process," which means a piecemeal, gradual transformation of world society from a capitalist to a socialist system.* World politics is a struggle between socialism and imperialism. In this struggle the first imperative is the security, prosperity, and cohesion of the Soviet motherland of socialism; a close second is

---

*In Brezhnev's speech to the Twenty-Fifth Party Congress in Moscow in February 1976, "the world revolutionary process" was the final topic of his foreign policy discussion, giving it major importance. In his Twenty-Sixth Party Congress address (February 1981), peace and disarmament came last, and the world revolutionary process took considerably less space. Africa got two sentences. Times change. The Brezhnev Politburo has stressed Leninist orthodoxy at home and abroad. The volumes of Brezhnev's speeches are entitled *On Leninist Course*.

the necessity to defend the gains of socialism in other countries of the Socialist Community, now defined to include Mongolia, Cuba, Vietnam, and Laos, as well as the Warsaw Pact nations of Eastern Europe. Protection of existing socialism takes precedence. Risking existing positions in pursuit of further gains is "adventurism," a Leninist sin. However, if the security of the existing base is not threatened, the Leninist imperative becomes the effort to promote— by whatever means and wherever possible—the "liberation" of what Lenin called the "colonies and semicolonies." Such an effort is particularly salient during periods of detente, in which the Soviet Union and (since 1945) its Socialist Community allies are less directly threatened. Hence in the 1920s the Comintern promoted revolution in China. In 1955-62 Nikita Khrushchev pursued entente with Egypt, Indonesia, India, Ghana, and Guinea, and attempted to intervene in the Congo (now Zaire).* Like in the 1920s and 1950s, Soviet policies of the 1970s follow the pattern of liberation combined with detente.

THE CHANGING CORRELATION OF FORCES

Since at least 1968 the Brezhnev Politburo has pursued an integrated, consistent set of policies which for a time achieved great success. The key to understanding Soviet policy is to recognize the complementary fit of constant military buildup, detente with NATO Europe and the United States, and the promotion (in response to opportunity) of liberation by means of armed struggle or military intervention in Asia and Africa. Detente has meant several things. First, it has meant strategic arms control and trade with West Germany, the rest of Western Europe, and the United States. These were essential to Soviet economic well-being and national security. Second, detente has meant Western recognition of the East European status quo, formalized in the Helsinki Agreement of 1975. Between the invasion of Czechoslovakia in 1968 and the signing of the Helsinki

*The botched Soviet effort to undercut African-Western cooperation through the United Nations during the Congo crisis of 1960-62 was, along with the 1962 Cuban missile crisis, an outstanding example of failed adventurism. The Congo experience may influence present Soviet caution toward interfering with cooperation between the Frontline States and the West.

Agreement, the Soviets consolidated the institutions of political, military, and economic integration in Eastern Europe. The Warsaw Pact Political Consultative Committee took responsibility for overseeing joint Socialist Community foreign and internal policy. The Council of Mutual Economic Assistance (CMEA) Comprehensive Program of 1971 encouraged joint planning and began a transition toward full economic integration—a necessary adjunct to the development of East-West trade, just as military integration among Warsaw Pact countries and the "Brezhnev Doctrine" were necessary adjuncts to a relaxation of political tension.

Third, detente has been intrinsically related to the "upsurge of the world revolutionary movement." It has encouraged West Europeans to remain uninvolved in Asian and African issues, and it has encouraged the Americans—if they needed further urging after the Vietnam war—to avoid containment or counterintervention in response to initiatives in Asia and Africa by the Soviets or Soviet allies. Vietnam was the first salient case of detente working to Soviet advantage in the Third World. Soviet-American detente was cemented by the SALT I and Anti-Ballistic Missile (ABM) treaties and the agreement on principles to prevent escalation of tension—all signed in 1972. These preceded the American withdrawal from Vietnam and the continued Soviet arming of the North Vietnamese Army for its successful invasion and conquest of South Vietnam in 1975. The other salient case is Cuba. After Fidel Castro's ten million ton sugar harvest failed in 1969, Cuba came to depend almost entirely on Soviet subsidies while detente and Soviet military power protected the Cuban revolution. In 1975 Cuba held its first full-fledged Communist Party congress and, like Vietnam, was welcomed as a full member of the Socialist Community.

These two cases provided the backdrop to the successful Angolan adventure which brought Soviet power to southern Africa. Soviet statements after 1975 made the claim that true liberation was possible only with a Soviet connection, with Soviet arms and military protection, which an increasingly powerful Soviet Union could now effectively provide.* All together—East European consolidation, detente,

---

*The authoritative *Vneshniaia Politika Sovetskogo Soiuza* (Foreign policy of the Soviet Union) states the following: "The decisive successes in the struggle for freedom and independence which the national liberation movement in Asia and Africa attained *were predetermined by the growth of the might of the USSR*" (Moscow, 1976; p. 101; my translation; emphasis added).

and the successful pursuit of liberation in Asia and Africa—were summed up by the Soviets in that most optimistic, even boastful, phrase of the 1970s, "the changing correlation of forces." In the Soviet view growing military clout came increasingly to be seen as the sine qua non for the continued success of all other elements of policy.

OBJECTIVES OF LIBERATION

Soviet support for liberation is assumed to have three consequences, which are Soviet objectives. First, it should weaken the imperialist enemy. The process of armed conflict between Third World peoples and Western nations or their (assumed) proxies, such as Israel, South Africa, or local regimes of the "reactionary national bourgeoisie," provokes hatred of the West among Third World peoples and may create dissension in the West—as in France during the Algerian war or in the United States and Europe during the war in Vietnam. The enemy may be weakened even if the liberation movement is unsuccessful; the case of the Palestinians is an example. Second, successful liberation should end Western control of natural resources, markets, and investment outlets on which the Western economy is assumed to depend. Third, liberated nations are expected to become friends, allies, and ultimately partners in an expanded Socialist Community. To the extent this occurs, they may provide economic resources, military bases, diplomatic support, and armed forces in the service of a constantly expanded world socialist network held together by "proletarian internationalism" under Soviet guidance. Cuba and Vietnam are cases in point.

Two corollaries to the Soviet view of liberation must be emphasized. First, Leninists assume that imperialism versus liberation is a dialectic—no stable or lasting compromise is possible. Thus in Africa movements, leaders, and governments must ultimately choose between joining the world socialist camp or becoming neocolonial extensions of world imperialism. "African socialism" or nonalignment are but way-stations toward socialism or indications of arenas of continuing struggle. Ultimately the only question is, "Which side are you on?" Soviet policy in the "countries-in-process-of-liberating-themselves" (the literal translation of the Soviet term *osvobodiashchiesia strany*)

191

is to choose the time, place, and means whereby the struggle in one country or another can be tipped in the socialist direction. Second, the Soviet Union and other socialist countries are the natural allies of liberation because while the impulse to be liberated springs from local reaction to "exploitation," the anti-Western interest is identical.

THE IMPORTANCE OF SOUTHERN AFRICA

Southern Africa is important to Soviet world policy in some ways, and quite unimportant in others, and it is essential to understand which is which.

Southern Africa is utterly unimportant to Soviet and Socialist Community security. Naval patrols in the south Atlantic and intelligence ships which monitor the flow of supplies and naval activity are useful adjuncts to Admiral Gorshkov's scope of operations but are not worth major risks or much expenditure of political capital or military or economic resources. The important places for Soviet security are Poland, China, the Islamic borderlands, and of course Western Europe, which must be prevented from rearmament and anti-Sovietism. Among the Third World outposts of socialism, Cuba and Vietnam have first claim on Soviet attention and resources, followed by Ethiopia and South Yemen, which are more useful than southern Africa for harassment of Western resource supply. Mozambique and Afghanistan are both labelled countries of "socialist orientation," but the Afghan counterrevolution threatened to create a Pakistan-Afghanistan-Iran bloc of Islamic states linked to China and the West and bordering forty million Soviet Moslems. Hence the invasion in December 1979 to prevent it. Commitments and resources to preserve or expand Soviet presence and influence have been and will be made and expended according to Soviet security concerns.

Southern Africa *is* important to Soviet policy basically because it is the last area in Asia and Africa where Leninism still makes sense and the Soviets really are the natural ally. Throughout the developing world, liberation against the West has gradually been achieved. Resources have been nationalized by governments of all ideological stripes and political affiliations. The Group of 77 may use the rhetoric of "exploitation" to bargain with Western governments and corporations, but this is a form of bargaining within the Western-based world

192

economy, not a process of splitting the developing nations from that economy and into a world socialist camp. It has become increasingly and brutally obvious that Soviet-style socialism is an economic failure, and that the Soviet camp has little except guns to spare for its friends.

Simultaneously, local conflicts—often ethnic and national disputes of long standing—reemerge. The formerly oppressed start oppressing each other. In such circumstances Soviet military aid may be useful, but it builds little long-term loyalty or permanent connections. Anti-Western ideology and the acceptance of Soviet support become increasingly a matter of convenience. In China-Vietnam-Kampuchea-Thailand, Ethiopia-Somalia, India-Pakistan, Greece-Turkey, or Iran-Iraq, intervention of either superpower simply polarizes neighboring countries and internal opposition toward the other side. The united front of socialism and oppressed peoples against Western imperialism is becoming a tenuous, archaic, even absurd perception, but it is one to which a stultified Soviet communism remains wedded.

Soviet policy thus swims upstream against the historical current. The Soviets have an overwhelming interest in not becoming, or being seen as, just another white European imperialist power presiding over a shaky empire held together or expanded by coercion and violence. In East Asia the tireless efforts of China to portray the Soviets as such were confirmed by the Vietnamese invasion of Kampuchea in December 1978. In Africa the Soviet betrayal of Somalia and the Eritreans and the massive military airlift to Ethiopia in 1977 led to African accusations of imperialism, which the Soviets have tried to refute in shrill and defensive propaganda. In the Islamic world the invasion of Afghanistan caused an even more severe reaction; the Ayatollah Khomeini declared that "The danger of communist powers is not less than that of America."[1] Such setbacks heighten the importance to the Soviets of the few remaining situations in which they may act as a disinterested ally against the oppression of the West.

Southern Africa fits. Africans are united (with varying degrees of commitment) in favor of liberation, and liberation is seen as a good cause throughout the world. As both Western and Soviet writers constantly emphasize, resources from southern Africa are essential to Western security. European and American investments have been highly profitable, and much of that profit comes from the low wages paid to African workers kept in check by a police state. The last anticolonial struggle—against the Portuguese—merged into the struggle for liberation against the white minority regimes in Rhodesia and South Africa (including Namibia). The experience of these struggles seemed to demonstrate the indispensable Soviet role as the natural ally of liberation.

Because of the importance of southern Africa to the West, a small Soviet investment in liberation might produce great gains. The Soviets would lose no friends by an active policy skillfully pursued. They might succeed in provoking a U.S. policy of aid to colonialists and racists, which would permanently polarize the region and bring within reach the long-range goal of a southern Africa united under "socialist orientation." Western attention might be diverted from matters more important to the Soviet Union, such as the rearming of China or the management of conflict in the Middle East. If Soviet presence and influence could be established, access to ports by the Soviet navy and establishment of intelligence facilities would increase the Soviet capability for naval harassment in time of crisis or war.[2] (However, naval reach is a welcome side effect, not the basis for policy.)

Once presence and influence are established, the transition to communism in southern Africa might be achieved at low cost and with relative ease. The Soviets and particularly their Cuban and East German allies are very good at building a strong centralized state: party organization, police training, a disciplined national army, and management of information. In southern Africa (apart from South Africa, which is different) the impact and staying power of such Soviet-sponsored efforts could be great. (The problem is getting local national leaderships to maintain the Soviet connection, to take the Cuban rather than the Chinese path, after state-building has been accomplished.) The dialectics of backwardness, first proposed by Trotsky as the "law of combined development," in which the communist vanguard in power can build socialism from any level of social and economic organization, reach their furthest extension in a country like Mozambique.

The Soviet Union could easily provide the one thing that the liberation movements need—guns. By the mid-1970s, with the burdens of Cuba and Indochina and an increasingly shaky economy at home (in which economic growth is stifled by 12-15 percent of GNP being spent on the military), Soviet abilities to prop up friendly governments with cash, food, or consumer goods were almost nil.

Expansion of Soviet presence and influence therefore depended on a local need for weapons or military protection. By becoming the armorers in southern Africa, the Soviets could expose Chinese support for liberation as ineffective and wean the liberation movements away from China. Southern Africa was thus a no-lose opportunity as long as involvement there did not overstrain resources or threaten a greater confrontation with the West than was desirable.

THE STRATEGY OF LIBERATION: PROLETARIAN INTERNATIONALISM AND SOCIALIST ORIENTATION

In the 1970s the Soviet Union developed a network of allies cooperating to establish a permanent Socialist Community presence in new countries. In turn, these countries, candidate members of the Socialist Community called countries of "socialist orientation," provide bases, sanctuaries, and resources with which the Socialist Community can further expand its influence and presence. The Soviet Union is coordinator, weapons supplier, and ultimate decision-maker, particularly in risky circumstances where failures may threaten Soviet security. The extent of direct Soviet involvement and hands-on Soviet control of decisions varies in proportion to Soviet security concerns, ranging from miniscule (El Salvador) to limited (southern Africa) to significant (Ethiopia) to total (Afghanistan). In southern Africa the limited direct Soviet role is designed to minimize risks and avoid direct confrontation with the West.

"Proletarian internationalism," one of the oldest Leninist ideas, was reemphasized in the 1970s. It means simply that all communist countries will cooperate, under Soviet direction, to promote "the world revolutionary process," with each contributing what it can. It is Soviet language for what Americans call a "proxy" relationship. It includes a CMEA undertaking to build a natural gas pipeline from the Urals to Berlin, the cooperation of Cubans and East Germans with the Soviet Union in arming and training the South West Africa People's Organization (SWAPO), or making "socialist orientation" irreversible in Angola (see below). "Proletarian internationalism" has long applied to liberation movements or civil wars—witness the Comintern operatives in Shanghai in the 1920s and the International Brigades of the Spanish civil war.

The Soviets do not control all decisions in joint Socialist Community ventures—they consult with Cubans, East Germans, Vietnamese, and other allies—but, "proletarian internationalism" requires an integrated policy. Disagreements must never surface in public; hence we know little about them. The Soviet Union must always be applauded and never criticized. For example, Fidel Castro praised proletarian internationalism in Moscow just as communist policy in the Horn of Africa switched from support of Somalia and the Eritreans to Ethiopia—a decision whose wisdom Castro apparently doubted (see p. 209 below). Furthermore, any policies counter to Soviet interests are out of bounds, and the Soviet Union maintains a veto over all joint decisions. Drawing new governments and leaders of liberation movements into the network of proletarian internationalism is a Soviet goal. How far the Soviets are willing to go to enforce proletarian internationalism depends on the time, place, and circumstances.

Along with the revival of "proletarian internationalism," the Soviets developed a major new concept and policy in the mid 1970s—"socialist orientation." This is the latest attempt to make Soviet and allied influence permanent in countries which (temporarily) invite it and eventually add them to the Socialist Community. "Socialist orientation" developed from the experience of previous failures and successes. Economic and military aid to Third World nationalists without an implantation of Soviet and allied presence within those countries was a failure. Egypt is one example. China, communism notwithstanding, is another—and the most important—and the list is long. Soviet policymakers quite reasonably concluded that unless the first stage of liberation—the "national democratic revolution" led by "revolutionary democrats"—came to depend on Soviet and allied support and internal presence, a country would not follow through to communism on its own. In Cuba and Vietnam communism did become entrenched. As noted above, these countries waged armed struggle directly against the imperialist enemy, and the Soviet Union became the necessary provider of weapons and diplomatic protection. Castro is the perfect model of a "revolutionary democrat" turned communist by "imperialist aggression." Certainly southern Africa offered a possibility for success if and when a connection could be established with the Movimento Popular de Libertação de Angola (MPLA), the Frente de Libertação de Moçambique (FRELIMO),

SWAPO, the Zimbabwe Patriotic Front, or the African National Congress (ANC) in South Africa.

In the mid-1970s the International Department of the CPSU Secretariat, in its search for a way to stay in Africa, began to promote "socialist orientation." After the establishment of Soviet and allied presence in Angola, Mozambique, and Ethiopia and connections to the southern African liberation movements, "socialist orientation" was touted as the wave of the future for all Africa.

The first requisite of socialist orientation is the acceptance of a strong Soviet and allied presence and influence in both internal evolution and foreign policy.[3] Internally leaders must be willing to become a "vanguard" dedicated to "scientific socialism." How the leadership gained power or who the leaders are does not matter as long as they make a commitment to eventually become communists and accept Soviet and allied socialist aid in making their parties communist. Aid in party-building is designed to inculcate "scientific socialism" as well as to create an effective organization under central discipline which will eliminate factional quarrels and which will have effective contact with and control over the population.

Second, socialist orientation involves training, staffing, and maintaining security forces loyal to the state and to the party. Security police and internal intelligence are one component; the national army is another. All are to be trained and supplied by the Socialist Community. Ideally they will be sufficiently integrated with the party leadership to avoid factional plots and coup attempts, although this is no small feat in Africa. The experiences of the People's Republic of the Congo, which has been a scene of intrigues, plots, assassinations, and attempted coups since 1963, amply illustrate the point that rhetorical adoption of Marxism-Leninism and the presence of Cubans and Soviets in military, police, and militia training are not a guarantee against turmoil. The Congo proclaimed its socialist orientation in 1969—before the term came to be used—but has still not stabilized the factional politics of its coercive forces.

Third, socialist orientation countries are expected to make genuine efforts to meet the basic economic needs of the peasantry. Soviet as well as Western analysts well understand that an African regime isolated in a capital city and incurring peasant resentment born of neglect may become a target for a coup or insurgency regardless of rhetoric. Thus the Socialist Community will provide Cuban doctors and literacy experts, East German teachers, Soviet agricultural specialists, or other technicians.

Western readers may by now sense an interesting irony. Soviet notions about building effective socialism in Africa are much like Western ones about how to stabilize developing countries under an effective autocracy. The key in each case is stability, defined as internal security against subversion and disorder, plus a party with roots among the people, plus meeting enough peasant needs to gain some legitimacy among the people.

The final element of socialist orientation is crucial: the regime should cooperate with Soviet international policy in return for Socialist Community aid and protection. Socialist orientation is cemented by Soviet "Treaties of Friendship and Cooperation," which include clauses on military aid and joint consultation in the event of threats. The treaties may justify, although they do not require, Soviet intervention to aid friendly regimes. The Soviets make no firm commitment to defend "gains of socialism." Conversely, no *unilateral* Soviet intervention is implied in the wording. Nonetheless, the treaty with Afghanistan—almost identical in its relevant sections to those with Ethiopia, Angola, and Mozambique—was explicitly cited by the Soviets as the basis for their invasion.* Currently the Soviet Union has eight airborne divisions and a large and increasing fleet of long-range aircraft (which, if need be, could refuel in socialist Ethiopia) which could reach southern Africa.[4]

The Soviets have made clear that socialist orientation carries the obligation to devote economic resources to the Socialist Community. However, Western trade or investment may be encouraged if it serves

*The Soviet treaties with Angola and Mozambique both provide for "cooperation in the military sphere"; both cite "unbreakable" friendship with the Soviet Union; both pledge Soviet respect for Angolan/Mozambican nonalignment; and both include a key clause on cooperation in time of crisis: "In the event of any situation arising that may create a danger to peace or disturb peace, the High Contracting Parties shall immediately establish contact with each other in order to coordinate their positions in the interests of removing the danger or restoring peace" (Angolan treaty, 26 October 1976, article VII). Soviet treaties with Afghanistan and Vietnam are almost identical in wording, illustrating the flexibility of their application. (For text of the Soviet-Angola treaty, see *Africa Contemporary Record 1976-77*, ed. Colin Legum, pp. C151-53; for the Mozambican treaty, see *ibid.*, *1977-78*, pp. C17-18.)

overall socialist purposes. Hence Gulf Oil continues to run the Cabinda fields in Angola and, incidentally, to finance the Angolan revolution.

Socialist orientation also includes whatever cooperation "proletarian internationalism" may require—for example, making pro-Soviet statements, voting correctly in the United Nations and other international bodies, offering diplomatic mediation, providing sites for Soviet intelligence facilities, arranging Soviet access to ports and airports, and granting sanctuary for Soviet-aided liberation movements and exile groups. At least one official Soviet writer has noted that armies of socialist orientation nations may be used to help establish or defend similar regimes elsewhere.* The Soviets denounce Western attempts to use African forces—such as the Moroccan troops sent to Shaba (Zaire) after the rebel attack in March 1977—but such policies are a mirror of Soviet hopes.

To make socialist orientation irreversible is an important Soviet objective in southern Africa. But unlike in Afghanistan, the costs of heavy-handed behavior outweigh possible gains. Unilateral Soviet intervention would alienate Africans and confirm perceptions of Soviet imperialism, would alarm Europe and thus threaten detente, and would add to Soviet costs already overextended in support of Poland, Indochina, Cuba, Afghanistan, and elsewhere. Thus Soviet policy must elicit, not impose, African cooperation for party-building, ideological instruction, security force training, and international alignment. The best way to elicit cooperation and extend it to new countries is to further a polarized southern Africa which pits "liberation" against "the West."

THE NATURAL ALLY ARRIVES: 1975-78

In their first venture in Africa—the Angolan civil war—the Soviets took care to appear legally correct in their involvement,

---

*General V. G. Samoilenko wrote: "The external function of these armies of countries of socialist orientation is firstly to defend independence and national sovereignty of their countries from imperialist encroachment; secondly to *render possible military support and help to other peoples*, struggling for their political independence" ("Social Essence of Modern Wars and Armies"; mimeo, 1978, p. 15; emphasis added).

recognizing the MPLA government and sending most of their sophisticated weapons and military advisors only after the official date of independence, 11 November 1975. The large-scale Soviet airlift of Cuban soldiers followed the invasion of Angola by South African troops, which swung African support to the MPLA.[5] Richard E. Bissell is probably correct in suggesting that the Soviet decision to intervene depended on an assumption that the United States would not respond[6]—an assumption which was soon confirmed by the U.S. Congress. It probably also depended on pressure to intervene from Castro, the long-standing political-military ally of the MPLA via the Cuban establishment at Brazzaville.*

In any case, Brezhnev had a victory in his pocket for the February 1976 Twenty-Fifth Party Congress (compare Poland, Afghanistan, and other unresolved problems confronting the Twenty-Sixth Congress of February 1981) which could justify to Soviet skeptics the utility of continued military buildup and detente, now demonstrated not to inhibit gains of socialism in Africa as well as in Indochina.

Once victoriously entrenched in Angola, Soviet activity developed a rapid momentum on three fronts: a weaving together of presence and influence in Angola and Mozambique to include the East Germans and Cubans; an accelerated recruitment of Zimbabwean, Namibian, and South African liberation forces to Soviet and allied weapons and training; and an evolution and broadcast of a policy framework to match the activity—with references to the upsurge of liberation, the "natural ally," and a new stage of development called socialist orientation. The theme of the natural ally was introduced before the summer 1976 summit of the nonaligned nations at Colombo but following the intervention in Angola. Throughout 1976 the Soviet press made Angola a centerpiece of its attention, emphasizing the Soviet role as natural ally and denigrating China, the United States, and South Africa as equally natural enemies whose efforts (mercenaries, invasions) to overthrow the true Angolan revolution had met defeat at the hands of principled socialist cooperation.

President Agostinho Neto of Angola came to Moscow in May 1976 and signed a declaration on friendly relations and economic aid

*The Cubans had been working with the MPLA and also the PAIGC (the anti-Portuguese guerrilla forces in Guinea-Bissau) since 1965 (see William J. Durch, "The Cuban Military in Africa and the Middle East: From Algeria to Angola," *Studies in Comparative Communism*, Summer 1978, pp. 47-49).

agreements, and he returned in October to sign the Soviet-Angolan Treaty of Friendship and Cooperation, the first of its kind with an African nation.

Socialist cooperation, according to the Soviets, was far less important than the Soviet role. An authoritative Soviet publication chose to quote Neto stating that Soviet arms were "necessary for the liberation of the Angolan people." Only secondarily, after Soviet military aid, the "necessary" part, was there mention of Cuba, which sent "at the needed time its best sons."[7] However, Neto had met with Castro at Conakry in March 1976 to discuss (among other things) the coordination of aid to liberation movements. In July and in November Neto had gone to Havana. Cubans trained the Angolan army in the use of Soviet equipment, which the Cubans had used to roll back the forces of the União Nacional para a Independência Total de Angola (UNITA) in January and February. In summer 1976 Cuba sent the first wave of medical technicians, who were followed in 1977 by a wave of teachers for the Angolan literacy campaign. (Castro initially emphasized literacy and health in the Cuban revolution.) International experts were recruited to guide the show trial of mercenaries of June 1976.[8] The first independence congress of the MPLA in December 1977 formally adopted Marxism-Leninism as its ideology in the Soviet format of a Central Committee document which declared, 'There is capitalism and there is socialism . . . there is no other way."[9]

Angola provided a dramatic illustration of the need for internal security, party-building, centralization, and discipline, which became crucial to the socialist orientation concept. A first challenge came from the left—from one group calling itself the Organization of Angolan Communists and another called Active Revolt (associated with the first president of the MPLA, Mario de Andrade). Nito Alves, then Interior Minister of Internal Administrations, returned straight from the Twenty-Fifth Congress in Moscow to purge the left, which had been agitating against centralized discipline over the workers in factories.* It seems likely that Soviet counsel urged the purge. A 1978 manifesto of African communists, a key document probably produced under Soviet sponsorship, makes clear that the duty of all

---

*The Soviets often apply—or misapply—lessons of their own history. In 1921 Lenin put down a workers' rights movement led by left communists in somewhat similar circumstances.

African communists is to cooperate with and work through "the national-democratic revolution."* Left factionalism is out. Purges of the independent left in Ethiopia in 1977 following those in Angola point to Soviet policy against independent communist factions in the interest of centralization and stability.

Alves was imprisoned in early 1977. In May his followers staged a coup which failed. The episode fully established the authority of the pro-Soviet MPLA faction. By late 1977, when Marxism-Leninism was officially adopted by the MPLA-Party of Labor (the title Party of Labor was added at the independence congress), Cubans, East Germans, and a small number of Soviets were training party cadres, the police, and the army.

Mozambican President Samora Machel's first visit to Moscow came in May 1976 and resulted in Soviet-Mozambican agreements on air service, fishing, public health, and education. That year the Soviet Union replaced China as Mozambique's major donor of foreign aid.† Socialist orientation was confirmed at the Third Congress of FRELIMO on 3-7 February 1977, which adopted Marxism-Leninism, constituted FRELIMO as a "vanguard party," and affirmed the socialist countries as the "natural ally" and the "liberated zone of our planet." In March 1977 Castro visited the country; as a result, Cuban medical, educational, and agricultural technicians were sent to Mozambique, and about 1,200 Mozambicans went to study in Cuba. Machel visited Cuba in October 1977 and signed a twenty-year Cuban-Mozambican treaty, which included bilateral military cooperation.

In late March 1977, just after Castro's visit, Soviet President Nikolai Podgorny arrived in Maputo on a tour of Mozambique,

---

*The manifesto, clearly intended to guide the next stage of African revolution, in which communist groups are to emerge within "national-democratic" parties, is called "For the Freedom, Independence, National Revival, and Social Progress of the Peoples of Tropical and Southern Africa." Published in New Delhi by the Communist Party of India in September 1978, its authors are "A number of communist and workers' parties of Africa [who] met and elaborated the following document," which "provides a basis for discussion among all parties, militants, patriots, progressives, revolutionaries, and Marxists in Africa" (p. 3). Phrases in the document (e.g., "life itself demonstrates," "the capitalist-oriented states") point to a Russian-language origin or translation. (Cited hereafter as "Africa Manifesto.")

†In 1970-76 Chinese aid to FRELIMO amounted to $59 million; Soviet aid was $3 million (*Africa Contemporary Record 1977-78*, p. C148).

Zambia, and Tanzania—nations previously closely aligned with China and currently cooperating to unite the Zimbabwe liberation movements under the auspices of the Organization of African Unity (OAU) liberation committee based at Dar es Salaam. During Podgorny's visit Mozambique signed its Treaty of Friendship and Cooperation, which (like all the others) provided for mutual consultations and military aid in the face of threats. Soviet military aid began to arrive that same year, including some outmoded T-34 tanks, MiG 17's, and 122-mm rockets. However, the Soviets did not see fit to provide Mozambique with the sophisticated air defense which would be necessary to deter the intermittent and destructive raids by the Rhodesian air force.

Soviet policies in Angola and Mozambique were not parallel. On the one hand, Angola was an example of everything the Soviets wished to see. On the other, in the Soviet view FRELIMO's Chinese, Zambian, and Tanzanian connections, its home-grown Marxism with a Maoist peasant-participatory tilt,[10] its emphasis on the OAU and the United Nations (Machel urged and won passage of a General Assembly resolution calling for international aid against Rhodesian attacks in June 1977), and its continued economic ties with Portugal, Western Europe, and South Africa made Mozambique less aligned and less reliable.

Both Neto and Machel professed nonalignment as the basis of their foreign policy. From the Soviet viewpoint, their stance was useful. The Soviet version of nonalignment, first promoted in the early 1960s through such organizations as the Afro-Asian People's Solidarity Organization, is to equate "nonaligned" with "anti-imperialist." Only anti-Western nations can be truly nonaligned, and the Soviet Union is thus their natural ally. Castro, the most anti-American, is the most steadfastly nonaligned of all. The verbal logic may be twisted, but the political logic is impeccable. The Soviets probably encouraged Neto and Machel to declare nonalignment while adopting socialist orientation, and thus lend their prestige in support of Cuban claims to nonalignment as well.

The second stage of Soviet and allied activity in southern Africa, beginning in 1977, was to arm and train effective forces for the liberation of Namibia, Zimbabwe, and (eventually) South Africa. This effort depended on Angolan, Mozambican, and Zambian cooperation. In March 1977, during a meeting of the Frontline States at Luanda, Castro met with liberation leaders Sam Nujoma of SWAPO,

Joshua Nkomo of the Zimbabwe African People's Union (ZAPU), and Oliver Tambo of the ANC. Cuban training of their forces, with some Soviet and East German participation, accelerated. Cubans staffed the Voice of Namibia liberation radio from Angola. Nujoma, Nkomo, and Tambo visited East Germany and the Soviet Union that year, and articles by all three appeared in *World Marxist Review* in February 1978. East Germans began actively to train security police in Angola (with the Cubans) and Mozambique and to work with SWAPO in Angola. In addition, they managed the Voice of Zimbabwe from Maputo and began to print ANC and ZAPU propaganda in East Berlin.[11]* Soviet arms shipments to the liberation movements matched the level of recruitment and training. By 1978 the Zimbabwe People's Revolutionary Army (ZIPRA), the military arm of ZAPU, fielded some 8,000-10,000 men based in Zambia but trained in Angola, while SWAPO fielded some 3,500 in its Angolan camps and an estimated 2,000 inside Namibia.[12]

To coordinate much of this activity Vasili Solodovnikov, Director of the African Institute of the Soviet Academy of Sciences, became Ambassador to Zambia in 1976.† Since then the Soviet mission in Lusaka has grown to be the largest in black Africa. Lusaka became a crucial spot as the political-military headquarters of ZAPU and as a center of Soviet activity outside the Soviet-linked countries, thus legitimizing Soviet cooperation with *all* the Frontline States and the OAU.

Part of Solodovnikov's crucial task was to try to wean Zambia, Tanzania, FRELIMO, and the Zimbabwe African National Union (ZANU), led by Robert Mugabe, away from their connections with China. The Angola events were a windfall for Soviet policy in that task: Chinese aid to the Frente Nacional de Libertação de Angola

---

*Like the Cubans, the East Germans have been active in Africa since the mid-1960s. Their involvement built up in 1977-78, culminating in Chairman Erich Honecker's visit to Angola, Mozambique, and Zambia in February 1979. *Sechaba, African Communist* (the South African Communist Party journal), and ZAPU's *Zimbabwe Review* have been printed in East Berlin since 1969. Hard information on East German military involvements through Angola with SWAPO is hard to come by.

†Solodovnikov is still there, in the Soviet pattern of establishing able ambassadors for long tenure—witness Anatoly Dobrynin as Dean of the Diplomatic Corps in Washington.

(FNLA) and to UNITA (via Zambia) could be associated with the FNLA Western mercenaries—the "whores of war," reviled in Africa since the time of Moise Tshombe's Katanga secession of 1960-62—and with South Africa, which aided UNITA. Soviet media lost no opportunity to denounce "the Maoists" as handmaidens of the most degenerate sort of imperialist aggression—and ineffective ones to boot.[13] Podgorny's 1977 trip legitimized Soviet cooperation with the formerly pro-Chinese Frontline States, and as socialist orientation supplanted Chinese with Soviet and allied aid in Mozambique, Zambia began to accept the Soviet-Cuban-ZAPU connection. Although it was clear that Soviet arms and propaganda mainly supported the ZAPU wing of the Patriotic Front,* the Soviets did send limited military aid, and Cuba and East Germany did provide some training, to ZANU in Mozambique. Here too the Soviets demonstrated cooperation with OAU policy supporting the ZAPU-ZANU coalition and cooperation with Tanzania and Mozambique, which tilted toward Mugabe and ZANU.

A third stage of Soviet activity, toward the eventual establishment of a South African communist regime, began to appear in 1978 along with the increase in military training in Angola for ANC guerrillas. On Radio Moscow in May 1978 Secretary-General Alfred Nzo of the South African Communist Party (SACP) made the now well-known statement that the South African people "knew that the USSR was their natural ally."[14] The unspecified "African communists" who wrote the 1978 "Africa Manifesto" were probably led by the SACP, and the manifesto outlined a specific strategy for South Africa (see pp. 224-28 below). At the present stage all African communists are to cooperate within "national-democratic" organizations, but eventually—and not only in South Africa—they are to emerge from within the ruling party as the true vanguard of their countries.

In December 1978 a meeting of world communist and allied parties at Sofia, Bulgaria, was called to examine "existing socialism" and take stock of the world communist movement and its future development. Present were leaders of FRELIMO (Sergio Vieira, head of FRELIMO's central committee secretariat for defense and security), ZAPU (Nkomo), SWAPO (Nujoma), and the ANC (Tambo). All

*On the creation of the Patriotic Front, see p. 231 below.

made speeches following the conference. All, presumably, were part of "existing socialism" as far as the Soviet Union was concerned.[15]

Except for Cuban expeditionary forces in Angola, the natural alliance was quite cheap. Through 1978 the Soviet Union had transferred about $410 million in arms to Angola, $180 million to Mozambique, and $40 million to Zambia, plus the costs of arming and training the fewer than 20,000 SWAPO, ZAPU, ZANU, and ANC guerrillas with surplus and relatively simple equipment; at most the cost equalled that of one of the Soviet army's 170 divisions.[16] The cost of Soviet economic aid was also low. In Angola in 1976 East Germany gave $10 million for relief while the Soviets paid only for technicians. How much the Soviet Union contributed for the Cuban soldiers, advisors, and medical and education teams is not known, although Castro affirmed in December 1979 that the Cuban budget would be short of foreign exchange and dependent on Soviet oil, and that Cuban workers would go to Siberia to cut lumber to recompense the Soviet Union for its generosity.[17]

By the end of 1978 Soviet objectives for southern Africa seemed to be

(1) A deepening of socialist orientation in Angola and Mozambique which would eventually make the Socialist Community presence and influence permanent while avoiding any commitments to those countries;

(2) Promotion of the liberation war against Rhodesia using Angola, Zambia, and Mozambique as staging grounds and sanctuaries and gradually drawing Zambia into cooperation with the Soviet-aided military effort; encouraging dependence of the Patriotic Front on Soviet and allied aid; alienating the Patriotic Front and the Frontline States from Western initiatives toward compromise; eventually establishing socialist orientation in liberated Zimbabwe;

(3) Promotion of the liberation war in Namibia which would fully commit SWAPO to armed struggle; discrediting of the Western "contact group" (Canada, France, United Kingdom, United States, and West Germany) mediating between SWAPO and South Africa through the United Nations and the Frontline States as closet supporters of South Africa; ultimate liberation

of Namibia ending all South African support through Namibia for UNITA;

(4) The establishment, link by link, of a bloc of southern African frontline states of socialist orientation dependent on Soviet arms and Socialist Community military, political, and technical cadres, confronting the "bastion" of South Africa. The meaning of "Frontline States" would change; they would shift toward the "natural alliance" and away from the influence of fuzzy-headed populists like Julius Nyerere of Tanzania or Kenneth Kaunda of Zambia, who maintain untenable concepts of "African socialism" and who consort with the Chinese;*

(5) The gradual development of a strong united front for armed struggle in and against South Africa, including communists within the ANC. Eventually protracted struggle would polarize South Africa between the regime and a united opposition led by the SACP-ANC (Soviet sources put the SACP first). Ultimately a "people's democracy" would emerge which would become the political and economic center for the less developed surrounding countries of socialist orientation.

All these objectives involve the encouragement of polarization. The more communist the liberation movements and the Frontline States become, the more the West is expected to oppose them. The more this occurs, the less likely is it that settlements will be negotiated, and the stronger will grow local dependence on Soviet arms. The more pro-Soviet the South African united front, the more the Frontline States will be influenced to accept Soviet patronage, and the more the West will be pressured to support South Africa. The policy was (is) in fact simple: do whatever is useful and possible to induce the West into alliance with Rhodesia and South Africa as a complement to direct Soviet participation as the natural ally of liberation.

These were (are) objectives, not expectations, however. Soviet policymakers have probably never been overly optimistic about their

---

*The "Africa Manifesto" denounces "African socialism" as a deviation (p. 22). In Soviet perspective Nyerere, Kaunda, and others like them are populists similar to the Russian *narodniks*, whose peasant socialism had to be replaced by "scientific socialism." Nyerere's concept of *ujamaa* is actually quite similar to the ideas of the narodniks, who wished to build socialism through the traditional peasant communes of Russia.

prospects. Results depend on cooperation of the liberation movements and the Frontline States, and also on the United States, Western Europe, and South Africa, which must play their proper (hostile) roles.

SOVIET DIFFICULTIES SINCE 1978

On a world scale evidence of mounting Soviet difficulty since about 1978 is now clear. In addition to a continuing campaign against UNITA, Soviet-supplied allies are bogged down in counterinsurgency warfare in Kampuchea, Eritrea, and the Ogaden. The Soviet army has been using helicopter gunships, the burning of crops, and forced depopulation to subdue the *mujahiddin* (Islamic rebels) of Afghanistan. Western Europe is increasingly uneasy, China remains implacable, and the unpredictable Americans are once again on the anti-Soviet warpath. Soviet consumers are hungry for goods—or just plain hungry—in a run-down economy. Iran had the wrong revolution. Polish workers are doing just what Karl Marx said they should—organizing to confront a repressive state following a period of rapid industrialization and social change. That the Solidarity movement is far more truly socialist than the communist establishment, makes it doubly dangerous to Soviet interests.

In southern Africa skepticism of Soviet intentions, Soviet failure to provide resources, and the natural pull toward exclusive cooperation among Africans have eroded Soviet influence and continue to do so.* The Zimbabwe settlement of 1979 and the emergence of the Mugabe government in 1980 were a serious blow to Soviet global policy and a disaster to its policy in southern Africa. The settlement demonstrated almost everything the Soviets had hoped to prevent:

---

*To describe the tendency toward cooperation among Africans to the exclusion of outsiders as "natural" is simply to argue that experience of shared nationalist struggle, long-standing exchange of pan-Africanist ideas, and institutionalized cooperation through the OAU and other mechanisms including Frontline States consultations have made it very difficult for any outside power to polarize African regimes against each other as part of the East-West struggle. Probably the most basic underlying rule of African interstate relations is that in the long run disputes among Africans are better settled within the African family. Outsiders may be used, but they are not to dominate.

liberation under Western auspices in cooperation with the Frontline States; an orderly transfer of power via free elections; the persistence of a Chinese connection in southern Africa; rejection of socialist orientation in favor of Western-connected development and "African socialism"; and—above all—the fact that the Soviet Union could be used as the armorer of liberation then tossed aside as irrelevant. Furthermore, the events in Zimbabwe were not an isolated case. None of the Soviet policies in the region—the consolidation of socialist orientation in Angola and Mozambique, the liberation of Namibia by armed struggle, and the beginning of a protracted struggle for South Africa—have been going very well.

A TARNISHED IMAGE

African perceptions of Soviet motives began to shift soon after the Angola windfall. Unlike Soviet intervention in Angola, their intervention in Ethiopia in 1977 was a clear case of self-interest—a grabbing of political and strategic advantage in a situation of revolution, civil war, and interstate war among Africans. Most serious was the betrayal of former friends and allies—the Somalis and the Eritreans, including the Marxist Eritrean People's Liberation Front (EPLF), whose forces had been trained by Cuba as the Somalis had been trained and supplied by the Soviets. Castro's personal mediation failed to end the fighting in the Horn of Africa, and Cuban prestige suffered as well. Under Idi Amin, Uganda had been armed (via Libya) with Soviet weapons (an estimated $80 million in arms from the Soviets and $10 million from Czechoslovakia, of a total $95 million)[18] and had off and on welcomed Soviet friendship, but Amin's cruelties did not help the Soviet image. Neither did Francisco Macias Nguema, the tyrant of Equatorial Guinea, who had also received Soviet weapons. Soviet haughtiness in Addis Ababa (the Cubans were different) as the Dergue went about liquidating its enemies was watched by the African delegations at OAU headquarters and at the Economic Commission for Africa. None of this Soviet behavior looked much like that of a natural ally and disinterested friend of liberation, and much of it looked like the sort of great power imperialism with which Africans are far too familiar. In 1977 Guinea denied Conakry as a base for Soviet military flights into the Atlantic. The Vietnamese invasion of Kampuchea and the Soviet invasion of Afghanistan encouraged further distrust if not outright hostility.

SCARCE RESOURCES

In the late 1970s the economic squeeze on the Soviet Union intensified for reasons including Soviet military costs and the continuing necessity of large subsidies to Cuba, Vietnam, and (recently) Afghanistan and Poland. Most Soviet and East European credits now require repayment in hard currency. The CMEA is supposed to coordinate aid to socialist orientation countries, but so far the Soviets have had little success in persuading the East Europeans (apart from the East Germans) to contribute. Bulgaria has sent a few technicians to Mozambique. Angola became an observer in the CMEA in 1978 and Mozambique in 1979. In 1980 the Soviet journal *Foreign Trade* described CMEA policy toward aid to socialist orientation countries as follows:

> Interested CMEA countries are rendering large-scale assistance to rehabilitate and develop the national economies of Laos, Angola, Mozambique, Ethiopia, Democratic Yemen, Kampuchea, and Afghanistan. Development of cooperation with these countries rests on a *realistic basis* and is of *reciprocal interest* for those countries and the CMEA countries.[19]

In other words, not all CMEA countries are interested, and few handouts ("realistic basis") and hard-nosed bargains ("reciprocal interest") are the socialist economic style. In 1979 the only major Soviet-East European projects in Africa were the development of Guinean bauxite; a Nigerian oil refinery, pipeline, and metallurgical complex; an Ethiopian oil refinery; and a Mali cement factory.[20] A large project to develop Moroccan phospates (and ship them to Eastern Europe) began in 1979 and proceeds in spite of Morocco's war in the Western Sahara or its "puppet" role in the "imperialist aggression" in Zaire's Shaba Province. In Angola and Mozambique the only resource or industrial projects announced were for coal mining in Mozambique and phospates in Angola.

In recent years Soviet trade with southern Africa has been unimportant: in 1978 and 1979 it was only 0.12 percent of total

Soviet trade (see Table 1). Note that exports to Angola were more than twice those to Mozambique; Angola has hard currency earnings with which to pay.

MAINTAINING CONNECTIONS

The policy of socialist orientation is an attempt to make Soviet and Socialist Community connections permanent. Like earlier attempts to extend the Socialist Community to the Third World, it has fundamental problems which are present in Angola and particularly in Mozambique. First, the Socialist Community is poor and cannot finance effective development or provide needed technology as well as "imperialism" can. To the extent that economic needs supersede military and security needs, the natural course is to push the East out and get the West back in. Second, local conflict or cooperation with neighbors takes precedence over opposition to the West, and international alignments thus become a flexible response to local conditions. The particular southern African variant of this problem is the strong pressure for cooperation among the Frontline States, and between them and the rest of Africa. Any Soviet impulses to divide Africans of socialist orientation from others, be they Tanzanian *narodniks* or Zairean stooges of neocolonialism, fall afoul of what George Padmore called in 1956 pan-Africanism, which he set as an alternative to communism.[21] Economic pressures and African solidarity impel exactly that "third way" which Soviet policy so explicitly rejects.* Finally, the "organizational support" in party, police, and military training which Brezhnev promises creates the very stability which makes outside protection and influence unnecessary. If secure, even a thoroughly communist Angolan or Mozambican regime may dispense with the Soviet connection. After all, Tito and Mao were communists too.

---

*It is worth noting that Soviet writings take pains to mention Nigeria favorably in deference to Nigeria's key role in the OAU and its active policy in support of liberation—for example, it has consistently favored the MPLA in Angola. However, Nigeria in ideological terms remains a capitalist bourgeois democracy.

Table 1

SOVIET TRADE WITH SOUTHERN AFRICA, 1975-79

(*Million rubles*)

Country[a]	1975		1976		1977		1978		1979	
	Imports	Exports	Imports	Exports	Imports	Exports	Imports	Exports	Imports	Exports
Angola	—	—	14.4	5.3	10.2	69.2	9.6	47.8	11.8	52.4
Mozambique	—	—	—	—	—	5.9	0.8	17.4	0.9	20.3
Zambia	—	7.5	—	2.3	0.4	1.4	0.8	0.6	4.4	1.9
Tanzania	5.9	2.6	2.8	1.2	3.5	1.2	3.4	6.2	4.4	3.4

Source: USSR Ministry of Foreign Trade, *Foreign Trade of the USSR in 1977, 1978, 1979, 1980: Statistical Summary* (Moscow, 1978-81; in Russian).

[a]Botswana, Rhodesia/Zimbabwe and South Africa are not listed, and presumably there was no trade with them. The Soviet Union was accused of buying Rhodesian chrome through Mozambique in 1979; the charges were denounced but not totally repudiated.

MOZAMBIQUE

Since February 1977 the Leninist rhetoric and effusive praise of the Soviet Union offered by Samora Machel and other Mozambican leaders has been quite remarkable. They have endorsed such Soviet ventures as the invasion of Afghanistan and Soviet proposals for an Indian Ocean "zone of peace." Denunciations of imperialism come easily to leaders who for years fought the Portuguese army in the bush. Mozambican rhetoric has confused people who equate such rhetoric with Soviet domination.

Mozambique's real needs and present struggle are economic. Speaking in Moscow in 1979, FRELIMO security chief Sergio Vieira followed the usual attacks on imperialism with a plea for development aid that was almost a warning to his Soviet hosts: "Economics is the key to a revolution's viability. We would not like to be a model of 'poor socialism.' This is a particularly sensitive question in Africa."[22]

Mozambique remains an almost destitute country which has not yet recovered from its liberation war against the Portuguese or from devastation inflicted by some 350 Rhodesian attacks against the sanctuaries of Mugabe's Zimbabwe African National Liberation Army (ZANLA) guerrillas. Its main export is cashew nuts. Its best friends are Tanzania and the ZANU government of Zimbabwe. Mozambique is threatened by the South African military and remains dependent on South African cash. In these circumstances it is little wonder that Soviet writings pay Mozambique little notice. Mozambique represents problems of socialist orientation which Soviet policy finds hard to solve.

In November 1980 Machel visited the Soviet Union, bringing "warmest greetings from the Mozambican communists." An agreement was signed between FRELIMO and the CPSU "to increase cooperation in preparing party cadres" and "to develop cooperation between party press agencies and other mass media." Machel said his talks with Brezhnev were "a guarantee that socialism will be consolidated." In other words, lots of politics. However, Machel left little doubt about the present nature of the struggle in Mozambique:

The armed struggle is the highest form of our culture. And we are winning ideologically. Our current enemy is making its appearance. Our current enemy is underdevelopment. We are fighting against poverty, against misery. And when we say that we mean: hunger in our country, organized by the exploiters, by the colonialists, the racists. That is what we are fighting against. Against privation, against lack of shelter. We are fighting for building schools, for building a hospital. In short, the happiness and well-being of each citizen.[23]

Despite the economic emphasis, Machel's visit did not produce any major Soviet development aid—only agreements for "continued cooperation" in fishing and agriculture and "broadened" Soviet assistance in vocational training. East Germany has sent the largest number of Socialist Community technicians, working in the Moatize coal fields and throughout the country. Romania has sent oil technicians. Although these technicians are essential to Mozambique, they do not generate funds for imports, including food imports. Proletarian internationalism did not, or could not, extend to feeding the hungry during the serious famine of 1977.

Mozambique's major sources of hard currency—80 percent of it in 1977—are railroad and port user fees and payments for Mozambican contract workers from South Africa.[24] South Africa is the largest single source of imports, although Europe as a whole provides about half of Mozambique's trade.[25] The Soviet share of imports is well under 10 percent of the total. Lines of credit include $100 million from Brazil, $130 million from Britain, and $25 million from France. The United States has sent about $50 million in humanitarian aid since 1975.[26] In November 1980 the Southern African Development Coordination Conference, held at Maputo, was expected to approve some $800 million for Mozambican transport and communications development.

Internal economic policy seems to resemble Tanzania's (and potentially Zimbabwe's). The *aldeias comunais*, or communal villages, staffed by FRELIMO cadres, clearly owe their inspiration to Mao and to Nyerere's *ujamaa vijijini*. Most remain woefully impoverished. In summer 1980, as part of a general policy of relaxation after the end of the Zimbabwe war, Machel promoted the revival of small capitalist businesses and invited the Portuguese back to manage them.

Mozambique's African policy does not always follow Soviet guidelines, rhetoric aside. In spite of Mozambique's strict adherence to the Moscow line on Kampuchea and Afghanistan, it continues to maintain connections with China. While China was not invited to the FRELIMO congress in February 1977, Machel visited Peking in May 1978. Chinese Vice-President Li Xiennien returned the visit in January 1979, went on to Lusaka, and found the time to consult with ZANU, the ANC, and SWAPO. Establishment of the ZANU government of Zimbabwe—Mugabe has maintained cordial relations with China throughout—restores the possibility of an active Chinese policy including Mozambique, Tanzania, Zambia, and Zimbabwe. So far Mozambique has apparently not ruled this out.*

Mozambican-Soviet differences result in part from the Soviet failure to provide Mozambique with an effective defense against the disruptive Rhodesian attacks of 1977-79, in spite of the Friendship and Cooperation Treaty mandating joint consultation in response to threats. (Mozambique also has friendship treaties with Angola, Cuba, Bulgaria, and North Korea.)

As a Frontline State, Mozambique has consistently promoted use of the United Nations toward a Namibian settlement. Relations with Tanzania remain very close. (Tanzania provided sanctuary, training bases, and a conduit for Chinese arms during Mozambique's liberation war.) Mozambique stresses its participation in the OAU as well as, or perhaps balanced with, socialist solidarity. Above all, Mozambique welcomed the Lancaster House settlement for Zimbabwe because it ended war on its soil, and it has established close relations with the Mugabe government, which through 1980 had no formal relations with the Soviet Union at all.†

The natural ally of liberation may soon have another chance to provide defense for Mozambique. In 1978 Maputo became a site for

*In southern Africa Chinese and United States policies have been parallel since 1975. The Chinese have since then largely confined themselves to diplomatic contacts. Chinese and American policies may diverge, however, and China has kept open its options for an independent and more significant role.

†The November 1980 communique signed by Machel during his Moscow visit did mention Zimbabwe. It seemed to include a Soviet pledge not to fish in potentially troubled waters on behalf of Nkomo and ZAPU. The two sides "expressed their satisfaction over the gaining of independence by Zimbabwe . . . and declared their consistent support for the freely and democratically elected government of Zimbabwe and its people. The sides expressed the confidence that the people of Zimbabwe will be able to maintain its unity" (TASS [Moscow], 23 November 1980; in English).

ANC activities and for operations into South Africa. In February 1981 the South African Defense Force (SADF) raided ANC camps there. South Africa also can cut off much of Mozambique's foreign exchange if it chooses to expel Mozambican workers and forego rail and port traffic through Maputo. Certainly the Frontline States—now including Zimbabwe—will have to coordinate a strategy toward the ANC and South Africa taking into consideration both South African military retaliation (for which the February 1981 raid was probably a signal) and the flow of cash, goods, and people between them and South Africa. The cautious strategy would be to concentrate on a Namibian settlement rather than on South Africa, thus allowing Zimbabwe and Mozambique a respite from conflict. But if Mozambique suffers further attacks, the potential Soviet and East German role as protector will again become important. Since the first battles between Cuban and South African soldiers in central Angola in late 1975, the Soviets, Cubans, and East Germans have shown no inclination whatsoever to directly confront Rhodesian or South African forces. Whether lack of effective defense will allow South Africa to "Finlandize" Mozambique remains to be seen.

ANGOLA

The death of President Agostinho Neto in Moscow in September 1979 did not change the basic lines of Angola's foreign policy. Neto's successor, Eduardo dos Santos, continued to emphasize Angola's nonalignment and desire for good relations with the West—particularly an opening of diplomatic relations with the United States. At the same time, like Neto, dos Santos firmly maintained that Cuban troops would remain as long as they were needed—presumably until the UNITA insurgency ended and until South African raids on SWAPO camps inside Angola ceased.

The Soviet presence in Angola is not large: perhaps two to three hundred military, political, and technical advisors. Cuba maintains approximately 20,000 troops and a large contingent of educational and health technicians.* The Cubans have left the fighting in central and southern Angola against UNITA bands to the Angolan army

*In January 1980 Jonas Savimbi, the leader of UNITA, claimed 34,000 Cubans and 5,000 military men "from Warsaw Pact countries" were in Angola (*New York Times*, 19 January 1980, p. 5).

FAPLA; the purpose of their troops is to prevent significant UNITA gains in the event of FAPLA defeats and to provide defense against a South African invasion to overturn the regime or to detach the Ovimbundu areas of central and southern Angola for a separate UNITA-governed state. Cuban airplanes and artillery provide cover and support. In 1979 Jonas Savimbi claimed that 3,000 Cubans had been killed by his forces but this figure cannot be confirmed.[27]

In 1979-80, if anything, the war in Angola intensified, with the involvement of SWAPO and South Africa. South African planes and commandos conducted raids, some apparently coordinated with UNITA. On a visit to New York in November 1979, Savimbi pledged to continue (or intensify) the war. In the following month dos Santos went to Moscow and consulted with Brezhnev, Defense Minister Dmitri Ustinov, Foreign Minister Andrei Gromyko, and Central Committee Secretary Boris Ponomarev, who holds responsibility for the socialist orientation countries. A major Soviet military mission to Angola followed. After the mission, Soviet-Angolan agreements were signed, including one on publishing (with propaganda implications) and one permitting the Soviet Academy of Sciences to maintain "a station for photographic and laser observation of satellites" in Angola which may well have military purposes.[28]

The fighting in southern Angola and the Cuban, Soviet and South African involvement could be ended by a Namibian settlement, which would get SWAPO out of southern Angola, end the South African raids, and cut UNITA off from its supplies and sanctuaries. According to a July 1980 statement of the Angolan Foreign Minister, Namibian independence would impel Angola to reduce the number of Cubans in the country.[29] UNITA, which has hindered traffic on the Benguela railway from Zambia and Zaire and which can disrupt if not dislodge MPLA control of the Ovimbundu areas, would clearly lose from a Namibian settlement, as would the Soviet Union, whose military aid would be less necessary.

Soviet relations with Angola also depend on Angola's economic ties to the West. Since independence, oil has been Angola's only significant export and source of revenue, and most Angolan oil goes to the United States.* Gulf Oil, which was for many years accused of

*IMF statistics for 1979 show the first three recipients of Angolan exports as the Bahamas ($701 million), the United States ($316 million), and the Virgin

subsidizing the Portuguese through royalty payments from Angola's Cabinda oilfields, now finances the Angolan revolution by its cooperation with the MPLA government, which it considers "a reliable partner." Gulf paid about $320 million to Angola in 1979 and plans to double oil production there by 1985.[30] Soviet policy welcomes the contribution, which allows Angola to pay for Soviet aid (and Cuban troops) with hard currency.

Other sectors of the Angolan economy have fared very poorly. In the central regions, where insurgency continues, hunger is widespread. Angola now imports 90 percent of its food[31] (apart from black market transactions) although it was once nearly self-sufficient; most foreign exchange goes to buy food. Coffee and diamond exports are at about one third of preindependence levels. As in other countries, such as Mozambique, the Soviet Union cannot—or will not—help.

In a December 1979 speech in Moscow, dos Santos indirectly affirmed his policy of an economic opening to the West: "The development and expansion of economic ties with a view to the solution of individual problems of national reconstruction is now a matter of vital importance to the People's Republic of Angola."[32] In early 1981 Planning Minister Roberto Antonio de Almeida stressed the lack of products for peasants to buy, the lack of transportation to the villages, and a need for foreign, Western technicians and experts particularly to clear the bottleneck in the port of Luanda. West Germans are flying Boeing jets for the Angolan airline; French experts are helping to manage state farms. Brazilians and Portuguese, who can communicate with the local population (as most Russians cannot), are most welcome. Texaco and French oil companies are negotiating new oil contracts. Angola's sources of non-weapons imports in 1979 were (in order) South Africa, Portugal, the United States, West Germany, other European countries, and Brazil.[33]

Soviet commentary has consistently emphasized a Soviet-Cuban-MPLA-SWAPO alignment versus a presumed alignment of the United States-China-South Africa-UNITA. As in other situations, confrontation at the expense of development has been the key to Soviet policy.

Islands ($126 million). In the Bahamas and the Virgin Islands oil refineries process Angolan oil for the North American market (IMF, *Direction of Trade Annual 1980*, pp. 66-67).

The Soviet press noted in November 1979 that Savimbi had been received in the United States by then National Security Advisor Zbigniew Brzezinski, as well as by Alexander Haig (then president of United Technologies Corporation). Savimbi was described as "an agent of the former Portuguese secret police who was bought by the American CIA."[34] In July 1980 the Soviet Union accused the United States of training UNITA forces in Namibia along with the South Africans. It labelled China as the chief arms supplier, along with the United States, Britain, and Portugal. The Soviets fear a coalition or compromise between MPLA and UNITA which would make them unnecessary. The Soviet effort to increase influence, which began after Neto's death, depends on a military connection, which in turn depends on the policies of the West and the United States.

The Reagan administration faces a relatively clear choice. It can work for a Namibian settlement, an internal Angolan compromise between the MPLA and UNITA, and expanded Western investment, trade, and technical assistance. This policy implies recognition of the MPLA government, which the Reagan administration might accomplish more easily than the Carter administration would have, for it is less likely to be accused of coddling Cuban and Soviet imperialism. Alternatively, it can pursue a policy of nonrecognition of the MPLA, together with the encouragement of UNITA's insurgency, through greater cooperation with South Africa or by directly providing American military training and supply. Aid to UNITA would be consistent with a general U.S. (and Chinese) policy of military rollback of Soviet influence, including aid to the Afghans, the Eritreans, and the Kampuchean guerrillas. Confrontation in Angola would increase Soviet influence, bolster the need for the Cuban presence, and alienate Zambia (which wants regular traffic over the Benguela railway) and other African states. It would also increase demands on the Soviets and Cubans for effective military protection, which is implied by the Soviet-Angolan friendship treaty and by the entire framework of socialist orientation.

NAMIBIA

Soviet policy toward Namibia has been flexible, uncommitted, and derivative from the positions of SWAPO, the Frontline States, the OAU, and the United Nations, which Soviet writers usually echo.

In an interview in February 1978 Sam Nujoma declared in *World Marxist Review* that SWAPO "has no alternative but to step up its struggle" and that "scientific socialism" would guide a liberated Namibia.[35] By then Cubans and East Germans were training the People's Liberation Army of Namibia (PLAN)—the military arm of SWAPO—in Angolan camps. PLAN presumably remains a small force with some 3,500 men in Angola and perhaps 2,000 inside Namibia under constant harassment from the South Africans, who raid the camps in Angola. Nujoma attributed the expansion of armed struggle to the liberation of Angola, but cited the help of African states, along with "socialist countries," and praised UN initiatives. He claimed that the only two forces involved in Namibia were SWAPO and the South Africans, thus giving no legitimacy to the South African-sponsored Democratic Turnhalle Alliance (DTA), which SWAPO rejects. However, he did not rule out negotiation: "We will continue to take part in serious diplomatic and political struggles. This is precisely why SWAPO has agreed to the main imperialist powers searching for a peaceful settlement in Namibia. We favor such a settlement."[36]

When the Frontline States including Angola and Mozambique arranged mediation on Namibia through the Western contact group, the Soviet Union stood aside. The American chairman of the group, Donald McHenry, met with SWAPO leaders in Luanda in July 1978 to present Western proposals for mediation. These became the Waldheim plan for elections in Namibia, with SWAPO participation, to be policed by a 7,500-man UN force. South Africa rejected the Waldheim plan, with then Defense Minister P. M. Botha citing the fear of Soviet control of SWAPO "terrorists," as he continues to do as Prime Minister.

The South African decision to hold elections in December 1978 excluding SWAPO led SWAPO Vice-President Mishake Muyongo to appeal to the Soviet Union, East Germany, and Cuba for "all-out military assistance" against "the maneuvers of the racists of Pretoria and their American patrons, directed toward the establishment in Namibia of a puppet regime."[37] East Germany responded with military training.

It is interesting to note that in spite of some obvious differences—chiefly South African military presence and the UN role in Namibia—

both the Soviets and the South Africans drew parallels between Namibia and Zimbabwe. In each case the alternatives were: (1) a "moderate" regime managed largely by whites; (2) a Western-arranged electoral transfer of power to the nationalist movement; and (3) continued armed struggle. In Namibia, the Soviets viewed the DTA as an attempt to hijack true liberation by the use of stooges, and they saw the Abel Muzorewa government of Zimbabwe the same way. The December 1978 Namibian election followed announcement of the Rhodesian internal settlement and preceded the April 1979 Zimbabwe election, which brought Muzorewa's "moderate" government to power. Ultimately in Zimbabwe the Soviet Union was unable or unwilling to prevent the second alternative, and in Namibia it has no power to do so. In Zimbabwe the transfer of power succeeded, while in Namibia it has foundered on South African intransigence.

The Soviet Union approves all SWAPO's demands concerning Namibia—particularly the incorporation of Walvis Bay into an integral Namibian state. Anatoly Gromyko and others refer to Namibia's "great strategic significance."[38]* Indeed if one were looking for a base for influence in twentieth-century Africa, Namibia would be ideal—a sparsely populated treasure house of key minerals with a fine port for naval activity.† This is what South African defense planners and some Western analysts say the Soviets are after, and the Soviets say the West wants Namibia for the same reasons.** *Pravda* and

*Anatoly Gromyko, son of the Foreign Minister, now heads the African Institute of the Soviet Academy of Sciences (the post held before 1976 by Ambassador to Zambia Solodovnikov). His *Konflikt na Iuge Afriki* (Conflict in southern Africa) (Moscow, 1979) summarizes the official Soviet view of Western imperialism as the root of conflict in southern Africa. While Gromyko's book shows major influence from Western sources, his interpretation does not contradict in any significant way that presented by Soviet leaders or in other Soviet writings.

†In 1976 the Namibian population was given as 860,000, of which 46.5 percent were Ovambo, 11.6 percent white, 8.8 percent Damara, 7.4 percent Herero, and the rest several smaller groups. A 1975 DTA plan for ethnic homelands reserved 44 percent of the land for whites and 39 percent for the Ovambo (see R. T. Libby, *Toward an Africanized U.S. Policy for Southern Africa* [Berkeley: Institute of International Studies, 1980], p. 33; Policy Papers in International Affairs, no. 11).

**Tarabrin cites Maxwell Taylor, "National Policy Too Lightly Armed," in *Grand Strategy for the 1980s*, ed. Bruce Palmer, Jr. (Washington, D.C.: American

Izvestia refer to the "robbery" and "plunder" of resources by Western corporations, including the Rio Tinto uranium mine, and *Pravda* notes a 1978 SWAPO statement that liberated Namibia might not honor uranium contracts.[39]

The Soviets consider SWAPO a "national-democratic" or "patriotic" organization, not a Marxist-Leninist vanguard. They are also sensitive to claims that SWAPO represents only the Ovambo of northern Namibia. Gromyko argues that SWAPO has extended beyond its Ovambo base and has support throughout the country. While the Soviets oppose Western efforts "to foist on SWAPO compromises equivalent to total capitulation,"[40] the Namibia question has special characteristics which restrain Soviet pressure for more armed struggle. The United Nations has jurisdiction in Namibia, and if Soviet policies were seen as scotching African-sponsored initiatives at the United Nations, it would alienate the Frontline States and the OAU. Conversely, UN resolutions may be very useful in legitimizing Soviet military aid to SWAPO and internationally discrediting any American campaign to oppose "terrorism" and liberation struggles. Isolating the Reagan administration policies as internationally illegitimate is a very important Soviet objective, and Namibia may be useful in this regard quite apart from any specific outcome of armed struggle there.

Faced with South Africa's formidable ground force (70,000 regular troops) and air power against SWAPO's Angolan camps, the Soviets have shunned any commitment to direct confrontation with the SADF. As long as the Frontline States support a linkage of SWAPO-Frontline States-United Nations-Western powers-South Africa toward a negotiated solution, the logical Soviet policy is not to push armed struggle in Namibia too hard. The East German soldiers and advisors reportedly aiding SWAPO in Angola may push harder for armed struggle, but "proletarian internationalism" allows East Germany little independence if Soviet interests are affected.*

Enterprise Institute, 1978), to show that U.S. policy is based on control of resources and that American strategy tries to pit Africans against each other while depriving them of their natural ally (E. Tarabrin, "Africa: The Liberation Struggle and the Intrigues of Imperialism," *Mirovaia Ekonomika i Mezhdunarodnaia Otnosheniia*, June 1980, p. 67).

*Namibia was, after all, originally German South-West Africa, and Soviet treatment of the West German role there is interesting as part of the long-standing

Recent *Pravda* commentary illustrates the tenor of Soviet policy:

Pretoria's racists, with the open connivance of the West and its all-round support, have denied the people of Namibia their right to independence . . . .

The West has waged such a persistent struggle to maintain control over Namibia due to its vast reserves of strategic raw materials . . . .

[South Africa's] tactics are evoking the harsh condemnation of world public opinion . . . . "A just settlement of this problem," the UN document says, "is possible only with the participation of the South-West Africa People's Organization (SWAPO) which is the only true representative of the Namibian people."[41]

Unlike "Hands off socialist Vietnam!" or the "irreversibility" of the revolution in Afghanistan, this sort of language signals a low level of commitment and a reactive policy. Gromyko describes the Namibian situation as "fluid and complex." The Soviets will maintain a low level of arms shipments, encourage the radicalization of SWAPO, and fall in behind whatever the Frontline States and Nujoma agree to try. If South Africa proceeds with a formal transfer of power to the DTA, the Soviets may seek legitimacy through the United Nations for military aid to SWAPO and armed struggle. Namibia is a small pawn in the world revolutionary process, useful particularly to harass the West given the military dominance of the SADF, which prevents any clear military victory.

Soviet campaign against West German "militarism." Soviet statements about West German activities mirror Western alarm over the East German "Afrika Corps" aiding SWAPO. Soviet writers have noted West German investments in uranium in Namibia as well as in South Africa, and also the West German firm OTRAG's concession (for rocket testing?) in Zaire: "The basic interest of the militarist circles [of West Germany] concerns the uranium deposits of southern Africa." The clear implication is that West Germans are using Namibia, South Africa, and Zaire to build nuclear weapons. Gromyko also mentions German "colonists" in Namibia, who conduct "noisy demonstrations under racist, nationalist, and anticommunist slogans." Thus in southern Africa, focused on Namibia, both East and West use the enemy Germans to revive the old fears of the second world war. (Quotation from Gromyko, *Konflikt na Iuge Afriki*, p. 182; various *Pravda* commentaries echo the theme of West German involvement.)

SOUTH AFRICA

According to the "Africa Manifesto," "There can be no detente and no coexistence with . . . racist colonialist regimes."[42] The campaign for "mass unremitting struggle" against apartheid has three complementary strategies. The first is the dissemination of propaganda and analysis which establish that the West—primarily the United States, but also Britain, France, and West Germany—is responsible for South Africa and its policies. Thus South Africa can be used as an effective instrument of Soviet-Third World "anti-imperialist" bridge-building. The second, barely begun, is the training, arming, and organizing of "patriots" to wage "armed struggle" within and against the Republic— including the building of an underground organizational base as well as acts of violence designed to provoke official repression, advertise the struggle, and polarize the population in the classical pattern of communist (or any) insurgency. The third would establish the South African Communist Party as the "vanguard" of the entire liberation struggle by promoting the African National Congress as the sole legitimate and effective liberation movement while at the same time ensuring the dominant role of the SACP within it.*

The key to understanding Soviet and SACP policies (they are the same as far as an outsider can tell) is to realize that unlike other African nations, South Africa is considered a *developed* country. Its

---

*The discussion in this section is focused on the ANC and the SACP because these are the organizations to which the Soviet Union is connected. The importance of the ANC-SACP relative to that of the Pan-Africanist Congress, the Black Consciousness movement, or other black South African organizations is outside our subject. I have found no evidence of Soviet support for or connection to any South African organization or movement other than the ANC-SACP.

In addition to the goals noted, the Soviet Union has a direct economic interest in reducing the supply of South African minerals or ultimately controlling that supply. Presently the prices received by the Soviet Union for its exports of gold, chrome, platinum, vanadium, industrial diamonds, and other minerals follow world prices. Soviet trade officials wait for world prices to be set by South Africa and other suppliers, then sell as much as necessary to meet foreign exchange targets. Higher prices help both the Soviet Union and South Africa. Economic sanctions against South Africa, or internal disruption which would cut production and hence raise world prices, would benefit the Soviet economy. (See G. Ariovich and H. F. Kenney, "The Implications for the South African Economy of Russia's Trade Policy," *International Affairs Bulletin* 4, 2 [1980]: 18-37.)

THE NATURAL ALLY: SOVIET POLICY IN SOUTHERN AFRICA

economy is part and parcel of "monopoly capital," and its white ruling class is not a dependent neocolonial "national bourgeoisie." South Africa's economy depends on a proletariat which should provide the base for communist and united front activities, including union organizing:

> The South African working class, which is increasingly concentrated at large mining, industrial, and manufacturing enterprises, is the leading force not only in the vitally important spheres of production but also in the liberation struggle. Lately it has repeatedly staged general political strikes and convincingly demonstrated its ability to head the revolutionary struggle and lead it to victorious consummation. In many rural areas the people have also taken part in various militant struggles.[43]

South Africa has a long-standing communist party, organized by white workers in 1921, participant in the Comintern since 1926, currently led by an Asian medical doctor (Yusuf Dadoo) and an African Secretary-General (Alfred Nzo), with members of all races in exile and underground in the country. South Africa has the unique system of apartheid, which the Soviets and the SACP call "colonialism of a special type," which is "fascist" as well as "racist." The antidote is anti-racist, anti-fascist, and anti-colonial—a multiracial communist movement.

In these circumstances, communist policy becomes orthodox, even traditional. Its basic elements are the united front, the proletarian base and the worker-peasant alliance, the gradual escalation of armed struggle, the rejection of spontaneous revolutionary action, the rejection of national (ethnic) deviations, and reliance on the Soviet Union and the world communist movement. The main danger over the long run is not repression by the regime. That can be useful. The main danger is the emergence of a middle class which supports the regime. (Lenin recognized tsarist minister Stolypin's attempt to create a prosperous peasant class as the one strategy which might avert revolution in Russia.) The threat in South Africa is the evolution of a black middle class in the cities and homelands—a "black bourgeoisie" of "collaborationists."[44] According to Dadoo, "The imperialists are feverishly preparing all kinds of reformist prescriptions."[45]

The major obstacle to revolution in South Africa is its initial success, not its development. (Friendly regimes will frequently come to power in less developed African countries; the problem there is keeping them in power and maintaining the Soviet connection. In South Africa the problem is taking power.) Once established, the SACP-ANC united front should have the necessary organizational capability and economic resources to quickly create (with Soviet help) a "people's democracy" which would become the leader and patron of the less developed socialist orientation countries on its periphery.*

The SACP is to work within the ANC while retaining its own party organization. This is a united front of the classical type, first developed in China in the 1920s, when the fledgling Chinese Communist Party worked within the Kuomintang. At a 1973 Morogoro (Tanzania) conference of the ANC, the SACP was given a "vanguard role" within the movement.[46] SACP leaders consider the "revolutionary democrats" of the ANC welcome allies, and "the Party has no immediate interests different from those of the ANC."[47] The key word is "immediate." Long-term interests may diverge.

The preconditions for the ANC-SACP united front are ANC acceptance of Marxism and the Soviet connection and its rejection of black racialism. "Reactionary bourgeois nationalists" such as Chief Buthelezi and his Inkhata movement are unacceptable partners. Within the united front "social-democratic reformism" must be resisted; the "Africa Manifesto," among other writings, explicitly denounces African socialism and those who espouse it. Black consciousness is particularly dangerous because it violates proletarian internationalism—in other words, it excludes white Soviets and white South Africans. Black consciousness is a national deviation of a special type, be it expressed by the Pan-Africanist Congress with its Chinese connections or by Steve Biko's Black Consciousness movement. Biko and his sympathizers may be useful martyrs, but they are all the more useful if dead or jailed.

The Soviets clearly do not expect—or want—much to happen within South Africa soon; rather they are counting on "protracted" polarization. A gradual struggle better fits strained Soviet resources and acknowledges South African military and police power. Only a

---

*South Africa's dominant position is never stated, but it must follow in any reasonably orthodox communist analysis. Vietnam in relation to Kampuchea and Laos—not to mention the Soviet Union in Eastern Europe—is a parallel case.

long process of slowly escalating violence and government repression can be expected to turn nonwhite South Africans, particularly industrial workers, toward an organized and disciplined national liberation front. And only a protracted struggle can convince the ANC to accept the organizational discipline and reliance on military training which the communists within it can provide. Liberation by spontaneous uprising would not serve Soviet purposes, any more than it did in Iran. Lenin inveighed against Russian spontaneity as likely to fail to seize power and unable to follow through to socialism.

The ANC went underground in 1961, when it was banned following the Sharpeville pass-book riots and the shooting of demonstrators by the police. (The SACP has been underground since passage of the Suppression of Communism Act of 1950.) Since then, the ANC and SACP have cooperated through the armed wing of the alliance, the Umkonto we Sizwe, whose first leader was Nelson Mandela. In what is perhaps a slip (or perhaps not), Anatoly Gromyko describes Umkonto we Sizwe as the armed wing created by the SACP.[48] Dadoo and Tambo describe it as part of the ANC. The rebellion in Soweto in 1976, a failed spontaneous uprising, began a new era: "Hundreds of young workers and students are leaving the country illegally to join the ANC and its military wing Umkonto we Sizwe in order to acquire the political and military skills with which to confront the enemy."[49]

> The initiative has inexorably passed into the hands of the people. . . . [Future success depends on] the economic, political, and moral strength and influence . . . by the socialist world and in particular by that great bastion of freedom and democracy, the Soviet Union. Without their support, national and social liberation in the conditions of unceasing imperialist aggression is merely an illusion.[50]

In 1978, amidst the high hopes following establishment of socialist orientation in Angola and Mozambique and the escalation of the war in Zimbabwe, Dadoo claimed "an effective *beginning* to the armed struggle. And there is already public evidence that units of Umkonto we Sizwe . . . have begun to act against the enemy."[51] Dadoo continues according to the classical strategy of armed revolution: "To ensure that armed activities have a firm basis in every part of the country and to give direction and leadership to mass discontent and militant actions of the people we need to strengthen our underground structures," particularly among youth who seek "political and military skills." Armed struggle must be combined with "the intensification of mass action," including strikes and protest demonstrations.[52]

The network of Soviet and East German contacts with the ANC-SACP has widened, but only to a point. East Germany finances the ANC magazine *Sechaba*. Tambo went to East Berlin in 1978 to open an ANC office, after his visit to Moscow to see Ponomarev, who heads the CPSU Secretariat's International Department. Following the 1976 Soweto uprising young men crossed into Swaziland, then to Mozambique, and were flown to Luanda for training: *Africa Contemporary Record* reports that in 1979 some 2,000 ANC guerrillas were under training in Angola, Mozambique, and Tanzania, where the ANC camp at Morogoro provided a locale for Soviet-ANC contacts before the liberation of Portuguese Africa. Guerrilla training was part of the outburst of Soviet-based activity of 1977-78 (see pp. 203-5 above), to which South Africa responded by accelerating its military buildup and by focusing policy on the Soviet threat.[53]

Testimony at the Silverton Siege Trial of November 1980 indicates the present level of armed struggle. During 1980 guerrillas attacked a bank, oil storage tanks near Johannesburg, and a rural police station, destroying three oil storage tanks but failing in the other attempts.* All of the nine guerrillas on trial had been trained in Angola and had infiltrated from Mozambique. One had been to East Germany, another to the Soviet Union. They had Soviet weapons and apparently could move without difficulty across the South African border.

> If testimony at the trial indicated the movement's effectiveness, it is relatively successful in logistics, in moving arms, explosives, and men across South Africa's borders, but chronically unable to coordinate them in any kind of operation.[54]

On 31 January 1981 South African commandos attacked an ANC camp in Mozambique, killing thirty people. The attack occurred two days after Prime Minister Botha had called for elections to take place

*The oil tanks were part of the South African oil-from-coal installation. Cutting off South Africa's energy supply by sanctions on oil imports—or by blowing up the internal substitute facilities—is seen as an effective strategy.

in April 1981 and less than a week after Secretary of State Haig's announcement at a press conference that "opposition to terrorism [now] replaces human rights" in U.S. policy. At the November 1980 trial convicted men (three were sentenced to hang) and spectators sang the ANC anthem. This is what protracted polarization is all about.

The Soviet Union is at least two steps removed from direct involvement in South African affairs: the SACP within the ANC-SACP alliance and socialist allies (East Germany, Cuba) in the training camps in Angola and Mozambique are buffers. Faced with the formidable South African military machine, the Soviet Union will avoid having its prestige backed into a corner by any direct confrontation. The Soviet goal is to link the West with South Africa's white regime, create a united front *of Africans* to oppose it, and then wait for Africans to turn toward their natural ally.

ZIMBABWE: THE FULCRUM

ZANU won fifty-seven of one hundred seats in the Zimbabwe elections of March 1980. Mugabe, the new Prime Minister, announced rapprochement with whites who wished to remain in the country, continued trade with South Africa, encouraged aid and investment from Europe and the United States—and glaringly failed to allow the Soviet Union to open an embassy in Salisbury! His first trips outside Africa were to Europe and the United States—and to China, where he was greeted by Premier Zhao Ziyang and Chairman Hua Guofeng.*

Mugabe's development concepts are an exact repudiation of socialist orientation: "Our only model for Zimbabwe is Zimbabwe. True, we have certain Marxist principles. People are frightened of the word—they see in it all the evil behind the system in Russia[!] But no, that's not what we have in mind."[55] Mugabe then mentioned "African traditions," "Shona traditions," and "Christian humanism,

---

*Mugabe's 1980 China visit followed consultations in North Korea, where economic agreements were signed. North Korea has also provided aid to Mozambique and Tanzania. This is not Soviet-sponsored activity. If anything, the North Koreans are closer to China: they denounce "dominationism" (meaning either Soviet or Chinese big-power domination) and oppose the Vietnamese invasion of Kampuchea, playing host to Prince Sihanouk.

too" as a basis for policy.[56] Among the liberation movements and the Frontline States, anti-Sovietism, Chinese influence, African socialism, and acceptance of Western and white Rhodesian economic enterprise were what the Soviets least wanted from a liberated Zimbabwe, particularly in light of its potential influence. Mugabe continued close rapport with Mozambique, opened cordial relations with Angola, and established his position in African diplomacy.

Ambassador to Zambia Solodovnikov visited Salisbury in October 1980, but he was not received by Foreign Minister Simon Muzenda, let alone the Prime Minister, although by then Mugabe had said the Soviets were free to open an embassy. (East Germany, whose advisors had helped the ZANLA guerrillas and had run Zimbabwean propaganda from Mozambique, did reach agreement on full diplomatic relations in October.)

Zimbabwe is central to the future of southern Africa, and its orientation makes a tremendous difference. Excepting South Africa, it is the most developed country of the region. It has a potential agricultural surplus useful to Zambia and to economically beleaguered Mozambique. Zambia depends on transshipment of food and goods through Zimbabwe from South Africa. A Zimbabwe of socialist orientation, accepting the presence and influence of the Soviets and Cubans and East Germans, could have created a Soviet-linked bloc across southern Africa, drawing in the Zambians as well.* Conversely, Mugabe's policies reinforce Zambia's own Christian humanism and African socialism, impel Mozambique to become more nonaligned and more inexorably drawn into a Western economic orbit, and recreate the possibility of a Tanzania-Zambia-Zimbabwe group of Frontline States receptive to renewed Chinese influence.

As is well known, Soviet military aid and attention after 1976 went largely to Nkomo and ZAPU—probably because ZAPU was weaker than ZANU, had no Chinese ties to break, and therefore

---

*Whether Nkomo and ZAPU, in power, would have accepted significant Soviet or Cuban or East German influence is another matter entirely. Nkomo did what was necessary to obtain Soviet support—for example, writing in *World Marxist Review* (sponsored by the International Department of the CPSU Secretariat) and attending international communist meetings. But how much of a Marxist Nkomo is remains at best an open question, and the pressures for accommodation with white Rhodesians and toward economic relations with South Africa would affect any Zimbabwean government.

sought Soviet help through Lusaka to even the scales. Nkomo's ZIPRA guerrillas were more isolated from their ethnic base in Matabeleland, while Mugabe's ZANLA forces in Mozambique bordered their north-eastern Shona base and had an easier source of recruits and easier infiltration routes. Soviet weapons and Cuban training built ZIPRA from less than a thousand men in 1974 to a major (in local condi-tions) force of about 12,000 by 1978. ZIPRA received tanks and some aircraft. This equipment could not match the Rhodesian air force, but it might serve well in a post-liberation power struggle.

While the Soviets armed ZIPRA and consistently favored ZAPU in their propaganda, Soviet policies toward the Zimbabwe liberation struggle were always consistent with those of the Frontline States. The Soviets accepted the ZAPU-ZANU Patriotic Front, which had been formed in Maputo in 1976 under pressure from the Frontline States and the OAU to end fratricidal factional struggles. The Soviets began supplying weapons only after the failure of the 1976 Geneva conference.*

With the Frontline States, the Soviets rejected the internal settle-ment of March 1978 which brough Muzorewa and former ZANU leader Ndabaningi Sithole to Salisbury to cooperate with Ian Smith. To the Soviets it was a Western-sponsored plot to forestall true liber-ation by phony reforms. The April 1979 elections were denounced as the farcical creation of a black puppet government just as guerrillas (mostly ZANLA) won control of the countryside. Nkomo, writing in *World Marxist Review*, predicted "war to the end."[57] War to the end was certainly the Soviet preference.[†]

---

*For details on the Geneva conference, see Chapter 1 above.

[†]Soviet commentary on the Lancaster House negotiations went from confi-dent warnings to the Patriotic Front to fantasy in its insistence on the treachery of the West. In August, when negotiations began, *Izvestia* wrote that the British plan "envisions the isolation and ultimate elimination of the Patriotic Front." In November *Pravda* denounced the "all-powerful rule of the British Governor" intended "to preserve the privileges and de facto domination of the white com-munity and the imperialist monopolies." In December, when it appeared the conference would fail, *Pravda* predicted that "the colonial war in Rhodesia will be conducted under the British flag." On 23 December, after the agreement had been signed, *Pravda* was reduced to arguing that Lord Soames would try to rig the spring elections to favor Ian Smith and Muzorewa (see *CDSP* 31, nos. 33, 46, 50, and 51).

In spite of the dogged Soviet refrain that armed struggle must continue and imperialist schemes be rejected, the Soviet Union apparently had no discernible effect on either Nkomo or Mugabe. The Patriotic Front strategy of talk-fight needed the Soviets only for the fight part. The Patriotic Front had nothing to lose by negotiation, for if dissatisfied with the results, it could count on further Soviet military aid. Any arm-twisting of the Patriotic Front leaders by the Soviets or their allies—or worse, any effort to split them—would just deepen mistrust of Soviet intentions. Lancaster House turned out a success, and the Soviets, having served their necessary role as armorer, were excluded from the settlement.

Loose talk before the settlement saw Cuban columns driving across the Zambian border into Rhodesia. In 1979 such adventurism was utterly out of the question; 1979 was a year of zero economic growth in the Soviet Union. Aid even to Cuba was being cut. Allies with Soviet support were fighting in Indochina, Ethiopia, and Angola, and intervention against the Afghan rebellion looked increasingly necessary. The South Africans had already put in an appearance in Rhodesia and threatened substantial intervention. Apart from providing arms and training, Soviet military power had reached its limits. For Zimbabwe in 1979, as today for the ANC in Mozambique and the SWAPO bases in Angola, the military question was not how far Socialist Community forces would move south, but how often and how far the South Africans would move north.

Since the establishment of the Mugabe government, some Western commentators have feared a Soviet-encouraged putsch by Nkomo's men-at-arms.[58] Certainly attempts are possible, and the Mugabe government has kept the Soviets, Cubans, and East Germans at arm's length partly for this reason. Solodovnikov acknowledged these fears in Salisbury, in October 1980, saying that the Soviet Union had stopped military aid to ZAPU after the election and wished to cooperate with the government while keeping a political relationship with ZAPU.[59] The Soviet-Mozambican communique of November 1980 pledging "consistent support" for "unity" in Zimbabwe made the commitment more official. The Soviets wish to maintain respectability according to OAU guidelines (for example, justifying their Ethiopian venture as preservation of territorial integrity). A ZAPU coup might require significant Soviet assistance against ZANU, which might receive South African or Chinese arms. ZANU's MaShonaland base is a natural area for guerrilla warfare, be the enemy the Rhodesian army or a ZAPU regime. For the Soviets, one counterinsurgency war in southern Africa (the MPLA against UNITA) is quite enough.

It would be far better for Soviet fortunes if Mugabe's development policies were to fail—particularly if they were seen to fail owing to insufficient Western aid and understanding. In conditions of economic stringency and disorganization, a perceived need for tougher control could impel a change toward socialist orientation, whoever its leader might be. At that point the Soviets would be happy to come forward as natural allies, one step at a time. Promoting or preventing such an outcome depends on Western, not Soviet, policy.

Another external variable is Zimbabwe's relations with South Africa. If Zimbabwe were faced with South African air attacks and commando raids, it would be likely to turn to the Soviets for surface-to-air missiles and other military gear, as Zambia did in early 1980. But while Soviet influence could profit from confrontation with South Africa, confrontation is not an option the Soviets control.

SOVIET PROSPECTS

In southern Africa the growth or decline of Soviet influence depends mostly on what other actors do. The Soviet and Socialist Community role is established. The Soviets will attempt to maintain socialist orientation in Angola and Mozambique; they will work in acceptable ways (diplomacy, military aid) to increase their rather minimal influence in Zambia and Zimbabwe; and they will persist as the armorer and natural ally of liberation of Namibia and South Africa, but not in ways which would draw them into a serious commitment of power or risk major loss of prestige.* Pressing problems elsewhere now demand Soviet attention and scarce resources. As the United States rearms, China develops, the Middle East bubbles, and Eastern Europe grows increasingly restless, it seems unlikely that southern Africa will increase its importance in Soviet policy—except as a highly useful way to score political points against the West. As the Reagan administration prepares its counteroffensive to Soviet

---

*Although the KGB is certainly present in southern Africa, no developments since 1976 indicate covert operations against black African governments.

activity, the likely Soviet response will be the usual one in such circumstances: hold on to existing positions and go over to the offensive in the battle for hearts and minds.

After 1978, as the Soviets and their allies expanded their influence and sent weapons into southern Africa while the Carter administration's emphasis on human rights and negotiated solutions (e.g., Zimbabwe) took hold, the Soviets became shrill and defensive. They exhorted Africans to resist anticommunism and anti-Sovietism and the "myth of the Soviet threat." Soviet writings accused "imperialists" of plotting to roll back socialist orientation in Africa. Carter administration policies worried the Soviets, but the Reagan administration may help them. If the United States sells arms to South Africa, forgets Namibia, refuses to aid or deal with Angola and Mozambique, and abandons Zimbabwe, the Soviets will make good use of it. They may convince wavering Africans that Washington's war on terrorism is but a euphemism for imperialist attack using South Africa as proxy, convince Africans and Western liberals that the United States was never serious about human rights, and convince everyone that the Americans, not the Soviets, are militarists and aggressors. The Soviet game in southern Africa is polarization and confrontation of Africans against the West. Polarization is necessary because the Soviets cannot fully dominate African governments and movements—even the Angolans. How influential and entrenched they become will depend on how much they are needed. Ultimately the African governments and movements will decide whose side, if any, they are on. If they turn against the United States and the West, the Soviets will find just enough resources for arms aid, technical assistance, and state-building to minimally fill African needs. Zambia and Zimbabwe are cases in point.

How much the Soviets and their friends are needed will depend in turn on whether the West—particularly the United States—offers alternatives. The Frontline States need prosperity and security. Zimbabwe seeks prosperity through Western trade, aid, and investment. Angola and Mozambique seek an alternative to state-managed poverty. (For Angola, Gulf Oil advocates U.S. recognition and expanded trade.) For all the Frontline States, American ability to restrain South Africa from military adventures and destabilization is a partial alternative to Soviet weapons and Cuban and East German military advisors. Furthermore, both prosperity and greater security

234

reduce the need for and incentive toward the creation of a police state, which is what the Socialist Community can teach governments to build.

Western-sponsored negotiations recognizing the legitimacy of the liberation movements ultimately provided the alternative to armed struggle in Zimbabwe, but Namibia may be a more intractable situation. For nonwhite South Africans, the alternative to going underground with the ANC and its communist "vanguard" is white evolution out of the Afrikaner laager. As Chester Crocker has argued, there are ways for the United States to promote that evolution without throwing South Africa into chaos.[60] Developing such alternatives would limit or erode the sources of Soviet influence. Rhetoric is unimportant. Angola and Mozambique would keep cordial Soviet and particularly Cuban connections, and Zambia and Zimbabwe may develop some. That is nonalignment. If prosperity and security develop, economic exchange with South Africa and the West will take command.

Leninists expect the West to dig its own grave even as it multiplies its armaments. In southern Africa the United States could easily oblige by falling into the polarization trap—that is, by adopting a policy of confrontation against the liberation movements, the socialist orientation governments, and the other Frontline States. Such a policy would reject collaboration with the Frontline States and SWAPO concerning Namibia, would forego aid to or investment in "Marxist" Angola, Mozambique, and Zimbabwe; and would establish close relations with South Africa, including arms sales in defiance of the UN arms embargo in order to encourage South Africa to police the region against communist influence. Such a policy would confirm the Soviet claim that the United States is South Africa's patron, and it would preclude any American interference with Soviet and Socialist Community influence or an influx of Soviet weapons. The South African raid into Mozambique in January 1981, just after Secretary of State Haig announced "opposition to terrorism" as the new basis for policy, was a perfect rehearsal for polarization.

South Africa may try to dominate the region even without overt support from the United States. Efforts to do this by economic and diplomatic means before 1976 failed. After the recent and ongoing South African military buildup, more coercive means of threat and intervention may now be used. A policy of intervention would not rule out, and might accompany, a relaxation of apartheid within South Africa. Any Soviet claim to protect liberation against "imperialist aggression" by military means is hollow. The Soviets will not make commitments, nor will they allow trip-wires which force escalation. The Cubans, who may be more willing to take risks, would be unable to sustain a defense without Soviet help. As Richard Bissell has pointed out, Soviet military assets are highly portable.[61] What then prevents South Africa from invading Angola, destroying SWAPO's base, and delivering ultimatums (however sugar-coated) to Salisbury and Maputo? Apart from common sense, the major restraint on South African military threats and interventions is the United States. The presence of a few Soviets, Cubans, and East Germans is more an inducement. In common sense terms, four million South African whites may have enough difficulty policing South Africa without taking on another twenty-five million Africans in surrounding countries.

The 1981 fashion in Washington is to justify aid to pro-Western dictatorships because they are better than communists. Jeane Kirkpatrick, now U.S. Ambassador to the United Nations, promoted this policy in her 1979 article "Dictatorships and Double Standards," which was reprinted in the establishment journal *South Africa International*.* (The distinction between purportedly irreversible communist

---

*Naturally the South Africans were heartened by the argument that "totalitarian client states" of the Soviet Union are ipso facto more repressive than other states. (That Mozambique or Angola are more repressive than South Africa is highly dubious.) Kirkpatrick mentioned South Africa as a country which the Carter administration was trying to reform while that administration appeased communist China, Cuba, and Vietnam; the implication was that American interests are better served by leaving friendly regimes like South Africa alone (see Kirkpatrick, "Dictatorships and Double Standards," *Commentary*, November 1979; reprinted [in part] in *South Africa International*, April 1980). Another intellectual influential with (although not in) the Reagan administration, Ray S. Cline, argued in 1980 for inclusion of South Africa in a formal "All-Oceans Alliance" led by the United States. Cline cited South Africa among those nations "friendly to and anxious to be allied with the United States, whose individual economic or security problems, over which they do not have full control, hold them back from otherwise desirable guarantees of civil liberties and representative government . . . . We should be leading them toward mutual security and political freedom in our alliance system, not coldly rejecting them as we sometimes appear to do" (Ray S. Cline, *World Power Trends and U.S. Foreign Policy for the 1980s* [Boulder, Colo.: Westview Press, 1980], p. 187; published in cooperation with the Center for Strategic and International Studies, Georgetown University, Washington D.C.).

dictatorships and more flexible "autocracies" was first made by Carl Friedrich and Zbigniew Brzezinski in 1956.[62] Notwithstanding its age and the fact that the authors were talking about Stalin's Soviet Union, it seems ironic that Brzezinski's distinction would inspire the Reagan administration.) In southern Africa—quite apart from the costs of forfeiting "a decent respect to the opinions of mankind"— American encouragement of South African racism and repression helps no one so much as the Soviets. The United States acts out the Soviet image of it, and provides the evidence for Africans to believe it. Trying to make conditions in Soweto seem benevolent by references to Soviet-supported "terrorism," or to the iron rule of some future communist dictatorship, does not convince Africans—or anyone else who matters.

A United States policy toward the Frontline States of recognition, trade, aid and investment, negotiation, and balanced emphasis on human rights and economic progress would accelerate the decline of Soviet influence. Leaving southern Africa to the National Party of South Africa would give Soviet and allied influence a tremendous boost. It would justify, enhance, and restore the Soviet role as natural ally. The effects might not be evident for some time, but the Soviets are patient. They understand American failure to pursue good policies consistently. Let the hearts and minds polarize for a time, and when history provides the opportunity, the natural ally will be very much present for the next revolutionary upsurge.

Chapter 7

SOUTHERN AFRICA: ISSUES FOR U.S. DEVELOPMENT ASSISTANCE POLICY

Raymond W. Copson

INTRODUCTION

Southern Africa is of considerable importance to the United States, but the policy instruments available to this country for use in the region at present are markedly circumscribed. Economic assistance is one instrument that has been employed in the past, and many believe it could be used with greater effect in the future.

Advocates of increased U.S. development assistance to southern Africa hold a variety of expectations with respect to the ability of aid to further U.S. policy aims, arguing that it could be used to promote a peaceful settlement of the conflicts in the region, reduce Soviet and Cuban influence, promote U.S. access to mineral resources, and foster regional economic development. However, the limited volume of U.S. assistance now available for southern Africa, the overall orientation of the aid program toward agricultural and rural development, and various legislative restrictions and administrative practices that affect the use of aid raise questions about the U.S. ability to advance its interests through development assistance.

Despite the limitations on U.S. capabilities in the region, it is striking that the particular strategic and economic factors which make southern Africa important to the United States reflect major concerns of the new Reagan administration. Prominent foreign policy analysts influential with—and in some instances members of—the

---

The views expressed in this paper are entirely those of the author and are not to be attributed in any way to the Congressional Research Service or to the Library of Congress.

administration are deeply worried by what they perceive as the possibility of a global resource war, perhaps involving minerals produced in southern Africa, and by growing Soviet and Cuban influence in the Third World, including southern Africa. They often stress the importance of maintaining the security of vital shipping lanes, such as those off southern Africa's coasts. Thus it seems certain that this region will be a significant focus for U.S. diplomacy over the next few years, just as it was during the Carter administration, and Reagan administration proposals indicate that foreign aid will be a major instrument of policy in the area.

THE ASSISTANCE PROGRAM IN SOUTHERN AFRICA

VOLUME OF ASSISTANCE

Those who take an interest in southern African development look with some envy on the large amounts of U.S. economic assistance flowing to the Middle East—a projected $785 million to Israel and $850 million to Egypt in fiscal 1981—and ask why a comparable effort could not be mounted in southern Africa. However, while southern Africa—here taken to include Tanzania and Zaire*—falls far below the Middle East on the scale of U.S. aid priorities, the U.S. assistance program to the region has undergone a major expansion as well as a substantial restructuring in recent years.

The highest levels of the U.S. government were first awakened to the importance of southern Africa by the Angolan civil war of 1975-76. The Carter administration, coming into office in January 1977, held positions on human rights and the value of good relations with Third World nations that further enhanced southern Africa's significance in American eyes. Substantial increases in U.S. economic assistance to southern Africa were posted in 1977 and 1978 (see Table 1). In 1977 Zaire was the principal recipient of U.S. aid in southern Africa, accounting for about one third of the program. Other funds went to a modest assistance program for the region as a whole, while Botswana, Lesotho, Malawi, Swaziland, and Zambia received small

*The Bureau for Africa of the Agency for International Development (AID) does not classify Tanzania or Zaire as part of southern Africa, but they have significant economic and political ties to the region and are included here.

RAYMOND W. COPSON

Table 1

U.S. ECONOMIC AID TO SOUTHERN AFRICAN REGION, FISCAL 1977-82[a]
(Millions of dollars)

Type of Aid	1977	1978	1979	1980[b]	1981[c]	1982[d]
Development assistance	$ 16.0	$ 19.1	$ 54.8	$ 43.4	$ 44.7	$ 49.8
Economic Support Fund	54.0	110.7	45.0	68.0	80.0	135.0
Public Law 480 (Food for Peace)	59.2	51.6	63.7	87.1	62.4	59.0
Peace Corps	6.3	6.7	8.5	8.3	9.3	9.4
TOTAL	135.5	188.1	172.0	206.8	196.4	253.3
Change from previous year	+75%	+39%	-9%	+20%	-5%	+29%

Sources: U.S. AID: Bureau for Program and Policy Coordination, *U.S. Overseas Loans and Grants and Assistance from International Organizations. Obligations and Loan Authorizations, July 1, 1945-September 30, 1979* (Washington, D.C.: AID, 1980); Bureau for Africa, *Congressional Presentation*, fiscal 1982 (Washington, D.C.: AID, 1981), main volume, amended version.

[a] Includes Tanzania and Zaire.

[b] Preliminary figures.

[c] Projected figures.

[d] Figures proposed by Reagan administration.

amounts of development assistance and food aid. Tanzania received somewhat larger amounts of aid. The Carter administration boosted Tanzania to a leading recipient in 1978 and focused substantial Economic Support Fund (ESF) aid on Zambia and Botswana.* A major obligation was undertaken under the regional aid program for the construction of a southern perimeter road in Lesotho. By fiscal

*The ESF is administered by AID but, distinct from development assistance, it is aimed directly at promoting economic and political stabilization (see below).

1980 Zaire had fallen behind Zambia and Tanzania as a recipient of U.S. aid, and it will fall another notch in fiscal 1981 as Zimbabwe benefits from a $25 million ESF program.

Aid to southern Africa as a whole fell somewhat in 1979 but exceeded $200 million in 1980 as food shortages in the area resulted in unusually large food shipments for Mozambique, Tanzania, and Zambia under Public Law (PL) 480—the Food for Peace program. Aid for the region was expected to drop slightly in fiscal 1981, but it will resume its upward movement in fiscal 1982. A large new commitment is proposed for Zimbabwe, and the United States is participating in a new cooperative regional development scheme that has been launched by the black-governed states in the area; thus the Reagan administration projects that aid for southern Africa will exceed $250 million in fiscal 1982—29 percent of U.S. aid to sub-Saharan Africa.

The Reagan administration proposal for aid to southern Africa hardly differs from the Carter administration's proposal, except that $5 million was reprogrammed from Mozambique's bilateral account to the southern African regional program and development assistance for Tanzania was cut by $8 million (see Table 2). The Mozambique cut followed an incident in March 1981 in which four U.S. diplomats and two spouses were expelled from the country as alleged spies. The Tanzania cut is in line with the Reagan administration pattern of seeking to reduce planned overall foreign aid expenditures by eliminating a few proposed projects and deferring spending on some current projects. Despite the cut, aid to Tanzania in fiscal 1982 will exceed that in fiscal 1981.

Southern Africa has been protected from major aid reductions because the Reagan administration shares the view of the two previous administrations that this is a critical region for U.S. foreign policy. Indeed the centerpiece of the administration's Africa policy has been an attempt to achieve a negotiated settlement in Namibia that would help to stabilize the region. One immediate aid-related result of the administration's focus on southern Africa was a promise of $225 million in aid for Zimbabwe for fiscal 1982-85 made at a pledging conference in Salisbury at the end of March 1981.

Continuing growth in the volume of U.S. aid for southern Africa is probable, but unforeseen developments in this volatile region could interfere with administration plans. The expulsion incident in Mozambique led to a cutoff in PL 480 aid and derailed (at least for the mo-

Table 2

U.S. ECONOMIC AID TO COUNTRIES IN SOUTHERN AFRICA, FISCAL 1980-82

(Millions of dollars)

Country	1980[a] Total[b]	DA[c]	ESF	PL 480	PC	1981[d] Total	DA	ESF	PL 480	PC	1982[e] Total	DA	ESF	PL 480	PC
Angola	$ 4.9			$ 4.9		$ 1.1			$ 1.1		$ 1.1			$ 1.1	
Botswana	19.7		$13.0	5.3	$1.3	16.0		$10.0	4.4	$1.5	13.2		$ 10.0	1.8	$1.4
Lesotho	19.1	$ 9.8		7.9	1.4	19.4	$ 9.3		8.7	1.5	20.0	$ 9.9		8.8	1.4
Malawi	5.5	4.4		.7	.4	11.8	5.0		6.4	.4	13.8	7.2		5.9	.6
Mozambique	17.5			17.5		8.1			8.1		11.5			11.5	
Swaziland	9.0	7.5		.1	1.4	9.4	7.5		.4	1.6	9.2	6.8		.7	1.7
Tanzania	28.4	14.9		13.3	.3	27.0	13.5		13.2	.3	25.7	15.9		9.2	.5
Zaire	27.0	6.8		16.6	3.5	23.5	9.4		10.0	4.0	23.8	10.0		9.2	3.8
Zambia	43.0		24.0	19.0		30.1		20.0	10.1		30.0		20.0	10.0	
Zimbabwe	24.7		22.9	1.8		25.0		25.0			75.0		75.0		
Southern African regional program	8.1		8.1			25.0		25.0			30.0		30.0		
TOTAL	206.8	43.4	68.0	87.1	8.3	196.4	44.7	80.0	62.4	9.3	253.3	49.8	135.0	59.0	9.4

Source: AID, Congressional Presentation, fiscal 1982, main volume, amended version.

[a]Preliminary figures.

[b]Totals may not tally because of rounding.

[c]Key to headings: DA—Development Assistance; ESF—Economic Support Fund; PL 480—Public Law 480 (Food for Peace); PC—Peace Corps.

[d]Projected figures.

[e]Figures proposed by Reagan administration.

ment) a long-standing effort to establish a U.S. development assistance program there. This incident may be a harbinger of other difficulties in the region which could be exacerbated by the possibility (some would say probability) that the Reagan administration's policy toward southern Africa will be somewhat at odds with regional aspirations for Namibia and South Africa. In addition, strains in the U.S. relationship with Angola could damage the U.S. aid program in the region. Should Prime Minister Robert Mugabe of Zimbabwe, President Kenneth Kaunda of Zambia, or other leaders oppose U.S. policy on Namibia, South Africa, and Angola, relationships in the economic field could be harmed. Outspoken African criticism of the United States could lead to aid reductions by the U.S. Congress even if the administration sought to maintain its aid program.

DIRECTION OF AID

The U.S. development assistance program in southern Africa, administered by AID, operates in Lesotho, Malawi, Swaziland, Tanzania, and Zaire. As noted, it is heavily oriented toward projects in the rural sector, particularly those aimed at increasing food production by small farmers. In fiscal 1980, 52 percent of the development assistance funds went to a program in Agriculture, Rural Development, and Nutrition, which included projects aimed at extending credit to small farmers, promoting the use of new crops, improving small-farmer crop-marketing systems, and otherwise enhancing the productive capacity in the rural sector. Projects in Education and Human Resources Development absorbed 29 percent of the assistance funds; much of this program was also rural in focus, providing training in rural development (including rural construction and irrigation). The Health program, which received 17 percent of the assistance funds, was also closely connected to rural development, funding projects for potable rural water systems and other rural health improvements.

The orientation of the development assistance program in southern Africa reflects the concerns of the New Directions or basic human needs philosophy of development assistance that was first made a part of the Foreign Assistance Act in 1973. New Directions represented a major change in the U.S. aid program, shifting aid away from a commitment to rapid economic growth through technical assistance and support for infrastructure and large-scale agricultural enterprises

243

toward an amelioration in the living conditions of the poor—particularly the rural poor—who were seen as the victims of development. (The philosophical underpinnings of this shift were the same as those which underlay the War on Poverty, launched in the United States in the late 1960s.)[1] Thus projects to support highway or rail construction, port development, industrialization, or telecommunications could not be funded (except in unusual circumstances) because according to New Directions philosophy, they benefited primarily the better educated, wealthier segments of society—including commercial and other elites—who were best equipped to take advantage of them.* It was argued that benefits reaching the poor through such projects would do so only indirectly, through a process of "trickle down."

Southern African programs have been less affected by New Directions legislation than some others, however, because much U.S. aid to the region falls under the ESF—$68 million (33 percent) in fiscal 1980 and a proposed 53 percent in fiscal 1982.† The ESF was created by Congress in recognition of the fact that the national interest might require assistance for stabilization purposes to countries or in amounts not justified under the New Directions mandate; it is used at present to provide aid only to Zambia, Zimbabwe, and Botswana, as well as to the southern African regional program.** According to

---

*The New Directions legislation, with some alterations since 1973, reads in part as follows: "United States development assistance should focus on critical problems in those functional sectors which affect the lives of the majority of the people in the developing countries: food production and nutrition; rural development and generation of gainful employment; population planning and health; environment and natural resources; education, development administration, and human resources development; and energy development and production (Foreign Assistance Act of 1961, amended; PL 87-185, sec. 102). (Cited hereafter as Foreign Assistance Act.)

†Chapter 4 of the Foreign Assistance Act, providing for "Security Supporting Assistance" was entirely amended and retitled "Economic Support Fund" in 1978 (PL 95-384, sec. 10).

**Lesotho and Swaziland received ESF funds in 1978, but the House Africa Subcommittee recommended in 1979 that programs in these countries, as well as in Malawi, be funded from AID's regular development assistance accounts. This recommendation was accepted by the Committee on Foreign Affairs and has been followed by AID since that time (U.S. Congress, House Committee on Foreign Affairs, International Development Cooperation Act of 1979, Report of

legislation, assistance from the ESF is to be guided by the New Directions requirements to the "maximum extent feasible," but it is generally considered that the executive branch has wide flexibility in providing ESF assistance. Thus a large-scale "action-first" project, such as a $125 million commodity import program in Zambia in 1977, could be launched quickly despite the New Directions orientation toward carefully planned, small-scale projects in the rural areas that directly involve the poor. In addition, the ESF has made possible a rapid commitment of U.S. funds to Zimbabwe.

Like regular AID programs, most of the projects undertaken through the ESF have a predominantly rural and agricultural orientation. For example, the Zambian commodity import program has been used to bring in fertilizer and seed (among other commodities), and a large part of the funds allocated to Zimbabwe is going toward rural rehabilitation, resettlement, and health. However, the ESF has at the same time opened the way for AID to move into infrastructure development, particularly in the transport field. The trend is particularly evident in Zimbabwe, where one new project will provide technical assistance, training, and capital support in railway maintenance and services, and another will help to resurface a section of the Salisbury-Lusaka road. Furthermore, it is expected that $25 million pledged by the United States at the November 1980 Southern African Development Coordination Conference (SADCC) meeting in Maputo will go toward development of the transport sector in southern Africa.

In addition to the New Directions mandate and the ESF, a major component of the U.S. aid program in southern Africa is PL 480 assistance. Food aid—$87 million—constituted 42 percent of U.S. aid to the southern Africa region in fiscal 1980—far above initial estimates as drought plagued this region of rapidly expanding populations. Development experts have long been concerned over the possible effect of food aid in discouraging local agricultural production, but in view of the agricultural crises facing Zambia and Tanzania (among other countries), in the short run there may be no alternative to providing large amounts of this type of assistance.

the Committee on Foreign Affairs together with Supplemental Views on House Report (HR) 3324; HR 96-79, 96th Congress, 1st sess. [Washington, D.C.: Government Printing Office, 1979], p. 33). ESF aid to Zaire was switched to the regular development assistance accounts at the same time.

Certain critical development needs in southern Africa are receiving little attention under the existing U.S. program in the region. For example, there is only limited activity in the field of population planning under AID's centrally funded (as opposed to bilateral) programs, despite rapid population growth in several countries. The population field is politically sensitive in this part of Africa (as in other areas), and it is one which AID has largely chosen to avoid.

There is a serious need in the region for a rapid expansion of employment opportunities, and many countries would welcome assistance that might help them to become independent of South African manufactures. However, with the exception of some expenditures for management and clerical training under the Education and Human Resources Development program, few funds are going toward industrial development. Furthermore, while AID is active in the transport sector—increasingly so under the ESF program—some aspects of transport seem to be neglected. Railway locomotives and cars are in short supply throughout the region, and trackage systems need to be expanded and repaired. The repair and expansion of port facilities is recognized as a critical need by development experts and by the SADCC. Improvements are needed in telecommunications as well—a field in which the United States has great capabilities—but telecommunications projects do not yet form a part of the U.S. aid program in southern Africa.

CONGRESSIONAL ACTIONS ON AID FOR SOUTHERN AFRICA

Aid for southern Africa is affected by a number of actions taken by Congress. Some are general requirements that apply to all U.S. aid programs—for example, engineering and financial planning must be completed in advance of any grant in excess of $100,000,[2] and equipment for projects may be procured outside the United States only if the executive issues a waiver stating that such procurement "will not result in adverse effects" on the U.S. economy.[3] Critics have long held that such requirements are unnecessary restrictions on AID that inhibit its flexibility and responsiveness. They note that the procurement requirement can cause delays when equipment must be brought from the United States and cannot be purchased within the recipient country until the waiver procedure has been followed. Critics also maintain that the advanced planning requirement may be inappropriate in complex and changing Third World environments. However, others see these requirements as a valid exercise by Congress of its responsibility to oversee the implementation of U.S. programs, and they argue that most such requirements amount to an insistence on proper management and responsiveness to U.S. interests. While this debate will not soon be resolved, it seems unlikely that Congress will in the near future alter the major requirements it has imposed on AID.

Congress has enacted some requirements that apply specifically to southern Africa. For example, a prohibition on assistance to Angola has been in force since 1977,[4] and aid to Mozambique was banned from 1977 until 1980, when it was to be permitted if the executive issued a waiver stating that such aid would further the foreign policy and national interests of the United States.[5] (Such a waiver was issued by President Carter prior to leaving office.) If aid is given to Zimbabwe, the fiscal 1981 foreign assistance authorization law requires the President to issue a report every sixty days on the internal situation in that country, assessing the implementation within it of the Declaration of Rights in the Zimbabwe constitution as provided in the Lancaster House agreement, which ended the Zimbabwe civil war in December 1979.[6]

Arguments against country-specific restrictions are essentially the same as those against programwide restrictions—i.e., they inhibit the ability of AID to respond to regional development needs. In particular critics maintain that regional transport problems cannot be resolved unless railway, highway, and port development occurs in Angola and Mozambique—coastal countries through which exports from land-locked Zimbabwe, Malawi, and Zambia must pass. In addition, they suggest, the reporting requirement for Zimbabwe and the waiver requirement for Mozambique are the sort of Congressional demands that add another layer of paperwork to AID's load and tie down administrators in unnecessary tasks.

The force of these arguments is weakened, however, by the fact that the restrictions reflect deeply rooted concerns in the United States that would almost certainly be taken into account by AID even in the absence of Congressional action. For example, the presence of Cuban troops in Angola would make it difficult for any administration to provide development assistance or ESF funding to that country even if it wished to do so. It should be noted that the Carter administration had not recognized the post-independence Angolan government prior to leaving office, despite a "process of reconciliation" that was under way in 1980.[7] With recognition still an issue, aid—apart from humanitarian food assistance—remains very much a decision for the future. Similarly, reservations about the policies of Zimbabwe and Mozambique extend well beyond the Congress and would have been taken into account by AID in establishing relations with these countries.

Although Congressional restrictions reflect U.S. concerns, the general point that Congressional actions can complicate executive branch foreign policy plans is nonetheless well taken—as is clear from a 1977 debate over the multilateral Zimbabwe Development Fund (ZDF). This fund of $1-1.5 billion was proposed by Secretary of State Henry Kissinger as part of the peace initiative he launched during a visit to Africa in September 1976; it was to be used to facilitate a negotiated transition to majority rule in Zimbabwe. Many members of Congress were wary of the proposal, fearing that the ZDF might be used to finance a "buyout" of white farmers emigrating from Rhodesia. In addition, some argued that it represented an overconcentration of U.S. resources on a comparatively wealthy country at a time when the needs of other African countries were greater. State Department spokesmen insisted that the fund would not be used in a "buyout," but rather would support a general restructuring of the Zimbabwe economy that would promote prosperity, assure whites of Zimbabwe's good prospects, and encourage them to stay. Congress decided to support the ZDF, but in the fiscal 1978 international security assistance authorization (passed in July 1977), it stipulated that it would permit appropriations for the fund only when progress had been made toward an internationally recognized Rhodesian settlement;[8] mention of the fund was dropped in subsequent authorizations.

By the time the Congressional debate on the ZDF was under way, settlement negotiations at Geneva among the major participants in the Zimbabwe conflict—sparked by Kissinger's diplomatic offensive— had broken down and a new administration was in office, working with the British government on what became known as the Anglo-American plan for settlement. Thus on the one hand, the Congressional impact on the Zimbabwe peace initiative launched by Kissinger should not be exaggerated. On the other hand, however, the ZDF proposal was for many months an irritant in U.S. relations with independent Zimbabwe, where there was a belief—inaccurate though it might have been—that the United States had promised aid in exchange for a peace settlement. Only in 1981, when several Western donors pledged more than $1 billion in new aid to Zimbabwe, has this irritant become less significant.

In the recent past criticism against Congress has centered around its failure to enact foreign assistance appropriations bills for fiscal 1980 and 1981. The debate over appropriations for multilateral development institutions stymied efforts to enact appropriations legislation and meant that foreign assistance programs were funded under "continuing resolutions." The fiscal 1981 resolution was enacted more than two months after the beginning of the fiscal year.[9] Some in the executive branch complained that their work was made more difficult by the delay and uncertainty surrounding the appropriations process. An appropriations bill for fiscal 1982 has been enacted into law (PL 97-121).

AID ADMINISTRATION

Bilateral development assistance for southern Africa (as for other regions) is affected by the administrative procedures of AID. The planning and implementation of a development assistance project can take many months and even years from initial conceptualization until the beginning of work. The process begins with the submission of a Project Identification Document (PID) for a review that is normally expected to take about thirty days. Following PID approval, a Project Paper (PP) containing an operational project design is prepared over a period of approximately three to six months. Delays can arise as AID administrators, facing a number of other priorities, make arrangements for preparing the PP within AID or for recruiting contractors to write all or part of it. Scheduling and travel arrangements for design experts to visit a potential recipient country can cause further delays, and these can become significant when (as at present) travel funds are restricted by budgetary constraints. Once complete, the PP must be reviewed and possibly revised, and these steps can consume several weeks prior to final authorization. After authorization, additional months may be needed to make practical arrangements for implementation. Formal agreements with a host government may be required if that government is to secure rights of way, acquire land, assure the cooperation of local authorities, or fulfill other commitments essential to the project. If a U.S. contractor must be selected to implement the project, time is needed to post notifications, allow for the preparation of bids, conduct pre-award audits of bidders, and prepare the final contract.[10]

Some critics see this design and implementation process as unnecessarily time-consuming, and as another example of a tendency of bureaucrats to create procedures that rationalize their employment and (perhaps) perpetuate or expand their roles; others view this sort of process as essential to good management. The merits of the alternative views lie beyond the subject matter of this chapter, but it should be noted that AID procedures do have an effect on the rate at which assistance funds flow to southern Africa. According to AID's most recent *Congressional Presentation* on active projects—i.e., those which have passed at least the PID stage—at the end of fiscal 1980, an estimated $140 million in development assistance and ESF funds that had been fully approved and obligated for the region remained unspent in the aid "pipeline."[11]* This amount is greater than AID's total projected new obligations for the region in fiscal 1981.

Whether the quantity of aid in the pipeline can or should be reduced is an issue that is frequently debated. Careful planning and management would seem to require an assurance that funds are available for a project before it is under way and that the funds are expended only as the project moves forward according to preplanned stages. To try to spend development funds rapidly in a less developed region with a limited capacity to absorb them can easily lead to waste, although many observers believe that pressing political interests of the United States, as well as the economic needs of the states in southern Africa, require a rapid expenditure of aid.

The issue is particularly relevant at present to Zambia, where funds have been spent rather rapidly in an effort to stave off economic crisis. Through fiscal 1980 a support program in Zambia had received $83 million of $90 million obligated under active ESF projects, leaving only 8 percent of the aid funds in the pipeline. In retrospect it may be seen that the rapid delivery of U.S. aid played a role in rescuing the Zambian economy and political system. However, a few observers question whether adequate controls have been exercised over the ex-

*This estimate may be somewhat inflated because it includes funds for Zimbabwe which, according to AID, have been expended more rapidly than anticipated.

penditure of the funds. They are concerned that when AID evaluates its performance in Zambia, it will be able to point to few lasting achievements. Thus there has been a recent emphasis at AID on restructuring the support program in Zambia into a creditable long-term development strategy.

ENDS AND MEANS IN AID POLICY

The existing U.S. aid program in southern Africa raises questions about the relationship of ends and means in the making of aid policy. As we have noted, policymakers are aware of the region's importance to the United States, and many have broad expectations of the ability of aid to promote desirable political and economic changes in the region. Thus southern Africa receives a substantial proportion of U.S. aid for Africa, and the quantity of aid for the region has increased significantly in recent years. However, owing to fiscal and political constraints within the United States, the quantity of aid has never been large in absolute dollar terms, limiting its usefulness. In addition, because aid is oriented toward the rural areas and food production, other fields, in which a variety of possible projects would enhance U.S. interests and get a favorable reception among governments in the area, have been neglected. An examination of the goals that policymakers have hoped to achieve through development assistance in southern Africa may help to suggest the issues that must be clarified if aid is to be placed within the context of a coherent foreign policy for the region.

PROMOTING INTERNAL STABILITY

There is a firm belief among policymakers and others who take an interest in U.S. policy toward the region that the United States has an important stake in the internal economic and political stability of the southern African countries. It is generally considered that economic stability requires an easing of the balance of payments difficulties faced by the governments of the region, a reduction in unemployment, and an improvement in economic management capabilities, and that political stability requires governments that are strong enough to resist factional violence while at the same time maintaining popular legitimacy based on responsiveness to public needs. If the United States could contribute to the creation of such conditions of stability, it is argued, the Soviet Union would be deprived of opportunities to expand its influence in the region, and the doors to mutually beneficial economic relations (including Western imports of the region's minerals) would remain open.

The U.S. concern over regional stability is clearly reflected in the large volume of assistance that has been made available in southern Africa through PL 480. This concern is the motivating factor in the large-scale Zambian support program, which is aimed directly at easing the country's balance of payments difficulties and shoring up an overstrained budget, as well as in the substantial contribution to Zimbabwe's development. However, there are several threats to internal stability in southern Africa which may not be receiving adequate U.S. attention at present.

Rapid population growth may be the greatest long-term problem the region faces, but (as noted above) it is receiving little emphasis in the U.S. aid program. While southern Africa has the resources needed to support a very large population for a long time, several countries are experiencing population growth rates that could severely strain administrative, political, and economic capabilities in the short run. The populations of Zambia, Malawi, and Tanzania are growing at rates in excess of 3 percent annually; if these rates are sustained, the populations will approximately double in twenty-five or thirty years. With peace in Zimbabwe, that country's population may soon begin to grow at a comparable rate. How governments that have great difficulty in responding to current national needs will meet the demands imposed by doubled populations is not easy to imagine.

A rapid expansion of employment opportunities in the modern sector of the economy might be one answer to the population problem, but the U.S. assistance program does not make a major direct contribution toward industrial development. It has been argued that an essentially rural program holds out the greatest hope of providing new employment opportunities and of improving living standards because the populations of the area are predominantly rural and likely to remain so for many years. There is merit in this argument, and it is clear that any development program aimed at increasing employment will have to have a large rural component. However, the problems of unemployment, underemployment, and population growth are great, and an expansion of the industrial sector would seem essential as part of the response to these problems.

252

U.S. participation in industrial development, and in the development of infrastructure to accompany industrial growth, would of course be expensive—particularly under the difficult conditions likely to be encountered in Africa. In Zaire a 1,100 mile power transmission project (from the Inga dam to Shaba Province), initially funded by a U.S. Export-Import Bank loan of $238 million, encountered numerous construction delays owing to the terrain and to guerrilla incursions into Shaba Province from Angola. The debt was twice rescheduled and additional loans were required, bringing the cost up to $400 million in 1979, when construction was not yet complete. [12]

If current constraints on the U.S. foreign aid budget dictate that substantial assistance cannot be marked for infrastructure and the modern industrial sector, it may be necessary (as some suggest) to develop ways of using aid to attract private investment. However, private investors are likely to be most attracted by an aid program that promises cheap and reliable electricity, rapid transport, and trouble-free communications—in other words, a program whose orientation would be quite different from that of the current U.S. program. In any event, there is as yet no clear U.S. policy on working with private investors, although the Reagan administration has commissioned a study aimed at identifying ways in which government and private-sector cooperation in development can be expanded.

PROMOTING REGIONAL PEACE

Advocates of increased development assistance to southern Africa attest to the value of aid in promoting peace in the region. While the means by which aid will have this effect are not made explicit, one expectation seems to be that aid will demonstrate the commitment of the United States to the viability and independence of the black-governed states. It is evidently hoped that such a demonstration will discourage South Africa from armed attacks and subversion against its neighbors by suggesting that such attacks would meet with strong disapprobation from the donor. Although there is some validity to this expectation, limitations on the use of aid for deterrence purposes are readily apparent. An aid relationship is not a military guarantee and might not be strong enough to deter South Africa if its leaders feel that vital security interests are at stake. Moreover, it is not clear what quantity of aid is needed before it can begin to have a deterrent value. At existing levels of U.S. aid, South Africa could entertain doubts about the strength of U.S. opposition to attacks on its neighbors—particularly Angola and Mozambique, which have received only PL 480 assistance. In the case of Zimbabwe, however, it may be that the U.S. aid relationship is strong enough to have some deterrence value.

An alternative expectation of aid to southern Africa is that it will help South Africa's neighbors to prosper, thus demonstrating to South African whites that black majority rule is viable and beneficial. In addition, some proponents of aid hope that prosperity will make South Africa's neighbors reluctant to run the risks of confrontation with South Africa. Both of these expectations depend on rapid economic growth in southern Africa, and it is clear that large volumes of aid over many years would be required to bring about such growth. In any event, while there may be merit in the argument that prosperity can contribute to peace, it is far from certain that prosperity alone could defuse regional attitudes and ideologies to the degree necessary to assure peace.

PROMOTING ECONOMIC INDEPENDENCE

Some policymakers consider that development assistance to the countries of southern Africa is a way of promoting the economic independence of South Africa's neighbors or—in less ambitious visions—reducing their dependence on Pretoria. In fiscal 1981 AID cautiously argued the latter position, stating that aid could be "effectively used . . . in encouraging regional economic cooperation toward a more balanced economic interdependence in the area."[13] A major AID study of the development needs of southern Africa put it as follows: "A rational diversification of the economic relationships of the majority-ruled states may serve to strengthen their economies by reducing excessive vulnerability to the events affecting other nations in the region."[14] In their public statements the black-governed states in southern Africa strongly favor economic independence from South Africa, but they are probably as realistic as AID in recognizing that such independence is years in the future—if it can be achieved at all. Nonetheless, U.S. aid that seems to be making a contribution toward independence is likely to be well received and politically popular in the area.

One difficulty of promoting economic independence is the issue of whether the United States should be helping to do so. Some critics ask whether the United States should be supporting an assistance program that could make it easier for the recipients to pursue confrontation with South Africa. In response, AID officials and others who seek to expand U.S. support for regional cooperation schemes emphasize that independence is a distant prospect, while a more immediate effect of improved regional transport and communications is likely to be increased interest in the region in avoiding a destructive conflict. A substantial U.S. contribution to regional development will depend on the success of this argument, as well as on moderation in the rhetoric and conduct of the recipient governments.

Another difficulty for the United States in contributing to projects intended to enhance economic independence is that support for such projects could require a significant expansion of the existing transport program. Transport is the single most important dependent relationship in the region. Zambia, Zimbabwe, Malawi, Botswana, Lesotho, and Swaziland are heavily—and in some cases exclusively—dependent on South African highways, railways, and ports for importing vitally needed food, fertilizers, and equipment and for exporting agricultural products and minerals. If these countries are to decrease their dependence on South Africa, they will above all need assistance in building, repairing, and expanding modern transport facilities.*

A program oriented toward rural and agricultural development cannot address transport needs.[15] As noted above, the Carter administration gave some indication in its proposed fiscal 1982 program of moving away from the predominantly rural orientation with proposals for railway maintenance and road projects, and the Reagan administration has continued to support these projects. On the one hand, a major shift in the direction of transport aid could encounter opposition from supporters of New Directions and might be considered at odds with the "maximum extent feasible" clause of the ESF legislation. On the other hand, many who have been sympathetic to the

---

*In addition to assistance with transport facilities, the southern African states will need significant strengthening of the industrial sector to produce substitutes for South African manufactures.

goals of New Directions over the years are also supporters of enhanced economic independence in southern Africa, and it may be that an evolution toward major involvement in the transport sector would not encounter serious political opposition.

CONCLUSION

The effectiveness of foreign aid depends on a close connection between ends and means in aid policy, reflected in the structuring of programs and projects to correspond to policy needs and in sustained funding adequate to the realization of policy goals. There is reason to doubt that the U.S. aid program in southern Africa has fully met these criteria. If the United States intends through its development assistance program to promote internal stability and regional peace in southern Africa, encourage enhanced economic independence of countries in the region from South Africa, and foster regional economic development, it appears that substantially larger aid funding will be required, and increased aid for projects in the transport and telecommunications sectors, as well as industrial development, will be necessary.

Creating circumstances that would make possible a large-scale, sustained U.S. development effort in southern Africa will not be easy. Close consultations between Congress and the executive branch will be needed to establish a common understanding of regional needs and of U.S. interests in the area. The utmost in diplomatic skill will be required if destructive confrontations with recipient governments are to be avoided, and these governments will have to avoid statements and actions that would damage working relationships or undermine Congressional support for aid to the region. Even if all of these conditions are met, unforeseen events—for example, a renewal of Soweto-type uprisings in South Africa leading to demands for a U.S. response against South Africa and a potential polarization of U.S. relations with key leaders in the black-governed states—could disrupt an aid program. However, a major aid program that would complement U.S. interests in the area is worth consideration.

APPENDIX

———

Excerpts from

IMPORTS OF MINERALS FROM SOUTH AFRICA BY THE UNITED STATES AND THE OECD COUNTRIES

Prepared for the

SUBCOMMITTEE ON AFRICAN AFFAIRS

of the

COMMITTEE ON FOREIGN RELATIONS
UNITED STATES SENATE

by the

*Congressional Research Service
Library of Congress*

September 1980

Appendix

SUMMARY

South Africa possesses major reserves of many of the world's mineral commodities and is the fourth largest producer of nonfuel minerals. Substantial quantities of South African minerals are exported to the United States and to other OECD countries,[1] and several of these minerals have vital industrial and military applications. Because of the importance of these applications, and because there is a possibility that mineral supplies from South Africa will be interrupted, this study of South African minerals has been undertaken.

Principal Findings

1. South African supplies of chromium, manganese, vanadium, and the platinum group metals are of significant importance to the United States and other OECD countries.

2. In general, the United States has stockpiles that are more nearly adequate than are those of other OECD countries, and would thus suffer less immediate impact on productive capability than would some European countries and Japan.

3. The major immediate impact of disruptions in the supply of South African minerals on the United States would be indirect, taking the form of higher inflation rates and economic disruptions resulting from the direct impact on production in other OECD nations.

4. In the short term of 3 to 5 years, U.S. stockpiles, the capacity for technological innovation, and the ability to reduce consumption for non-essential purposes would enable U.S. industry to obtain adequate quantities of these minerals or acceptable substitutes—albeit in the context of higher world market prices—in the wake of interruptions in the supply of South African minerals.

5. For chromium and manganese, the medium term of 5 to 10 years after an interruption would be critical as industry moved to adapt to new technologies, secondary recovery, and new supply sources. If these adaptations were not successful, serious medium-term dislocations in the production of stainless and other hardened steels could result. Over the long term, there is no alternative to reliance on chromium imports from southern Africa. However, a new source of supply has opened up in Zimbabwe since the independence of that country in 1980.

6. An interruption in the supply of platinum-group metals would be unlikely to pose a serious problem because of the possibility of adopting alternative technologies for automobile emission control and because prospects for efficient secondary recovery seem good.

7. An interruption in the supply of gold from South Africa would not result in direct industrial damage, but it could lead to monetary instability and contribute to global inflation.

---

[1] The Organization for Economic Cooperation and Development, made up of developed countries, includes the United States together with Australia, Austria, Belgium, Canada, Denmark, Federal Republic of Germany, Finland, France, Greece, Iceland, Irish Republic, Italy, Japan, Luxembourg, the Netherlands, New Zealand, Norway, Portugal, Spain, Sweden, Switzerland, Turkey, and the United Kingdom.

8. South Africa's economic health is heavily dependent on trade with the United States and other OECD countries and on the investment it receives from them. Because of this interdependence, a South African decision to deny minerals to the OECD countries is highly unlikely and would probably be made only after extreme provocation.

9. Economic sanctions might be imposed against South Africa for a number of reasons, including new incidents of racial violence in South Africa; the acquisition of nuclear weapons by South Africa; South African intervention in Zimbabwe or Angola; or a South African refusal to grant independence to Namibia. Such sanctions could take the form of a trade embargo that would interrupt mineral supplies. Although the United States has the power to veto mandatory sanctions at the U.N. Security Council, moral and diplomatic considerations might persuade it to support sanctions proposals.

10. Revolutionary violence within South Africa is a continuing possibility and one which could at least temporarily endanger mineral supplies.

11. Although various mineral supply interruption scenarios can be imagined—involving both the current and/or successor regimes in South Africa—a long-lasting and complete cutoff of South African minerals seems the least likely possibility.

BACKGROUND

South Africa produces four minerals that are of particular importance to the industries of the United States and the other OECD countries: chromium, manganese, vanadium, and the platinum-group metals. In addition, gold, which is also exported by South Africa, is a critical mineral in the global economy because of its continuing importance as a store of value. South Africa and the Soviet Union dominate world production of these minerals and have the largest part of the world's reserves (table 1). Since the Soviet Union is not an acceptable alternative long-term supplier of critical minerals, there is added reason for concern over possible interruptions in South African supplies.

TABLE 1.—SOUTH AFRICA AND THE SOVIET UNION: 1978 PRODUCTION AND RESERVES OF 5 CRITICAL MINERALS AS A PROPORTION OF GLOBAL PRODUCTION AND RESERVES [1]

[In percent]

	South Africa	Soviet Union	Total
Reserves:			
Chromium	68	<1	[2] 69
Manganese	37	[3] 50	87
Vanadium	19	74	93
Platinum-group metals	73	25	98
Gold	48	[4] 22	70
Production:			
Chromium	34	[4] 32	66
Manganese	23	[3] 43	66
Vanadium	39	31	70
Platinum-group metals	46	47	93
Gold	58	[4] 21	79

[1] Source: U.S. Bureau of Mines. Mineral Commodity Summaries, 1979 [Washington, 1979].
[2] An additional 30 percent of global chromium reserves are held in Zimbabwe.
[3] The manganese data are for the "Central Market Economies" as a group, reflecting the Bureau of Mines reporting procedure. According to the Bureau, "the U.S.S.R. and the Republic of South Africa account for more than 80 percent of the world identified resources."
[4] Data are for the Central Market Economies as a group, again reflecting the Bureau of Mines reporting procedure.

Chromium is essential in the production of stainless steel and of other hardened and specialty steels. As far as is known, the United States has only small, primarily low-grade chromium resources, and it produces virtually no chromium at the present time. South Africa is the principal supplier of imported chromium, and the Soviet Union is another major source. But U.S. short-term and medium-term reliance on imported supplies is offset by its ability to eliminate non-essential uses, by the availability of stockpiles and inventories, and by new technological capabilities.

Over the long term, design changes and process improvements—as yet unknown or undeveloped—would be needed before all of the chromium in stainless steel could be replaced. Moreover, some 20 percent of the chromium used in wrought and cast steel, as well as the chromium used in tool steel and some other limited applications, may be irreplaceable. For these applications, alternative sources of supply in the Philippines, Turkey, and perhaps Zimbabwe might be used together with conservation and recycling. A doubling or tripling of chromium prices might also bring U.S. reserves back into production.

Manganese is also used in the production of steel, including stainless and tool steels. In most of its principal steel-making applications, there are no known substitutes for manganese at the present time. All manganese consumed in the United States is imported, either in the form of ore, of which South Africa supplies 9 percent, or of ferromanganese, with South Africa directly supplying 30 percent. Half or more of the ferromanganese imported by the United States may actually originate in South Africa, before it is processed in other countries.

Although the United States has only low-grade, uneconomic manganese ores, higher grade reserves are found in a number of countries and on the sea floor. Brazil, Gabon, and Australia are major suppliers of manganese ore, and the United States has a significant stockpile of this metal. Consequently, the United States would be capable of off-setting an interruption in the supply of South African manganese.

Vanadium is used as an addition to iron and steels, and is particularly important in the production of high-strength steels in applications where weight reduction is a consideration. Vanadium is also used to produce titanium alloys with important applications in the defense sector.

While South Africa supplies more than half of the vanadium imported by the United States, and although South Africa has more than 70 percent of the known vanadium reserves in the non-Communist world, the United States itself has large reserves of this metal. In addition, vanadium is available from several foreign sources, and from U.S. stockpiles of vanadium. Thus adaptations could be made to an interruption in supplies from South Africa.

Platinum-group metals are used as catalysts in automobile emission control systems, petroleum refining, and the chemical industry. In addition, platinum, like gold, is sometimes held as a store of value. The United States produces very little platinum, and South Africa is the leading supplier of imported platinum. The U.S.S.R. is the second-most important supplier. South Africa and the U.S.S.R. hold 98 percent of the world's known platinum-group reserves.

Despite South Africa's dominance in the platinum field, adaptations to an interruption in supply seem possible. The enhancement of secondary-recovery techniques holds out the possibility of recapturing most of the platinum used for catalytic purposes. New or existing technology could eliminate the use of platinum in auto emission-control devices. Moreover, the United States has some low-grade, subeconomic platinum resources that might be called into production in the event of a platinum shortage.

Gold is used primarily in jewelry and the arts, although 27 percent of the gold consumed in the United States is used in industry, primarily in the electronics industry. South Africa accounts for over 70 percent of gold production in the non-Communist world, and holds more than 60 percent of the non-Communist world's reserves, but the OECD countries have ample gold in stockpiles or in reserves for meeting industrial needs.

The use of gold as a store of value, however, holds open the possibility of international monetary instability if South African supplies were cut. Even the prospect of an interruption could reduce new investment by prompting private investors and speculators to tie up large amounts of capital in gold holdings, lead to sudden international capital shifts as buyers sought gold, and contribute to inflation by damaging the value of paper currencies. Speculation in platinum and in gem diamonds, produced in South Africa and Namibia, as well as in gold, could also be anticipated.

Gold-price increases might be countered by sales from the reserve stocks held by the U.S. Treasury, although the decision to make such sales could be politically difficult. New investment might be stimulated by reducing interest rates, although this step could add to the inflation caused by rising gold prices. In sum, the loss of South African gold might lead to a period of instability in international capital markets and contribute to global inflation.

U.S. AND OECD IMPORTS OF CRITICAL MINERALS FROM SOUTH AFRICA

The United States imports 7 of the 27 critical minerals and 2 key alloys from South Africa: Chromium, both as chromite ore and ferrochromium; manganese and ferromanganese; vanadium; copper; gold; the platinum group metals; and coal (table 6). Copper and coal imports, however, make up only a small part of U.S. consumption. Because of this, and because ample supplies of these two materials are available to the United States and the other OECD countries from other sources, neither receives further discussion in this report. Table 7 reports imports from South Africa as a proportion of U.S. consumption.

TABLE 6.—SOUTH AFRICAN EXPORTS OF MAJOR INDUSTRIAL MINERAL COMMODITIES TO THE UNITED STATES IN 1978 [1]

[In short tons, unless otherwise noted]

Mineral commodity	U.S. reported consumption during 1978	U.S. mine production during 1978	U.S. imports	
			Total dur- ing 1978	Sources (percent of total, 1974–77)
Ferrous metals:				
Chromite	1,000,000	(²)	1,000,000	South Africa (35), U.S.S.R. (18), Philippines (16), Turkey (13), other (18).
Manganese ore	1,350,000	(²)	600,000	Gabon (36), Brazil (33), Australia (13), South Africa (9), other (9).
Vanadium [3]	[4] 6,300	5,250	2,300	South Africa (56), Chile (25), U.S.S.R. (9), other (10).
Nonferrous metals:				
Copper	[5] 2,350,000	1,485,000	[6] 620,000	Canada (28), Chile (21), Peru (13), Zambia (10), South Africa (3), other (25).
Gold [7]	4.84	0.97	4.68	Canada (44), U.S.S.R. (17), Switzerland (mostly South African origin) (16), other (23).
Platinum group [8,9]	2,100,000	5,000	2,700,000	South Africa (42), U.S.S.R. (26), United Kingdom (42), other (15).
Fuels: Coal, bituminous and Lignite [10]	618,089,000	653,800,000	[11] 3,403,105	Poland (34), South Africa (32), Australia (30), Canada (2),[11] other (2).
Processed mineral commodities: [12]				
Ferrochromium [13]	480,000	------------	300,000	South Africa (38), Zimbabwe (23), Japan (15), other (24).
Ferromanganese [14]	900,000	------------	675,000	France (32), South Africa (30), Japan (14) other (24).

[1] Estimated.
[2] None.
[3] Data in short tons of contained vanadium.
[4] Consumption of intermediate vanadium products.
[5] Consumption of refined copper.
[6] Total imports of refined and unmanufactured copper.
[7] Data in million troy ounces.
[8] Platinum group includes platinum, palladium, iridium, osmium, rhodium, and ruthenium.
[9] Data in troy ounces.
[10] Source: U.S. Department of Energy, Monthly Energy Review, June 1979, p. 56.
[11] Bureau of the Census, personal communication, Aug. 27, 1979.
[12] These processed mineral commodities are a significant part of total consumption and are, therefore, included in the table, even though they are not mined.
[13] Ferrochromium is typically from 36 to 70 percent chromium content while chromite ore typically ranges from 22 to 38 percent manganese content.
[14] Ferromanganese typically ranges from 74 to 95 percent manganese content while manganese ore typically ranges from 35 to 54 percent manganese content.

Adapted from: U.S. Bureau of Mines, Commodity Data Summaries, 1979, p. 190, and other sources.

TABLE 7.—CRITICAL MINERAL IMPORTS FROM SOUTH AFRICA AND U.S. IMPORT DEPENDENCE

	1974–77 average	
Mineral	Total imports as percent of apparent consumption	Imports from South Africa as percent of total imports
Chromium	90	
Chromite		35
Ferrochromium		38
Manganese	98	
Ore		9
Ferromanganese		30
Vanadium (contained vanadium)	36	56
Platinum-group metals	88	42
Gold	59	[1] 16

[1] Refers to imports from Switzerland, which are reported to be mostly of South African origin.

Adapted from U.S. Bureau of Mines, Mineral Commodity Summaries, 1979.

Several OECD countries, including France and Britain, import uranium from South Africa and Namibia, but global resources of this element are large. Of greater concern for these countries, as for the United States, are imports of chromium, manganese, vanadium, and the platinum-group metals, each of which has important industrial and defense-related applications. Imports of gold are also a matter of concern because of the continuing role of this metal as a store of value. OECD data on critical minerals imports from South Africa are not available, but the imports of the European Community are given in table 8. Japan, which depends on imports for all of its chromite ore,[1] took 52 percent of its imports of this commodity from South Africa in 1978,[2] in addition to 71 percent of imported ferrochromium. Thirty percent of Japan's imported manganese came from South Africa, as did large amounts of the platinum-group metals.

TABLE 8.—EUROPEAN COMMUNITY [1] CRITICAL MINERALS IMPORTS [2]

Mineral or alloy	Net imports, 1977 [3] (1,000 metric tons)	Import dependence [4] (percent)	South African share of imports (percent)	Soviet share of imports (percent)
Chromite ore	1,111	100	49	11
Ferrochrome	274	([5])	44	4
Manganese	2,288	100	41	<1
Ferromanganese	508	([5])	8	1
Platinum-group metal and alloys, unworked	0.051	100	[6] 18	24
Gold:				
Unworked	1.034	([5])	57	1
Coin	0.075	([5])	44	17

[1] The members of the European Community are Belgium, Denmark, Federal Republic of Germany, France, Irish Republic, Italy, Luxembourg, the Netherlands, and the United Kingdom.
[2] Vanadium data are not available. Over 90 percent of European imports of vanadium, however, are believed to come from Australia and Norway.
[3] European Communities, statistical office, analytical tables of Foreign Trade, 1977, Luxembourg, European Communities (1978).
[4] Crowson, Phillip, British Foreign Policy to 1985: Nonfuel Minerals and Foreign Policy, London, Royal Institute of International Affairs (1977).
[5] Not available.
[6] This figure represents direct imports from South Africa. Additional platinum that originated in South Africa is reexported from the United Kingdom and other countries.

[1] Crowson, Phillip. British Foreign Policy to 1985. Non-fuel Minerals and Foreign Policy. London, Royal Institute of International Affairs [1977], Annex A.
[2] Japan Tariff Association. Japan Exports and Imports, December 1978.

As noted above, only the United States and France among the major Western industrial powers are currently stockpiling critical materials,[3] although the Federal Republic of Germany announced in June 1979 that it would begin to build a stockpile of its own. The reluctance many governments have shown toward stockpiles enhances the vulnerability of the OECD countries to an interruption in mineral supplies from South Africa. Even if the United States were able to protect its own industry against the effects of an interruption in South African supplies, its economy might still be damaged indirectly if the economies of its major trading partners in the OECD suffered. This stockpile problem is one that might be rather easily dealt with if the U.S. partners in the OECD were willing to take the necessary action. According to a 1977 estimate, the European Community could stockpile a 1-year strategic stockpile of chromium, manganese, vanadium, and their ferroalloys, together with the platinum-group metals, for $870 million plus storage costs,[4] or less than one-tenth of 1 percent of GNP.

Another source of worry is that the Soviet Union is a major producer of each of the critical materials imported from South Africa and holds a significant portion of the world's reserves in each case. The largest deposits of chromium outside southern Africa are in the Soviet Union, and that country has three-fourths of known vanadium reserves as well as large reserves of manganese, the platinum-group metals, and gold. Thus an interruption in the supply of critical minerals from South Africa would raise the prospect of dependence on the Soviet Union—a prospect most OECD members would wish to avoid.

It is fortunate that in the case of each of the critical minerals imported from South Africa, means are available for dealing with an interruption without depending on the Soviet Union as an alternative supplier. These means may be costly, and they cannot in all cases be implemented without disruption. But in general, the disruptions can be minimized if preparations for a possible cutoff in South African supplies are made in advance.

CHROMIUM

The United States, as far as is known, has only small, primarily low-grade, subeconomic chromium resources, and it imports virtually all of the chromium it consumes. Chromium imports are in the form of chromite ore, which must be processed before use, and of ferrochromium, which has been processed abroad and is ready for use in the metals industry.

Chromium plays a critical role in industry. Its principal use is in the manufacture of stainless steel, a material that is vitally important in the defense, aerospace, power-generation, and transportation industries where high-strength, corrosion-resistant materials are needed. In addition, chromium is used to increase the hardness of wrought and cast steel; in the manufacture of tool steel; and in lining refractory vessels used in the steel industry. Chromium also has a number of applications in the chemical industry, where among other purposes it is used in leather tanning and in wood preservatives.

---

[3] For the data on U.S. stockpiles and private inventories of critical minerals imported from South Africa see appendix 6.
[4] Crowson, British Foreign Policy to 1985, Annex B.

South Africa is the principal supplier of chromium to the United States, providing 35 percent of U.S. chromite imports from 1974 through 1977, and 38 percent of ferrochromium imports over the same period.[5] Imports of chromium from South Africa are increasing rapidly, and in 1978 South Africa supplied 48 percent of chromite imports and 78 percent of imported ferrochromium.[6] These increases result in part from the 1977 termination of imports of chromium from Zimbabwe, which had been permitted under the Byrd Amendment to the Fiscal Year 1972 Armed Forces Appropriation Authorization (Public Law 92–156).[7]

But increased importation of chromium from South Africa also results from South Africa's policy of encouraging local processing of raw materials. A program of incentives launched in 1975 offered low-cost loans, tax concessions, and other benefits intended to step up local processing. Taking advantage of these incentives, together with lower labor costs and the savings which result from shipping processed material rather than ore, Union Carbide has completed a $50-million ferrochromium processing facility in South Africa that is able to undersell U.S. producers in the U.S. market.[8] President Carter has given U.S. processors some relief from South African competition by granting a small tariff increase,[9] but the effects of this increase—much less than U.S. processors sought—are not yet known.

Over the long-term, the United States and the other OECD countries have no alternative to reliance on chromium from two countries in southern Africa—South Africa and Zimbabwe. Together, they hold over 99 percent of known chromium resources, amounting to nearly 25 billion tons of ore in South Africa and 10 billion in Zimbabwe—amounts that would meet global demand for centuries.[10] If these resources were unavailable, chromium resources in the rest of the world would be exhausted in 21 years at 1975 rates of consumption[11]—a possibility that has led a committee of the U.S. National Materials Advisory Board (NMAB) to conclude that the United States is strategically more vulnerable to a long-term chromium embargo than to the embargo of any other natural resource including petroleum.[12]

Despite this long-term dependence on southern African sources, an interruption in supply from South Africa need not be disastrous. As will be seen in the final section of this report, none of the plausible scenarios that might lead to an interruption would be likely to last for a period of time approaching 21 years; nor would it necessarily be the case that chromium supplies from Zimbabwe and South Africa would be interrupted at the same time. Moreover, technical means are available for achieving major reductions in chromium consumption even though consumption cannot be eliminated entirely.

[5] U.S. Department of the Interior. Bureau of Mines. Mineral Commodity Summaries, 1979. p. 35.
[6] Calculated on the basis of data provided by the U.S. Bureau of Mines.
[7] This Act became law on November 17, 1971.
[8] "The Ferrochromium Caper." Forbes, v. 122, Sept. 18, 1978: 116.
[9] U.S. Congress. House of Representatives. Import Relief Action, High-Carbon Ferrochrome. Communication from the President of the United States. January 15, 1979. Washington, U.S. Government Printing Office, 1979. (96th Congress, 1st session. House Doc. No. 96–28).
[10] Mineral Commodity Summaries, 1979: 35.
[11] U.S. National Academy of Sciences. National Materials Advisory Board. Contingency Plans for Chromium Utilization. Washington, U.S. National Academy of Sciences [1978] p. 37.
[12] Ibid., p. 16.

According to the NMAB report cited above, an immediate reduction
of 31 percent in chromium consumption is possible using functionally
acceptable substitutes currently available.[13] If a reasonably well-
funded and well-staffed investigation [14] were undertaken, chromium
consumption could be reduced by 35 percent from current levels within
5 years and by 64 percent within 5 to 10 years. After 10 years, however,
only an additional 1-percent reduction in chromium consumption
would be possible. The NMAB report notes that a crash program
supported by Government and industry might be able to reduce
chromium consumption at a faster rate than this schedule suggests.[15]

Examining particular industries, the NMAB committee found that
60 percent of the chromium used in stainless steel could probably be
replaced without unacceptable performance degradation,[16] while all
but 20 percent of the chromium in wrought and cast steels could be
replaced.[17] Chromium used in tool steels appears irreplacable, however,
and practical substitutes for most chromium applications in the
chemical industry do not seem likely to be developed. Thus the United
States would have a continuing need after 10 years for about 404
million pounds of chromium per year, or about 35 percent of present
consumption.

These NMAB estimates suggest that if U.S. imports of chromium
from South Africa were running at their 1974–77 levels of 35 percent
for chromite and 38 percent for ferrochromium, adjustment to an
interruption in supplies from South Africa need not cause severe
dislocations. The U.S. stockpile now contains about a 2½-year supply
of chromium, and this, combined with reliance on alternative sources
of supply in Turkey and the Philippines, and the measures for an
immediate 35 percent reduction in consumption proposed by the
NMAB, should make it a relatively simple matter to adjust to a cutoff in South African supplies.

With the higher levels of imports from South Africa that are now
emerging, an interruption in supplies could have a more serious immediate impact. Even so, after an initial jolt, an adjustment should
be possible. In addition to the use of the stockpile and alternative
suppliers, U.S. resources might be brought into production as prices
rise.

For the OECD countries lacking chromium resources and stockpiles, the disruptions following an interruption in supplies from
South Africa might be more severe. But presumably they too would
be able to implement conservation measures and turn to alternative
suppliers to last out the emergency. It should be noted that if Zimbabwean chromium were available after an interruption in supplies
from South Africa occurred, the emergency would not be great.

In any event, it would seem highly advisable for the United States,
perhaps in cooperation with its OECD partners, to begin implementation of the NMAB recommendations on chromium. These include
appointing a high-level design team to develop industrial processes
consuming less chromium than is now the case and offering incentives

---

3 Calculated on the basis of data appearing in ibid., p. 9.
4 Ibid.
5 Ibid., p. 9.
6 Ibid., p. 10.
7 Ibid., p. 11.

to encourage design changes and recycling. Preventive action taken now could minimize damage to vital chromium-consuming industries in the future.

Summary.—Although there seems to be no long-term alternative to reliance on chromium imports from South Africa and Zimbabwe, stockpiles, conservation, process changes, and other adaptations could permit an adjustment to short- and medium-term interruptions.

MANGANESE

Manganese is an essential element in the production of nearly all steels, in which it is a desulfuring, hardening, and conditioning agent, and there are no satisfactory substitutes in these applications at the present time. By far the largest part of the manganese consumed in the United States goes to the steel industry, but manganese is also used in the manufacture of dry-cell batteries and in other chemical applications.

The United States has no manganese resources that can be exploited economically and is almost totally dependent on foreign sources of supply. The Republic of South Africa and the Soviet bloc countries hold over 30 percent of world reserves, and in 1978 they accounted for two-thirds of world mine production. South Africa itself has 36 percent of known reserves and 75 percent of known resources in the non-communist world.[18]

Manganese is imported both as manganese ore and as ferromanganese, which has already been processed. South Africa is a minor supplier of manganese ore, providing 9 percent of U.S. imports from 1974 through 1977, but it supplied 30 percent of ferromanganese imports over the same period.[19] Half or more of the ferromanganese imported by the United States may originate in South Africa, however, before it is processed in other countries.

Despite the importance of South Africa as a supplier of manganese, the United States and the OECD countries need not suffer severe dislocations following an interruption in South African supplies. Gabon, Brazil, and Australia are major suppliers of manganese to the United States, and each of these countries, in addition to India, has substantial manganese reserves. Of even greater potential significance are the manganese deposits in metal-bearing nodules on the seabed. The obstacles to exploiting these resources are partly legal—an international agreement on deep seabed mining has not yet been reached—and partly technical. Nonetheless, in the event of a manganese-supply crisis these seabed resources could possibly be developed fairly quickly, particularly if Government incentives were provided for a development program in advance of any cutoff.

The U.S. stockpile of manganese is currently in a deficit position, containing about a 1.8-year supply of manganese ore and an 8-month supply of ferromanganese.[20] But the Government also holds some manganese ore which is below stockpile grade, and there are additional stocks in private hands. Meeting the 3-year stockpile goal in manganese would significantly reduce the dislocations likely to result from a loss of South African manganese supplies. In addition, as in the case of

---

[18] Mineral Commodity Summaries, 1979, p. 95.
[19] Ibid., p. 94.
[20] Calculated on the basis of data appearing in Mineral Commodity Summaries, 1979, p. 95.

chromium, a research and development effort directed toward reducing manganese consumption and encouraging recycling would be well-advised, as would an acceleration of seabed mining programs.

Summary.—The exploitation of seabed resources, turning to alternative suppliers, and possible design changes should permit an adaptation to an interruption in manganese supplies from South Africa. That adaptation would be eased by an increase in the manganese stockpile.

VANADIUM

Vanadium is used as an alloy in the iron and steel industry, and is particularly useful in producing high strength, lightweight steels. It is also used to produce vanadium-aluminum alloys which are in turn incorporated in titanium-based alloys. As an alloy, vanadium finds its way into jet engines, airframes, and pipelines, and it has a number of other applications in the transportation, construction, and defense fields.

The United States produces 73 percent of the vanadium it consumes and imports the remainder. South Africa supplied more than half of this imported vanadium from 1974 through 1977, with most of the rest coming from Chile and the Soviet Union. South Africa and the Soviet Union possess about 93 percent of global vanadium reserves, with South Africa holding over 70 percent of reserves among non-communist countries. South Africa is the world's most important producer, annually accounting for 39 percent of global production.[21]

But despite the importance of South Africa in vanadium production, an interruption in supplies would not be critical because of the large vanadium reserves held by the United States and other countries. U.S. reserves in deposits now being worked are equal to more than 20 years' consumption at current rates.[22] Resources in the United States are vast, amounting to nearly 10 million tons—an ample supply when measured against a projected 1990 consumption of 10,300 tons.[23] Large deposits of vanadium also exist in Australia, Canada, China, and Japan, and there are smaller resources in several black African countries and Scandinavia.

At the present time, the U.S. vanadium stockpile is in deficit, but this is not likely to cause a major problem in view of the reserves that are available. Columbium, molybdenum, and other metals can be used as substitutes for vanadium in some applications.

Summary.—Vanadium reserves and resources in the United States and other countries would minimize the impact of an interruption in supplies from South Africa.

PLATINUM-GROUP

The platinum-group metals—platinum, palladium, rhodium, ruthenium, iridium, and osmium—commonly occur in the same deposits and are mined together. Platinum-group metals are used as catalysts, or substances that promote chemical reactions without themselves being altered. Seventy percent of platinum-group consumption in the United

---

[21] Mineral Commodity Summaries, 1979, p. 177.
[22] U.S. National Academy of Sciences. National Materials Advisory Board. Vanadium Supply and Demand Outlook. Washington, National Academy of Sciences [1978] p. 14.
[23] Ibid p. 2.

States is for catalytic purposes in automobile emission-control systems, petroleum refining, and chemical processing.[24] The balance of consumption is used in dental supplies, glass and ceramics, and electronic and electrical equipment.[25]

The United States imports all but a tiny fraction of the platinum it consumes, and South Africa is the leading supplier, providing 42 percent of imports directly.[26] Additional platinum from South Africa enters the United States from the United Kingdom after processing. The Soviet Union is the second most important supplier, accounting for 26 percent of imports.

U.S. resources of platinum are potentially significant, but they are classifed today only as hypothetical,[27] meaning that they are poorly known and that there is no assurance of development. The great bulk of the world's known reserves, some 73 percent, are in South Africa, while 25 percent are in the Soviet Union. Canada, the United States, and Colombia together have only 1.3 percent.

The ability of the United States and the other OECD countries to deal with an interruption in platinum shipments from South Africa arises from the potential for reducing consumption and for recycling. Japanese demand for platinum is typically 40 percent of world demand, but more than 70 percent of Japanese consumption goes for jewelry. In other words, 28 percent of global production is for a non-essential purpose in Japan alone.[28]

In the United States, which itself consumes nearly one-third of global platinum production,[29] much of the platinum used is involved in the automotive pollution control program. Thirty-seven percent of platinum consumption goes directly to the automotive industry for emission-control devices.[30] Yet alternative technologies for controlling emissions, including the stratified charge ignition system, already exist, and others, notably the computer-controlled ignition system, are under development.

Platinum also contributes to automotive pollution control through the petroleum industry where it is used in platinum catalyzed reforming—a method of refining that increases gasoline octane ratings without lead anti-knock compounds. The development of lean-burn engines capable of using low octane gasoline, and the possible substitution of non-platinum catalysts, could eliminate this use of platinum.

The demand for newly mined platinum can also be offset by the secondary recovery of platinum from scrap. The potential for recycling is great because, when used as catalysts, the platinum-group metals are not consumed. As noted above, 70 percent of platinum consumption in the United States is for catalytic purposes, and it is estimated that from 70 to 80 percent of the platinum catalysts now scrapped are salvageable.

The U.S. stockpile of platinum contains less than a 1-year supply at present rates of consumption. Enlarging the stockpile to a 3 year

[24] U.S. Department of Commerce. Personal communication.
[25] Mineral Commodity Summaries, 1979, p. 116.
[26] 1974 through 1977. Ibid.
[27] U.S. Department of the Interior. Bureau of Mines. Mineral Facts and Problems, 1975 edition. Washington, U.S. Government Printing Office [1976] p. 839.
[28] Engineering and Mining Journal, v. 179, March 1978: 183.
[29] Calculated on the basis of data in Mineral Commodity Summaries, 1979, pp. 116 and 117.
[30] Ibid., 116.

supply level could ease the adjustment to any interruption in South African supplies.

Summary.—Recycling, conservation, and the development of alternative technologies in the automotive and petroleum industries would permit adaptation to an interruption in platinum-group supplies from South Africa. Adaptation could be facilitated by a conscious policy of increasing stockpiles prior to any cutoff.

GOLD

An interruption in the supply of gold from South Africa would probably not have any significant direct effect on industry because of the potential for reducing nonessential uses, recycling, turning to substitutes, and drawing down the U.S. Treasury stockpile. Some 56 percent of the gold used in the United States each year is for jewelry or for other artistic purposes [31] which could easily be eliminated. Sixteen percent of gold consumption goes into dental applications for which substitutes are available.

Only 27 percent of the gold consumed in the United States, or about 1.5 million troy ounces, is for industrial purposes,[32] primarily in the electronics industry where base metals clad with gold alloys are increasingly being substituted for pure gold. U.S. production of gold is approximately .97 million troy ounces, but reserves total 100 times that quantity or 110 million ounces. In addition, the U.S. Treasury stockpile contains 275 million ounces. Thus there is no doubt that the United States could easily meet its own industrial demand for gold and assist other OECD countries in meeting their industrial needs.

Nonetheless, the continuing importance of gold as a store of value means that an interruption in South African supplies could have disruptive economic effects on the United States and other OECD countries. South Africa produces 58 percent of the world's gold, or 71 percent of the gold produced in non-communist countries. It has about half of world resources, and an additional 15 percent is found in the Soviet Union.[33] Consequently, any interruption in South African mineral supplies, or even the rumor of interruption, would inevitably lead to an increase in the price of gold. In addition, increases in the prices of gem diamonds and of the platinum-group minerals, both of which are produced in South Africa and are also used to store value, could be anticipated.

The size of the potential gold price increase and its effects on the global economy are difficult to assess, because of the importance of psychological considerations in such a situation. It is possible that a panic mentality would set in and drive gold prices higher than strictly rational considerations would justify. The relevant rational considerations include the following: U.S. Treasury stockpiles of gold are equivalent to 12 years of South African production and could be used to combat drastic price increases; any interruption in South African supplies would likely be of limited duration, holding out the prospect of a fall in gold prices when South African supplies returned to the

---

[31] Mineral Commodity Summaries, 1979, p. 62.
[32] Ibid.
[33] Mineral Commodity Summaries, 1979, p. 63.

market; and finally, higher gold prices could lead to increased production in the United States, Canada, and other countries with gold reserves and resources, further restraining prices.

If, despite these considerations, a drastic increase in gold prices should occur, large sudden capital shifts could be anticipated as buyers sold other assets to buy gold. These capital shifts might be made by governments as well as by corporate and private investors. The IMF abolished the official selling price for gold on April 1, 1978, ending a long process of demonetization designed to free the world's currencies from dependence on gold as a reserve. Nonetheless, a number of European central banks, together with the governments of several oil exporting countries, continue to purchase gold as a reserve, evidently regarding it as the only secure store of value.[34] These purchasers could be expected to join private and corporate purchasers in a quest for gold, promoting some instability in world capital markets as assets were shifted into the precious metal. Some depressing effect on economic activity could also be expected as large amounts of capital were tied up in nonproductive assets.

Although an interruption in South African supplies of gold could, as a result of these effects, create an atmosphere of economic crisis, the means of dealing with such a crisis appear to be at hand. Sales from the U.S. stockpile can indeed have a calming effect, although experience has shown that regular monthly sales can excite speculation and drive up the price of gold. By announcing a recent sale only one week in advance, the U.S. Department of the Treasury precipitated a $17 drop in the price of gold futures.

To counter the depressive effects of a gold-price run-up, new investment might be spurred if central banks were to lower interest rates and if the International Monetary Fund acted to increase international liquidity by issuing new Special Drawing Rights (SDR's). (Such steps would, however, have some inflationary effects.) Over the medium term of 3 to 5 years, as gold prices rose, gold production could be expected to increase in the United States—which has 13 percent of global resources—and in other non-communist countries with gold reserves amounting to 20 percent of the world total.[35]

Summary.—Gold sales from reserves, an expansion in gold output capability, and the manipulation of interest rates and the money supply could be used to counter the economic dislocations resulting from an interruption in gold supplies from South Africa.

---

[34] Business Week, June 4, 1979: 76.

[35] In the short term, higher gold prices may mean a decrease in gold output because producers will process low-grade, previously uneconomic ores to take advantage of the price situation. This shift to lower-grade ores reduces the output of refined gold because the ore "throughput" capability remains the same. One mining company in the United States was recently reported to be processing 11 tons of low-grade ore to extract one ounce of gold (New York Times, November 1, 1979.) If gold prices remain high, producers can be expected to invest in expanded throughput capacity, increasing output in the medium term.

NOTES

Introduction

1. See Kenneth Grundy, *Confrontation and Accommodation in Southern Africa* (Berkeley: University of California Press, 1973); and Gwendolen Carter and Patrick O'Meara, *Southern Africa: The Continuing Crisis* (Bloomington: Indiana University Press, 1979).

2. See Committee on U.S. Policy Toward Southern Africa, *South Africa: Time Running Out* (Berkeley: University of California Press, 1981); Robert Price and Carl Rosberg, eds., *The Apartheid Regime: Political Power and Racial Domination* (Berkeley: Institute of International Studies, 1980); Heribert Adam and Hermann Giliomee, *Ethnic Power Mobilized: Can South Africa Change* (New Haven: Yale University Press, 1979); and Theodore Hanf et al., *South Africa: The Prospects for Peaceful Change* (Bloomington: Indiana University Press, 1981).

Chapter 1: Clough, "From Rhodesia to Zimbabwe"

1. For a more detailed discussion of bargaining, see the following: Glenn Snyder and Paul Diesing, *Conflict Among Nations* (Princeton: Princeton University Press, 1977), chs. 1 and 2; Fred Ikle, *How Nations Negotiate* (New York: Praeger, 1967); Thomas Schelling, *The Strategy of Conflict* (Cambridge, Mass.: Harvard University Press, 1960); Robert Jervis, "Bargaining and Bargaining Tactics," in *Coercion*, eds. J. Roland Pennock and John W. Chapman (New York: Lieber-Atherton, 1972; Nomos Series, no. 14); and William Fellner, *Competition Among the Few* (New York: Kelley, 1949).

2. See Schelling.

3. Snyder and Diesing, pp. 189-95.

4. *Ibid.*

5. See Kenneth Waltz, "The Myth of Interdependence," in *The Multinational Corporation*, ed. Charles Kindleberger (Cambridge, Mass.: MIT Press, 1974).

6. For general discussions of decolonization, see Rudolf von Albertini, *Decolonization* (Garden City, N.Y.: Doubleday, 1971), and William Roger Louis, *Imperialism at Bay* (London: Oxford University Press, 1978).

7. For a discussion of British decolonization policy, see Louis; see also David Goldsworthy, *Colonial Issues in British Politics, 1945-61* (Oxford: Clarendon

Press, 1971), and J.M. Lee, *Colonial Development and Good Government* (Oxford: Clarendon Press, 1967).

8. For discussion of the decline of British power, see Harold and Margaret Sprout, "Retreat from World Power," *World Politics* 15 (July 1963), and "The Dilemma of Rising Demands and Insufficient Resources," *ibid.*, 20, 4 (July 1968). For discussion of French foreign policy after World War II, see Alfred Grosser, *French Foreign Policy under De Gaulle* (Westport, Conn.: Greenwood Press, 1967), and Edward Kolodziej, *French International Policy under De Gaulle and Pompidou* (Ithaca: Cornell University Press, 1974).

9. See Ian Drummond, *Imperial Economic Policy, 1917-39* (London: Allen and Unwin, 1974); for a contrary view, see Walter Rodney, *How Europe Underdeveloped Africa* (Washington, D.C.: Howard University Press, 1974).

10. See Colin Leys, *Underdevelopment in Kenya* (Berkeley: University of California Press, 1975); Gary Wasserman, *The Politics of Decolonization* (Cambridge: Cambridge University Press, 1976); and Michael Barratt Brown, *After Imperialism* (New York: Humanities Press, 1970).

11. Quoted in Tony Smith, *The French Stake in Algeria, 1945-62* (Ithaca: Cornell University Press, 1978), p. 49. On the symbolic importance to France of its colonies, see also Alistair Horne, *A Savage War of Peace* (New York: Viking, 1978), and D. Bruce Marshall, *The French Colonial Myth and Constitution Making in the Fourth Republic* (New Haven: Yale University Press, 1973).

12. Quoted in John Marcum, *The Angolan Revolution* (Cambridge, Mass.: MIT Press, 1978), vol. 2, p. 297. For further discussion of Portuguese colonial policy, see the following: David Abshire and Michael Samuels, eds., *Portuguese Africa* (New York: Praeger, 1969); James Duffy, *Portugal in Africa* (Cambridge, Mass.: Harvard University Press, 1962); and Gerald Bender, *Angola under the Portuguese* (Berkeley: University of California Press, 1978).

13. Quoted in Marcum, p. 294.

14. See Louis.

15. For a discussion of French decolonization of West Africa, see Michael Crowder and Donal Cruise O'Brien, "French West Africa, 1945-60," in *History of West Africa*, eds. J.F. Ade Ajayi and Michael Crowder (New York: Columbia University Press, 1973); Guy De Lusignan, *French-Speaking Africa Since Independence* (New York: Praeger, 1969); and Marshall.

16. See Gerald Bender, "Portugal and Her Colonies Join the Twentieth Century," *UFAHAMU* 4, 3 (Winter 1974); Elizabeth Morris, "Portugal's Year in Africa," in *Africa Contemporary Record, 1972-73*, ed. Colin Legum (cited hereafter as *ACR*); and Marcum, pp. 241-43.

17. See Donald Rothchild, "Racial Stratification and Bargaining," *Canadian Journal of African Studies* 7, 3 (1973), and Wasserman.

18. On the pre-UDI period, see: James Barber, *Rhodesia: The Road to Rebellion* (London: Institute of Race Relations, 1967); Robert Blake, *A History of Rhodesia* (New York: Knopf, 1978); Larry Bowman, *Politics in Rhodesia* (Cambridge, Mass.: Harvard University Press, 1973); Martin Looney, *White Racism and Imperial Response* (Middlesex: Penguin Books, 1975).

19. See Bowman.

20. On UDI, see the following: Robert Good, *UDI: The International Politics of the Rhodesian Rebellion* (Princeton: Princeton University Press, 1973); Elaine Windrich, *Britain and the Politics of Rhodesian Independence* (New York: Africana, 1978); James Barber, *South Africa's Foreign Policy, 1945-70* (London: Oxford University Press, 1973); and Sam C. Nolutshungu, *South Africa in Africa* (New York: Africana, 1975).

21. See Anthony Lake, *The "Tar Baby" Option: American Policy Toward Southern Rhodesia* (New York: Columbia University Press, 1976), pp. 35-59; Harry Strack, *Sanctions: The Case of Rhodesia* (Syracuse: Syracuse University Press, 1978); and Good.

22. See Barber, *South Africa's Foreign Policy*, pp. 177-80, and Nolutshungu, pp. 174-90.

23. On the development of black nationalism in Rhodesia, see the following: Wilson Nyangoni, *African Nationalism in Zimbabwe* (Washington, D.C.: University Press of America, 1978); Lawrence Vambe, *From Rhodesia to Zimbabwe* (Pittsburgh: University of Pittsburgh Press, 1976); Masipula Sithole, "Ethnicity and Factionalism in Zimbabwe Nationalist Politics;" paper presented at Tenth Annual Congress of the Association for Sociology in Southern Africa, Maseru, Lesotho, 26-28 June 1979; and Bowman, pp. 45-61. For a specific discussion of the early development of the liberation movements, see Anthony Wilkinson, "From Rhodesia to Zimbabwe," in Basil Davidson et al., *Southern Africa: The New Politics of Revolution* (New York: Penguin Books, 1976), and Richard Gibson, *African Liberation Movements* (London: Oxford University Press, 1972), pp. 143-84. On the weakness of the nationalist movements at the time of UDI, see Good, *UDI*, pp. 82-83.

24. See Jorge Jardim, *Sanctions Double-Cross: Oil to Rhodesia* (Bulawayo: Books of Rhodesia Publishing Co., 1978); Strack; and Lake, pp. 158-97.

25. See Robert Good, "Rhodesia: Towards a New Policy Context," *Africa Today* 13, 4 (1971): 7, and Lake, pp. 60-122.

26. See Windrich, pp. 76-161.

27. See Mohamed El Khawas and Barry Cohen, eds., *The Kissinger Study of Southern Africa* (Westport, Conn.: Lawrence Hill, 1976); Roger Morris, *Uncertain Greatness: Henry Kissinger and American Foreign Policy* (New York: Harper and Row, 1977), pp. 107-20; and Lake, pp. 123-57.

28. See Good, *UDI*, pp. 303-9; Looney, pp. 170-82; and Windrich, pp. 162-85.

29. See "Report of the Commission on Rhodesian Opinion under the Chairmanship of the Right, Hon. the Lord Pearce," May 1972; "Rhodesia," in *ACR, 1972-73*; and Windrich, pp. 186-200.

30. *Ibid.*, pp. 201-20.

31. See A.K.H. Weinrich, "The African National Council: Past Performance and Present Prospects," *Africa Today*, 1974-75; "Rhodesia," in *ACR, 1972-73*, pp. B449-50.

32. *Ibid.*, pp. B488-94.

33. In 1965 one ZANU member wrote, "The present tendency . . . is to hate each other more than we hate the real enemy" (Nathan Shamuyarira, *Crisis in Rhodesia* [Central Islip, N.Y.: Transatlantic, 1965], p. 191). For partisan account of divisions in nationalist movement, see Masipula Sithole, *Zimbabwe Struggles within the Struggle* (Salisbury: Rujeko Publishers, 1979). For attempts to explain cleavages in nationalist movement, see Barry Schutz, "The Colonial Heritage of Strife: Sources of Cleavage in the Zimbabwe Liberation Movement," *Africa Today* 25, 1 (January-March 1978), and Julian Henriques, "The Struggles of the Zimbabweans," *African Affairs*, October 1977.

34. See Wilkinson, pp. 232-46.

35. For a discussion of the evolution of liberation strategy, see Selma Waldman, "Armed Struggle in Zimbabwe," *UFAHAMU* 3 (1975); Nyangoni, pp. 93-138; and Wilkinson, pp. 256-75.

36. See *ACR, 1972-73*, pp. B451-52.

37. *Times* (London), 7 February 1974.

38. See *ACR, 1973-74.*

39. See Good, *UDI*, and Windrich.

40. *Africa Research Bulletin*, 1-30 June 1975, pp. 3654-57 (cited hereafter as *ARB*); *Africa Report*, May-June 1975, pp. 2-17; and *ACR, 1975-76.*

41. See R.W. Johnson, *How Long Will South Africa Survive?* (London: Oxford University Press, 1977), p. 113, esp. footnote 61.

42. *Ibid.*, pp. 114-15, 129-32.

43. See Otto Geyser, *Detente in Southern Africa* (Bloemfontein: Institute for Contemporary History, 1976), and Nolutshungu.

44. For an account of the negotiations between South Africa, the Frontline States, and the Rhodesian parties in 1974-75, see Colin Legum, "The Secret Diplomacy of Detente," in *ACR, 1974-75*; *ARB*, 1-31 December 1974, pp. 3466-73; and *New York Times*, 20 December 1974.

45. See Legum, "Secret Diplomacy," and *ARB*, 1-31 December 1974, p. 3467.

46. See *ACR, 1975-76*, pp. B644-51; *ARB*, 1-31 August 1975, pp. 3737-41; and *New York Times*, 29 August 1975.

47. See *ACR, 1975-76*, pp. B651-53.

48. *Ibid.*, pp. B641-43.

49. *New York Times*, 10 March 1976.

50. *Manchester Guardian*, 13 June 1976.

51. *Ibid.*, 26 April 1976.

52. *ARB*, 1-31 December 1975, p. 3867.

53. See *ACR, 1975-76*, and *ARB*, 1-28 February 1976, p. 3939.

54. *Ibid.*

55. *Ibid.*, 1-31 March 1976, pp. 3969-70.

56. *Ibid.*, pp. 3971-72.

57. *Department of State Bulletin*, 31 May 1976.

58. See Colin Legum, *Southern Africa: The Year of the Whirlwind* (New York: Africana, 1977), and Johnson, pp. 220-53.

59. See Legum, *Southern Africa*; Johnson, pp. 1-16; and *Times* (London), 25 January 1977.

60. *ARB*, 1-31 January 1977.

61. *ACR, 1974-75*, p. A14.

62. Legum, *Southern Africa*, p. 29.

63. See Lake, pp. 198-238.

64. For details of Kissinger's dealings, see Legum, *Southern Africa*, pp. 40-43, and testimony of William Rogers, United States Senate, Committee on Foreign Relations, Subcommittee on African Affairs, *South Africa, Hearings*, September 1976.

65. See Kissinger's testimony, United States Senate, Committee on Foreign Relations, June 1976.

66. *Washington Post*, 3 July 1979.

67. *ARB*, 1-30 November 1976.

68. *International Herald Tribune*, 20 November 1976.

69. See *Daily Telegraph* (London), 25 March 1977; *Manchester Guardian*, 10 April 1977; *Financial Times* (London), 21 April 1977; and G.M.E. Leistner, "Can Rhodesia Survive Economically?," *Bulletin of the Africa Institute of South Africa*, nos. 3 and 4, 1977.

70. See Michael Clough, "From South West Africa to Namibia," in this volume.

71. *Department of State Bulletin*, 21 February 1977, p. 137.

72. *Manchester Guardian*, 29 January 1977.

73. *Rhodesian Herald*, 11 February 1977.

74. Quoted in *Daily Telegraph* (London), 15 February 1977.

75. *Times* (London), 11 May 1977.

76. *Rhodesia: Proposals for a Settlement* (London: Her Majesty's Government, September 1977); see also *ARB*, 1-30 September 1977, pp. 4571-78.

77. *Manchester Guardian*, 19 July 1980.

78. *Times* (London), 27 July 1980.

79. *Manchester Guardian*, 29 November 1980.

80. *Ibid.*, 14 January 1978.

81. *New York Times*, 23 March 1978.

82. *Department of State Bulletin*, 21 February 1977, p. 137.

83. *Congressional Record*, 15 March 1977, p. S4309.

84. *ARB*, 1-31 January 1978, p. 4718.

85. *Ibid.*

86. See, e.g., "Spoiler's Role in Rhodesia," *Washington Star*, 31 January 1978.

87. *New York Times*, 9 March 1978.

88. *Ibid.*, 28 March 1978.

89. *Public Papers of the Presidents, Jimmy Carter* (Washington, D.C.: Government Printing Office, 1978), pp. 664-65.

90. See *Washington Post*, 19 April 1978; *New York Times*, 19 April 1978; and *Financial Times* (London), 19 April 1978.

91. *ARB*, 1-30 April 1978, p. 3828.

92. *Daily Telegraph* (London), 25 April 1978.

93. *ARB*, 1-31 May 1978, p. 4863.

94. *Manchester Guardian*, 16 June 1978.

95. *ARB*, 1-30 June 1978.

96. *New York Times*, 4 September 1978; *ARB*, 1-30 September 1978, pp. 4994-95; *Washington Star*, 4 September 1978.

97. *Christian Science Monitor*, 6 September 1978.

98. *Washington Post*, 14 September 1978.

99. *Congressional Quarterly Almanac* 34 (1978): 419.

100. *New York Times*, 18 July 1978.

101. *Congressional Record*, 26 July 1978.

102. *ARB*, 1-31 July 1978, p. 4934.

103. *Times* (London), 8 August 1978.

104. *Manchester Guardian*, 8 August 1978.

105. *ARB*, 1-28 February 1978, p. 4757.

106. For details of the difficulties this invitation caused the Carter administration, see articles in State Department *AF Press Clips*, 4 October 1978.

107. *ARB*, 1-31 October 1978, p. 5032. For analysis of the visit by the Salisbury leaders, see *Washington Star*, 13 October 1978; *Baltimore Sun*, 15 October 1978; and *Washington Post*, 15 October 1978.

108. *ARB*, 1-31 October 1978, pp. 5033-34. For a determination of who supported an all-parties conference at various times, see Library of Congress, Congressional Research Service, "A Chronology of Statements on a Rhodesian Peace Conference and Related Events," 16 May 1979.

109. Letter from Hughes to Prime Minister Callaghan.

110. *ARB*, 1-30 September 1978, pp. 4998-99.

111. *Ibid.*, 1-31 October 1978, p. 5035.

112. See *Washington Post*, 3 and 4 December 1978, and *Observer* (London), 3 December 1978.

113. *Daily Telegraph* (London), 21 December 1978.

114. *New York Times*, 26 January 1979; *Washington Post*, 18 December 1978.

115. *ARB*, 1-31 December 1978, p. 5105.

116. *New York Times*, 19 February 1979.

117. *Washington Post*, 31 January 1979.

118. See Deon Geldenhuys, "South Africa's Regional Policy," in this volume.

119. *Washington Post*, 15 March 1979.

120. *ARB*, 1-30 April 1979, p. 5240.

121. *Manchester Guardian*, 1 December 1978.

122. For a discussion of the constitution agreed to by the internal parties, see *Washington Post*, 25 June 1979.

123. See *ARB*, 1-30 April 1979, pp. 5240-41, and 1-31 May 1979, pp. 5276-77; *New York Times*, 22 April 1979; *Washington Star*, 29 April 1979; and Testimony before Africa Subcommittee, Committee on Foreign Affairs, House of Representatives, 14 May 1979.

124. For example, see Martin Dickson in the *Financial Times* (London), 24 April 1979, and *Washington Post*, 9 and 27 April 1979.

125. *ARB*, 1-30 April 1979, p. 5241.

126. *Washington Star*, 29 April 1979.

127. *ARB*, 1-31 May 1979, p. 5280.

128. *Manchester Guardian*, 15 May 1979.

129. *Washington Star*, 23 May 1979.

130. *Daily Telegraph* (London), 5 May 1979.

131. *New York Times*, 8 April 1979.

132. *Washington Post*, 25 April 1979.

133. *Ibid.*, 22 May 1979, and *Manchester Guardian*, 24 May 1979.

134. *New York Times*, 17 May 1979.

135. *Ibid.*, 23 May 1979.

136. *Times* (London), 27 May 1979.

137. For a review of Congressional response, see Robert Cabelly, "Congress and the Rhodesian Situation" (Washington, D.C.: Government Research Corporation, 22 March 1979), and *African Index*, 16-30 April 1979.

138. *New York Times*, 9 June 1979.

139. *Ibid.* For an analysis of Carter's decision, see *ibid.*, 10 June 1979.

140. *Washington Post*, 8 June 1979.

141. Vance presented Congressional testimony on 12 June 1979; see *Department of State Bulletin*, July 1979.

142. Quotes in this paragraph are from *ibid.*

143. See *African Index*, 16-30 June 1979.

144. *Financial Times* (London), 26 June 1979.

145. See "Nigeria: Africa's Pacesetter on the Rhodesian Sanctions Issue," *African Index*, 1-15 June 1979.

146. *ARB*, 1-31 July 1979, p. 5346.

147. Based on the author's interviews with government officials in Salisbury at the time of the Commonwealth conference.

148. For details of the Commonwealth conference, see *African Index*, 1-15 August 1979; *New York Times*, 6 August 1979; *Washington Post*, 8 August 1979; and *ARB*, 1-31 August, pp. 5358-64.

149. This section draws heavily on Michael Clough, "The First Five Weeks of the Carrington Show," *African Index*, 1-15 October 1979.

150. *Ibid.*, p. 70.

151. *Times* (London), 12 August 1979.

152. Foreign Broadcast Information Service (FBIS), *Africa, Daily Report*, 9 August 1979, p. E2.

153. See "Rhodesia's New Black Rulers in Trouble on Peace Pledge," *Washington Star*, 18 June 1979; "New Rhodesia Remains Run by Whites," *ibid.*, 22 July 1979; "Blacks See Few Changes by Muzorewa," *Washington Post*, 1 August 1979; "A New 'Crisis of Confidence' Faces the Muzorewa Regime," *New York Times*, 12 August 1979; "Rhodesia Failing to Spark

Defections from Guerrillas," *Washington Star*, 2 September 1979; and "Rhodesia War: Outlook Bleak," *New York Times*, 27 April 1979.

154. *Washington Star*, 22 July 1979.

155. *Ibid.*

156. Clough, "The First Five Weeks," p. 70.

157. For a discussion of the Lusaka Manifesto, see Michael Clough and John Ravenhill, "Regional Cooperation in Southern Africa: The Southern African Development Coordination Conference," in this volume.

158. See "Why Salisbury Is Squeezing Kaunda," *Financial Times* (London), 24 October 1979; "Botswana Uneasily Shelters Zimbabwe Refugees," *Christian Science Monitor*, 31 October 1979; and "Kaunda's Agony," *Sunday Times* (London), 29 October 1978.

159. See Clough and Ravenhill.

160. Clough, "The First Five Weeks," p. 69.

161. *Time*, 20 August 1979.

162. *Washington Post*, 16 August 1979.

163. FBIS, *Africa, Daily Report*, 9 September 1979.

164. *Daily Telegraph* (London), 19 September 1979; see also *Christian Science Monitor*, 19 September 1979, and Clough, "The First Five Weeks," p. 71.

165. *Times* (London), 12 September 1979.

166. *Ibid.*, 13 September 1979.

167. Clough, "The First Five Weeks," p. 71.

168. *Washington Post*, 15 September 1979.

169. See *Washington Star*, 29 September 1979; *Washington Post*, 9 October 1979; and *New York Times*, 15 November 1979.

170. Clough, "The First Five Weeks," p. 72.

171. *Ibid.*

172. Quotes in this paragraph are from *ibid.*

173. *Ibid.*

174. *New York Times*, 16 October 1979.

175. *Times* (London), 16 October 1979.

176. See Michael Clough, "Peace in Rhodesia?," *African Index*, 1-17 December 1979, and "Progress Toward a Rhodesian Ceasefire," *ibid.*, 1-15 November 1979.

177. See Michael Clough, "The Mugabe Landslide," *ibid.*, 7 March 1980.

178. *Ibid.*, and *ARB*, 1-28 February 1980, and 1-31 March 1980.

179. *Washington Post*, 3 July 1979.

Chapter 2: Clough, "From South West Africa to Namibia"

1. The best historical overviews of the South West Africa/Namibia issue are the following: Gail-Maryse Cockram, *South West African Mandate* (Cape Town: Jutas Press, 1976); Solomon Slonim, *South West Africa and the United Nations: An International Mandate in Dispute* (Baltimore: Johns Hopkins Press, 1973); and John Dugard, ed., *The South West Africa/Namibia Dispute: Documents and Scholarly Writings on the Controversy between South Africa and the United Nations* (Berkeley: University of California Press, 1973).

2. Dugard, p. 73.

3. Quoted in Slonim, p. 37.

4. *Ibid.*, p. 76.

5. For a discussion of the significance of the 1948 election, see T.R.H. Davenport, *South Africa: A Modern History*, 2nd ed. (Toronto: University of Toronto Press, 1978), pp. 257-76, and T. Dunbar Moodie, *The Rise of Afrikanerdom: Power, Apartheid, and the Afrikaner Civil Religion* (Berkeley: University of California Press, 1975), pp. 234-58.

6. See Slonim, pp. 180-84.

7. *Ibid.*, p. 313.

8. On the Odendaal strategy, see Wolfgang H. Thomas, *Economic Development in Namibia* (Munich: Chr. Kaiser Verlag, 1978), pp. 49-56.

9. The ICJ decision is reprinted in Dugard.

10. *UN Monthly Chronicle*, March 1972, pp. 3-52.

11. See J.H.P. Serfontein, *Namibia?* (Randburg: Fokus Suid, 1976), pp. 68-91.

12. *Ibid.*, p. 82.

13. *Ibid.*, p. 91.

14. On the evolution of nationalist movements in Namibia, see the following: Richard Gibson, *African Liberation Movements* (London: Institute of Race Relations, 1972), pp. 107-41; Hidipo Hamutena and Gottfried Geingob, "African Nationalism in Namibia," in *Southern Africa in Perspective: Essays in Regional Politics*, eds. Christian Potholm and Richard Dale (New York: Free Press, 1972); Gerhard Totemeyer: *South West Africa/Namibia: Facts, Attitudes, Assessment and Prospects* (Randburg: Fokus Suid, 1977), and *Namibia Old and New: Traditional and Modern Leaders in Ovamboland* (New York: St. Martin's Press, 1978); and Serfontein, pp. 134-91.

15. *Ibid.*, pp. 96-100.

16. *UN Monthly Chronicle*, January 1975, pp. 15-27.

17. See OAU Declaration of Dar es Salaam on Southern Africa, reprinted in *Africa Contemporary Record 1974-75*, ed. Colin Legum, pp. C71-75 (cited hereafter as *ACR*), and Colin Legum, *Southern Africa: The Secret Diplomacy of Detente* (New York: Africana, 1975).

18. Quoted in Serfontein, p. 107.

19. *Ibid.*, p. 250.

20. *Ibid.*, pp. 250-51.

21. Quoted in *ibid.*, p. 110.

22. *Ibid.*, pp. 110-11.

23. For accounts of the conference, see *ACR, 1975-76*, pp. B557-58; Thomas, pp. 56-68; and Serfontein, pp. 262-98.

24. *Africa Research Bulletin*, 1-30 September 1975, p. 3770. (Cited hereafter as *ARB*.)

25. *Ibid.*, 1-31 August 1976, pp. 4136-38.

26. *Ibid.*, 1-31 March 1977, pp. 4370-71.

27. *ACR, 1977-78*, p. B843.

28. See R.W. Johnson, *How Long Will South Africa Survive?* (London: Oxford University Press, 1977), and Colin Legum, *Southern Africa: The Year of the Whirlwind* (New York: Africana, 1977).

29. *ACR, 1977-78*, p. B844.

30. *UN Chronicle*, February 1976, pp. 18-28.

31. *ARB*, 1-28 February 1978, pp. 4759-60.

32. *Ibid.*, p. 4760.

33. *Ibid.*, 1-30 April 1978, p. 4829, and 1-31 July 1978, p. 4935.

34. *UN Chronicle*, August-September 1978, pp. 5-20.

35. *ARB*, 1-31 July 1978, pp. 4936-38.

36. *UN Chronicle*, August-September 1978, pp. 5-20.

37. *ARB*, 1-30 September 1978, p. 4999.

38. *Ibid.*, p. 5000.

39. *UN Chronicle*, October 1978, pp. 5-16.

40. *ARB*, 1-31 October 1978, pp. 5038-39.

41. *Ibid.*

42. *Ibid.*, 1-31 December 1978, p. 5103.

43. *Ibid.*, pp. 5103-4.

44. *ACR, 1977-78*, p. B847.

45. *Southern Africa Record*, no. 15 (April 1979): 2-4.

46. *Ibid.*

47. *Ibid.*

48. See André du Pisani, *A Review of the Diplomatic Efforts of the Western Contact Group on Namibia, 1976-80* (Johannesburg: South African Institute of International Affairs, Occasional Paper, October 1980).

49. *UN Chronicle*, September-October 1980, pp. 18-19.

50. *Christian Science Monitor*, 31 October 1980.

51. See Michael Clough, "Namibia, 1981?," *African Index*, 17 December 1980.

52. *Ibid.*

53. Foreign Broadcast Information Service (FBIS), *Daily Report*, 25 November 1980, p. U1.

54. *Ibid.*, 7 January 1981, p. U1.

55. *Windhoek Advertiser*, 15 January 1981.

56. *Die Transvaler*, 25 March 1981. The quotes in the remainder of this paragraph are from this article.

57. *Rand Daily Mail*, September 1980.

58. *Windhoek Advertiser*, 31 December 1980.

59. *Times* (London), 14 January 1981.

60. *Africa Confidential*, 14 January 1981.

61. *ARB*, 1-31 November 1980.

62. *Rand Daily Mail*, 16 June 1980; *Washington Post*, 1 June 1981.

63. FBIS, *Sub-Saharan Africa Report*, 2 July 1980, p. 67.

64. *Windhoek Observer*, 4 April 1981.

65. *Windhoek Republikein*, 4 September 1981.

66. *Die Transvaler*, 25 March 1981.

67. See *The Star* (Johannesburg), 27 May 1980, and *Windhoek Observer*, 11 April, 10 and 17 May, and 23 August 1980.

68. See Michael Shannon McCrary, "Guerrilla Warfare in Namibia and Associated Implications for External Military Involvement"; Masters thesis, Naval Postgraduate School, March 1979.

69. *ARB*, 1-31 January 1981.

70. *Windhoek Observer*, 17 January 1981, and *Windhoek Advertiser*, 23 December 1980.

71. *Africa Confidential*, 20 May 1981.

72. *Die Burger*, 4 August 1980.

73. *Sunday Times* (Johannesburg), 17 August 1980.

74. *Windhoek Advertiser*, 3 September 1981.

75. For details, see Chapter 1 above.

76. *Department of State Bulletin*, October 1981, p. 27.

77. See *New York Times*, 23 January 1981, and *Washington Post*, 25 April 1981.

Chapter 3: Green, "One Namibia, One Nation"

1. Union of South Africa, *House of Assembly Debates*, 1947 (Pretoria: Government Printer), col. 5557.

2. Told to author by the Namibian.

3. Lusaka, 1976.

4. Interview with Nujoma in R. H. Green, M. L. and K. Kiljunen, *Namibia: The Last Colony* (London: Longmans, 1981).

5. *Ibid.*, pp. 11-14.

6. Author's discussions with SWAPO personnel and fragmentary accounts from visitors to SWAPO-controlled areas.

7. For detailed statistical estimates and political-economic description, see the following: R. H. Green, *Namibia: A Political Economic Survey* (Sussex: Institute of Development Studies, 1979; Discussion Paper 144); W. S. Barthold, *Namibia's Economic Potential and Existing Economic Ties with the Republic of South Africa* (Berlin: German Development Institute, 1978); and W. H. Thomas, *Economic Development in Namibia: Towards Acceptable Development Strategies for Independent Namibia* (Munich: Kaiser/Grunewald, 1978).

8. See W. G. Clarence-Smith and R. Moorsom, "Underdevelopment and Class Formation in Ovambo-land, 1845-1915," *Journal of African History* 16, 3 (1975); U. Al-Nagar, "African Initiative in Namibia in the Pre-Colonial Period"; paper presented at International Conference on Southern African History, University of Lesotho, Roma, August 1977.

9. See H. Bley, *South West Africa under German Rule* (London: Heinemann, 1971); Republic of South Africa, *Report of the Commission of Enquiry into South West African Affairs, 1962-1963* (the Odendaal Report) (Pretoria: Government Printer, 1963); Department of Foreign Affairs, *South West Africa Survey*, 1967 and 1974 (Pretoria: Government Printer, 1967 and 1974); R. First and R. Segal, eds., *South West Africa, Travesty of Trust* (London: Deutsch, 1967); R. H. Green and K. Kiljunen, "Unto What End: The Crisis of Colonialism in Namibia," and M. L. Kiljunen, "The Land and its People," in Green, Kiljunen, and Kiljunen.

10. See G. and S. Cronje, *The Workers of Namibia* (London: International Defence and Aid Fund, 1979); R. Moorsom, "Underdevelopment, Contract Labour and Workers' Consciousness in Namibia 1915-72," *Journal of Southern African Studies*, October 1977; "Focus on Namibia," *South African Labour Bulletin* 4, 1-2 (January-February 1978); R. Voipio "Con-

tract Work as Seen Through Ovambo Eyes," in Green, Kiljunen, and Kiljunen; UNIN, *Manpower Estimates and Development Implications for Namibia* (Lusaka, 1978; Namibia Studies Series No. 1).

11. In an article on the Namibia budget (17 September 1980), the *Financial Times* uses a figure of R1,300 ($1,725) million for GDP. More recent official figures (for 1979) exclude Walvis Bay and agricultural output used by the producing household or ranch. If adjusted for coverage, they appear to be within 2 to 3 percent of the estimates we have cited.

12. The South African population estimate of 1.0 million is too low. See UNIN, *Manpower Estimates*, pp. 7-15, for a fuller discussion.

13. Additional abbatoir capacity is apparently about to be built (*Windhoek Advertiser*, 17 September 1980). Negative weather and price patterns are reviewed in "Farm Industry Plagued by Drought," *Financial Times*, 12 November 1981.

14. For more detailed discussion see "Namibia," in *Africa Contemporary Record, 1977-78, 1978-79,* and *1979-80* (London: Africana).

15. For a more detailed breakdown of the secondary and tertiary sectors, see Green, *Namibia: A Political Economic Survey*.

16. *Windhoek Advertiser*, 19 May 1978; University of Port Elizabeth Study.

17. See UNIN, *Manpower Estimates*, esp. chs. 3 and 4.

18. R. Murray, J. Morris, J. Dugard, and N. Rubin, *The Role of Foreign Firms in Namibia* (London: Africana Publications Trust, 1974); Commonwealth Secretariat, *The Mineral Industry of Namibia: Perspectives for Independence* (London, 1978).

19. "Discussion Paper on the Constitution of Independent Namibia, 1975"; reprinted in U. Lissner, *Namibia 1975: Hope, Fear and Ambiguity* (Geneva: Lutheran World Federation, 1976); SWAPO, *Political Programme* (Lusaka, 1976); "SWAPO Political Programme" (Lusaka, 1976).

20. See Cronje and Cronje, esp. ch. 7, ap. B, "Focus on Namibia."

21. SWAPO, *Political Programme*.

22. *The Herald* (Salisbury), 10 November 1981.

23. *Ibid.*

24. See C. Collins, "SWAPO's Images of a Future Society: Women in Namibia," *Issue* 7, 4 (Winter 1977). This paragraph draws on two 1979 presentations by and discussions with Martha Ford, then SWAPO Women's Secretary.

25. SADCC (Lusaka, 1 April 1980); the document is known as the "Lusaka Declaration."

26. The farm planning mechanism is detailed in C. Nixon, "Land Use and Development in Namibia"; mimeo, 1978; see also S. Mshonga, *Toward Agrarian Reform* (Lusaka: UNIN, 1979; Namibia Studies No. 3).

27. See D. Geldenhuys and D. Venter, "Regional Cooperation in Southern Africa: A Constellation of States," *International Affaris Bulletin* (South African Institute of International Relations, December 1979); R. H. Green: "Constellation, Association, Liberation: The Struggle for Southern African Development Coordination," *Africa Contemporary Record, 1979-80*; and "Southern African Development Coordination: The Struggle Continues," *ibid., 1980-81*.

28. For example, there was a December 1980 seminar at the Royal Swazi Spa for world businessmen organized by Business International SA and featuring a bevy of South African quasi-private (possibly ongoing Muldergate project-financed) consultancy, trade, and academic bodies.

29. "Southern African Development Coordination."

30. See SADCC Council of Ministers, "Communique" and "Statement," 18 November 1981; SADCC, *Conference Communique* (Blantyre, 20 November 1981); and J. Hanlon, "Forgetful Donors Reminded to Honour Promises," *Guardian*, 24 November 1981.

31. See SADCC: *Southern African Development Coordination—Toward Economic Liberation* (London: Rex Collings, 1981), and *Southern Africa: Toward Economic Liberation: Maputo Conference* (London,1981).

32. SADCC-2, "Communique," Conferencia do Maputo, 28 December 1980; included in SADCC, *Southern Africa: Toward Economic Liberation*.

33. *Ibid.*

34. SADCC-2, "Transport and Communications Projects" (1980), in *ibid.*, and parallel Blantyre conference paper, 1981.

35. SADCC-2, "Southern Africa: Regional Food Security" (1980), in SADCC, *Southern Africa: Toward Economic Liberation*, and parallel Blantyre conference paper, 1981.

36. SADCC-2, *Report of (Salisbury) Ministerial Meeting* (1980).

37. See R. H. Green, "Economic Coordination, Liberation and Development: Botswana/Namibia Perspectives," in *Papers on the Economy of Botswana*, ed. C. Harvey (London: Heinemann, 1981); "Armageddan: Maputo and Walvis Bay Race for Botswana Coal Exports," *Windhoek Advertiser*, 24 October 1980.

38. See reports on UN Council for Namibia 1980 uranium hearings—e.g., *Rand Daily Mail*, 5 and 12 July 1980; *Guardian*, 11 July 1980; SWAPO, *Information and Comments* 2, 5 (July 1980).

39. See Collins.

40. *Sunday Express*, 30 November 1980.

41. *Rand Daily Mail*, 9 and 20 October 1980.

42. Quoted in *Windhoek Advertiser*, 8 June 1979.

43. *Sunday Express*, 30 November 1980.

44. For example, see "Armageddan," *Windhoek Advertiser*, 24 October 1980.

45. Heard by author.

46. *Sunday Express*, 30 November 1980.

47. *Ibid.*

48. See *Windhoek Advertiser*, 4 and 27 July 1980; *To the Point*, 15 August 1980.

49. See Theo Ben Gurirab (SWAPO representative to the United Nations), "Statement at Uranium Hearings, July 7, 1980," in SWAPO, *Information and Comments*, 2, 5 (July 1980).

50. See interview with Moses Garoeb in *The Herald* (Salisbury), 10 November 1981.

51. Position conveyed to SWAPO participants at international seminars and meetings.

52. The threat was made to the Namibian Council of Churches when it pressed for South African withdrawal. The Republic's Prime Minister said that if pressure continued, RSA would withdraw but would take all the assets it had created and destroy the rest—citing the building in which they were meeting as an example. The religious leaders responded that nothing could be worse than continued South African occupation, and Botha stormed out of the meeting.

Chapter 4: Geldenhuys, "South Africa's Regional Policy"

1. See W. J. Breytenbach, ed., *The Constellation of States: A Consideration* (Johannesburg: South Africa Foundation, 1980). It should be pointed out that in this study Transkei, Bophuthatswana, and Venda are referred to as "independent" solely in the sense that this status has been conferred on them by acts of the South African Parliament—i.e., *Status of Transkei Act* (No. 100, 1976), *Status of Bophuthatswana Act* (No. 89, 1977), and *Status of Venda Act* (No. 107, 1979).

2. Quoted in G. S. Labuschagne, *Suid-Afrika en Afrika: Die staatkundige verhouding in die tydperk 1945-1966* (Potchefstroom: Sentrum vir Internasionale Politiek, 1969), p. 16.

3. Quoted in J. C. Smuts, Jr., *Jan Christian Smuts* (London: Cassell, 1952), p. 447.

4. Quoted in E. A. Walker, *A History of Southern Africa* (London: Longmans, 1968), p. 685.

5. Labuschagne, p. 19.

6. G. M. Cockram, *Vorster's Foreign Policy* (Pretoria: Academica, 1970), p. 116.

7. Labuschagne, p. 19.

8. South Africa, *Debates of the House of Assembly (Hansard)*, vol. 64, 1 September 1948, cols. 1325-26; vol. 68, 12 May 1949, cols. 5561-62; vol. 82, 11 August 1953, cols. 1327-28. (Cited hereafter as *HA Deb.*)

9. D. J. Geldenhuys, "The Effects of South Africa's Racial Policy on Anglo-South African Relations, 1945-1961"; unpublished Ph. D. dissertation, Cambridge University, 1977, pp. 242ff.

10. *Ibid.*, p. 245.

11. *Ibid.*

12. Labuschagne, p. 35.

13. Geldenhuys, "Anglo-South African Relations," p. 269.

14. G. C. Olivier, *Suid-Afrika se Buitelandse Beleid* (Pretoria: Academica, 1977), pp. 220-221.

15. See Geldenhuys, "Anglo-South African Relations," pp. 26, 27, 268ff. The sense of identity with whites elsewhere in Africa dates back to the 1920s, when Prime Minister Hertzog took an active interest in their position in Kenya.

16. Quoted in J. Barber, *South Africa's Foreign Policy 1945-1970* (London: Oxford University Press, 1973), p. 106.

17. S. C. Nolutshungu, *South Africa in Africa: A Study in Ideology and Foreign Policy* (Manchester: Manchester University Press, 1975), pp. 58, 76.

18. Labuschagne, pp. 34, 55-56.

19. M. E. Muller, *Suid-Afrika se Buitelandse Verteenwoordiging (1910-1972)* (Pretoria: J. L. van Schaik, 1976), pp. 82-90.

20. See Nolutshungu, p. 75, and *HA Deb.*, vol. 95, 10 June 1957, col. 7633.

21. *Ibid.*, vol. 99, 27 January 1959, cols. 60-65, and vol. 107, 10 April 1961, col. 4174.

22. *Ibid.*

23. L. E. Neame, *The History of Apartheid* (London: Pall Mall Press, 1962), p. 160.

24. *HA Deb.*, vol. 99, 27 January 1959, col. 64.

25. *Ibid.*, vol. 107, 10 April 1961, col. 4191.

26. *Ibid.*, vol. 101, 4 May 1959, cols. 5254-55, and South Africa Department of Information, *Dr. H. F. Verwoerd on I. Crisis in World Conscience II. Road to Freedom for Basutoland, Bechuanaland, Swaziland* (Pretoria, n.d.; Fact Paper 106), pp. 14-15.

27. T. D. Venter, "Confederal Association of States or Federation? A Future Political Dispensation for South and Southern Africa: Theoretical Perspectives for South African Party Politics," *South African Journal of African Affairs*, no. 1-2 (1976): 137.

28. A. Guelke, "Africa as a Market for South African Goods," *Journal of Modern African Studies* 12, 1 (1974): 70. The inclusion of the Congo was probably ⸍ not unrelated to South Africa's attempts in 1960 to forge a (covert) relationship with breakaway Katanga (see Nolutshungu, pp. 86-87).

29. Quoted in Cockram, p. 186.

30. See *ibid.*, p. 120.

31. See Labuschagne, p. 69, and G. D. Scholtz, *Dr. Hendrik Frensch Verwoerd, 1901-1966* (Johannesburg: Perskor, 1974), vol. 2, pp. 275-76.

32. Labuschagne, p. 69.

33. Quoted in Cockram, p. 151.

34. Barber, p. 23.

35. N. M. Stultz, "The Politics of Security: South Africa under Verwoerd, 1961-6," *Journal of Modern African Studies* 7, 1 (April 1969): 3-20.

36. See B. J. Vorster, *South Africa's Outward Policy* (Cape Town: Tafelberg, 1970); lecture originally delivered at the Annual General Meeting of the Suid-Afrikaanse Akademie vir Wetenskap en Kuns on South Africa in the World, Pretoria, July 1969; and C. W. De Kiewiet, "The World and Pretoria," *Africa Report* 14, 2 (February 1969): 48-49.

37. See Olivier, pp. 135-44.

38. See S. Ettinger, "The Economics of the Customs Union between Botswana, Lesotho, Swaziland and South Africa"; unpublished Ph. D. dissertation, University of Michigan, 1974.

39. Cockram, pp. 116ff.; W. J. Breytenbach, *South Africa's Involvement in Africa* (Pretoria: Africa Institute, 1978), and G. M. E. Leistner, *South Africa's Development Aid to African States* (Pretoria: Africa Institute of South Africa, 1970).

40. Nolutshungu, pp. 173, 263.

41. *Ibid.*, pp. 181-82.

42. G. K. H. Tötemeyer, *Namibia Old and New: Traditional and Modern Leaders in Ovamboland* (London: C. Hurst and Co., 1978), p. 194.

43. K. W. Grundy, *Confrontation and Accommodation in Southern Africa: The Limits of Independence* (Berkeley: University of California Press, 1973), pp. 41-46, and Nolutshungu, pp. 166-67.

44. See H. R. Strack, *Sanctions: The Case of Rhodesia* (Syracuse: Syracuse University Press, 1978), pp. 85-189.

45. *HA Deb.*, vol. 30, 15 September 1970, col. 4208.

46. *Ibid.*, col. 4207.

47. See C. J. A. Barratt, *Dialogue in Africa* (Johannesburg: South African Institute of International Affairs, 1971).

48. *Southern African Record*, no. 2 (June 1975): 1-7.

49. *Ibid.*, no. 3 (October 1975): 31-35.

50. *Bulletin van die Afrika-Instituut* 11, 9 (October 1971): 384

51. See C. Legum, *Vorster's Gamble for Africa: How the Search for Peace Failed* (London: Rex Collings, 1976), pp. 13-14.

52. *Ibid.*, p. 16.

53. South Africa, *Senate Debates*, 23 October 1974, vol. 2, cols. 3340, 3346.

54. "Statement by Ambassador R. F. Botha, Permanent Representative of South Africa to the United Nations, to the Security Council, 24 October 1974," *Southern Africa Record*, no. 1 (March 1975): 21.

55. "Uittreksels uit 'n toespraak deur die Suid-Afrikaanse Eerste Minister, Sy Edele B. J. Vorster, tydens 'n vergadering te Nigel op 5 November 1974," *ibid.*, pp. 39-40.

56. *Ibid.*, no. 2 (June 1975): 39.

57. Legum, *Vorster's Gamble*, pp. 23-25.

58. See Tötemeyer, pp. 136ff.

59. *Die Transvaler*, 23 December 1974.

60. "Uittreksels uit 'n toespraak deur . . . B. J. Vorster . . . op 5 November 1974," p. 47.

61. *Uittreksels uit 'n toespraak deur die Eerste Minister, B. J. Vorster, tydens die Eeufeesvierings te Sterkstroom, 13 September 1975* (Department of the Prime Minister), p. 11.

62. C. Legum and T. Hodges, *After Angola: The War Over Southern Africa* (London: Rex Collings, 1976), pp. 13-14.

63. *Ibid.*

64. *Ibid.*, pp. 15-17.

65. *HA Deb.*, vol. 64, 27 January 1976, col. 112.

66. Republic of South Africa, *White Paper on Defence 1977* (tabled in the Senate and the House of Assembly by the Minister of Defense), p. 6.

67. *HA Deb.*, vol. 64, 27 January 1976, col. 110.

68. *Ibid.*

69. *Ibid.*

70. *Ibid.*, col. 113.

71. See Legum and Hodges, pp. 14-15.

72. *HA Deb.*, vol. 64, 27 January 1976, col. 116.

73. See Legum and Hodges, pp. 37-38.

74. See *HA Deb.*, vol. 64, 27 January 1976, cols. 112, 132.

75. *Ibid.*, col. 116.

76. *Ibid.*, col. 114.

77. *Ibid.*, col. 117.

78. See J. Stockwell, *In Search of Enemies: A CIA Story* (London: André Deutsch, 1978), pp. 186ff.

79. Legum and Hodges, pp. 31-32.

80. *Ibid.*

81. See *HA Deb.*, vol. 64, 30 January 1976, col. 375.

82. See *ibid.*, col. 372.

83. *Ibid.*, vol. 50, 30 August 1974, col. 1858.

84. *Ibid.*, col. 1860.

85. *Ibid.*, vol. 51, 10 September 1974, col. 2594.

86. *Ibid.*, vol. 64, 27 January 1976, col. 132.

87. *Ibid.*, col. 372.

88. *Ibid.*, vol. 51, 10 September 1974, col. 2591.

89. See *ibid.*, vol. 64, 27 January 1976, col. 110.

90. See *ibid.*, 30 January 1976, col. 374.

91. See *ibid.*, vol. 50, 30 August 1974, cols. 1857-60, and vol. 51, 10 September 1974, cols. 2589-91.

92. See Cockram, pp. 160-72.

93. *HA Deb.*, vol. 64, 30 January 1976, cols. 357-58.

94. *Ibid.*

95. *Ibid.*, col. 375.

96. *Ibid.*, 27 January 1976, col. 112.

97. *Ibid.*

98. C. Legum, ed., *Africa Contemporary Record, 1976-77* (London: Rex Collings, 1977), vol. 9, p. A7.

99. See *HA Deb.*, vol. 60, 4 March 1976, cols. 2494-95, and vol. 66, 28 January 1977, cols. 397-404.

100. See D. G. Baker, "Kissinger . . . Carter: Two Views of Southern Africa," *Africa Institute Bulletin* 15, 8 (1977): 196-202, and R. W. Johnson, *How Long Will South Africa Survive?* (Johannesburg: Macmillan, 1977), pp. 209-42.

101. See *ibid.*, pp. 243-86, and "Address to the Nation by the Prime Minister, the Hon. Ian D. Smith, on 24 September, 1976," *Southern Africa Record*, no. 7 (December 1976): 39-44.

102. See Johnson, pp. 1-16.

103. See *HA Deb.*, vol. 66, 11 February 1977, col. 1284.

104. R. F. Botha in *ibid.*, vol. 69, 14 June 1977, col. 10085. Botha succeeded Muller as Foreign Minister on 1 April 1977.

105. *Ibid.*, vol. 69, 27 May 1977, col. 8712.

106. *Ibid.*, col. 8711.

107. *Ibid.*, vol. 69, 14 June 1977, col. 10085, and vol. 74, 6 June 1978, col. 8589.

108. *Ibid.*, vol. 72, 30 January 1978, col. 68.

109. *Ibid.*, vol. 74, 6 June 1978, col. 8589.

110. *Ibid.*

111. *Ibid.*

112. D. J. Geldenhuys, *The Neutral Option and Sub-Continental Solidarity: A Consideration of Foreign Minister Pik Botha's Zürich Statement of 7 March 1979* (Johannesburg: South African Institute of International Affairs, Occasional Paper, 1979), pp. 4-5, and T. D. Venter, "South Africa: A Non-Aligned Posture in Foreign Policy?," *South African Journal of African Affairs*, no. 3-4 (1979): 178-85.

113. On the pariah option, see P. C. J. Vale, "South Africa as a Pariah International State," *International Affairs Bulletin* 1, 3 (1977): 121-41. On Vorster's visit to Israel, see *HA Deb.*, vol. 61, 22 April 1976, cols. 5200-2. During the visit, the two countries signed an agreement which provided (*inter alia*) for economic, industrial, and technological cooperation.

114. "Uittreksels uit 'n toespraak deur die Suid-Afrikaanse Minister van Buitelandse Sake, Sy Edele dr Hilgard Muller, voor die Constantia-klub, Pretoria (22 Oktober 1976)," *Southern Africa Record*, no. 8 (March 1977): 20.

115. *Address by the Honourable P. W. Botha, Prime Minister, Minister of Defence and of National Security, on the Occasion of a National Party Congress in Durban on 15 August 1979* (Prime Minister's Office), p. 26.

116. See *HA Deb.*, vol. 74, 5 June 1978, cols. 8442-8557; 6 June 1978, cols. 8857-97, and vol. 81, 5 June 1979, cols. 7794-7962.

117. For the acts conferring independence, see footnote 1 above.

118. *Address by the Hon. R. F. Botha, South African Minister of Foreign Affairs, to Members and Guests of the Swiss-South African Association in Zürich, on 7th March 1979* (Berne: South African Embassy, Press Section), pp. 17-18.

119. See *HA Deb.*, vol. 79, 7 February, col. 229, and vol. 80, 19 April 1979, col. 4459; see also P. W. Botha's interview with the *New York Times*; quoted in *The Citizen,* 17 May 1979.

120. *HA Deb.*, vol. 80, 3 April 1979, col. 3919.

121. *Ibid.*, vol. 81, 5 June 1979, col. 7801.

122. *Ibid.*, vol. 81, 6 June 1979, col. 7940.

123. *Address by the Honourable P. W. Botha, Prime Minister, Carlton Centre, Johannesburg: 22 November 1979* (Department of Foreign Affairs), pp. 7-14. (Cited hereafter as *Carlton Address.*)

124. *HA Deb.*, vol. 81, 6 June 1979, col. 7940.

125. *Ibid.*, vol. 79, 7 February 1979, col. 249.

126. See *Address by the Hon. P. W. Botha, MP, DVD, at Pietersburg on 25 August 1979* (Prime Minister's Office), pp. 18-19.

127. See Grundy, pp. 28-82, and G. M. E. Leistner, "Economic Interdependence in Southern Africa," *Africa Institute Bulletin* 15, 9-10 (1978): 311-17.

128. *Address by the Hon. R. F. Botha... in Zürich,* p. 17.

129. *Carlton Address,* pp. 7-14.

130. *Rand Daily Mail,* 23 November 1979.

131. *HA Deb.*, vol. 81, 5 June 1979, col. 7804.

132. *Address by the Honourable P. W. Botha... National Party Congress in Durban,* p. 24, and *HA Deb.*, vol. 79, 9 February 1979, col. 3919.

133. *Address by the Hon. P. W. Botha... at Pietersburg,* p. 19, and *Carlton Address,* p. 36.

134. *HA Deb.*, vol. 81, 6 June 1979, col. 7884.

135. *Die Vaderland,* 20 April 1979, and *Die Transvaler,* 13 June 1979.

136. *The Star,* 8 April 1980, and *Rand Daily Mail,* 17 April 1980.

137. See *HA Deb.*, 6 February 1980, cols. 248-51 (at the time of this writing, 1980 issues of *HA Deb.* had not yet been bound into volumes); *Toespraak deur Sy Edele P. W. Botha, DVD LV, Eerste Minister, Minister van Verdediging en van die Nasionale Intelligensiediens, tydens 'n openbare vergadering te Fauresmith op 25 April 1980* (Department of Foreign Affairs and Information), pp. 24-27; *Toespraak deur Sy Edele P. W. Botha, DVD LV, Eerste Minister, Minister van Verdediging en van die Nasionale Intelligensiediens, tydens 'n openbare vergadering te Potchefstroom op 14 Augustus*

1980 (Department of Foreign Affairs and Information), pp. 19-22; "Konstellasie 'n tree nader," *Beeld*, 16 February 1980; "Second Step toward 'Constellation,'" *The Citizen*, 16 February 1980; "Carlton-beraad vorder goed," *Die Vaderland*, 16 May 1980; "Economic Union: P. W. Plans to Push Ahead the Carlton Way," *Sunday Times*, 18 May 1980; "P. W. roep 4 state byeen," *Beeld*, 18 July 1980; and "PM to Meet Black Leaders," *Rand Daily Mail*, 18 July 1980.

138. See the contributions from the government benches in the House of Assembly debates on foreign affairs in *HA Deb.*, 19 May 1980, cols. 6573-6712, and 20 May 1980, cols. 6714-53; see also comments of P. W. Botha reported in *Rand Daily Mail*, 30 June 1980.

139. *The Star*, 22 October and 26 November 1980; *Rand Daily Mail*, 22 October 1980; *Beeld*, 24 November 1980.

140. See, for example, *HA Deb.*, 19 May 1980, col. 6650.

141. *Address by the Honourable P. W. Botha . . . National Party Congress in Durban*, p. 26.

142. *Address by the Honourable P. W. Botha, MP, Prime Minister, Minister of Defence and of the National Intelligence Service, at the Opening Ceremony of the Summit Meeting in Pretoria on 23 July 1980* (Department of Foreign Affairs and Information), p. 7.

143. *Address by the Honourable P. W. Botha . . . National Party Congress in Durban*, p. 24.

144. *HA Deb.*, vol. 79, 7 February 1979, col. 248.

145. *Die Transvaler*, 7 and 10 August and 9 November 1979; *Beeld*, 10 and 13 August and 19 September 1979, and *The Star*, 30 October 1979.

146. On the dilemmas, see Breytenbach, *Constellation*, pp. 44-47, and D. J. Geldenhuys and T. D. Venter, "Regional Co-operation in Southern Africa: A Constellation of States?," *International Affairs Bulletin*, 3, 3 (December 1979): 59-60.

147. See comments of R. F. Botha reported in *The Citizen*, 29 August 1980, and of P. W. Botha reported in *Beeld*, 2 September 1980.

148. On South Africa's economic ties with black states in southern Africa, see Leistner, pp. 311-17; T. Malan, "Mozambique's and Zambia's Economic Relations with South Africa," *ISSUP Strategic Review*, January 1981; and *The Economist* Intelligence Unit, *Economic Reviews of Southern Africa*— various issues.

149. *HA Deb.*, 19 May 1980, col. 6651.

150. *The Star*, 4 March 1980.

151. *Ibid.*

152. *Rand Daily Mail*, 5 March 1980.

153. *Ibid.*

154. "Joint Statement Issued by the Governments of South Africa and Zimbabwe on 3 September 1980" (on trade representation), *Southern Africa Record*, no. 21 (October 1980): 47-48.

155. See "Extract from an Address by the Prime Minister of Zimbabwe, the Hon. Robert Mugabe, to the OAU 17th Ordinary Session of the Assembly of Heads of State and Government, in Freetown, Sierra Leone, on 2 July 1980," *ibid.*, pp. 35-37.

156. *HA Deb.*, 19 May 1980, cols. 6649-50.

157. *Ibid.*

158. See A. Du Pisani, *A Review of the Diplomatic Efforts of the Western Contact Group on Namibia, 1976-1980*, (Johannesburg: South African Institute of International Affairs, Occasional Paper, 1980).

159. See Otto Krause: "Nuwe opset kan ons bevry," *Die Transvaler*, 3 April 1980, and *The Star*, 3 September 1980.

160. *HA Deb.*, 6 February 1980, col. 251.

161. *Ibid.*, 19 May 1980, col. 6627.

162. *Ibid.*, vol. 80, 24 April 1979, col. 4803, and 1 May 1980, cols. 5296-97.

163. See *ibid.*, col. 5296.

164. See *ibid.*, cols. 5296-97.

165. *Ibid.*, vol. 60, 30 January 1976, col. 366.

166. See D. J. Geldenhuys, "Some Strategic Implications of Regional Economic Relationships for the Republic of South Africa," *ISSUP Strategic Review*, January 1981.

167. Comments of Pietie du Plessis, Minister of Agriculture, reported in *The Star*, 9 December 1980.

Chapter 5: Clough/Ravenhill, "Regional Cooperation in Southern Africa"

1. For a brief discussion of the Conference of Heads of State as an institution, see Kenneth Grundy, *Confrontation and Accommodation in Southern Africa* (Berkeley: University of California Press, 1973), pp. 113-17; for a history of PAFMECSA, see Richard Cox, *Pan-Africanism in Practice—An East African Study: PAFMECSA, 1958-64* (London: Oxford University Press, 1964), and Joseph Nye, *Pan Africanism and East African Liberation* (Cambridge, Mass.: Harvard University Press, 1965), pp. 119-28.

2. See Deon Geldenhuys, "South Africa's Regional Policy," in this volume.

3. For background on black African support for "dialogue" with South Africa, see the following: Carolyn McMaster, *Malawi—Foreign Policy and Develop-*

ment (New York: St. Martin's Press, 1969); T. David Williams, *Malawi— The Politics of Despair* (Ithaca: Cornell University Press, 1978), pp. 301-24; Sam C. Nolutshungu, *South Africa in Africa* (New York: Africana, 1975), pp. 191-295; and Grundy, pp. 118-51. On talks between Zambian and South African leaders, see Douglas Anglin and Timothy Shaw, *Zambia's Foreign Policy: Studies in Diplomacy and Dependence* (Boulder, Colo.: Westview, 1979), pp. 272-309. For texts of letters exchanged between President Kenneth Kaunda and Prime Minister B.J. Vorster on the subject of a regional modus vivendi, see *Southern Africa Record*, no. 11 (January 1978): pp. 27-52.

4. *Africa Research Bulletin*, 1-30 April 1969, pp. 1371-72. (Cited hereafter as *ARB.*)

5. The text of the Lusaka Manifesto is included in Grundy, pp. 315-23; see also Nathan Shamuyarira, "The Lusaka Manifesto," *East African Journal*, November 1969.

6. Passages from the Lusaka Manifesto in this paragraph are quoted in Grundy.

7. See James Barber, *South Africa's Foreign Policy, 1945-70* (London: Oxford University Press, 1973), pp. 271-72, and Nolutshungu, pp. 2666-68.

8. See various issues of *ARB*—1970, pp. 1921-24; 1971, pp. 2037-88, 2063-36, 2126-67, 2189-91; see also John Barrett, "Dialogue in Africa: A New Approach," *South Africa International*, October 1971.

9. *ARB*, 1-31 October 1971, pp. 2247-49.

10. *Ibid.*

11. *Ibid.*, 1-30 September 1972, pp. 2591-94.

12. *Ibid.*, pp. 3355-56.

13. See Colin Legum, *After Angola: The War Over Southern Africa* (London: Rex Collings, 1977), pp. 28-35, and John Marcum, *The Angolan Revolution* (Cambridge, Mass.: MIT Press, 1977), vol. 2.

14. For a discussion of the emergence of the Frontline States, see Colin Legum: *The Secret Diplomacy of Detente* (London: Rex Collings, 1975), and "Southern Africa: How the Search for Peaceful Change Failed," in *Africa Contemporary Record, 1975-76*, ed. C. Legum.

15. Quoted in Zdenek Cervenka, *The Unfinished Quest for Unity: Africa and the OAU* (New York: Africana, 1977), p. 127.

16. See Michael Clough, "From Rhodesia to Zimbabwe," in this volume.

17. Quoted in *ARB*, 15 June-14 July 1979, p. 5155.

18. *Ibid.*

19. For attempts to define the boundaries of a southern African region, see Grundy, and Kenneth Heard and Timothy Shaw, eds., *Cooperation and Conflict in Southern Africa* (Washington, D.C.: University Press of America,

1977). On the general problem of defining regions, see Richard Falk and Saul Mendlovitz, eds., *Regional Politics and World Order* (San Francisco: W.H. Freeman, 1973).

20. See McMaster;Williams, pp. 301-24;Nolutshungu, pp. 191-295,and Grundy, pp. 118-51.

21. On the costs borne by Mozambique as a result of its support of the liberation struggle in Zimbabwe, see Peter Meyns, "Transforming Liberation Ideology into National Development Strategy: Experiences from Mozambique"; paper presented at the Zimbabwe Economic Symposium, Salisbury, 8-10 September 1980, and Mario Azevedo, "A Sober Commitment to Liberation: Mozambique and South Africa, 1974-79," *African Affairs*, Spring 1981.

22. *Africa*, July 1980.

23. *Afrique-Asie*, 7-20 July 1980, supplement, pp. vi-xi.

24. *Rand Daily Mail*, 25 February 1980.

25. *Afrique-Asie*, 7-20 July 1980, supplement.

26. *Washington Post*, 31 March 1980.

27. Conclusion based on interviews with southern African leaders in September-October 1980.

28. B.D. Giles, "A Macro-Economic Study of the Southern African Area"; mimeo, 16 October 1978.

29. "First Steps Toward Economic Integration: Interests, Institutions, Instrumentalities"; paper presented at SADCC, Arusha, July 1979, p. 2.

30. On SACU, see Paul Mosley, "The Southern African Customs Union: A Reappraisal," *World Development* 6, 1 (January 1978): 31-43; Peter Robson, "Reappraising the Southern African Customs Union: A Comment," *ibid.* 6, 4 (April 1978): 461-66; Pierre Landell-Mills, "The Southern African Customs Union: A Comment on Mosley's Reappraisal," *ibid.* 7, 1 (January 1979): 83-85; and Paul Mosley, "Reply to Robson and Landell-Mills," *ibid.*, pp. 87-88. On the Central African Federation, see Colin Leys and Cranford Pratt, eds., *A New Deal in Central Africa* (New York: Praeger, 1960). On the East African Community, see John Ravenhill, "Regional Integration and Development in Africa: Lessons from the East African Community," *Journal of Commonwealth and Comparative Studies* 17, 3 (November 1979): 227-46; and Christian P. Potholm and Richard Fredland, eds., *Integration and Disintegration in East Africa* (Washington, D.C.: University Press of America, 1980). An excellent discussion of the problems generated by customs unions among developing countries can be found in Lynn K. Mytelka, "The Salience of Gains in Third World Integrative Systems," *World Politics* 25 (1973): 236-50.

31. On the prospects for economic growth in Zimbabwe, see Colin Stoneman, "Zimbabwe's Prospects as an Industrial Power," *Journal of Commonwealth*

and *Comparative Studies* 18, 1 (March 1980), and Robert Rotberg and William Overholt, *A Symposium on Zimbabwe's Economic Prospects* (Mt. Kisco, N.Y.: Seven Springs, February 1980).

32. Background paper, "First Steps Toward Economic Integration," p. 10.

33. *Ibid.*

34. Opening Address, Arusha, Tanzania, 3 July 1979.

35. "Southern Africa: Towards Economic Liberation."

36. *Ibid.*

37. *Ibid.*

38. *Ibid.*

39. *Christian Science Monitor*, 4 April 1980.

40. Professor Richard Harlen, Head of the Department of Electrical Engineering at the University of Zimbabwe, quoted in *The Herald* (Salisbury), 8 August 1980.

Chapter 6: Singleton, "The Natural Ally"

1. Quoted in the *Times* (London), 22 March 1980.

2. On Soviet naval missions, see Admiral Sergei Gorshkov, *Morskaya Moshch' Gosudarstva* (The sea power of the state) (Moscow, 1976). The book has recently been translated into English. Gorshkov discusses the priority of naval missions as follows: (a) attacking the enemy with seaborne missiles; (2) sea denial; (3) helping repel "imperialist aggression" in local conflicts; and (4) enhancing Soviet prestige.

3. On socialist orientation, see Boris Ponomarev, "Existing Socialism and Its International Significance," *Kommunist*, no. 2 (January 1976): 29-30, and particularly R. Ul'ianovskii, "On the Countries of Socialist Orientation," *ibid.*, no. 11 (July 1979). (*Kommunist* is the journal of the Central Committee of the Communist Party of the Soviet Union [CPSU]). See also Anatoly Gromyko, "Socialist Orientation in Africa," *International Affairs* (Moscow), September 1979; S. P. Nemanov, "Vanguard Parties in African Countries of Socialist Orientation," *Narody Azii i Afriki* (Peoples of Asia and Africa), no. 2 (1979). (All except the Gromyko article are in Russian.) Gromyko notes that the Soviet Central Asian Republics and Mongolia provide useful examples for African nations developing into socialism: "Their experience is invaluable for the socialist-oriented African and Asian nations, which are studying it" (p. 96). (For background on Gromyko, see footnote on p. 221 below.)

4. On Soviet airborne capabilities, see Kenneth Allard, "Soviet Airborne Forces and Preemptive Power Projection," *Parameters*, December 1980.

5. On the Soviet intervention, see Jiri Valenta, "Soviet Decision-Making on the Intervention in Angola," in *Communism in Africa*, ed. D. W. Albright (Bloomington: Indiana University Press, 1980).

6. Richard E. Bissell, "Soviet Activity in Africa," *South Africa International*, April 1980, p. 206.

7. *Vneshniaia Politika Sovetskogo Soiuza 1978* (Moscow, 1978), p. 177.

8. On the trial and for the communist view of mercenaries generally, see Wilfrid Burchett and Derek Roebuck, *The Whores of War* (London: Penguin, 1977). Burchett and Roebuck considered mercenaries a serious threat to the liberation movements; their use in Rhodesia was expected.

9. *Africa Contemporary Record 1977-78*, p. B503.

10. See Marina Ottaway, "The Theory and Practice of Marxism-Leninism in Mozambique and Ethiopia," in Albright, ed., pp. 124-28.

11. On East German policy in southern Africa, see "The Two Germanies in Africa," *Africa Contemporary Record 1978-1979*, pp. A99-107.

12. *Ibid.*, p. A4.

13. For representative Soviet attacks on China in league with racists, fascists, and imperialists, see B. B. Bogoslavskii, *Proiski Pekina v Afrike* (Peking's intrigues in Africa) (Kiev, 1978); Amath Damsoko and Essop Pahad, "Maoism Self-Exposed in Africa," *World Marxist Review*, April 1976; and V. N. Sofinskii and A. M. Khazanov, "Policy of the PRC in Nations of Tropical Africa," *Problemy Dal'nego Vostoka* (Problems of the Far East), no. 2 (1978).

14. *Africa Contemporary Record 1978-79*, p. B868.

15. A list of the parties that attended is in *World Marxist Review*, February 1979, pp. 3-4; it omits mention of the MPLA, which is curious. The speeches were reprinted in *ibid.*, various issues, early 1979.

16. U.S. Arms Control and Disarmament Agency (ACDA), *World Military Expenditures and Arms Transfers 1969-1978* (Washington, D.C.: Government Printing Office, 1980), p. 161.

17. Castro's speech to the National People's Government Assembly, 27 December 1979; reprinted in *World Affairs*, Summer 1980, pp. 21-63. Castro mentions $250 million and $500 million in foreign exchange needs (p. 21) and a possible 10,000 men to cut lumber in Siberia (p. 41).

18. ACDA, *World Military Expenditures and Arms Transfers 1968-1977*, p. 151.

19. *Foreign Trade* (Moscow), October 1980, p. 7; emphasis added.

20. *Vneshniaia Politika Sovetskogo Soiuza 1978*, p. 187.

21. George Padmore, *Pan-Africanism or Communism? The Coming Struggle for Africa* (New York: Roy Publishers, 1956).

22. Quoted in *World Marxist Review*, March 1979, p. 60.

23. Quoted in *Noticias* (Maputo), 22 November 1980, pp. 3, 23-24; in Portuguese.

24. *Africa Contemporary Record 1977-78*, p. B333.

25. International Monetary Fund (IMF), *Direction of Trade Annual 1980*, pp. 267-68. In 1979 total imports to Mozambique reported by the IMF were $375 million, while imports from the Soviet Union were 20 million rubles.

26. *New York Times*, 13 October 1980, p. 5.

27. *Ibid.*, 8 November 1979, p. A2.

28. *Pravda*, 21 and 22 December 1979; translated in *Current Digest of the Soviet Press* 31, 51, pp. 14-15. (Cited hereafter as *CDSP*.)

29. See *Africa Index*, 18 October 1980, p. 2.

30. Congressional testimony of Gulf Oil Exploration and Production Company President Melvin Hill; cited in *ibid.*, p. 70.

31. *New York Times*, 2 February 1981, p. Y17.

32. *Pravda*, 22 December 1979; translated in *CDSP* 31, 51.

33. IMF, *Direction of Trade Annual 1980*, pp. 66-67.

34. *Izvestia*, 12 July 1980; translated in *CDSP* 32, 28, pp. 15-16. Meetings with Brzezinski and Haig reported in *Izvestia*, 18 December 1979; see *CDSP* 31, 51.

35. Sam Nujoma, "Namibia at the Threshold of Independence," *World Marxist Review*, February 1978, pp. 108-13. As an example of the Soviet echo, E. Tarabrin wrote that "in complex circumstances . . . the patriots have only one path—to strengthen the armed struggle" ("A New Round of the Liberation Struggle," *Mirovaia Ekonomika i Mezhdunarodnaia Otnosheniia* [World economy and international relations], February 1979, p. 46).

36. Nujoma, p. 111.

37. *Africa Contemporary Record 1978-79*, p. A6.

38. Anatoly Gromyko, *Konflikt na Iuge Afriki* (Conflict in southern Africa) (Moscow, 1979), p. 237.

39. *Pravda*, 11 May 1978, and *Izvestia*, 14 December 1979; translated in *CDSP* 29, 19 and 31, 50 respectively.

40. Tarabrin, "New Round," p. 46.

41. *Pravda*, 14 December 1979; translated in *CDSP* 31, 50.

42. "Africa Manifesto," p. 25.

43. *Ibid.*, p. 15.

44. Oliver Tambo in *World Marxist Review*, February 1978, p. 104.

45. Yusuf Dadoo in *ibid.*, July 1978, p. 25.

46. *Africa Contemporary Record 1978-79*, p. 380.

47. Dadoo in *World Marxist Review*, July 1978, p. 32.

48. "To this end in November 1961 the SACP created the armed organization 'Umkonto we Sizwe' " (Gromyko, *Konflikt na Iuge Afriki*, p. 214).

49. Dadoo in *World Marxist Review*, April 1977, p. 78.

50. Dadoo in *ibid.*, July 1978, pp. 24-25, 26.

51. *Ibid.*

52. *Ibid.*

53. On the South African military buildup, see Robert Jasters, *South Africa's Narrowing Security Options* (London: IISS, 1980; Adelphi Papers, no. 159).

54. Joseph Lelyveld in the *New York Times*, 27 November 1980, p. 3.

55. Robert Mugabe; quoted in *Financial Gazette* (Salisbury), 19 September 1980, pp. 1, 6.

56. *Ibid.*

57. Joshua Nkomo, "Zimbabwe: A Turning Point," *World Marxist Review*, February 1978, p. 113.

58. Brian Crozier, "What Next from Moscow?," *Soviet Analyst*, 6 August 1980; Martin McCauley, "East Germany on Safari," *ibid.*, 10 September 1980.

59. *The Herald* (Salisbury), 22 November 1980, p. 1.

60. Chester A. Crocker, "South Africa: Strategy for Change," *Foreign Affairs*, Winter 1980-1981. Crocker became Assistant Secretary of State for African Affairs in 1981.

61. Bissell, p. 209.

62. Carl Friedrich and Zbigniew Brzezinski, *Totalitarian Dictatorship and Autocracy* (Cambridge, Mass.: Harvard University Press, 1956).

Chapter 7: Copson, "Issues for U.S. Development Assistance Policy"

1. Donald R. Mickelwait, Charles F. Sweet, and Elliott R. Morss, *New Directions in Development: A Study of U.S. Aid* (Boulder, Colo.: Westview Press, 1979), p. 2.

2. Foreign Assistance Act of 1961, amended; PL 87-185, sec. 611.

3. *Ibid.*, sec. 604.

4. First enacted as sec. 114 of the Foreign Assistance Appropriations Act, 1978 (PL 95-148). Congress later allowed funding to continue for Angolan graduate students who had begun their training in the United States prior to fiscal 1978.

5. Sec. 101(b) of PL 96-369 is a "continuing resolution" on appropriations; it makes the waiver provision of the foreign assistance appropriations bill (HR 4473) applicable to fiscal 1981 programs.

6. PL 96-533, sec. 720.

7. Testimony of Richard M. Moose, Assistant Secretary of State for African Affairs, 30 September 1980 (U.S. Congress, House Committee on Foreign Affairs, Subcommittee on Africa, *United States Policy Toward Angola—Update*; Hearing, 96th Congress, 2d sess., 17 and 30 September 1980 [Washington, D.C.: Government Printing Office, 1980], p. 39).

8. PL 95-92.

9. PL 96-536 (House Joint Resolution [HJR] 644), approved 16 December 1980.

10. The paragraphs on the design and implementation process are taken from a forthcoming Congressional Research Service report on bilateral U.S. aid to Africa.

11. AID, *Congressional Presentation*, fiscal 1982, main volume, amended version.

12. U.S. Congress, Senate, Committee on Banking, Housing, and Urban Affairs, Subcommittee on International Finance, *U.S. Loans to Zaire*; Hearing, 96th Cong., 1st sess., 24 May 1979 (Washington, D.C.: Government Printing Office, 1979), p. 1.

13. AID, *Congressional Presentation*, fiscal 1981, annex 1, p. 444.

14. AID, *A Report to the Congress on Development Needs and Opportunities for Cooperation in Southern Africa* (Washington, D.C.: AID, March 1979), p. 7.

15. This fact emerges clearly in *ibid*.

LIST OF ACRONYMS

ACP: African, Caribbean and Pacific EEC Associates under the Lomé
            Treaty
AID: Agency for International Development
ANC:*   African National Congress
            African National Council
BENSO: Bureau for Economic Research: Cooperation and Development
BSAC: British South Africa Company
CAF: Central African Federation
CCTA: Commission for Technical Cooperation in Africa South of the
            Sahara
CMEA: Council of Mutual Economic Assistance
CPSU: Communist Party of the Soviet Union
CSA: Commission for Scientific Cooperation in Africa South of the
            Sahara
DTA: Democratic Turnhalle Alliance
EAC: East African Community
ECA: Economic Commission for Africa
ECOWAS: Economic Community of West African States
EEC: European Economic Community
EPLF: Eritrean People's Liberation Front
ESF: Economic Support Fund
FAMA: Fund for Mutual Assistance in Africa South of the Sahara
FAPLA: Forças Armadas Populare de Libertação de Angola
FLN: Front de Libération National
FLS: Frontline States
FNLA: Frente Nacional de Libertação de Angola
FRELIMO: Frente de Libertação de Moçambique
ICJ: International Court of Justice
IMF: International Monetary Fund
MPLA: Movimiento Popular de Libertação de Angola

*See footnote on p. 11 above.

305

LIST OF ACRONYMS

NNF:	Namibian National Front
OAU:	Organization of African Unity
PAC:	Pan-Africanist Congress
PAFMECSA:	Pan-African Freedom Movement of East, Central, and Southern Africa
PAIGC:	Partido Africano da Independencia da Guiné e Cabo Verde
PF:	Patriotic Front
PLAN:	People's Liberation Army of Namibia
SACP:	South African Communist Party
SACU:	Southern African Customs Union
SADCC:	Southern African Development Coordination Conference
SADF:	South African Defense Forces
SWA:	South West Africa
SWANU:	South West Africa National Union
SWAPO:	South West Africa People's Organization
TAZARA:	Tanzania-Zambia Railroad
TNC:	Transnational corporation
UANC:	United African National Council
UDI:	Unilateral Declaration of Independence
UNFP:	United National Federal Party
UNIN:	United Nations Institute for Namibia
UNITA:	União Nacional para a Independência Total de Angola
UNTAG:	United Nations Transitional Assistance Group
ZANLA:	Zimbabwe African National Liberation Army
ZANU:	Zimbabwe African National Union
ZAPU:	Zimbabwe African People's Union
ZDF:	Zimbabwe Development Fund
ZIPRA:	Zimbabwe People's Revolutionary Army

INSTITUTE OF INTERNATIONAL STUDIES
UNIVERSITY OF CALIFORNIA, BERKELEY

215 Moses Hall   Berkeley, California 94720

CARL G. ROSBERG, *Director*

Monographs published by the Institute include:

RESEARCH SERIES

1. *The Chinese Anarchist Movement*, by Robert A. Scalapino and George T. Yu. ($1.00)
7. *Birth Rates in Latin America: New Estimates of Historical Trends*, by O. Andrew Collver. ($2.50)
15. *Central American Economic Integration: The Politics of Unequal Benefits*, by Stuart I. Fagan. ($2.00)
16. *The International Imperatives of Technology: Technological Development and the International Political System*, by Eugene B. Skolnikoff. ($2.95)
17. *Autonomy or Dependence as Regional Integration Outcomes: Central America*, by Philippe C. Schmitter. ($1.75)
19. *Entry of New Competitors in Yugoslav Market Socialism*, by S.R. Sacks. ($2.50)
20. *Political Integration in French-Speaking Africa*, by Abdul A. Jalloh. ($3.50)
21. *The Desert and the Sown: Nomads in the Wider Society*, ed. by Cynthia Nelson. ($5.50)
22. *U.S.-Japanese Competition in International Markets: A Study of the Trade-Investment Cycle in Modern Capitalism*, by John E. Roemer. ($3.95)
23. *Political Disaffection Among British University Students: Concepts, Measurement, and Causes*, by Jack Citrin and David J. Elkins. ($2.00)
24. *Urban Inequality and Housing Policy in Tanzania: The Problem of Squatting*, by Richard E. Stren. ($2.95)
25. *The Obsolescence of Regional Integration Theory*, by Ernst B. Haas. ($4.95)
26. *The Voluntary Service Agency in Israel*, by Ralph M. Kramer. ($2.00)
27. *The SOCSIM Demographic-Sociological Microsimulation Program: Operating Manual*, by Eugene A. Hammel et al. ($4.50)
28. *Authoritarian Politics in Communist Europe: Uniformity & Diversity in One-Party States*, ed. by Andrew C. Janos. ($3.95)
29. *The Anglo-Icelandic Cod War of 1972-1973: A Case Study of a Fishery Dispute*, by Jeffrey A. Hart. ($2.00)
30. *Plural Societies and New States: A Conceptual Analysis*, by Robert Jackson ($2.00)
31. *The Politics of Crude Oil Pricing in the Middle East, 1970-1975: A Study in International Bargaining*, by Richard Chadbourn Weisberg. ($4.95)
32. *Agricultural Policy and Performance in Zambia: History, Prospects, and Proposals for Change*, by Doris Jansen Dodge. ($4.95)
33. *Five Classy Programs: Computer Procedures for the Classification of Households*, by E.A. Hammel and R.Z. Deuel. ($3.75)
34. *Housing the Urban Poor in Africa: Policy, Politics, and Bureaucracy in Mombasa*, by Richard E. Stren. ($5.95)
35. *The Russian New Right: Right-Wing Ideologies in the Contemporary USSR*, by Alexander Yanov. ($5.95)
36. *Social Change in Romania, 1860-1940: A Debate on Development in a European Nation*, ed. by Kenneth Jowitt. ($4.50)
37. *The Leninist Response to National Dependency*, by Kenneth Jowitt. ($3.25)
38. *Socialism in Sub-Saharan Africa: A New Assessment*, ed. by Carl G. Rosberg and Thomas M. Callaghy. ($12.95)
39. *Tanzania's Ujamaa Villages: The Implementation of a Rural Development Strategy*, by Dean E. McHenry, Jr. ($5.95)
40. *Who Gains from Deep Ocean Mining: Simulating the Impact of Regimes for Regulating Nodule Exploitation*, by I.G. Bulkley. ($3.50)

INSTITUTE OF INTERNATIONAL STUDIES MONOGRAPHS (continued)